The Popular Magazine in Britain and the United States

1880-1960

This volume is dedicated
to the memory of
Lee D Witkin,
without whose generosity
this study would
never have been started.

The Popular Magazine

in Britain and

the United States

1880-1960

DAVID REED

THE BRITISH LIBRARY
1997

© 1997 David Reed

First published 1997 by
The British Library
Great Russell Street, London WC1B 3DG

British Library Cataloguing in Publication Data
A catalogue record for this title is available from
The British Library

ISBN 0-7123-0417-7

Designed by John Mitchell
Laid out and typeset in Caslon 224 Book
by
The Author
Printed in England by
Henry Ling, Ltd, Dorchester

Contents

Illustrations

DR. WN. BY J. GILBERT.   GEORGE C. LEIGHTON, RED LION SQUARE.

While shepherds watched their flocks by night, — All seated on the ground.

Plate I

*By 1855, the **Illustrated London News** was selling 130,000 copies a week, ten times the daily sale of The Times, and had a strong claim to be considered the most important news medium of mid-Victorian Britain. It was the model for similar publications at home and abroad. Therefore, when it responded to the innovation of The Coloured Times, and published a special Christmas number with a colour cover of unprecedented excellence, it established a festive season tradition that continues down to the present day in magazines around the world. Its first example was printed by the Leighton Brothers of Lambs Conduit Street, London, using a combination of wood blocks and etching.*

Plate II
The Colored News only lasted for nine issues, with the first appearing on 4 August 1855. But this hitherto unknown weekly, of which only one, incomplete set appears to have survived, made its impact through its effect on others. Its colour was produced from wood blocks. It was one among a large number of publications launched that year after stamp duty was abolished, thereby allowing the industry to cut cover prices and expand sales to a new readership.

Plate III
Chromolithographs were increasingly used by magazines as occasional supplements to attract sales as the nineteenth century wore on. But the first to use them regularly was the New-York-based **Frank Leslie's Popular Monthly**, which included one in its first issue of January 1876 and every edition thereafter. In January 1880, it went one step further by binding in what appears to be the first full-colour advertisement in print, an innovation that seems to have escaped notice until this point.

DANS LES RUES DE LONDRES

Plate IV

*The labyrinthine procedures which enabled **L'Illustration** to publish colour illustrations from relief plates along with its letterpress type before it managed monochrome halftones are described on pages 38-9. The necessary skills were confined to one or two studios in the French capital, which did their best to keep their techniques secret and their prices high. In fact, Boussod, Valadon et Cie, who helped to develop the new process, were a major publisher of fine art reproductions, and it was in this area that colour gillotage gave the most profitable returns.*

"CHUMS"

Plate V
Chums *was a sixpenny weekly for juvenile minds that followed the sterling traditions of Boy's Own Paper in diverting attention away from disreputable, but seductive working-class villains intent on no good, towards splendid pink chaps resolutely defending the 'White Man's Burden'. The owners tried to increase sales by becoming the first publishers in the world, in August 1893, to use colour halftones on a regular basis. This involved having the plates made in Prague by Husnik and Hausler, the only company capable of producing them on an industrial basis at that time, and printing them in Britain, before they were bound into the magazine once a month.*

The Lettie Lane Paper Family

Presenting Lettie's Best Friend and Some of Her Pretty Dresses

By Sheila Young

Next Month We Shall Present Lettie's Brother

Cut along dotted lines in hats and slip doll's head into the slits thus made.   By pasting an inch-wide strip of cardboard at waist-line, slightly bent to form easel, the doll can be made to stand.

Plate VI

*Edward Bok, the editor of **Ladies' Home Journal**, the biggest selling magazine in the world in 1909, was always keen to substitute illustrations for words. Nor was he shy about using the latest technology, having introduced four-colour, wet-on-wet printing on one machine as early as the autumn of 1905. Because the covers were printed separately, it was easy to use the new technology on them, where it would be most noticeable to prospective purchasers. But by 1909, the process had made its way into the body of the monthly.*

Plate VII

*During the first decade of the twentieth century, **Collier's** was so politically influential that the weekly had a hand in changing the role of the Speaker of the American House of Representatives, as well as bringing down a cabinet minister. It also led the industry in the quality of its graphics, both inside and on the covers, as in this example from July 1910. Unlike its rival, the Saturday Evening Post, which ran similar images on a limited range of themes week after week, it chose diversity and a fresh, frequently stunning design to grace every issue.*

Plate VIII

The increasing use of colour during the first decades of the century by some of the most successful publishers in the United States changed the expectations of their readers and conditioned the potential audience to demand more of their magazines. But few publishers could afford the finest paper and creative compromises were necessary. The art staff of the Chicago-based **Woman's World** *realised that illustrations created using flat colour, rather than more illusionistic schemas employing shading, could look very attractive and be printed on less expensive paper than that used by the likes of the Ladies' Home Journal.*

Plate IX

Weldon's Ladies' Journal *was a British example of what is almost a sub-genre of fashion magazine: that owned by a publisher of paper clothing patterns, which is close to being a catalogue. What differentiated it in 1920 from its American peers, like The Delineator, was its use of photogravure, which had become a commercial process during the previous decade. In the years to come, this intaglio technology would dominate the London-based industry, while it had little impact among the best-sellers across the Atlantic, which had a tendency to be rather conservative about production processes.*

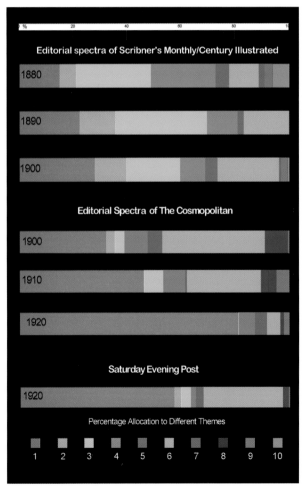

Editorial spectra of Scribner's Monthly/Century Illustrated

1880

1890

1900

Editorial Spectra of The Cosmopolitan

1900

1910

1920

Saturday Evening Post

1920

Percentage Allocation to Different Themes

1 2 3 4 5 6 7 8 9 10

Plate X

*In the years after Edward Bok retired, **Ladies' Home Journal** lost its way. The appointment in 1935 of Bruce and Beatrice Gould as the co-editors, a unique arrangement of a husband and wife team, completely revived the monthly. Their series 'How America Lives', launched in February 1940, was a tour-de-force of magazine journalism as it sub-sumed all aspects of women's magazines through an examination of one family every month. In the sixth, the Wright family of Burlington, Vermont is put under a benign microscope held by the Journal's staff with accompanying illustrations photographed by one of the leading fashion cameramen of his day, Martin Munkacsi, to resemble family snapshots.*

Plate XI

*Previous suggestions that the content of American magazines changed radically towards more populist themes during the 1890s are given the lie by this graph and the statistical analysis of the content of the magazines upon which it is based, which can be found in appendices I, X and XVII. **Century Illustrated** was always a balanced publication, an approach reflected in the range of articles pub-lished in **Cosmopolitan** in 1900. But the extra-ordinary success of the **Saturday Evening Post** and its emphasis on fiction affected many editors and encouraged them to build on its example, as can be seen in Cosmopolitan by 1920.*

Key:

1 Fiction
2 Travel and adventure
3 History and biography
4 Arts
5 Natural sciences
6 Modern life
7 Religion
8 Women's pages
9 Humour and enter-tainment
10 Miscellaneous

Introduction

THIS IS A MAPPING EXERCISE. Its object is to describe directly and by comparison; to refine the terms of the discussion; to outline some generic aspects of the modern magazine and establish a perspective on the changes wrought on those elements between 1880 and 1960. Unfortunately, like Renaissance navigators, we confront a world in which some fragments are visible but much is obscure. Work has barely begun on the most popular, modern British serials, while efforts in the United States over the last generation have been concentrated on fine details, with few studies of the overall situation based on serious research. But taking some general criteria as given without reflection can leave such studies of minutiae out on a limb if the broader picture has not been examined for over a generation.

To attempt a study of large-scale patterns is to confront the need to establish the parameters of the discussion and the terms in which it is couched. The manner in which problems are addressed when saying a great deal about very little, as in the overwhelming majority of academic studies, may not be appropriate in this context. Care needs to be exercised that analysis is pertinent to the period under discussion and does not continue to tackle publications of the modern period in ways more suitable to earlier times. Publishing in the twentieth century has increasingly come to resemble other large-scale industries. Rehearsing arguments and feigning conflicts with fellow students is inappropriate given the absence of fellow travellers on this plane. Indeed, it would bring us closer to the plain of la Mancha. The approach also needs to correlate the size of the endeavour with the realities of publication. It should also promote coherence and accessibility so that commentaries use a vocabulary which will suggest similarities and highlight differences across barriers which frequently inhibit the understanding of generic qualities. It will focus on the magazine as a manufactured object.

As this study covers eight decades, it is possible to subdivide the period in order to further the above objectives. By breaking it down into ten-year segments, the material is partitioned into elements which permit the consistent, recurrent analysis of magazines. Thus by repeating particular procedures for each decade, a series of cross-sections can be built up which outline parts of the periodical press over time. This frequency is sufficient to establish a clear overview without generating superfluous information which would camouflage the general picture. The matter is one of balance.

Once the decennial grid has been accepted, there is the matter of the analytical criteria to apply within it because the space in which to report is not boundless. They need to be applicable over as broad an area as possible if the study is to pin down the fundamentals of magazines published in different continents. It would also be helpful if they were accessible to those outside a specialist audience and related back to previous work. Such matters are far from simple because magazines are at the centre of a complex nexus of stimuli – cultural, technical, financial and commercial – which weigh heavily on the content and appearance of individual issues as mediated by the editorial staff.

In the past, commentators have yielded to the temptation to concentrate on matters which are attractive and easy to convert into a narrative, the context rather than the contents of the magazines, and have over-emphasized that element. Van Zuilen's in many ways estimable study *The Life Cycle of Magazines*, for example, devotes more than 300 pages to the business and social context of its theme between 1945 and 1972 but only 8.75 to the way in which content contributed to the cycle and was changed by it.[1] Then there is the appearance of a publication and the means of production. All three matters, content, context and form, are the arena of creation for a publisher's staff and define the persona of a title. Indeed, they are critical in holding a loyal readership because experienced staff are backed by theoretical analysis in suggesting that magazines offer more satisfying experiences than mere stimulation to their readers. They offer a cynosure, a parenthesis in which to shelter, a home from home.

Kenneth Purdy, a successful editor of *True*, a mark one version of the men's magazine, wrote to Theodore Peterson of his aims and those of his predecessor. 'When I came to the magazine in 1949, it seemed to me that little needed to be done to the basic policy. Williams' notion had been to furnish his readers with a refuge from women; to offer vicarious adventure, humor, and good writing.'[2] Cynthia White, in her study of the women's press, wrote, 'Turning the first page of a mass weekly is like entering a women's club – a woman knows she is on "home ground" in more senses than one. This is her territory, her profession; she knows the rules and she shares the implicit goals and values.'[3] Mary Dodge, from 1873 to 1905 the editor of *St Nicholas*, sometime described as 'the best magazine for children ever published in America',[4] wrote: 'Most children of the present day attend school. Their heads are strained and taxed with the day's lessons. They do not want to be bothered nor amused nor petted. They just want to have their own way over their own magazine. They want to enter one place where they can come and go as they please. Of course, they expect to pick up odd bits and treasures. A child's magazine is its playground.'[5]

Such market-orientated definitions of function are reflected in the more formal analysis of Waples, Berelson and Bradshaw, of the late 1930s, into the broader question of *What reading does to people*. They concluded that people read for five main reasons: 1) respite from tension; 2) aesthetic pleasure; 3) 'the reinforcement effect (e.g., reinforcement of an attitude or conversion to another attitude toward controversial issues)'; 4) for prestige; and 5) 'the instrumental effect (e.g. fuller knowledge of a practical problem and greater competence to deal with it)'.[6]

In 1976, Sara Zimet examined the interactions between books and their consumers. 'All the studies reviewed point to the importance of identification and projection in the response of readers and indicate, in effect, that the attitudes the reader brings to the printed page affect the strategies he or she uses in processing the message. In other words, as we read, we process the text in order to meet our own personal needs.'[7] That is, we filter out that which does not suit us and retain that which does.

Such a manipulation of the author's text by the reader is possible because of the reductive, indeterminate nature of words. As the Polish theorist Roman Ingarden was so keen to point out, the realisation of a passage in the imagination of a reader embeds the 'meaning units' in a field of experience and preconceptions which varies widely from consumer to consumer.[8] Thus, the reader is the arbiter.

One reason why the consumer should wish to exert such power is suggested by Leon Festinger's *A Theory of Cognitive Dissonance*, which outlines the need of individuals to protect themselves, to insulate themselves from 'outrageous fortune', rather than confront it. Essentially, the theory derives from the extensively documented human need to avoid contradiction, with either the self or others. As its author points out, it is a motivation of such strength that elaborate excuses are often constructed to explain away even trivial inconsistencies amongst one's ideas.[9] And, as what one 'knows' about one's environment is dependent on sensed-data, that is, is dependent on neurological signals internal to our own organism, our cognition of the world is a function of a system dedicated to avoiding contradiction, or what Festinger calls 'dissonance'. By adulthood, and probably a lot earlier, our curiosity is circumscribed by the need to avoid mental discomfort. The author suggests that two basic hypotheses follow. '1. The existence of dissonance, being psychologically uncomfortable, will motivate the person to try to reduce the dissonance and achieve consonance. 2. When dissonance is present, in addition to trying to reduce it, the person will actively avoid situations and information which would likely increase the dissonance.'[10] He then refines his theory, exploring its consequences, enumerating the experimental and survey evidence that tends to substantiate it. In doing so he exposes the psychological roots that nourish the fragmentation of the magazine trade into its special interest sectors, the cynosures that pad the mental cell. Women's magazines for women. Financial reports for financiers. Comics for kids, of all ages. In Britain there is even a monthly magazine for witches: *Wax and Wane*.

Then there is another element which arises from the cyclical production pattern of magazines. The serial format, returning every week or month, reassures its audience in the way that a mother reading or telling a story to her child over and over again reassures the infant that there is a base of reliability and predictability that can be touched in a dangerous and unstable world. In a life of mixed fortunes, the individual needs a reliable womb of conceits in which to rest its imagination and rejuvenate its will.

Thus, the importance of the magazine's persona, as defined by its content and the manner in which that content is presented to the readers, to which the audience can turn afresh every week or month, is a critical factor in holding those people. But few commentators have ever tried to examine content and those that have done so have treated one or two publications at best. Arthur John used a statistical approach at one point in *The Best Years of the Century* to analyse *Harper's Monthly* and *The Century Illustrated Monthly*.[11] But his approach was tentative and he relapsed into less precise methods which let him down to some extent, as we will see in chapter three. Mott, on the other hand, was very thorough in applying the schema he had chosen to structure his five volume set on magazines.[12] But he was already at work and established in his field before the quantitative analysis of content became an accepted technique and most of his comments on different publications again concern context rather than content.

So, both the need to establish a consistent analytical approach to the topic and to seek 'the discovery of new facts'[13] seem to be pushing in one direction. By building on the simple analysis of content used by John, and of course many others in the past, and enlarging on his series of categories to which content may be apportioned and applying them at ten year intervals to selected magazines over eight decades, a new type of framework can be constructed for a large scale study.

Unlike John, who varied the categories he used and the order in which they were presented,[14] the appendices listing the results here follow a precise, set format. The categories used were developed out of those employed by John; but when they were tested against a variety of magazines certain modifications were found to be necessary if they were to be applicable to the range of material considered. Most categories are self–evident, although one or two will benefit from a brief amplification. 'Social life and manners' always refers to such matters in the country of publication, while 'Foreign life' deals with the opposite setting. 'Public affairs' is the category for discussions of education, politics and law. 'Contemporary events' includes material which would have been on the news pages of the daily press. Where John used 'Women', 'Fashion', which means clothing presented for emulation, 'Domestic', which means work around the home, and 'Children' have been substituted. 'Humour and entertainment' includes competitions.

The basic unit of measurement in this study was the page. Subdivisions and fragments of a page were expressed as a percentage of the unit by measuring the area and calculating it in square millimetres. This was then divided by the area of the printed page and multiplied by 100 to record the result as a percentage of the unit. Each page or fragment was then allotted to a topic. An entire volume could be analysed in this way and then the whole numbers and percentages could be totalled to give the breakdown for that volume. The number of pages allocated to each topic in the volume was then divided by the total number of editorial pages that constituted that volume and multiplied by 100 to express the totals for each topic as percentages of the whole. This approach gave a uniform result which was independent of page size, type, leading and the number of pages in each volume and allows the reader to concentrate on the emphasis placed on each topic by each editor at the end of each decade.

It would appear that no previous historian in this field has employed the technique on the scale used here. This is hardly surprising for, without access to electronic pocket calculators, those tools of the 1980s, the volume of computation necessary would have been too intimidating to contemplate.

Yet, despite the levels of accuracy achieved in the calculations, it would be misleading not to acknowledge that the figures are challengeable from another direction. Consistency is essential in any analysis over such a wide range of material and that has been achieved here because it was conducted by one individual during a relatively short period and the categories used were very simple. No complicated questions were put to the subject matter which might encourage ambiguity or need elaborate verification procedures.[15]

These figures are employed as a *guide* to changes that occurred over decades. The work was carried out and the figures used because they are a better indication of what has happened than the loose adjectival definitions applied by other historians of this subject hitherto. To repeat, the intention here is to refine the conversation, to create an outline upon which others can build. As will be seen, the figures which have been produced have exposed some mistakes by previous workers.

Having established a modus vivendi, the next step was to select the magazines to which the analysis was to be applied. By opting for the most popular titles in both countries at the end of each decade the intention was again to establish a framework which was independent of the tastes of the researcher. This was seen to be particularly important in the light of Mott's last volume in which the selection of magazines seems very idiosyncratic.

An alternative approach would have been to pick a number of titles and follow them between 1880 and 1960. This tactic raises severe problems however. Only a very limited number of magazines survive across those eight decades and their durability might well be attributable to some eccentric financial or marketing arrangement rather than a popularity with the public. For example, a number of women's magazines were owned by the publishers of paper clothing patterns who used the publication to publicise their products. In one instance, *McCall's*, a take-over revealed that the monthly had been making a loss for years which the parent company had covered to keep its more important merchandise in the public eye.[16] Then there is the matter of a magazine which survives but sells far fewer copies than its most successful competitors; *Family Herald*, for example. Such a publication is going to reveal little about popular magazines for perhaps decades and studying it will demonstrate little relative to the effort expended.

In the light of these disadvantages, other criteria for selecting magazines were used. Choosing the best-selling publications from the end of each decade ensures that research is focused on the really popular magazines. It also ensures a precise criteria is used for selection while allowing the research the flexibility necessary to maintain its focus. This approach, however, comes with its own built-in problem: establishing accurate sales figures. Getting such dependable statistics about publications in the United States for the period under examination is not very difficult. Performing the same operation in Britain requires an entirely different level of research.

Reliable circulation figures for American magazines began to circulate at the end of the nineteenth century. But the first attempt to publish details of sales in a tabular form seems to have been initiated by Lay and Brother, a company that manufactured printers' inks in Philadelphia. Their single edition media directory, *The Newspaper Record*, appeared in 1856. Their intention had been to give a profile of each publication that included the size of its circulation, the name of its editor, its political persuasion and so on. But, 'after a stubborn trial of all the means in our power we were at length compelled to alter the original idea and give simply the name of periodicals and place of issue.'[17] Publishers regarded anything more as an unnecessary intrusion into their domain. Information was private property as far as they were concerned.

Another effort yielding only marginally better results was made by Daniel J. Kenny in 1861.[18] But the first really successful penetration of the publishers' secretive ways was achieved by George Rowell after the Civil War. His *American Newspaper Directory* was launched in 1869. It seems to have been an extension of his business as both an advertising agent and a publisher for that trade, as its preface indicates that it was intended as an annual supplement to his monthly, *The Advertisers' Gazette*.[19]

By the time Rowell took this initiative, advertising was starting to expand and become an important source of revenue for American weeklies and some of the more adventurous monthlies, as we will see in due course. As the cost of buying space in the different magazines related to their circulations, obtaining reliable figures was critical as far as the agencies and their clients were concerned.

From the first, the *Directory* carried publishers' advertisements, which made it a financial success. It also attempted to improve the quality of the information it contained, primarily the circulation figures. To this end, it harassed the publishers, refusing to print the sales they claimed without verification; substituting general ratings designated by letters which indicated that the circulation was probably above a certain figure. By understating the achievements of a particular publication, the agency tried to sting the owner into revealing more. This drive for greater accuracy continued for almost 30 years and makes Rowell's *Directory* the most useful source of accurate sales figures for the period.

Eventually the pressure backfired when, in 1898, the *Directory*'s most prominent advertisers, the major metropolitan newspapers, organised a boycott. They stuck to their guns and in 1908 the *Directory* had to be merged with that of another leading agency, N.W. Ayer, and published as the *American Newspaper Annual and Directory*.[20]

Yet, despite this setback, certain features were now part of the landscape. Rowell's financial success had caused his annual to be copied by a number of other prominent agencies, including Ayer. And the inclusion of publishers' advertisements in the *Directory* had not only increased Rowell's revenues; they had also implied approval by magazine owners, if only tangentially, of the idea that the publication of information, hitherto unquestionably considered private, was a legitimate activity. Now, it was very difficult for the magazine and newspaper publishers to deny the directory and its staff reasonable access to their sales figures. All that was now in question in the United States was accuracy and verification.

That being said, the citadel did not fall at the first trumpet blast; vested interest and pecuniary advantage encouraged the periodical publishers to resist this penetration of their walls of secrecy. However, the power of the advertisers was developing fast. Between 1865 and 1900, the volume of national advertising in the United States appears to have swollen from an estimated 10 million insertions to a volume about nine times that figure.[21] And *national* advertising became the key to the magazine owners' success. Until the advent of radio in the 1920s, they were the only uniform, nation-wide medium in the United States.

But such a strong position was a double–edged sword. For, if the advertisers were paying for a mass audience, they wanted to know the real size of that mass before they would cough up their money. So it is not surprising that the Association of American Advertisers, whose prime purpose was to drag accurate figures out of the publishers, was formed in June 1899.[22] Their power was such that they audited the figures of 400 publications within three years.[23] Thus, by the end of the first decade of the twentieth century, another barrier had been breached and any publisher who wanted advertising revenues on a large scale had to allow the advertisers, or their accountants, access to his books. The last redoubt contained only the standardisation of the process and regular publication.

During 1913, a number of internal changes took place within the Association that led to a flurry of political manoeuvres within the industry. In an attempt to broaden the Association's financial base, one group encouraged the involvement of agencies and even publishers. This led on to a conference and on 20 May 1914, the Audit Bureau of Circulation was formed from the tripartite combination of the agencies, the publishers and the advertisers.[24] Between that meeting and the middle of July, the steering committee met over 30 times and by 30 July the first ABC circulation statement blanks were sent to publishers. By the end of September the organisation employed 12 professional auditors to check the returns and the way they were compiled.[25] One problem that ABC did encounter was that many managements lacked the competence to actually prepare the figures in the proposed standard manner and the auditors had to be loaned out to teach them the necessary techniques.[26]

Within three years, the pace quickened after a new type of media information service was launched. Starting early in 1917, the *Barbour's Advertising Rate Sheets* were published every month and listed a substantial body of information about a wide range of publications, but did not include circulation figures.[27] That left the way open for the *Standard Rate and Data Quarterly*, the first edition of which was mailed to subscribers on 30 June 1919.[28] From this point, statistical data on magazines and newspapers published in the United States was not only accurate, available and comprehensive, but increased rapidly in its profusion. Thus, the Library of Congress stacks currently contain empty bays which have to be held in reserve for the vast volume of information exuded every month by commercial services. The situation could not contrast more poignantly with that prevalent in Britain.

Although directories of British serial publications did become established by the end of the nineteenth century, they did not embody the investigative attitudes of their American peers. When circulation figures were published among their pages they were isolated numbers which were very rarely authenticated by auditors and never part of a regularly published accounting procedure. And even when a third party had verified the figures, that particular figure was frequently reiterated year after year in the pages of the directory. For example, the magazine *Bow Bells* had its circulation checked by a firm of accountants and certified at 104,260 in July 1889. But that figure was still being quoted four years later.[29]

The first exception to this regrettable state of affairs was created by George Newnes who published vague assertions regarding the circulation of *Tit-bits* fairly regularly during the 1880s.[30] Then Alfred Harmsworth took a much more radical approach and, as the sales of *Answers* began to soar, he published its audited circulation figures every week on the magazine's front page, starting in January 1890. But although the weeklies were a market in which imitation was rife, this bold innovation went so much against the grain of British publishing that no other company followed his lead, despite his great success. Furthermore, once the circulation figures of his raft of cheap weeklies stabilised in the mid-1890s, he abandoned the practice and sales figures for publications from the Harmsworth stable are almost as difficult to obtain as those from their rivals: almost but not quite. The private papers that his heirs deposited at the British Library, which contain his early diaries and copies of some letters, do feature references to sales.[31] Unfortunately, these mentions tail off quite quickly during the early 1890s as Harmsworth became secure financially and no longer needed reassurances about cash flow.

Assembling a reliable list of circulation figures in these circumstances is difficult to say the least, though it would be foolish to deny the pre-eminence of *Tit-bits*. As the Harmsworth figures of the early 1890s were audited by chartered accountants, their status seems secure. The same seems to be true for the weeklies of the Religious Tract Society, *Boy's Own Paper* and *Girls' Own Paper*, for which we have a reference in the Society's minutes, as will be seen in Chapter 4. Other figures are far less reliable.

This situation was tackled by the Advertisers' Protection Society which was formed in 1900 and whose title indicates the alarm felt by the agencies and their clients in respect of their position. Their hitherto unexamined newsletter, of which only one incomplete set appears to exist, was used, amongst other things, to publish claimed circulation figures, the Society's estimates of circulation and the occasional audited figures either sent to them or obtained in the course of business by one of their members. Where audited figures did come to light, comparisons with the Society's approximations reveal that their guesses and the actual figures were relatively close.[32] This newsletter appears, therefore, to be the best available source so far uncovered for British circulation figures for the period leading to the 1914–18 war.

After the end of hostilities, the attitudes of some publishers changed abruptly for a brief period and audited net sales figures were published by the Incorporated Society of British Advertisers, the newly retitled organisation which succeeded the Advertisers' Protection Society, as well as by an annual for the advertising trade.[33] But although this spate of revelations allows the most accurate end of decade list of top selling magazines for Britain to be created so far, the tap was turned off very abruptly and no more figures of any reliability appeared for another five years.

The next clue to sales was produced in a totally different way and bypassed direct contact with the publishers altogether. *Press Circulations Analysed* was issued in 1928 as a result of an early market research exercise in which 20,140 people were interviewed by representatives of the London Research Bureau. This book did not try to suggest actual circulations. Instead it contented itself with listing the percentage of interviewees who mentioned different newspapers and magazines read in their home. It also separated the respondents into three categories: middle class, lower middle class and working class.[34] In doing this it revealed a major limitation.

Of the 20,140 interviewed, 5,020 were listed as being middle class, 6,290 as lower middle and 8,830 as working class. Expressed as percentages of the sample, they were 24.93%, 31.23% and 43.84% respectively. But this is not the percentage breakdown of these segments in society as a whole. For example, according to Routh the working classes constituted 78.29% of the employed in the 1921 census, and 78.07% in the 1931 census.[35] Clearly, there is no way of knowing how the Bureau defined each class for they do not list their definitions in the book and they have long since disappeared. Nevertheless, the balance of their samples is so far adrift from that suggested by the British census that the figures need to be adjusted if the three different samples for each publication are to be totalled to reveal the overall relative popularity of each publication in a way that approximates to reality. That being done, and it is discussed in greater detail in chapter six, the most successful of the magazines could be selected. (Again, it has to be emphasized that actual circulations and whether a publication is the best-selling weekly of the time or number three is irrelevant to this study. All we are creating here is a filter, which is used to separate a manageable group of about half a dozen magazines to study.)

However, this selection spotlights a problem with this publication: the Bureau excluded all specialist titles from its investigation and thereby left out *Radio Times* and *The Leader*, two of the best-selling weeklies of the 1920s.[36] So the list has to be used with caution and supplemented with information from other sources.

Three years later in 1931, a stronger form of illumination was focused on these dark recesses: the Audit Bureau of Circulation established itself in Britain, long after it was accepted in Europe and North America.[37] But even this acceptance was hampered by the magazine publishers. The organisation's private ledgers reveal that it was soon endorsed by the national and local newspapers but not the magazines. *Punch*, *Radio Times* and *Everybody's Weekly* were among the few which submitted to the independent audit during the 1930s. Only in the immediate post-World War II period did the magazine publishers relent and accept the inevitable. So it is solely with the last two decades examined here that British circulation figures are completely reliable and a selection can be made with some confidence.

ONCE THE CORE APPROACH IS ESTABLISHED of decennial selections from among the best-sellers in both countries, other layers of information can be built upon it. Production technology has received a considerable amount of attention because such matters have had a critical influence at key moments in magazine history. However, that influence, even at such times, has been complex and some previous assumptions can now be seen to have been too simplistic. Extensive work on this topic was also necessary because there is as yet still no general history of modern printing technology of any substance.

Attention has also been paid to the balance between artwork, both tone and line, and photography over the 80 years, together with the invasion of colour, in an effort to develop a general outline of the period. This topic has never been explored before and yet it is essential if more detailed studies are going to be made of visual styles in modern magazines.

The matter of the business context has also been detailed because such factors have profoundly affected every aspect of the modern magazine. Advertising revenue opened up the design field and the application of new technology among successful American magazines in a way that was not possible among their British counterparts in the early decades of the twentieth century. This emphasis on commerce also acts as a corrective to the overly literary or personalised approach to magazine history that has been adopted by some in the past. Every publication is an amalgam of business and editorial decisions and the latter cannot be discussed as though editors were autonomous men who conducted themselves with the freedom of authors. Nor is editorship merely an aspect of biography.

Exploring the above criteria over a period of 80 years is sufficient to concern us in one volume. Furthermore, these yardsticks can be discussed within such a time-scale in a manner which adds to the overall setting for other criteria not dealt with here. Enquiries which look at aspects of magazine fiction, for example, and other sub-elements of the structure of the magazine, such as stylistic changes in illustrations, need a narrower focus. Such research can best be applied to shorter periods or particular situations so that information can scrutinised in detail. The gains from a resolute study at this level of magnification can best be gauged from the recent fine work of Helen Damon-Moore.[38] This study aspires to examine broad tendencies within the industry as a whole.

This attempt to draw out the generic qualities of magazines has also led to a fresh approach to their overall classification. In the early days of the magazine, when the size of the readership and the volume of advertising were very limited when compared to their growth in the twentieth century, many editors and publishers relied on an editorial profile which was heavily dependent on fiction and a broad range of topics that counterpointed one another to generate sufficient sales to sustain publication. Their object was to attract as many customers as possible from an undifferentiated mass of people by publishing 'something for everyone' because survival was a problem for almost all serials, particularly in the United States. These are the mixed function magazines and it was their success which led to the mass magazine market of the twentieth century. In this tactic they were at one with the newspapers of the period which, from the 1870s, made a concerted move to publish a diversified content to catch as many readers as possible, changing the face of the American daily.[39]

Publishers and editors also realised that a separate body of titles could be developed by restricting their target audience purely to a select but large element of the market. Again, to make the venture a viable proposition the editors presented the intended audience with a range of material that included substantial quantities of fiction. The first sub-market to feature these restricted function magazines was that for women where the first publication appeared in 1693.[40] During the second half of the nineteenth century a mass market developed among young people that came to be exploited with particular effectiveness by British publishers, who targeted them with another group of magazines with a restricted function. In the 1890s, a third group of magazines arose, intended purely for a male audience, that in their articles and stories dwelt on tales of travel and adventure. All these restricted function magazines published fiction.

Magazines with a specialised function, unless they were restricted solely to stories, avoided fiction. In the nineteenth century, these specialised publications, again unless their field was fiction, were only able to sustain relatively small sales. But, as the twentieth century has developed so has their market, for reasons discussed below. Now, specialised magazines and those restricted to the women's market dominate the industry in both Britain and the United States.

These are the roots upon which the publishers, the money men, the promoters have grafted their enterprises. For, as Peterson has pointed out, commercial success in launching a twentieth–century magazine has depended, and continues to do so, on identifying a homogeneous reader group, capturing it and selling it to advertisers as a market.[41] In fact, it is the complete symbiosis of the two aspects of the magazine, that of the editor and the publisher, contributor and advertiser, mind and money, that makes the medium such a runaway, if ill-documented success since the 1890s.[42]

The Context

'Do you know why we publish the Ladies' Home Journal ?' Curtis asked an audience of advertisers at one point early in his career. 'The editor thinks it is for the benefit of American women. That is an illusion, but a very proper one for him to have. But I will tell you; the real reason, the publisher's reason, is to give you people who manufacture things that American women want and buy a chance to tell them about your products.'

Cyrus Curtis, the most successful magazine publisher of his day, quoted in,
The Story of Advertising, *James Playstead Wood, New York, 1958, p211.*

THE ECONOMIC AND SOCIAL FRAMEWORK that was the context for magazine production in the late nineteenth century in the two subject countries was the consequence of the differing development patterns of the United Kingdom and the United States during the earlier part of the century. 'British industry enjoyed benefits from coal and other tractable supplies of mineral ore, that spilled over into metallurgy and other heat-intensive industries. Spin-offs from the early and widespread deployment of a technology based upon cheap supplies of coal exercised an important and persistent influence on the country's industrial development.'[43] British industrialisation was a gradual, slow moving accretion of economic clinker that stretched back into the eighteenth century.

By way of contrast, the American industrial transition was late but explosive. Canals did not make any impact until the completion of the Erie in 1825, barely preceding the railways.[44] As late as 1850 less than 15% of the American working population were involved in manufacture, a date by which 60% of the British work force were so employed.[45] Yet, by 1890 America possessed an industrial machine that was already outperforming the British on such key industrial indicators as steel production.[46]

THE POPULATIONS OF EACH COUNTRY and their growth were, of course, the most general factor affecting the size of the domestic market. At the start of the nineteenth century, almost twice as many people lived in Great Britain as in the United States. A century later, the reverse was true and the numbers of citizens in both countries had increased spectacularly. During the first half of the century, the British population grew by 98% to 20.8 million,[47] while that of the US increased by 437% to just over 23 million.[48] During the second half, growth slowed a little to 78% and 328% respectively.[49]

However, from the point of view of an effective working economy, it was not just that those people existed but where they lived. In the US, for example, 'The number of cities with a population in excess of 25,000 was 52 in 1870; by 1900 there were 160 such urban areas': an increase of 208%.[50] In other words, the number of easily accessible markets surged ahead for both the manufacturer and the publisher in a very short time. The British urban explosion occurred between 1801 and 1851, when the number of towns with a population of more than 25,000 grew from 19 in the earlier year to 58 in the later: a 205% increase.[51] By the second half of the century, the time of the US expansion, the British momentum had slowed to a steady accretion. By 1871 there were 65 towns of 25,000 inhabitants in Britain and in 1901, 81: a percentage increase of only 24.6%.[52] Thus, the population of both countries came to be concentrated in cities. This meant that their citizens were grouped into more and more easily serviced units, which meant that the unit costs of distribution, whether for goods or magazines, were less onerous in those areas. As this process happened earlier in Britain than in America, it is not surprising that we find mass circulation magazines developing first in the old country.

Making these concentrated globules of population a practical, working proposition was the motivation for and the consequence of the transport transformation of the 19th, and 18th centuries. By the end of the latter period, the U.K., already a highly developed economy but relatively small in geographical scale, was evolving a road and canal infrastructure that supported this growing industrial and commercial framework. As Michael Freeman has pointed out, 'The sequence of highway legislation, river navigation schemes, turnpike and canal promotions and dock and harbour improvements represented a continuous drive to upgrade existing systems of transport. What we see in the fifty years from 1770 was the culmination of a long, at times uneven but nevertheless perceptible movement towards greater efficiency, both in terms of basic infrastructure (the provision of network and services) and in the institutional framework within which that infrastructure fell.'[53] The railways gave muscle, that is speed and power, to this already extant skeleton.[54]

In the US the railways, in conjunction with the telegraph, were not just the icing on the cake, they were the cake itself and they made the economic feast of the last half of the 19th century possible. Not surprisingly, the rail connection of the eastern and western seaboards, on 10 May 1869, received much publicity.[55] Yet, more to the point are the words of railway historian Robert Riegel. 'The construction of the transcontinental roads brought about the construction of other roads in the more populous portions of the West, so that there soon grew up complete systems in the more important commercial and agricultural regions.'[56] Thus, even before the transcontinental connection was completed, the agricultural production centres of the American hinterland were being connected to the consumer centres of the East. This began in the upper Mississippi Valley in the 1850s but only really made a vital difference in the 1870s, when the railway managements were able to organise efficient long-distance services.[57] In addition, regular railway services also meant regular and faster postal and small package services, important for both business communication and the distribution of magazines.

Until the Post Office Act of 1863, American postmasters were given considerable discretion in decisions as to whether a particular publication might gain the advantageous rates granted to newspapers. Although the new legislation attempted to define publications that might be sent second class as 'all mailable matter exclusively in print, and regularly issued at stated periods, without addition by writing, mark or sign', the law specifically discriminated against magazines, which had to be sent at one cent a copy, whereas the second-class rate was 0.38¢.[58] This encouraged the development of advertising circulars masquerading as newspapers during the 1870s.[59] This encouraged Congress to amend the law in 1879. During the intensive lobbying that preceded the bill's passage, the magazine publishers successfully induced the legislators to include their products within the definition of those entitled to second-class postage, while specifically relegating advertising circulars to third-class status. The former was charged at two cents a pound, while the latter cost one cent for two ounces: eight times as much.[60] This considerable advantage was a major coup for the publishers and only further encouraged the advertising trade to look to magazines as an attractive national medium. The position of the magazines was strengthened further in 1885, when the second-class rate dropped to one cent a pound, and in 1897, when rural delivery became free.[61] Another way in which the Post Office affected the industry came after 1875, when the department began using fast mail trains between the major cities. Within three years, over 60 per cent of all second-class post was sent from just six offices, indicating how the mail and its services had encouraged the centralisation of the publishing industry.[62]

Once the American railway network was in place, the developing technology of refrigeration and its application to wagons and warehouses in the early 1880s had remarkable consequences. After Gustavus F. Swift had hired Andrew J. Chase to design a refrigerated car to carry his dressed beef from Chicago to Boston in 1881,[63] the meat, beer and photographic industries were transformed into national operations, sometimes with international ramifications, through the application of this new technology.[64] As a result, the need for heavy capital investment in the special equipment and plant required, and the provision of new and reliable communication techniques to co-ordinate a steady flow of orders, products and raw materials over sometimes considerable distances, became paramount. Such expenditures and commitments discouraged the traditional middlemen and merchants, mainstays of the world trading system for centuries.[65] Furthermore, the American railway companies, anxious about losing livestock business, got cold feet about building and leasing the first fleet of wagons.[66] Thus, by necessity, large companies came into being in these developing industries, handling everything from the obtaining of the raw materials, through manufacture to the distribution of the finished product.[67]

Pressures of a different nature, though with remarkably similar consequences, arose within the next few years as highly mechanized, continuous processing developed within the food industries. The gross volume spewing from the ends of these new machines demanded efficient control of the raw materials and the well-managed distribution of the end products. Industrial milling of flour necessitated informed buying policies and a new marketing strategy to keep the rollers running, which is why the Pillsbury and Gold Medal brands came to the shop shelves.[68] When, in 1883, the Norton Brothers created the first 'automatic line' canning factory, disgorging containers at up to 4,400 per hour, it did not take long for Heinz and Campbell Soup to make a public appearance.[69] A quantum leap in the processing of oats had even more radical consequences at meal times as a new industry and a new habit, that of breakfast cereals, was born in the wake of the pioneer Quaker Oats.[70] With the distribution system in place, such packaged, branded products could be shifted wherever the railroad ran. Already the metalworking industries had developed techniques for the industrial production of firearms, agricultural implements, sewing machines, locks, scales and pumps.[71] Later they were joined by typewriters, bicycles and adding machines. A national distribution network meant that a national market was there to be exploited. But it all cost money. Thus, in American manufacturing as a whole, investment in capital per worker rose over 300% between 1879 and 1914, that is from $1,764 to $5,565, expressed in constant 1929 dollars.[72] In Britain, the lack of commitment to long-term technological investment at the tail end of the nineteenth century is notorious and those industries in which capital investment was forthcoming were frequently those such as flour, soap, sewing cotton and brewing in which marketing pressures were paramount.[73]

Superimposed upon these changes in production, collaboration between companies developed to aid the harassed capitalists deflect the sharper thrusts of competition. In the United States, loose confederations within particular industries were tried and found wanting.[74] Then Samuel Dodd, John Rockefeller's senior legal adviser at Standard Oil, invented the holding trust and in 1882 the bandwagon began to roll.[75] In 1889, business aggrandisement received its greatest infusion of blood when the state of New Jersey amended its laws to make company mergers possible. In little more than a decade, General Electric, American Telephone and Telegraph, International Harvester and US Steel grew to dominate their particular horizons.[76]

In Britain, the creation of the cotton giant J. & P. Coats proved to be the model that inspired Leverhulme on the path that later led to Unilever.[77] However, such aspirations were the exception rather than the rule. All too frequently the flurry of mergers that occurred in Britain round the turn of the century were a response to the waxing of share prices on the stock exchange.[78] Furthermore, Britain appears to have lacked the sizeable pool of managers necessary to run these companies, if the results are any criterion.[79] Only in the 1920s did the professional managerial skills become available in sufficient volume to make a wide variety of large companies a practical possibility.[80]

The department store had made its first appearance in Paris in the 1850s, demonstrating its success through the numbers of imitators of the original Bon Marché.[81] By 1914, '17% of the value of trade in Paris was in the hands of the department stores'.[82] Yet, although this was a substantial slice of the market, these establishments seem not to have had the dramatic impact of their transatlantic cousins. Perhaps their American counterparts further compounded the dislocation encouraged by the changes in production management detailed above that followed from technological development. Whatever the cause, the consequences were marked. For example, in 1899 one witness to the Industrial Commission of that year reported that whereas in 1880 'there had been dozens of dry goods jobbers in the wholesale section of Boston', only four now remained.[83] Of course, the advertising of the department stores was relatively local in scope.

Such a parochial scale of influence could not be ascribed to the mail order houses of the United States, which existed to serve a nation-wide clientele.[84] Nor the chains of stores that began to flourish in that country after the turn of the century. In Britain and France the chain stores developed somewhat earlier and in Britain seem to have catered to a particularly working class market. Nevertheless, that did not stop the owners from vigorously endorsing their merchandise.[85]

All these enormous investments in distribution, with the consequent technological development and managerial infrastructures, particularly in the newer production companies, led to debts that were only repayable in the medium to long-term. For example, the capital invested in American manufacturing more than doubled between 1879 and 1889, from $2,790 million rising to $6,525 million.[86] This meant that established selling procedures, which largely meant leaving matters to the initiative of middle men and shop keepers, were seen to be inadequate. A good return on this capital investment, as well as consistent and thus profitable production levels, required a stable and, preferably, steadily increasing demand. To stimulate such consumption the companies turned to advertising.[87]

There were few general and regular large advertisers in the 1870s and 1880s. Many business men and many companies thought advertising undignified, worse than that, disreputable, and worse even than that, an unnecessary expense. They manufactured to sell to jobbers. It was up to the jobber and then the retailer to move the stock.[88]

THUS JAMES WOOD SETS THE SCENE. Given that the largest advertisers were often selling spurious patent medicines, it is not surprising that established businesses should be so sniffy.[89] In the US, many monthly magazine publishers were reluctant even to accept advertisements despite the possible rise in revenue.[90] It was not until the early 1860s, fully 120 years after the first American periodical appeared, that one of these journals with aspirations to respectability, *Atlantic Monthly*, under the stimulus of a new and more commercially minded management, deigned to accept such vulgar additions to editorial matter in substantial quantities. By May 1866 its publishers, Ticknor and Fields, had gone so far as to use their entire back cover to display advertisements for photographic products. A four-page pink paper insert adjacent to the front cover emphasized their interest in and promotion of this growing source of revenue.[91]

However, many years passed before soliciting for advertising in earnest became fitting professional behaviour for sensitive American magazine publishers. Nevertheless, from its inception in 1870, *Scribner's Monthly* accepted some advertising. But it was not, apparently, until 1872, when Roswell Smith, the commercial mentor of the magazine, appointed Henry F. Taylor to the position of advertising manager, that the sale of space began to gather momentum. Smith and Taylor began soliciting for advertising and soon achieved pre-eminence in that field.[92] Eventually, in 1881, its leading competitor, *Harper's Monthly*, swallowed its pride and, allowing greed to supersede snobbery, followed its rival.

Those catering for less hidebound tastes, that is, the American weeklies, seem to have been less fussed by such pretensions to respectability. The very successful weekly *Youth's Companion* began carrying advertisements in January 1857 when new publishers took over its hitherto sanctimonious pages. To the end of the 1860s all insertions resembled the modern classified advertisement. However, at the turn of the decade, after what appears to have been the establishment within the magazine of an advertisement department, radical changes were initiated that turned it into a considerable selling medium. From 1871 it allowed its advertisers to use line blocks and within a few weeks the first instance of a two-column display had occurred. Although the latter portent remained generally underused and underdeveloped until the following decade, the weekly selling columns soon developed a strident, crude flavour that tended to overwhelm the elegant but staid pattern of the editorial section. In part the widespread use of bold or large type contributed to the imbalance. In part, the increasing use of illustrative figures had its effect. For, by 1883, 33% of the *Companion*'s insertions used a line block in one form or another: a precocity that contradicts established opinion on the inception of such devices.[93] Another ten years on and the proportion had risen to 60% of the 2808 insertions between 1 January and 30 June.[94] The consequence was some very ragged layouts.

Thus, once Cyrus Curtis had established his initial foothold in the magazine market with *Ladies' Home Journal*, it is not surprising that he sought to curtail the freedom of the advertisers, laying down limits to the graphic intrusions they could effect on his pages. In terms of industries, he actually closed his pages to the products of some entirely, in particular cosmetics and patent medicines, as he sought respectability. Such a move could have brought financial catastrophe, but because he was selling space in two of America's most successful magazines, the aforementioned *Journal* and, later, the *Saturday Evening Post*, he carried the day, and by 1910 he was in such a domineering position that he was able to issue edicts in the form of a leather-bound pocket book, that dictated precisely what he would permit in his magazines.[95]

It is interesting to note that Alfred Harmsworth, the progenitor of the Amalgamated Press and Curtis's British contemporary, demonstrated much the same paternal concern over the advertisements in his *Daily Mail* and *The Times*, bombarding editors with telegrams about transgressions.[96] This also helps to direct our attention to the differing channels that advertising took in the two countries. In America access could only be gained to a national market through the weekly and monthly magazines. In Britain the burgeoning mass circulation newspapers followed the lead of *The Times*, which throughout the first half of the nineteenth century had utilised the latest technology to dominate the demand for news and garner the lion's share of the published advertising into the bargain.[97] This gave the British advertiser a touch more respectability than his counterpart across the Atlantic.

It also meant that the newspaper was the medium of choice for national campaigns. Given the market penetration of *The Times* before 1860 and the waxing power of its rivals, such as the *Daily Telegraph* and the *Daily News*, as well as the Sunday press, after that date,[98] and the as yet still relatively latent requirements of British commerce, the quantity of advertising available to those periodicals of weekly, monthly or quarterly persuasion must have been limited. The scale of success of the daily newspapers in sopping up the amount of business on the streets can be gauged from a survey conducted in 1886. By that time 60.6% of the column space in the *Daily Telegraph* was given over to advertising. The figure for *The Standard* was 51%, that for *The Times* 49%, *The Scotsman* 40.5% and *The Scottish News* 26.5%.[99] Furthermore, a generation later, Robert Donald, in his presidential address to the Institute of Journalists in 1913, was decrying the efficiency of the national dailies, based in London, in attracting advertising and damaging the provincial newspapers.[100] Thus, it would appear that the skill of the advertising departments of Fleet Street was debilitating all serials other than their own, and the ability of the British magazines to gain income from any source other than their cover price, during the late nineteenth and early twentieth century, was somewhat circumscribed. Even the well-established *Illustrated London News*, which from the start had placed its advertising pages among the editorial matter and had never been adverse to their form of revenue, during the first 10 weeks of 1886 used only 21.6% of its column space to sell the wares of others.

So, to sum up, the dynamic of development within both Britain and the United States proved remarkably consistent whether judged from the point of view of an industrialist, an advertising executive or a magazine publisher. The energies of urbanisation were released in the first part of the nineteenth century in Britain and towards its end in the United States. The rise of the popular magazine was a part of this process in each country, as we will see. So, given the headlong economic momentum of American society in the 1890s, the established commercial strength of the British and the needs of their respective societies, it hardly seems surprising that these countries should have been the seedbed of so many concepts that have sustained the periodical world during the ensuing 60 years. Yet, before we detail those developments we need to uncover that other context in which the magazine is created, that of production technology.

NOTES

1. van Zuilen, A.J., *The Life Cycle of Magazines*, Uithoorn, Holland, 1977, pp112-120.

2. Peterson, Theodore, *Magazines in the Twentieth Century*, Urbana, Illinois, 1964, pp310-311.

3. White, Cynthia L., *Women's magazines 1693-1968*, London, 1970, p299.

4. Tebbel, John, *The American Magazine*, New York, 1969, pp148-149.

5. Ibid.

6. Waples, D., Berelson, B., Bradshaw, F.R., *What Reading Does to People*, Chicago, 1940, p13.

7. Zimet, Sara Goodman, *Print and Prejudice*, London, 1976, p16.

8. Ingarden, Roman, *The Cognition of the Literary Work of Art*, Evanston, Illinois, 1973, p53. Originally published in Polish in 1937. This is the only one among a number of books by European authors whose studies are considered to be relevant to 'reception theory' that have been found useful in this study.

9. Festinger, Leon, *A Theory of Cognitive Dissonance*, Evanston, Illinois, 1957, pp1-2.

10. Ibid, p3.

11. John, Arthur, *The Best Years of the Century*, Urbana, Illinois and London, 1981, pp43-44.

12. Mott, Frank L., *A History of American Magazines*, Boston, 1938-68, 5 Vols.

13. University of London, *Regulations for Internal Students*, 1991-1992, p1509.

14. John, op.cit., pp43-44.

15. Stempel, Guido H. and Westley, Bruce, H.(Eds.), *Research Methods in Mass Communication*, New Jersey, 1981.

16. Peterson, op.cit., p206.

17. Lay and Brother, The Newspaper Record, Philadelphia, 1856, p x. Quoted in Myers Jr., Kenneth H., *SRDS*, Evanston, Ill., 1968, p32.

18. Myers, ibid., p33.

19. Ibid., pp35-36.

20. Ibid., pp35 & 39.

21. Bennett, Charles O., *Facts Without Opinions*, Chicago, 1965, p15.

22. Ibid., pp16-17.

23. Ibid., p17.

24. Ibid., pp23-52.

25. Ibid., pp57-58.

26. Ibid., pp61-62.

27. Myers, op.cit., pp43-44.

28. Ibid., p57.

29. Browne and Co., T.B., *The Advertiser's ABC*, London, 1893, p40.

30. *Advertiser's ABC*, London, 1886, p470 cites a figure of 'over 320,000 copies' and the edition of 1889, p711 quotes 'above 350,000'.

31. British Library Manuscript Files 62153 to 62397.

32. *The Advertisers' Protection Society Monthly Circular*, No.49, London, May 1908 estimates the circulation of *Answers* to be 650,000. No.85, May 1911 publishes a certificate of average circulation for the weekly for 1910 of 716,998 and states that it was 830,318 for 1906. The collection of circulars is held by the Incorporated Society of British Advertisers at 44 Hertford Street, London W1.

33. *Incorporated Society of British Advertisers Monthly Circular*, No.10, London, March 1921. pp15-16; and Mather and Crowther, *Practical Advertising*, London, 1922, pp11-45. (This is an annual serial.)

34. London Research Bureau, *Press Circulations Analysed*, London, 1928, p133.

35. Routh, Guy, *Occupation and Pay in Great Britain 1906-79*, London, 1980, p5, table 1.1.

36. London Research Bureau, op.cit., p(v)

37. Nevett, Terence R., *Advertising in Britain*, London, 1982, p155 and White, op.cit., p117.

38. Damon-Moore, Helen, *Magazines for the Millions: Gender and Commerce in the Ladies' Home Journal and the Saturday Evening Post 1880-1910*, New York, 1994.

39. Baldasty, Gerald J., *The Commercialization of News in the Nineteenth Century*, Madison, WI, 1992, p125.

40. White, op.cit., p23-24.

41. Peterson, op.cit., pp69-73.

42. Ibid, p441.

43. O'Brien, P. and Keyder, C., *Economic Growth in Britain and France 1780-1914*, London, 1978, p192, paraphrasing J.R.Harris, Industry *and Technology in the Eighteenth Century: Britain and France*, inaugural lecture delivered in the University of Birmingham, 1971.

44. Heilbroner, Robert L. and Singer, Aaron, *The Economic Transformation of America*, New York, 1977, pp32-33. By this time Britain had been building canals for 60 years.

45. Ibid, p42.

46. U.S. Bureau of the Census, *Historical Statistics of the United States, Colonial Times to 1970*, Pt.II, Washington, D.C., 1975, Series P265, p694. Hereafter known as *Historical Statistics*. And, Mitchell, B R, *Abstract of British Historical Statistics*, Cambridge, 1962, p136. In 1880 the U.S. produced 1,247,000 tons of steel; in 1890, 4,267,000 tons. In 1880 Britain produced 1,295,000 tons of steel; in 1890, 3,579,000 tons

47. Mitchell, B. R., *European Historical Statistics 1750-1975*, 2nd Edition, London, 1981, p34.

48. *Historical Statistics*, op.cit., Pt.I, p8.

49. Mitchell, op.cit., p34 and *Historical Statistics*, op.cit., Pt.I, p8.

50. Porter, Glenn and Livesay, Harold C., *Merchants and Manufacturers*, Baltimore and London, 1971, pp154-155.

51. Mitchell, *British Historical Statistics*, op.cit., pp24-27.

52. Ibid. Measures of the numbers of people living in large towns are a more accurate indication of a potential urban market than figures expressing the percentage of the population living in towns in total.

53. Freeman, Michael J., 'Introduction' in *Transport in the Industrial Revolution*, Ed. by Derek H. Aldcroft and Michael J. Freeman, Manchester, England and Dover, New Hampshire, 1983, p3.

54. Hawke, Gary and Higgins, Jim, 'Britain' in *Railways and the Economic Development of Western Europe 1830-1914*, O'Brien, Patrick (Ed.), London, 1983, pp172-184. The extraordinarily detailed, year-by-year expenditures data on these pages quantifies in a quite remarkable way, even given the qualifying riders lain upon them, the concepts and beliefs about the development of transport previously subscribed to with little substantial evidence in support.

55. *The Times*, May 11, 1869, No.26434, p12, cl.1. Allowing for the difference in times zones and the time of the ceremony - 2.30pm locally - the story was telegraphed to London with some speed to be placed at the top of column one, in the listing of recent intelligence in the editions for the following day.

56. Riegel, Robert Edgar, *The Story of the Western Railroads*, Lincoln, Nebraska and London, 1964, p110.

57. Chandler, Alfred D., *The Visible Hand*, Cambridge, Mass. and London, 1977, p210.

58. Kielbowicz, Richard Burket, *Origins of the Second-Class mail Category and the Business of Policymaking, 1863-1879*, Columbia, South Carolina, Journalism Monographs No.96, 1986, pp4-6.

59. Ibid., pp13-14.

60. Ibid., p20.

61. Greene, Theodore P, *America's Heroes*, New York, 1970, p61.

62. Kielbowicz, op.cit., p17.

63. Chandler, op.cit., p299.

64. Porter and Livesay, op.cit., pp166-179.

65. Ibid.

66. Chandler, op.cit., p300.

67. Porter and Livesay, op.cit., pp166-179.

68. Chandler, op.cit., pp293-295.

69. Ibid., p253.

70. Ibid., p293.

71. Ibid., p271.

72. *Historical Statistics*, op.cit., pp666, 684-685, quoted in Pope, Daniel, *The Making of Modern Advertising*, 1983, New York, p32.

73. Hannah, Leslie, *The Rise of the Corporate Economy*, 2nd Edition, London, 1983, p16.

74. Heilbroner and Singer, op.cit., pp108-109.

75. Ibid, p109.

76. Ibid, p110.

77. Wilson, op.cit., Vol.1, pp70-71.

78. Hannah, op.cit., p59.

79. Ibid., pp74-75.

80. Ibid., pp78-81.

81. Caron, François, *An Economic History of Modern France*, Trans. by Barbara Bray, London, 1979, p92.

82. Ibid., p93.

83. Chandler, op.cit., p229.

84. Ibid, pp230-233.

85. Jefferys, James B., *Retail Trading in Britain 1850-1950*, Cambridge, Eng., 1954, pp24-32. Caron, op.cit., p92.

86. Presbrey, Frank, *The History and Development of Advertising*, New York, 1929, p337.

87. Porter and Livesay, op.cit., pp166-179 & 224.

88. Wood, Advertising, op.cit., p238.

89. Reed, David, Growing Up, *Journal of Advertising History*, Vol.10, No.1, 1987, pp21-23.

90. Presbrey, Frank, op.cit., p466.

91. Wood, Advertising, op.cit., pp195-197.

92. John, op.cit., pp99-101.

93. Reed, op.cit., pp25-28.

94. Ibid, p30.

95. Wood, James Playstead, *The Curtis Magazines*, New York, 1971, pp64-65.

96. Nevett, op.cit., pp82-83.

97. Lee, Alan J., *The Origins of the Popular Press in England 1855-1914*, London and Totowa, N.J., 1976, p47. By 1841 *The Times* 'sold twice the number of copies as the *Morning Post, Morning Herald* and *Morning Chronicle* put together, and by 1850 four times as many.'

98. Wadsworth, A.P., 'Newspaper Circulation 1800-1954' in *Transactions of the Manchester Statistical Society, Session 1954-55*, Manchester, pp20-23. '*The Daily Telegraph* which was 27,000 in 1856 and 30,000 in 1858, reached 141,700 by 1861; 191,000 by 1871; 242,000 by 1877; 250,000 by 1880; with a peak of 300,000 about 1888....*The Daily News*......touched 150,000 during the Franco- German war and settled at about 90,000....in 1890 it was 93,700.' *The Times* circulation peaked at 66,000 in the mid-1860s and held above 60,000 until 1879, then collapsed to 40,000 by 1890. *Lloyd's Weekly News* claimed 900,000 sales in 1890, *Reynold's News* 350,000. The other Sundays claimed substantially less.

99. Reid, A., 'How a provincial newspaper is managed', in *Nineteenth Century*, Vol.XX, 1886, p395, quoted in Lee, pp86-87.

100. Taylor, Henry Archibald, *Robert Donald*, London, 1934, p269, quoted in Lee, Alan J., Op.cit., pp216-217.

The Great Printing Revolution

THE RAW MATERIAL OF THE MAGAZINE manufacturing process is paper and its differing qualities are parameters that define many aspects of a modern publication's nature. Yet, in the mid-nineteenth century there were few alternatives available to any publisher, whether he was producing books, newspapers or magazines. Paper was made from rags and cotton waste. As demand for printed matter rose inexorably as the century unrolled, the demand for the raw material rose with it. And although the supply of these materials did increase, it was not fast enough to satisfy demand. In Britain the price of rags used in making 'ordinary printing paper' rose 28% during the early 1850s. By the early 1860s newspaper stock cost 25 cents a pound in the United States.[1] Not surprisingly, the search for a cheaper substitute was equally relentless.

Many unusual sources of vegetable fibre were tried, though the only two in which interest was sustained over the years were straw and esparto. The former is still used to make board. The latter, which comes from esparto grass, *Stipa tenacissima*, grows in the drier parts of Spain and North Africa, yielding a paper of the highest quality. First used in Britain during the period 1857-60,[2] and during the latter half of the nineteenth century, substantial quantities were imported; until the resources of the world's temperate forests were unlocked, that is.

Friedrich Keller of Hainichen, Saxony registered a patent for a wood-grinding machine in 1840. Six years later, Heinrich Voelter, a paper-mill director, also of Saxony, bought the patent and began designing and improving machinery that could be used in his mill. By 1852, two mills in Germany were regularly producing wood-pulp, although rag had to be added to reinforce the porridge of fibres that is known as the furnish.[3] In 1853 Charles Watt and H. Burgess obtained a patent for the manufacture and use of wood-pulp for paper-making in the United Kingdom.[4] While, in 1858 Voelter obtained a patent for his process in the United States, antedated to 29 August 1856.[5] Yet, it would appear from our present, somewhat sketchy knowledge, that the revolution that appears so inevitable with hindsight needed the combined stimulus of high prices, a competing process and the economic thrust of the dynamic, post-civil-war American economy to push it from the periphery to the centre of the stage.

On 12 April 1866 the plant of the American Wood Paper Company in Manayunk, Pennsylvania went on-stream. But it did not use the process already discussed. Instead, the equally new soda method, which reduced the wood to a fibrous slurry through the use of caustic soda, was employed. This pulp still needed the addition of rag and was mixed with straw pulp before a satisfactory product was obtained. Nevertheless, the company was successful and soon opened two additional plants.[6] Only on 5 March 1867, did the Voelter process begin producing wood pulp in the United States, at Curtisville, Massachusetts. Again, a percentage addition of rag was necessary to strengthen the end product.[7]

The paper from both forms of wood pulp took a while to overcome the reservations of consumers, and although the *Staats-Zeitung*, a New York daily for its German population, began using what came to be called newsprint on 7 January 1868, it was not until the early 1870s that its American-language competitors began the change over.[8] Doubtless, the economic incentive was the strongest, for already in 1869 the price of newsprint was down to 14 cents a pound. By 1897 it was two cents a pound and still falling.[9] Thus, the paper industry was propelled into a transformed situation, in which raw materials, far from being in restricted and expensive supply, were abundant and widely distributed. Now the only limitations on production were those of capital and the availability of management skills to exploit the situation. The firm of S. D. Warren of Boston, Massachusetts seems to have possessed both.

Having originated as paper dealers, the company expanded into rag importation and then paper manufacture. In 1873 Warren concluded that the days of rag pulp were numbered and that the new processes had proved themselves. So he began building wood pulp mills on carefully selected sites with considerably more acumen than many of his competitors. By 1880 he owned the largest paper mill in the world. More apposite to our purposes here, during the 1870s the company was already supplying paper to leading magazines, such as *Youth's Companion*, *Atlantic Monthly* and, in the 1880s, the *Century Illustrated Monthly Magazine*.[10] Moreover, Warren was far from content to rest on his laurels, and the company's continued commitment to innovation can be inferred from its position as the first manufacturer in the United States of coated paper on a commercial scale, in 1881.[11] Indeed, the company's involvement in product innovation and development may be particularly germane to the progress of this chapter for, in 1885, their client, the *Century Illustrated Monthly Magazine*, was one of the first periodicals in the United States to use the halftone process to reproduce an illustration;[12] a process which relies on paper with a smooth surface.

For much of their existence, halftones were illustrations which simulated a range of tones with very small specks of ink which were proportional in area to the intensity of the light reflected from the subject reproduced. From the 1890s until the process was computerised, they were, in the main, produced when a diamond-ruled lattice on a transparent sheet was interposed between a plate coated with a light-sensitive emulsion and a negative of the original during exposure to a light source. In this process, the light passed through the negative and the screen to reach the plate and the edge-effect of the lattice deflected the rays.

Thus, a very dark area on the original object was converted to a translucent area on the negative because little light reached the film in the camera from this particular area. When the printing plate was exposed, plenty of light passed easily through this translucent area and was spread by the lattice to create a relatively large dot of light on the plate emulsion. Conversely, bright areas of the original created dense sites on the negative which only passed a little light while the plate was being exposed. These faint rays were focused by the lattice as relatively small dots of light on the plate emulsion. The definition and precise size of the dots, large and small, could be modified by the operator by adjusting the position of the screen.

The quality of the result was also affected by the frequency of lines which formed the interposed lattice, which was known as the screen. The more lines per inch that were ruled on to the screen, the more dots per square inch formed the image on the plate and the finer the resulting reproduction. Modern newspapers tend to use screens ruled with 60-80 lines per inch. The highest quality can be obtained with screens of 300+ lines per inch, which needs to be printed on the finest art paper.

Once the plate had been exposed, the development and etching of the plate transformed the latent image, which was composed of dots of varying sizes, into a delicate relief of metal.[13] When it was eventually inked up, the large dot, of course, produced a relatively large, dark area on paper, and vice versa. Thus, if the quality of such printed images was consequent upon the efficient transfer of ink from tiny pinnacles of etched metal, it is evident that the quality of the paper surface was a critical element in getting the best from the plate.

By the end of the nineteenth century there were three types of paper that served the halftone plate particularly well. They are with us still, even if their number has received some additions and their relative importance has shifted. Super-calendered paper is produced by passing the slightly dampened web between rollers, the surfaces of which are alternately steam-heated metal and polished cotton paper. With the cylinders being driven at different speeds, the web slides between them and a highly polished surface is produced on both sides.[14] Surface finishes are varied by changing the pressure of the rollers. Produced directly from ground wood pulp, this is the cheapest material to give reasonable results with halftone blocks.[15] However, as Julius Beck revealed in the 1930s, even the best calendered paper, in which the surface is so smooth that investigation with scientific measuring devices is unable to detect any roughness, will still give uneven reproduction and absorption of the ink. This arises, apparently, because the 'ironing' process, to get the smooth surface, compresses some fibres much more thoroughly than others. The 'hills' are squashed more than the 'valleys' and in this way areas of differing absorptive powers are created.[16] Thus, although super-calendered paper is a cost-effective solution to the needs of the printer of halftone blocks, it is incapable of rendering the finest images.

Yet, it was an invaluable basis upon which to build the edifice of the illustrated magazine as it developed over the last dozen or so years of the nineteenth century. In Britain the list of mills producing super-calendered paper grew in parallel with the number of consumers. By 1885 there were two listed: J. and E. Thomas and Green of Beaconsfield, Buckinghamshire and Y. Trotter of Chirnside, Berwickshire in Scotland.[17] A year later John Dickinson of Croxley Green, Hertfordshire had been added to their number.[18] After another 12 months, Reed and Smith of Cullompton, Devon and William Tod and Son of Edinburgh had joined the fold.[19] By 1890, when the *Review of Reviews* began and *The English Illustrated Magazine* was in full flight, there were still only three suitably equipped mills in England, though the Scots now had five.[20] But in 1891 demand soared with the start of *The Strand Magazine* and its clones. So by 1894 there were 10 such mills in England and Wales, with a further eight in Scotland catering for this publication and its imitators, amongst others.[21] After the expansion of the periodical trade in the second half of the decade, the close of the century saw another jump to fourteen mills in England and Wales and eleven in Scotland.[22] Figures on the total unit volumes manufactured by these mills do not seem to have been accumulated.

Despite the efficacy of super-calendered stock, the finest reproductions were only possible on art papers. 'These consist of a body (or base) paper (preferably of esparto) to which a surface coating of mineral matter mixed with adhesive is applied in such a thickness that the fibres of the body paper do not show on the surface at all..... These art papers are usually super-calendered'.[23] (The mineral matter is kaolin.) In fact, this type of paper was the first of the modern, quality surfaces produced in volume.[24] As noted above, S. D. Warren began making it in the United States in 1881. It would appear that most of their output was produced for that sector of the industry using chromolithography.[25]

The third of our materials for rendering good-quality halftones is imitation art paper, which is intermediate in results and cost between the other two. It is made 'by adding a large quantity of mineral loading to the pulp in the beater. The resulting paper is water-finished or damped and super-calendered.'[26]

The significance of the invention of the halftone and its potential as perceived by publishers of the time can be inferred from the fact that all of these new papers were developed into commercial propositions within a very few years in the 1880s. The industry had never previously seen such radical innovations in the finished product in such a short time. This implies that the demand must have been insistent and substantial. This was certainly true of super-calendered and imitation art paper, which seem to have been developed as a direct consequence of the demand for an economic, smooth surface upon which halftones could produce results of quality.[27] On the other hand, one can also reasonably assume that Warren's initiation of art paper production in 1881 was a fortuitous coincidence, designed as it was for the chromolithography trade, for its potential does not appear to have been exploited by magazine publishers before the middle of the 1890s. All of these types of paper and later refinements upon them have been available to the modern magazine publisher and his printers.

THE BIRTH OF THE HALFTONE was a messy affair, the details of which are far from agreed. In part this stems from a lack of interest on the part of historians. However, this lack of agreement may also arise from a situation in which no one person can be credited with the entire creation of the final form of this crucial technique: evolution not revolution was the keynote. Fortunately, the first tremulous steps can, largely, be avoided by this narrative as they failed to achieve the maturity necessary to feature in the magazine printer's repertoire. Suffice to say that the first appearance of a halftone in a periodical seems to have occurred on 30 October 1869 at the launch of the *Canadian Illustrated News*.(Fig. 1) William A. Leggo and George E. Desbarats were responsible for the technique that made this advance a practical reality. They used glass plates coated with darkened collodion that were then scored through to make a crude cross-line lattice which was used to break down the image into small dots.(Fig. 2) The technique was

Figs 1 & 2 The world's first halftone, published on 30 October 1869, of Queen Victoria's youngest son, Prince Arthur, during his visit to the dominion, exhibits a regular structure quite unlike that created by other experimenters during the following years.

Figs 3 & 4 Frank Miles's drawing of Lillie Langtry was printed in Paris, although it was published as an insert in the London weekly, Life, on 6 September 1879. Its irregular dot structure is a typical product of an emulsion fragmented into tiny particles to produce dots on the printing plate that could create a facsimile of the original tones.

applied to lithographic plates which were called Leggotypes. The two men went on, in 1873, to found the *New York Daily Graphic*. Thus, it was their imprint and a derivative of their technique, apparently, that was used to produce the much vaunted 'Shanty-town' reproduction in the 4 March 1880 edition, which has been eulogised all too frequently as the world's first halftone reproduction in a periodical. Indeed, given the connection, one now wonders just how much credit Stephen Horgan should receive for his part in its production. What has been up until now virtually universal acclamation, might well be seen as a naïve endorsement by inattentive historians of a skilful piece of self-promotion by the American. It is particularly unfortunate that the information, regarding the connection between the Canadians and the American, though established by Kainen, should have lain dormant for so long.[28]

Meanwhile, in Europe, various experiments using reticulated gelatine emulsions to create a random grain structure that would give acceptable halftones bore fruit in the late 1870s.[29] At this time *L'Art Contemporain* began using the process to reproduce works of art, its almost exclusive function for the French. That title was one among a number owned by La société anonyme de publications périodiques of 13-15 quai Voltaire, Paris.[30] They also owned *Le Monde Illustré*, which on 26 July 1879 reproduced *Le Cadeau du Grand Père* by C. A. Pabst, using a block previously featured in the publisher's art magazine.[31]

On 6 September 1879 the British weekly, *Life*, began using the Parisian company to reproduce a sketch of a society woman, as a supplement, on a regular basis. The first subject was Mrs Lillie Langtry.(Figs 3 and 4) Alternating with the portraits were reproductions of works of art. But the latter sequence was discontinued within a year and *Life* soon began to reproduce

31

works from the studio of Fritz Zuber-Bühler, whose soft, retouched photographic portraits are difficult to distinguish from drawings. At the moment this would seem to be the first regular publication of halftones in a British, French or American magazine.

Nevertheless, despite the success of these first tentative steps, it was soon realised that a more regular grain structure would enhance and further define the tonal transitions of the reproductions. It would be necessary to interpose some sort of fine lattice of the type already described, between the negative of the original and the plate during the exposure of the latter, to get regularity. But such realisations were not enough. The problems were largely those of practice, as Kainen has pointed out. One snag probably arose from the difficulties inherent in etching the delicate dot structure of the plate.[32] Another problem was the need to control precisely the proximity of the screen or lattice to the negative in the exposure of the plate. Each minute gap between the lines acted as a lenseless aperture with the light being diffracted by its edges. As we have seen, the greater the amount of light passing from the negative, the larger the resulting dot of light on the far side of the screen that would affect the emulsion of the plate.[33] It followed that the quality of definition of the dots of light on the emulsion was a matter of some importance. Robert Faulkner was the first to realise this in 1872.[34] But it was another 10 years before technicians were able to exercise the control necessary to put his realisation into practice.

On 16 September 1882 a halftone produced via a primitive cross-line screen appeared on page 185 of *L'Illustration*. This appears to be the first to appear in a magazine in France. Comparison with an example of the work of Charles Gillot reproduced in *The Art Journal* for 1885 suggests that the Parisian engraver might well have had a hand in the production of this illustration, particularly as he was already closely associated with *L'Illustration*[35] and had learned how to control the etching process when he developed his father's gillotage process. Two months later, the issue for 25 November carried another halftone. This time it was printed from a block that had been made for a book. This cost-cutting exercise was repeated a year later, in the issue of *L'Illustration* for 17 November 1883. In this instance the original volume from which it had been borrowed concerned Japanese art. The image structure reflected the still experimental state of the art, for the screen used to create the halftone seems to have been composed purely of diagonal lines very closely set at a frequency of 150 per inch. Given their later association and the known evolution of Meisenbach's techniques, it is certainly possible that the Munich-based block maker created the plate from which the image was printed in the magazine.[36] At about the same time, in the first annual edition of *Le Figaro Illustré*, a drawing of a moonlit river scene was rendered by a primitive cross-line screen.[37] However, on 3 May 1884 the level of expertise employed in these periodicals made a very unexpected bound forward.

The Paris Salon was a great social event in that capital's year. On this occasion *L'Illustration* took the opportunity to devote its entire issue to the subject, all 32 pages. A sandwich design was used that alternated a two page picture spread with two pages of text. It seems likely that this tactic was chosen so that all the illustrations could be printed at one pass through the presses, while the text was printed on a second, or vice versa. Of the 53 works of art that were reproduced, an amazing 38, or 72%, were halftones, including the first page, a translation of Boulanger's *La Captive* into an image 199 x 267mm.(Fig. 5) In the shadow areas some signs of crude white line retouching can be seen. All the remaining 37 halftones were 1/4 page size or larger. They exhibit an image structure of well-defined, round dots on a clear ground,(Fig. 6) which resembles a present day halftone, suggesting that a device closely resembling a modern cross-line screen had been used in their creation. The line frequency used varied between 80 and 100 per inch, which is slightly finer than the average, modern newspaper halftone. The

Figs 5 & 6 The 3 May 1884 edition of L'Illustration featured a cover and many inside illustrations that were reproduced from halftone blocks by the Munich and London-based Meisenbach. Their clearly defined dot structure suggests that the German blockmaker had used an etched glass screen in their manufacture.

remaining 15 illustrations were all printed from line blocks about 120 x 80mm in size and were crammed on to the central double spread. Relative to the rest of the issue they are of minor importance and without them this would have been the world's first edition of a periodical wholly illustrated by halftones, at a time when very few editors and their design staff even knew of their existence.

Close examination of the lower right corner of some of the reproductions reveals exactly how the French weekly had made such an impressive technical advance. They feature the name 'Meisenbach', the Munich-based block maker. Not previously associated with Paris, although he set up an establishment in London in 1884,[38] the German's name does not occur in the *Annuaire-Almanach du Commerce*, the Bottin of 1884. It, therefore, has to be assumed, for the moment at least, that the Parisian journal had the originals photographed in the Salon and then sent these negatives to Munich, where blocks were made, which were then returned to Paris to be printed. Such a rigmarole only emphasizes the value that the editor must have placed on the attainment of quality achievable by the best halftones, and the advantages that would accrue from their use. For, although there was an international trade in blocks by this time, there is no evidence to suggest that it was conducted at this hectic pace.

Despite the advanced form of the image structure in this particular issue, subsequent usage in *L'Illustration* regressed into much cruder production techniques, when halftones were seen that is, for they were only used very sporadically during the following twelve months. It was only with the Salon of the following year, 1885, that another halftone-dominated edition was published. Again, this failed to emulate the technical apogee of the previous May and one can only assume that the *tour de force* had been too expensive to repeat. Meanwhile in April 1885, another magazine, the monthly *Paris Illustré*, in April 1885, had used a halftone with a clearly defined dot structure on its cover. Their oval reproduction was of a photographic portrait of a singer, Madame Krauss. She was surrounded by coloured artwork produced by Emile Grasset, which alluded to the roles and appurtenances of her working life.

Yet, despite such experiments and the quality of the results, *The Penrose Annual*, a decade later, in its first half dozen editions, contains many disparaging comments, usually by French printers, on the Gallic inability to utilise halftones and a general lack of skill. In fact, this apparent contradiction may be resolved if one accepts the judgement of the contemporary French observer Professor Leon Vidal, who acknowledged the skill and brilliance of a small number of companies, in particular Boussod, Valadon et Cie. He also related how that company had retained its secrets and its staff, leaving other interested companies to their own devices. Moreover, the company discouraged the spread of demand for the techniques from publishers by charging very high prices for their work. Without suppliers and promoters of the new technology in the form of a graphic supplies industry, the less fortunate firms were in a very weak competitive position, hence the poor overall state of French printing and the glory of the few exceptional companies.[39]

This observation is supported by the entry on Charles Gillot in the *Dictionnaire de Biographie Française*, which links this key technician to both *L'Illustration* and Boussod, Valadon.[40] Owning a print shop in his own right which he had inherited from his father, he engraved and printed *Paris Illustré*, the early issues of which must rank among the most exquisite of all magazines. His father, Firmin Gillot, had invented a technique for translating etched or lithographic plates into zinc relief plates that could be printed letterpress. It involved taking a very clean, grained or highly polished zinc plate, on to which an image, from whatever source, was reproduced via transfer paper. Ink, that incorporated an acid-resistant powder, was then applied to the plate so that it adhered to the image but left other areas clear. The plate was then immersed in a shallow bath of very dilute nitrous acid and the etching process begun. By proceeding through baths of increasing strength and renewing the resist, the image was transformed into a relief which could be used on a normal letterpress machine. The process came to be known as gillotage and was reported as being very popular in Paris, being used by, amongst others, Daumier, during the late 1860s. When the father died in 1872, Charles took over the family business and tried, by experiment, to extend his father's process through the use of photography. By 1875 Charles had succeeded and four years later began to produce line blocks for *L'Illustration* using this photo-mechanical process.[41] His abilities were to prove crucial in the utilisation of colour in the periodicals of the coming decade, as will be seen later.

In addition, Boussod, Valadon had the services of a M. Manzi, who had 'acquired his experience in the studios of Austria and Italy', apparently.[42] His importance to the firm may be implied from his appointment as a full partner in the reorganisation of 1897 when the company became Boussod, Manzi, Joyant, et Cie.[43] So, given access to such expertise, is hardly surprising that this company came to dominate On 6 September 1884 the first cross-line halftone seems to have made its debut in a British magazine when *The Graphic* published a 205 x 148mm reproduction of a photograph entitled *The Midnight Sun*, which had been taken at North Cape, Norway.[44] No engraving attribution appeared on the block. One year later, the same publication ran a four-page story, 'An Amateur Photographer at the Zoo'. It was illustrated by 15 cross-line halftone reproductions of photographs spread over four pages. It began with what is now known as an establishing shot, that is, a general view of the zoo, and continued with details of the

Fig.7 On 5 September 1885, The Graphic published what appears to be the world's first photographic picture story using blocks made by Meisenbach. For some reason, they seemed to have been embarrassed by the association for a crude attempt was made to erase his name from the blocks.

place.(Fig. 7) It thus has a substantial claim to be considered as the first photo-picture story to be published in any periodical in the world. A certain amount of retouching and some crude blocking out is noticeable in some reproductions. On one, Meisen-bach's name has been scratched over in a futile attempt to obliterate his responsibility for production of the blocks.[45]

On the same day, the 5 September 1885 issue of the *Illustrated London News* published a large, 446 x 335mm reproduction of a painting entitled *Fido's Lesson* by Munier as a special supplement. It was produced for them by Boussod, Valadon et Cie. under the name

of the phototype process, on paper of a much higher quality than the normal stock. The experiment was repeated four months later on 16 January 1886, when the weekly published *The Sedan Chair* by Kaenmerer. By 4 September 1886 the process had been integrated with the normal pagination, even if special paper had been used for the four full page illustrations. After another year, on 17 September 1887, the integration was taken further when a small halftone was slipped in among the usual line blocks on page 339. All of the examples were reproductions of art work or flat copy. None paralleled the tendency of *The Graphic* to print facsimiles of photographs that described the everyday world. In part this seems to have been a consequence of the suppliers chosen by the two magazines. Boussod, Valadon seem, almost entirely, to have used the new technology to reproduce art, both in their own country and for export, which is hardly surprising given their print publishing business. Meisenbach's work for the British magazines, on the other hand, seems to have been more concerned with the translation of images of the world at large into a type-compatible form that was printable on the normal pagination. A few weeks later the *Ladies' Pictorial*, a publication which is, so far, relatively obscure, began using halftones. Early in 1888, all three publications began extending their use of the process. Part of the inducement to participate in this technological initiative may well have been financial. At this time, *The Graphic* was spending around £500 a week on illustrations.[46] The changes may also suggest the increasing competence of the house of Meisenbach and the growth of a small but increasingly effective process engraving industry in London that was sufficiently well organised by 1888 to provide these blocks in quantity for magazines with weekly deadlines.[47]

Thus, Berry and Poole's report that the first edition of *The Strand Magazine* was 'the earliest to contain wood engravings, photographic line blocks and halftone illustrations in one issue', that of January 1891, is sadly misguided.[48] Even the Newnes organisation itself used such a mix a year earlier in the January 1890 edition of the *Review of Reviews*.

Throughout the nineteenth century, wood engraving had been the basis of most magazine illustration, but it could be a laboured and laborious process, particularly for those illustrations that filled the page. To ease this bottleneck, systems were devised for drawing the illustrations on to the whole block, cutting it into sections that were engraved by different craftsmen, which were then bolted back together again for printing.[49] Yet, maintaining a studio of men for such purposes, or contracting out the work, could be very expensive. For example, engravings probably cost the New York based publishers of *Century Illustrated Monthly Magazine* $8,000 per month by 1890.[50] At a time when advertising was still a relatively underdeveloped source of revenue, such expenses had to be reflected in the cover price. As a consequence, the well-illustrated American journals were priced at a level that only those with quantities of surplus disposable income, the middle and upper classes and their institutions, could afford.

The halftone changed all that. As Mott pointed out, 'When the *Century* paid up to $300 for a page-size woodcut ... it could buy a halftone for less than $20.'[51] Not surprisingly, such advantages encouraged experimentation with the process and Harper Brothers of New York appear to have been the first American magazine publisher to take the plunge. In the 8 April 1884 edition of *Harper's Young People*,[52] they used a reproduction of a picture of children and geese that employed a halftone with an irregular dot structure. The following month the company used a small cross-line halftone of a riverside scene in their *Monthly*.[53] Then, in October, *Harper's Young People* used another cross-line, at 110 lines per inch.[54] The following year *Century Illustrated* dipped its toe in the water and joined the photo-mechanical fold.[55] However, a few years passed before the Americans began using halftones on a large scale.

This lag may well have been a consequence of the considerable difficulties in making cross-line screens. However, the turning point came in 1890 when the Levy Brothers began manufacturing diamond-ruled, cross-line screens on an industrial scale at their plant in Sixth St., Philadelphia.[56] Within a few years most of the major magazines were making extensive use of halftones. By 1893, Mott reported, 30% of *Century Illustrated's* reproductions were produced in this manner, 50% of *Harper's*, 60% of *Scribner's* and 100% of *Cosmopolitan*.[57] Unfortunately, examination of the magazines in question completely contradicts Mott's figures for which no reference is given.

MEANWHILE, THE FRENCH WERE EXPERIMENTING WITH COLOUR. The *Illustrated London News* had been distributing colour supplements on an occasional basis since 1855,(Plate I) after its owners, the Ingram family, had felt the challenge of a new, but ephemeral weekly, *The Colored News*, which used coloured wood blocks.[58](Plate II) Initially, the printers of the *News*, Leighton Brothers of Lambs Conduit Street, London, used a combination of wood blocks and etched tone blocks. Later, in the 1880s, chromolithographs were substituted.[59] Such promotional ploys were a common event in the United States.[60] *The Christian Union* made good use of 'chromos' in 1871

Fig.8 Puck was the first successful American weekly to use lithographic reproductions of cartoons. As a result, it could feature bold drawings on its large 339 x 250mm pages to attract its readers.

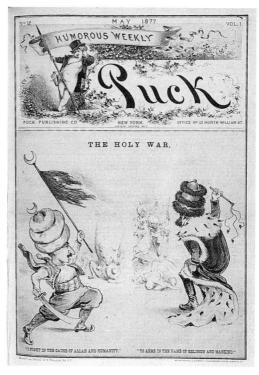

and 1872 to bolster its circulation,[61] though *The Aldine, Old and New* and *Punchinello* were less successful.[62]

In 1876, *Frank Leslie's Popular Monthly* began publication and from issue one adopted the procedure of binding in a chromolithograph of a quite respectable quality on a special paper stock just inside the front cover, thus achieving what might be described as an intermediate stage. The print was no longer easily slipped from between the covers to be displayed separately, the intended fate of so many of the promotional prints. Equally, it was still produced in a manner distinct from the rest of the publication by an outside agency. On the other hand, such inducements to readership loyalty were not occasional items but a regular feature in each edition.

The next move appears to have been made by *Puck* in 1877, when the New-York-based comic paper began using rather crude, solid, lithographed tints to embellish the caricatures that dominated the pages of its early editions.(Fig. 8) When *Judge* appeared four years later, its similarity to its rival and predecessor was reflected in its indulgence in brash coloured effects on four pages. In Britain, *The Little One's Own Coloured Picture Paper*, was that country's first regularly wholly chromolithographed periodical, in May 1885.[63] Yet, what the French did was quite different. They began using colour reproductions on the normal pagination, printed from relief not litho plates.

The breakthrough was achieved using gillotage, which has been described already, to make the relief plates, because the extensive use of chromolithography in magazines was not practical for economic reasons. It required coated or sized paper that would have been a prohibitively expensive raw material for magazine manufacture. Instead, *L'Illustration's* plate makers created a monochromatic image on a lithographic stone, the key. From this impressions were made on to transfer paper, one for each colour that was to be printed. The process that followed was similar to that outlined above under gillotage, with a number of significant modifications. The first step was to darken 'the zinc plate with chloride of antimony, which turns the plate a blue black colour. The transfer or drawing is made upon this, the ink dusted with resin, and the plate given a slight etch, just sufficient to remove the dark surface from the parts not covered by the ink of the resist. The latter is then cleared off, and the picture appears as a dark shining blue black image on the clean matted surface of the bare zinc. The plate is then put into a dusting box and a shower of resin allowed to fall upon it. When taken out of the box the plate will appear covered with a transparent white film the dark key showing through it. The resin grain is fixed by heat, and then the artist etcher (for he must be somewhat of an artist) proceeds to paint over with an acid-resisting varnish the parts which are to correspond to the colour in which the plate is to be printed. The plate is then etched to the colour of the darkest tone next to the solid colour which has been painted out. Another stopping out follows, and a further etching for the next tone. The sequence may be repeated several times. The plates for other colours are treated the same way.[64] As the colours of most pictures to be reproduced were not solid tints but intermingled amongst one another, it is clear that considerable skill was required and it is no wonder that it took three months to produce the very first examples in *L'Illustration* in December 1881.(Plate IV) And perfectly understandable that *Paris Illustré* was the only serial to attempt the use of this technique on a monthly basis for many years.

While these sterling efforts were being made with quite dazzling results in France, German chemists were involved in research that would, eventually, short-circuit such cumbersome rituals. In 1873 Professor Hermann Vogel of Berlin discovered the potential of certain dyes to extend the sensitivity of silver halide emulsions, which are the basis of all modern photographic and photo-mechanical processes, beyond their strong blue-orientated bias into the green, yellow and red areas of the spectrum.[65] In 1884 further experimentation of his, with quinoline red and quinoline blue, which could be mixed together to complement one another, yielded a product known as azaline, which was marketed as a method of extending the colour sensitivity of standard photographic emulsions as far as orange.[66] Further experimentation by other organic chemists produced other 'optical sensitizers' during the late 1870s and 1880s.[67] Complementing the physical research, in 1885 both Ernest Vogel, the son of Hermann, and Frederick Ives of Philadelphia independently developed theories of three-colour printing that were to prove fruitful once the technology had been further developed.[68]

This began to happen when, Robert Burch reports, the Munich printers, Messrs. Bohrer, Gorter and Company, began using four-colour collotype in 1888. They gave up in the face of consumer apathy.[69] Next to pick up the gauntlet was Emil Ulrich, a Berlin lithographer, who used three-colour principles in his experiments in colour collotype. He added a fourth, black plate for increased definition and exhibited a proof in Berlin during 1890, at the Photographic Congress.[70] In 1891 his work was seen in London at a highly publicised German exhibition, timed to coincide with the state visit to the city by the Kaiser, and he won a medal.[71] After he combined forces with Ernst Vogel to promote four-colour collotype[72], the pair sold the American rights to a New Yorker, William Kurtz, who found the process too temperamental in his native climate and adapted it to halftone letterpress.[73] In another version of the story, Kurtz paid Vogel junior $40,000 to cross the Atlantic to help him with the adaptation.[74] Either way, on 23 February 1893 Kurtz filed letters of application with the United States Patents Office. Surprisingly they only covered the matter of the relationships of the angles of the single line halftone screens he used so that interference effects, or Moiré patterns, were avoided. As others had, independently, solved that problem previously, his claimed innovation is of relatively little importance in itself.[75] Of much greater significance was the publication in the March 1893 edition of *The Engraver and Printer*, a specialist monthly periodical out of Boston, of a still-life reproduction that was very much the fruit of his labours. Examination confirms the approach detailed in his patent regarding the angles of the single line screens used to create each of the three-colour plates. It appears to be the first American colour halftone published, certainly in a magazine. As such, his achievement would soon have been widely known within the trade.

Even more effective as publicity was the exhibition by Kurtz of a colour reproduction at the Chicago World Fair in 1893.[76] Although it is implausible that more than a small percentage of the total of 21,477,212 visitors[77] saw his work, and even fewer appreciated its significance, it appears to have stimulated the local competition into emulating him. Sipley, for instance, reports that the Franklin Engraving Company formed a separate organisation, the Chicago

Colortype Company, directly as a result of their knowledge of Kurtz achievement. And three others, the Photo Colortype Company, the Osgood Colortype Company and the Moss Colortype Company appeared to have followed suit.[78] Certainly, the link with Kurtz seems inescapable for he had created the Coloritype Company in conjunction with the F.A. Ringler Company, described by a contemporary as 'the largest and most complete printing plate manufacturing establishment in the country'[79], during 1893 and assigned his patent to Coloritype during June/July of that year.[80] The similarity between this company's name and that of the others must count as substantial evidence of the influence of his achievement on them. Late that year, the Illinois Engraving Company managed to make a very poor three-colour, parallel line halftone separation that was published in *The Inland Printer*.[81]

By 1894, the Chicago Colortype Company, under the control of Gustav Zeese, was able to produce its own reproduction of a fruit picture.[82] However, some doubt must be expressed about the example printed opposite page 16 in Sipley. The only technological route to this result would have been to make the three separations direct from life, which could only have been an added difficulty in a very tricky process, quite apart from whether the strawberries in the picture could have withstood the intensity of light that would have been necessary to effect the exposure. As the example in the collection of the National Museum of American History's Department of Graphic Arts, given by the company, is merely a reproduction of a crudely hand-coloured, originally monochrome photograph, a question mark must hang over the authenticity of the date of Sipley's contender. Down in Pennsylvania, Epstean reports that the Philadelphia Photo Engraving Company was able to produce a set of useable three-colour plates by February, 1894.[83]

Meanwhile, Waterlows in London were conducting their own experiments with three-colour collotype. Fortunately, they published their results as supplements to *Land and Water*, a sporting periodical. On 2 August 1890 a yachting scene, *Rain and Sunshine* on the Solent appeared. On 21 March and 20 June of the following year, portraits of the Prince and Princess of Wales were reproduced.[84] Then, at last, in the 13 February 1892 edition of the weekly *Land and Water*, they produced what appears to be the first colour halftone published anywhere, certainly in a magazine, a supplement featuring a racehorse. Nevertheless, the difficulties were such that it proved impractical to move beyond the experimental stage at that moment and the company appears to have lost interest.[85] The same fate seems to have befallen the London firm of Gilbert Whitehead and Company, who in 1891 are reported to have experimented with three-colour collotype and letterpress, aided by Dr E. Albert.[86]

The race had now been well and truly joined. Late in 1893, the full details of Kurtz' parallel line process were published in the September/October edition of *The British Printer*. With its 'guaranteed circulation' of 12,500, it clearly attained an effective penetration of the printing community in the U.K.[87] Yet, the American disclosure was completely upstaged by the insertion in the same issue of a three-colour *cross-line* halftone. The plates had been produced in Prague by Husnik and Hausler but were printed with British inks by the De Montfort Press of Leicester, the company which published and printed this trade magazine.[88] The same Bohemian company were responsible for the three-colour halftones that began appearing in the weekly children's periodical *Chums* on 30 August 1893(Plate V), and not 1894 as reported by Burch.[89] Published weekly by Cassell and Co. at sixpence, its emphasis on words, the content and title, suggest that it was aimed at the very affluent adolescent. With the Harmsworth comics selling for a halfpenny, any broader market would probably have been too competitive. The three-colour reproductions were issued with slight irregularity for the first year, totalling 11 in all, and certainly constitute the first series of their kind. During the second year, to August 1895, nine were published. *The British Printer* for 1894 also showed a number of examples of the Bohemian

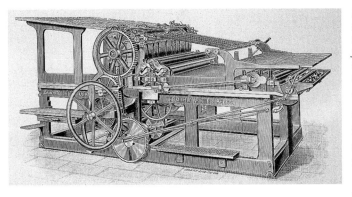

Fig.9 The high-quality registration achieved by the flat-bed presses of the Miehle Company opened the way for the commercial development of colour printing in the magazine industry on both sides of the Atlantic.

company's work, including impressions from the individual separations as well as the finished article.[90]

The following year saw the emergence of the Heliochrome Company of Elgin Crescent, Notting Hill Gate, London, when *The British Printer* featured five examples of their work as inserts beginning during the summer, including one still life taken direct from nature.[91] However, the stimulus for this apparently home-grown technology was not entirely British, as the managing director of the company, Martin Cohn, had trained with Dr Vogel in Berlin for seven years.[92] From there he had formed the Photochrome Printing Company of Belfast but that venture was not a success. Nor was his transplant to London.[93] Such a record only emphasizes the still experimental nature of the three-colour halftone business at that point.

Over in Paris, the success of the colour gillotage process obviated any need to employ colour halftones. With *Figaro Illustré* proceeding very nicely; with the Christmas special editions of *L'Illustration* produced by the same process, there was no need to change. Through 1895 and 1896 the former began increasingly to reproduce hand-coloured photographs, but the same process was used to take care of that as well.

Back in New York, America got its first regular use of three-colour halftones in a serial publication when *The Christian Herald* of 6 November, 1895 used one, 227 x 249mm, on its cover. Given the quality of the paper, which was reasonable but not outstanding, the quality of the parallel line halftone reproduction was amazing. Doubtless, much of the credit for this achievement must be laid at the door of the Miehle Company, whose well-regarded presses,(Fig. 9) with their then unprecedented accuracy of register, had been delivered to the publisher that autumn.[94] The following week a sombre print of the Florence Mission, New York graced the periodical's front cover. This used a cross-line screen, the form that prevailed from that point.

From 6 November until 26 February 1896 the sequence was unbroken. Perhaps, more importantly, at least for the accountants, the back cover of the 11 December edition sported what could well be the first three-colour halftone advertisement ever published, when the N.K. Fairbank Company took the entire page to promote its vegetable oil shortening, Cottolene. The second polychromatic promotion was situated on the back page of the edition for 19 February 1896, when the Leonard Manufacturing Company chose to 'puff' six 'full size teaspoons' for 99 cents. Meanwhile, that month's edition of *The Inland Printer* of Chicago had managed to pick up a couple of three-colour advertisements as well.[95]

However, back in New York, the glory was fading. *The Christian Herald* for 4 March 1896 could only manage a monochromatic image. After that, another four-week colour sequence was again terminated by a colourless conclusion on 8 April. From then on, the fall was rapid. The conversion had lacked true revelation. Monochrome was reborn. Only sporadically, for the next few years, did such technical glories rise up again. However, there could by no doubt that colour was in the air.

Already, in October 1895, a new magazine, *Black Cat*, had wrapped its recipe of short stories only in a cover fronted by a 'chromo'. Each month the design was changed but every one featured a representative of the title. Fashion magazines, such as *Mode de Paris*, with its English text, printed in Paris but aimed primarily at the New York market, had been using chromolithographed plates inset since 1890. *The Delineator*, with its enormously larger circulation, picked up that habit in July 1896. In August 1896, *Scribner's Magazine*, the New-York-based monthly, began using colour covers on an occasional basis. On initial examination the image structure appears to be compatible solely with the chromolithographic process, a judgement that is supported by a contemporary note. The cover was printed in twelve colours. A poster version in nine colours and gold was also produced, which only emphasizes the value the publishers placed on such a graphic device to attract readers despite its cost.[96] In December of that year, even Harpers Brothers were tempted by the new mood, when a rather discordant violet and gold confection graced their cover.

Yet, it was left to *Frank Leslie's Popular Monthly*, whose commitment to colour quality among the Anglo-Saxon publications was unparalleled, to introduce quality halftone colour on a regular basis to the ranks of the best selling journals. While the covers, from December 1896, only featured a series of somewhat unattractive designs reproduced through two-colour halftone, the regular, monthly chromolithographed frontispiece was replaced in January 1897 by a two-colour substitute. However, the following month Photo-Colortype of Chicago and New York took over responsibility for production and from that time the quality of the three-colour halftones matched that of their chromolithographed predecessors. It was no wonder that by May of that year, *The Inland Printer* felt sufficiently confident to publish a note that stated quite clearly that the Photo-Colortype Company of Chicago were, by then, making a financial success of their utilisation of the process.[97]

December 1896 would seem to have been the point at which the flood gates burst. Quite apart from *Leslie's*, the London-based *Navy and Army Illustrated* used a colour halftone reproduction of a painting of Field Marshal Lord Roberts, which was probably a supplement and not, as now, bound into the copy. In addition, *The English Illustrated Magazine* used a colour cover which, with a stipple structure, may have been printed by lithography or letterpress. In May 1897 *Cassell's Family Magazine* used their first full colour cover with a classic halftone structure. It was engraved and printed by André and Sleigh, of Bushey, Herts., whose three-colour halftone reproductions began appearing as inserts in *The British Printer* during 1896. Like *The Christian Herald*, the company were using the Miehle press.[98] Two months later this polychromatic addition became a regular feature in *Cassell's*.

Despite the growing use of colour, techniques were still at the tentative stage, as can be gauged from the following contemporary description of the vagaries of the making of separation negatives.

There are sundry chemical wrinkles. The red negative may be made with collodion tinged with aurine, but the negative must be soaked in alcohol to discharge all traces of aurine before development is attempted. The blue is given a preliminary bath in alcohol, then soaked in an alcoholic solution of chlorophyll until it takes on a sort of pea-green tint, then is drained and quickly bathed in distilled water, and the exposure is made.[99]

Others used different procedures and another contemporary used cyanine to sensitise a plate to red light. However, despite such measures, he still found it necessary to make an exposure of ten minutes in full sunlight for this plate, or even longer with a less intense source.[100] Unfortunately, that was not the end of the process engraver's tribulations. At that time, what William Gamble later called the 'Indirect Method' was the only way of making colour plates. The initial stage of this technique involved the hoop-la already indicated in getting the three separation negatives. The second stage was to make a same-size transparency from each negative. The third was to expose three plates, one to each transparency, through a halftone screen, either parallel or cross-line.[101] Then, and only then could a proof be contemplated. Clearly, with so many operations and so many 'wrinkles', at this moment such attempts were less an industrial technology, more an act of faith. The new century had been born before the German organic chemists were able to come up with dyes that made these ad hoc, primitive imprecisions a thing of the past and gave the printing industry a foundation upon which a standardised colour production technology could be erected.

As the nineteenth century drew to a close, the monochrome halftone process was itself further improved. By the April 1894 issue, contemporary observers noted that the block makers for *Harper's Monthly* had learned how to retouch a halftone.[102] By January of the following year, their rival, the *Century*, acknowledged its use of such techniques in an editorial.[103] By the issues for 1900, *Century Illustrated* seems to have been using screens as fine as 125 lines per inch, with some of 150, as was *Harper's*; though not 200 lines per inch as reported by an overawed contemporary.[104]

In 1899, on 15 February, the invention of an automatic etching process by Louis Levy was announced to the Franklin Institute in Philadelphia.[105] By the following year, competent workmen employed in the newspaper trade were able to use the process to etch a zinc halftone plate in one minute.[106] This was at a time when the average American 'wet-plate' operator was producing 20 to 25 plates a day, while his European equivalent produced 12 to 15 in the same period.[107] In other words, this was a time of rapid technological change in which production costs were being decimated.

Similar progress was being made with printing presses and typesetting machines, those other keys to the technical revolution of the late nineteenth century. Of course, as in every other sphere, progress was a cumulative accretion of half-steps. Nevertheless, a real landmark was reached when William Bullock installed his first web-fed, rotary perfecting press at the *New York Sun* in 1865, which initiated a great acceleration in production times because rolls of paper, the web, meant faster machines which could print both sides at one pass, the perfecting.[108] During the 1870s other manufacturers began installing similar machines in Britain.[109] With their short deadlines, it is not surprising that the newspapers were quick to pounce on the new technology. Yet, in 1886 R. Hoe & Co. built a rotary for the *Century* which could do ten times the work of a similarly sized flatbed press. That was the advantage for the magazines: increased productivity to cope with increased sales without a comparable increase in the size of the printing shop or its staff; that is, it effected a substantial saving in unit costs.[110] Four years later, the same manufacturer built a rotary press for the same magazine capable of printing the finest quality halftones then available from curved plates.[111]

By 1897 the circulation leaders of the two biggest British magazine publishers, *Tit-bits* and *Answers*, were being produced at 24,000 copies per hour on Hoe machines. The Newnes organisation also printed *The Strand* on Hoe's rotary perfecting presses.[112] The rival press makers, C.B. Cottrell & Sons were not slow to appreciate the scope of this market and in 1890 they produced their own web-fed rotary perfecting press which they sold to *Youth's Companion*, *Harper's*, *Lupton's*, *McCall's*, and other periodicals.[113] The year after, they signed up Howard M. Barker as their chief engineer. Throughout the nineties he worked on improving their rotary presses, and the first upgraded machine was sold to *Munsey's Magazine* in 1898.

Thereafter he developed two and three-colour presses with automatic folders that became the standard for the magazine industry, being bought by all the biggest selling periodicals of the day in the United States, such as *Munsey's, Youth's Companion, Everybody's, McClure's, Cosmopolitan, Saturday Evening Post, Ladies' Home Journal, McCall's* and many others.[114]

At the same time, between 1894 and 1900, Henry Wood of the Campbell Printing Press Company developed a machine that automatically cast and finished the curved stereoplates needed for the new rotary presses. His Standard Autoplate could, in fact, handle all four processes involved simultaneously and a one hour production process needing 35 men was replaced by this innovation which disgorged one plate a minute. It was installed at the *New York Herald* in 1900 and spread rapidly through the American industry.[115]

One technical development that was critical to the introduction of the increasingly fast presses that has, so far, received little attention, is the creation of new inks. As Frank Wiborg, one of the key figures in the American ink industry during this critical period has pointed out, 'the ink must be made to fit the paper stock.'[116] In other words, many of the innovations in this area were demand led, which is not to say, of course, that innovations independent of the industry did not make their own contribution.

First among the latter were the production of coal tar oils during the second half of the nineteenth century. Their physical properties facilitated the production, on an industrial scale, of finer and more consistent grades of lampblack, the basis of black ink at the time.[117] Then, around 1875, the burning of hydro-carbon gas began to be used to produce the pigment. The end product of this process was composed of the smallest particles then known to science and provided, without question, the densest black available to the printer.[118] The large circulation periodicals of the 1890s took advantage of the qualities of this new pigment. In particular, *Munsey's Magazine* was among the first to use it to cope with the demands of printing halftones on high speed presses.[119] Similarly, the accidental discovery of Mauveine by W.H. Perkins in 1856 and the work of Peter Griess in Germany in the decades that followed, led to the creation of the German dye industry. From that base, the potential was developed that made it possible for ink manufacturers to produce the coloured inks so essential to the twentieth-century printing and magazine trades.[120]

The other major innovation of the period, again originating in the United States but this time crossing the Atlantic quickly, concerned mechanical typesetting. The advantages of such a system were transparent and throughout the nineteenth century inventors had been fiddling with the possibilities. Yet, the modern systems did not materialise until the 1880s and it was a few years before teething troubles were ironed out and they began to be installed in commercial situations. For example, Ottmar Mergenthaler appears to have produced his first, flawed Linotype machine in 1883 but it was 1886 before the first successful model was sold,[121] and 1890 before they began to be installed in any numbers.[122] The introduction of Tolbert Lanston's Monotype took even longer. Having been first patented in 1885,[123] it was 1900 before it was installed in a commercial situation.[124]

A Linotype consists of a keyboard that calls up type matrices for individual characters and spaces which are added one to another until the line length is full. A fount of molten lead, integral to the machine, is then used to mould the entire length of the line in one piece from the assembled matrices. The cooled lump of lead is called the slug. This is added to the preceding lines which have already been set and the matrices are disbursed automatically to their storage points. The Monotype machine also features a keyboard but the output from this is only punched tape. This is fed into a second machine which moulds the individual characters from molten lead but leaves them distinct.[125]

The Linotype was first used in New York in 1886,[126] crossing the Atlantic the following year when James Gordon-Bennet launched a European edition of his *New York Herald* in Paris.[127] Its first user in London appears to have been *The Globe* in 1892, followed by the *Financial News*. By 1895 at least 250 machines were in use in the British provincial press.[128]

What attracted the owners of newspapers and other serials was the acceleration in type composition. For example, an experienced hand compositor could set about 1,000 ems an hour, where the early Linotypes, in the hands of skilled and experienced operators were capable of 4,000 to 5,000 ems per hour.[129] Indeed, a contemporary account records that one F.J.Smith of the *Toledo Commercial* set an average of 5755 ems per hour of corrected matter during a 45 hour week.[130] Later machines were much faster.[131] But this was not all.

Traditional forms of hand composition were not only slower and obviously more labour intensive during the creation of the text. Once the type had been used, the forme, which held it, had to be broken down and the individual characters redistributed to their founts. This was also labour intensive and required the maintenance of a vast stock of type for a major publication. Linotypes completely obviated this part of the process by melting down the used slugs each time. It followed from this that serials could increase their pagination without a comparable increase in compositors or space and the rent such space would require. For example, the daily edition of the *New York World* was able to grow from 16 to 24 pages very easily, its Sunday edition from 48 to 72 pages.[132]

THE SECOND HALF OF THE NINETEENTH CENTURY saw a complete transformation of the printing trade. After its existing techniques were upgraded during the previous 50 years through the mechanisation of paper making and the press itself, the decades that followed witnessed a revolution which turned publishing inside out.

The conversion of the bulk of the paper trade from a rag to a wood base precipitated a price collapse which transformed the economic structure of publishing. With a key item in their expenses wholesaling at a fraction of its former price, publishers could contemplate a choice between a cut in cover price or an enlargement of each publication without a corresponding price increase. Most, as we shall see, took the first option, increased sales and expanded their market.

The illustrations that graced those pages were completely different at the opening of the twentieth century from their predecessors of 1850. The industrialisation of the etching of metal plates made possible by the techniques of Gillot *père* allowed line work and then halftones to invade the publisher's pitch. Not only did spectacular price cuts for illustrative blocks increase their use, the halftone distributed an entirely new quality of information about people and places. The wood-block used hitherto had been a vague cipher for the original; the photographic reproduction became a recognisable cipher for the original. Now one's peers, one's monarch, their women and even their playthings could be recognised and turned into the subject of comment which was based upon far more specific information than hitherto. The power in society had shifted slightly.

Furthermore, the editorial staff had previously been constrained by the dimensions of the block as it was originally cut. Now the photo-mechanical reproduction of the original allowed the editorial staff the luxury and flexibility of being able to order a block to be made, or even remade, to a specific size which could be changed with circumstances. And it surely can be no coincidence that a new title, that of art director, made its appearance during the 1890s, the decade in which photo-mechanical reproduction took over.

This newly authorised individual had other new means at his disposal as the century ended that enormously enhanced the publication upon which he worked. Colour was transformed from its status as a luxury item in the 1850s to a regular decoration by 1900. From an annual event it became a monthly occurrence.

The last decade of the nineteenth century also saw another dream realised after decades of experimentation – mechanical composition. This, in the decades to come, would also enhance the control of the art director over the publication on which he worked. Before the Linotype and the Monotype reached the composing floor, vast stores of type had to be held for any type face that might be used. Now, all that was required were the moulds for each size of the face. Once the type had been used it could be melted down. This released the art staff from another of their bonds.

Each of these possibilities was presented to the editorial staff during the last two decades of the nineteenth century. It is not surprising that it took magazine staff some time to learn how to use them effectively. Although one or two publications glimpsed the potential quite quickly in one or two areas, the 1930s had arrived before the opportunity to transform the form and content of magazines was even half realised.

Notes

1. Hunter, Dard, *Papermaking*, London, 2nd revised edition 1957, p380, and Coleman, D. C., *The British Paper Industry 1495-1860*, Oxford, 1958, p338.

2. Hunter, p562.

3. Ibid., p376.

4. Clair, Colin, *A Chronology of Printing*, London, 1969, p150.

5. Smith, David C., *History of Papermaking in the United States (1691-1969)*, New York, 2nd edition 1970, p132.

6. Ibid, pp130-132.

7. Ibid., pp132-134. It should be noted that pulp produced from wood by mechanical grinding has always needed additional material to be added. The cellulose fibres produced by this process alone are not long enough to sustain the web under any form of stress. Current practice adds at least 10% sulphite pulp to the furnish.

8. Hunter, op.cit., pp381-382.

9. Ibid., p380.

10. Smith, op.cit., p159 et seq.

11. Hunter, op.cit., p574.

12. Mott, Frank Luther, *A History of American Magazines*, Boston, 1938-1968, Vol.4, p153-154, reports that the *Century* was the very first. Examination of the material has drawn a complete blank in the search for Mott's examples. No halftone reproduction has been found in the pages of this magazine before Vol.29, No.3, January 1885, pp393-395.

13. Verfasser, Julius, *The Half-tone Process*, London, 1904; Gamble, William, *Modern Illustration Processes*, London, 1933, p149 et seq.; Chambers, Eric, *Camera and Process Work*, London, 1964, p89 et seq.

14. Sykes, Philip, *Albert E Reed and the Creation of a Paper Business 1860-1960*, privately produced, 1982?, pp92-94. A bound typescript of this volume is available at the British Library. No other copy is known.

15. Grant, Dr J. & Battle, S., The Nature and Uses of Paper and Board, in *Paper and Board Manufacture*, Various editors, London, 1978, p34.

16. Beak, Dr Julius, Coated and Uncoated Papers for Half-tone Printing, in *The Penrose Annual*, Vol.38, London, 1936, pp101-102.

17. *Directory of Paper Makers of the United Kingdom*, London, 1885, pp3-43.

18. Ibid, 1886, pp3-47.

19. Ibid, 1887, pp3-49.

20. Ibid, 1890, pp3-51.

21. Ibid, 1894, pp3-59.

22. Ibid, 1899, pp3-51.

23. Grant and Battle, op.cit., p34.

24. Beak, op.cit., p99.

25. Marzio, Peter C., *The Democratic Art*, London, 1980, p78.

26. Ibid.

27. Beak, op.cit., p99.

28. Kainen, Jacob, The Development of the Halftone Screen, *The Smithsonian Report for 1951*, Washington, D.C., p415, 418. Compare Clair, op.cit., p159.

29. Ibid, pp413-416.

30. *Annuaire-almanach du commerce de l'Industrie*, Paris, 1880, p2199.

31. *Le Monde Illustré*, Paris, No.1165, July 27, 1879, supplement.

32. Kainen, op.cit., p416.

33. Ibid, p409.

34. Ibid, p416.

35. Hodson, J. S, Modern Processes of Automatic Engraving, *The Art Journal*, London, 1885, pp 58-60.

36. Kainen, op.cit., p 418 mentions that 'Meisenbach's earliest work was in single-line halftone, with the screens moved slightly during exposure, and it is possible that cross-line results were not obtained until 1883.'

37. *Le Figaro Illustré*, Paris, Winter 1883-84, p11. As the British Library copy is date stamped 3 December 1883, it seems reasonable to assume that it was actually published during October or November of that year. The first seven issues of this title were annual, but the second series, beginning April 1890 was a monthly publication.

38. Clair, op.cit., p160.

39. Vidal, Leon, Applications and Progress of Photo-mechanical Processes in France, *The Process Year Book for 1896*, London, pp42-43. The situation had only begun to change in 1893/4 when the screens of the Berlin house of Gaillard began to be imported into France. See Fabrication de Plaques Lignées sur Verre par M Edm. Gaillard á Berlin, *3mme Annuaire Général et International de la Photographie*, Paris, 1894, p52.

40. *Dictionnaire de Biographie* Française, Vol.15, Paris, 1982, p86 (this volume has strange double pagination)

41. Cate, Phillip Dennis, *The Color Revolution, Lithography in France 1890-1900*, Santa Barbara and Salt Lake City, 1978, pp4-5; Anon., Automatic Engraving Processes, *The Printing Times and Lithographer*, London, 15 October 1874, pp 178-179; Hodson, op.cit., pp58-60.

42. Vidal, op.cit., p42. In fact, this author refers to a M. Menzi, but the cover of *Le Figaro Illustré*, No.4, 1886-87, credits 'Procede Manzi' so it seems probable that the later writer was guilty of a simple spelling error.

43. Wakeman, Geoffrey and Bridson, Gavin D.R., *A Guide to Nineteenth Century Colour Printers*, Loughborough, Leics., 1975, p14.

44. *The Graphic*, London, Vol.30, p260.

45. Ibid, Vol.32, 5 September 1885, pp 269-272.

46. Thomas, W.L., The Making of the 'Graphic', *The Universal Review*, Vol.2, No.5, Sept.1888, London, p82.

47. The existence of companies other than Meisenbach's is inferred from the varying dot structures and halftone patterns of the reproductions that can be found in the three publications at this time.

48. *The English Illustrated Magazine*, London, Vol.7, pp747-752. Berry, W. Turner and Poole, H. Edmund, *Annals of Printing*, London, 1966, p262.

49. Clair, op.cit., opposite p153 in the author's annotated copy held by the British Museum. This attributes the invention of the composite block to Charles Wells in 1860. This is wrong because I have found examples of composite blocks in *Frank Leslie's Illustrated Newspaper* published in New York in 1855.

50. John, Arthur, *The Best Years of the Century*, Urbana, Ill., and London, 1981, p182.

51. Mott, op.cit., Vol.4, p5.

52. *Harper's Young People*, New York, Vol.5, No.232, p361, 8 April 1884.

53. *Harper's Monthly*, New York, May 1884, Vol.68, No.408, p871.

54. *Harper's Young People*, New York, Vol.5, No.259, p792, 14 October 1884.

55. Mott, op.cit., Vol.4, pp153-154. The reproduction occurred on pp 393-395, Vol.29, No.3, January 1885.

56. Anon., Death of Max Levy, *The British Printer*, Vol.39, No.230, Jul-Aug.1926, Leicester and London, p82. Berry and Poole, op.cit., pp260-261 reports that manufacture began in 1888 but the unreliability of this source, in combination with the detail furnished in the obituary, enhances the plausibility of the latter. Kainen, op.cit., p420, gives a very clear description of the details of the Levy's method of manufacture.

57. Mott, op.cit., Vol.4, pp153-154.

58. Wood, Franklin, A Century of Progress in the Graphic Arts, 1842-1942, *The British Printer*, Vol.55, No.329, March 1943, London, p150.

59. Burch, Robert, *Colour Printing and Colour Printers*, 1910, London, 1911, New York, pp 147-148.

60. Mott, op.cit., Vol.3, pp7 and 191.

61. Ibid, p425.

62. Ibid., pp411, 437, 442 respectively.

63. Burch, op.cit., p210.

64. Gamble, William, *Line Photo-engraving*, London, 1909, p288.

65. Eder, Josef Maria, *History of Photography*, New York, 1945, p459.

66. Ibid., pp460-461.

67. Ibid., pp464-471.

68. Ibid., p653 for information on Vogel, and Berry and Poole, op.cit., p257, for Frederick Ives.

69. Burch, op.cit., p227.

70. Eder, op.cit., p653.

71. Cohn, Martin, Three-colour Process: its history and adaptability to printing methods, *The Process Year Book for 1896*, London, pp33-34.

72. Eder, op.cit., p653.

73. Cohn, op.cit., pp33-34.

74. Sipley, Louis Walton, *A Half Century of Color*, New York, 1951, p16.

75. The Letters Patent No.498,396 were granted on 30 May 1893. According to Stephen H. Horgan, *Horgan's Halftone and Photomechanical Processes*, Chicago, 1913, p127, Frederic Ives had known that such a disposition of angles between the lines was necessary. And both Dr E.Albert in Germany in 1891, and Du Hauron in France in 1892 had actually patented the procedure.

76. Epstean, Edward, The Beginnings of the Three-Color Process in the United States, in *The Photo-Engravers Bulletin,* September 1940, p22.

77. Badger, Reid, *The Great American Fair*, Chicago, 1979, p131.

78. Sipley, op.cit., p21.

79. Anon., F.A.Ringler Company, *The Inland Printer*, Vol.11, No.2, May 1893, Chicago, p159.

80. Sipley, op.cit., p22.

81. *The Inland Printer*, Vol.12, No.3, December 1893, opposite p201.

82. Sipley, op.cit., p26,

83. Burch, op.cit., p237.

84. Ibid., p227.

85. Cohn, op.cit., pp33-34.

86. Gamble, William, 'Modern Colour Processes', in Burch, op.cit., p255.

87. Anon., Photo-Mechanical Colour Printing, *The British Printer*, Leicester, Vol.6, No.35, pp365-366.

88. Ibid., opposite p364.

89. Burch, op.cit., pp238-239.

90. *The British Printer*, Leicester, 1894, Vol.7. Examples appear opposite pages 20, 44, 314, with another example, together with the impressions from the three separation plates, between pp378-379.

91. Ibid, Vol.8, opposite pages 202, 268, 274,344 and 358.

92. Ibid, Vol.9, No.49, Jan-Feb. 1896, p7.

93. Burch, op.cit., p256.

94. Anon., *The Inland Printer*, Vol.16, No.1, October 1895, p92.

95. Ibid., No.5, February 1896, opposite pages 556 and 608.

96. Anon., The August 'Scribner' Poster, *The Inland Printer*, Vol.17, No.3, June 1896, p301.

97. Anon., Three-Color Process, *The Inland Printer*, Vol.19, No.2, May 1897, p223.

98. Anon., *The British Printer*, Vol.10, No.57, May-June 1897, p147, reports this and other British users of the press, as well as technical details of how it achieved its excellence.

99. Snow, C. Ashleigh, Zinco-chromatic Methods in the United States, *The Process Year Book for 1896*, London, p51.

100. Hyslop, W.H., Three-Color Half-Tones, in *The Inland Printer*, Vol.14, No.1, October 1894, p28.

101. Hyslop, op.cit., p28 and Gamble in Burch, op.cit., pp256-257, quite separately confirm these details and one can reasonably assume that such elaborate procedures were common to both continents.

102. Brown, M. Lamont, Engraved Half-tones, in *The Process Year Book for 1897*, London, p34.

103. Mott, op.cit., Vol.4, pp153-154.

104. Brown, M. Lamont, Process Work in the States, in *The Process Year Book 1910*, London, p102, reported that these magazines were already using screens of 200 lines per inch, an assertion completely confounded by examination.

105. Levy, Max, A New Method of Etching, in *The Process Year Book for 1899, Penrose's Pictorial Annual*, London, p104.

106. Levy, Max, The Levy Acid Blast and the New Process of Etching, in *Penrose's Pictorial Annual, The Process Year Book for 1900*, London, pp101-102.

107. Schmidt, Herman J., American and European Process Notes, in *The Process Year Book 1901*, London, p65. This information was gathered by a well-informed contemporary observer who toured both continents to revue current developments.

108. Comparato, Frank E., *Chronicles of Genius and Folly*, Culver City, California, 1979, pp313-322.

109. Moran, James, *Printing Presses*, London, 1973, p196. The American press makers, R. Hoe & Co., installed their rotaries at *Lloyd's Weekly* first, then the *Standard, Daily Telegraph* and *Liverpool Mercury*.

110. Peterson, Theodore, *Magazines in the Twentieth Century*, Urbana, Illinois, 1964, p5.

111. Ibid.

112. *Newsagents' Chronicle*, No.57, 5 June 1897, p5.

113. Ibid.

114. Comparato, op.cit., p613.

115. Ibid, pp617-618.

116. Wiborg, Frank, *Printing Ink*. A History, New York, 1926, pp110-111.

117. Ibid., pp156-160.

118. Ibid., pp162-163.

119. Gamble, William, The Editor's Notebook, in *Penrose's Annual*, Vol.31, London, 1929, p178.

120. Wiborg, op.cit., pp173-176, 179.

121. Clair, Colin, *A History of European Printing*, London and New York, 1976, p379

122. Larken, H.W., A Century of Compositors, in *Printing World: a Century in Print*, Various editors, London, 1979, p31.

123. Ibid.

124. Moran, op.cit., p12.

125. Clair, *European Printing*, op.cit., pp379-381.

126. Ibid., p379.

127. Bellanger, Claude (Ed.), *Histoire générale de la presse française*, Paris, 1972, Vol.3, p383.

128. Clair, *European Printing*, op.cit., p379. *The British Printer*, Leicester, Vol.7, No.42, Nov-Dec. 1894, p48 of the advertising section, lists some of the publications using the Linotype. It is noticeable that the provincial press had been very quick to take advantage of this advance while no major London newspaper or periodical publisher was yet listed.

129. Bakeless, John, *Magazine Making*, New York, 1931, p55.

130. Anon., *The British Printer*, Vol.5, No.25, January-February 1892, p116.

131. Bakeless, op.cit., p55.

132. Pickett, Calder, *Six New York Newspapers and Their Response to Technology in the Nineteenth Century*, University of Minnesota PhD thesis, Ann Arbor, Michigan, pp377-378.

American Periodicals 1880–1900

IT IS FREQUENTLY ALLEGED that American popular culture experienced a crucial change of emphasis in the 1890s; that the old, 'gentlemanly' standards relinquished their pre-eminence to more energetic, frequently more vulgar models. For example, in his book, *Magazines in the United States*, James Playstead Wood, states, `It was *McClure's*, with *Munsey's* and *Cosmopolitan*, which marked the shift in magazine content from poetry, literary criticism, and the formal essay to light fiction and journalistic reporting of contemporary events.'[1]

Unfortunately, analysis fails to confirm this hypothesis about these leading magazines of the 1890s. The situation was much more complex than this simplistic scenario suggests. As we will see, *Munsey's* was one of the most conservative of the popular monthlies, while some of the publications we will examine were already shifting their editorial position before the 1890s opened. Others never assumed a 'gentlemanly' posture in the first place. To quote just one example, twenty years before the heyday of the three periodicals Wood mentions, Frank Leslie launched his *Popular Monthly* in January 1876. The very first article in the very first issue, `The Centennial of 1876', very fully illustrated, featured a description of a contemporary event. It was followed by a poem, a paragraph of diverting fact, a page long article about Japanese childhood and an adventure story: in other words, its approach was remarkably similar to that editorial mix which previous commentators have insisted burst on the American magazine world in the 1890s.[2]

This contradiction of conventional wisdom about the development of the popular magazine in the second half of the nineteenth century in the United States is confirmed by detailed examination of some of the most popular publications of the period. The most solidly established of the best sellers of the time was *Harper's New Monthly Magazine*, which was launched in June 1850. From a start of 7,500 per month, it claimed to have reached a circulation of 50,000 per month by the end of its first year and to have continued upwards towards 200,000 by the beginning of the Civil War.[3] With claimed sales of that order, one can hardly quibble with the judgement that it was 'the outstanding publishing success of the period in the monthly field,'[4] or that it marked the beginning of a new era.[5]

Analysis of the contents of volumes 1 and 21, that is, for the June to November periods in 1850 and 1860, combined with a similar analysis by Arthur John for the years 1871 and 1880, contradicts further the hypothesis that the editorial attitude of the modern American magazine was transformed in the last decade of the nineteenth century.(see Appendix II) Thus, it can be suggested that the mixed function magazine, which aspired to a large readership through its use of an editorial formula that used contrast and counterpoint over a wide range of topics, as defined in the introduction, a light and attractive miscellany, was certainly in existence in the Ante-bellum period.

Doubtless, much of the popularity of *Harper's Monthly* derived from its leavening of the text with copious numbers of illustrations, for a monthly magazine of the period that is. By 1880,

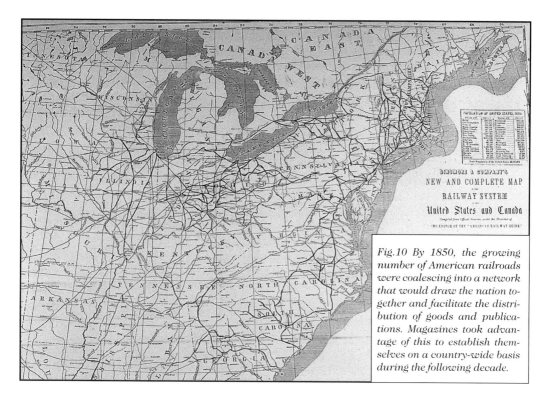

DIXILON & COMPANY'S
NEW AND COMPLETE MAP
of the
RAILWAY SYSTEM
of the
United States and Canada

Fig.10 By 1850, the growing number of American railroads were coalescing into a network that would draw the nation together and facilitate the distribution of goods and publications. Magazines took advantage of this to establish themselves on a country-wide basis during the following decade.

volume 61, it used 434 among 960 pages, or 0.45 per page overall. However, any discussion of the causes of volume sales of a magazine must be larger than a discussion of the mere virtues of the product at the time. In this instance, it also needs to take account of the developing railroad system.

The year 1850 was one of the earliest in which something approaching a network could have been said to exist in the United States, as an examination of the railway maps of the period demonstrates very clearly.(Fig. 10) Through this transportation linkage, the disparate elements of the middle class, scattered throughout the cities east of the Mississippi, were being integrated into one market. This developing network of effective and timely distribution provided by the railroads may well have inspired other publishers in the decade 1850–1860, for *Atlantic Monthly, Harper's Weekly* and *Frank Leslie's Illustrated Weekly* all began their lengthy careers at this time.

Another aspect of the American magazine market during the latter days of the nineteenth century also deserves our attention. Although, as already discussed in Chapter 1, pressures were mounting on publishers to reveal their precise circulation figures and make them available to external auditors, such practices were not yet universal. This means that absolute reliance cannot be placed upon the available figures which are used to select the best-selling magazines of the period. However, the format adopted by the Rowell organisation does clearly indicate which figures have been audited, while the remainder are treated with caution. Furthermore, as the precise scale of a magazine's sales is not in itself an issue here but a filter used to separate the most successful from the less, whether a publication sells an average 263,215 every month or about 250,000 is not a matter of paramount importance. This study is concerned primarily with the identity of the best-selling publications, not their pecking order.

*Fig.11 In its very first volume,
Scribner's Monthly's innovations
in page layout, with clearly defined
titles above larger type and a greater
space between the lines, established
new standards in commercial
graphic design in the United States.*

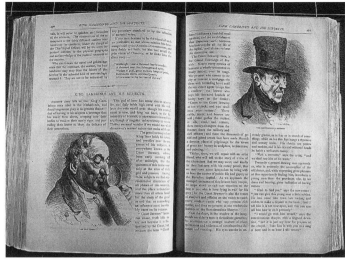

Those selected for study
which were published during
the 1880s were all credited
with average sales of more than
75,000 per issue by the ultra
cautious *American Newspaper Directory* at the decade's
end.[6] Some, such as *Ladies'
Home Journal, Youth's Companion* and *The Delineator*,
were already selling consider-
ably more than this figure. By the end of the nineties, the considerable increase in circulation
among the most successful magazines means that the cut-off point is twice the earlier level; a
choice which can be exercised with more reliability because audited sales figures were
becoming the accepted standard in the American publishing industry.

The only exception to the above rules has been applied to a monthly publication known as
Comfort. Mott was prepared to accept that every issue of this monthly was distributed to over
one million homes during the 1890s,[7] but a serious question mark must be registered as to
whether this was prepaid circulation compatible with other magazines included herein, and
whether *Comfort* can be considered to be a magazine rather than an advertising flyer for a large
number of clients. Even Dorothy Sayward, who wrote the only known study of this publication,
goes no further in its defence than to call it a mail-order magazine because it was used by
advertisers who 'wished to by-pass both jobber and retailer and sell to the consumer directly'.[8]
Indeed, its primary purpose was as a vehicle for cheap advertisements and its classification as
a magazine, which permitted it to use the US Post Office for its distribution at special rates, was
challenged in the American Congress as early as 1895.[9] Another challenge in 1907 was
successful and it was stricken from the list of qualifying publications. It only survived by
dropping its price to 15¢ a *year*.[10] As it would appear that its circulation figures were never
audited and its claims to be considered as a magazine are limited, it has been decided to exclude
this publication from further consideration.[11]

IN 1880, HARPER'S MOST SERIOUS AND SUCCESSFUL RIVAL among the American monthly
magazines was *Scribner's Monthly*. It had first appeared in November 1870, enclosed in a blue
cover. Its genesis is described in admirable fashion by Arthur John,[12] who uses simple content
analysis to illustrate the differences between the two competitors.

The influence of *Scribner's* original editor, Josiah Holland, was apparent from the first in the
magazine's emphasis on a broad range of non-fiction. Whereas, after twenty years, *Harper's* was
still promoting fiction to the extent of using 33% of the regular page space, its interest in such
matters as public affairs, religion, social manners and problems was absolutely minimal. At

Scribner's the latter topics were allocated 16% of the page space in 1871 on average(see Appendices I & II).[13]

As John has pointed out, Holland's primary editorial problem was developing his list of contributors. *Harper's* had an arm lock on much of the best of British fiction, while the *Atlantic Monthly* had cornered the market in the literature of New England; still at that time regarded as the centre of American writing of quality. Unfortunately, as Holland's modest talents were of a sentimental nature, his involvement in the project alienated the stern literary youth of New York, that is before they saw the colour of his money. Thus, initially frustrated in his choice of authors, it is not surprising that he should opt to emphasize the appearance of the magazine in order to gain an edge: 'I would make it as handsome a magazine as America produces.'[14]

From the first, that aspiration has to be taken seriously. Comparison of volume 1 with volume 43 of *Harper's*, which was published at the same time, reveals some similarities but important differences as well. The frequency of illustrations was very similar between the two publications. *Harper's* was using 0.39 reproductions per page at this point while *Scribner's* began with 0.37. Like *Harper's*, *Scribner's Monthly* also tended to group its illustrations at the front of each issue.

On other matters it was more individual. That *Scribner's* used paper of a quality superior to that of its rival is obvious both to the eye and the touch. Although that first volume was published before even the days of super-calendering, the paper surface is smoother and, over a century later, it remains both whiter and more durable than the stock used by *Harper's*. The typographic design also demonstrated a substantial improvement in clarity over its older rival. Not only is the face larger but fewer lines to the column afford greater legibility. Wherever possible, articles begin at the top of a page and the heading is invariably laid out across both columns, creating a clear distinction between items.(Fig. 11) Many of *Harper's* headings were small and remained contained within the single column ruling.(Fig. 12) Clearly, the launch of *Scribner's* in 1870 endorsed a new standard in graphic design in American popular periodicals which both boosted the importance of page layout and demonstrated how typography could be used to direct the reader's attention.

A decade later in 1880, both *Harper's* and *Scribner's* had availed themselves of the smoother stock which had reached the manufacturer's catalogue. In *Harper's*, the habit of condensing the illustrations into the front of each issue was further reinforced by the use of a higher quality paper in that part of the magazine. As the success of letterpress reproductions is dependent on the surface properties of the paper used, the company was able to maximise image quality in the front section. Conversely, it printed the latter part of each issue on cheaper stock, thus minimising ex-

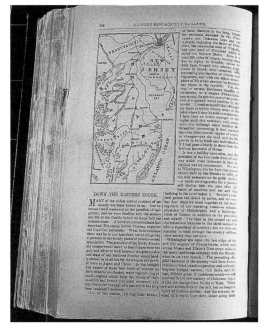

Fig.12 The incoherent, confusing layouts of Harper's Monthly, in which titles were easy to confuse with the captions, looked old-fashioned once Scribner's appeared late in 1870.

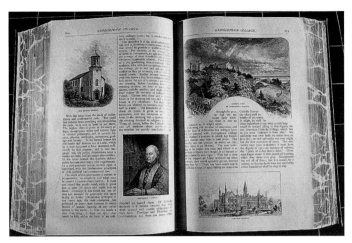

Fig.13 By 1880, the design of Scribner's Monthly had assumed new levels of fluency that were to influence all aspiring popular monthlies in the United States in the decades to come.

penses. With a similar cover price to its rival, now 35¢ a copy, but without advertising revenue, all costs, particularly large and unavoidable ones like paper, needed to be contained.

Scribner's, by way of contrast, having taken the lead in soliciting advertising as mentioned in Chapter 1, had invested this revenue in paper stock and was able to use the same superior grade throughout each issue. This allowed it greater latitude in placing illustrations, a possibility that it employed in a shift away from its previous bias towards the front of each issue for their deployment.(Fig. 13) While volume 61 of *Harper's Monthly*, that for June to November 1880, used 94% of all its illustrations in the first half of every issue, *Scribner's*, although still weighted towards the front, spread 98% of its reproductions through the initial 74% of each issue, on average. Indeed, a pattern was set up whereby the initial dozen or so pages of each edition were extensively illustrated. A verbal bridge followed. Then the pictorial emphasis was resumed and continued up to the end of the third quarter of the magazine. Thus, the flow of revenue from advertising, by allowing the use of a better paper stock throughout, gave the editor a freer hand in the distribution of his material and made a noticeable difference to the overall design of *Scribner's*.

There was also a considerable difference in the editorial content of the two publications. *Harper's Monthly* ploughed on with its interest in fiction and that aspect of non-fiction listed here under travel and adventure. In fact, from a combined total of 52%, they had now risen to 61% of page space by 1880. In complete contrast, the same combination of fiction and travel and adventure in *Scribner's* used only 21% of the page space during the same period. That publication's main focus was history and biography, while its taste for matters that would appeal to the well educated that it derived from the broad curiosity of its first editor, the arts, descriptive sciences and information on contemporary society, remained steady at 40%. The same group of topics rated only 26% of the page space in *Harper's Monthly* during 1880.(see Appendices I & II)[15]

Frank Leslie's Popular Monthly was another rival to *Harper's* by 1880. Its paper size, 280 x 199 mm, was larger than *Scribner's* at 239 x 165 mm, or *Harper's* at 245 x 167 mm, though it only gave 128 pages against their average of 160. When *Leslie's* was launched in 1876, it was priced at 20¢ a copy or $2.50 a year, as against the 35¢ a copy or $4 a year of its two senior rivals. But that did not last and by 1880 it was selling for 25¢ a copy or $3 a year. By 1884 it was claiming a readership of 100,000, that is, about the same as its rivals.[16] By way of contrast, in Germany, at this time, the periodical *Gartenlaube* claimed 400,000 subscribers, which probably made it the largest selling magazine of the period.[17]

Frank Leslie's new monthly was profusely illustrated for the period. Its 768-page first volume, January to June 1876, was graced by 540 illustrative figures, many of them full page, at a density of 0.70 per page, a hitherto unprecedented level in the American monthly. In addition, elaborately illuminated capitals were frequently used to begin an article, while each issue began with an inserted frontispiece, the first four of which in volume one of 1876 were chromolithographs. Despite this, the paper stock was of poorer quality than that of the other illustrated monthlies already discussed and the copies which remain are devoid of any advertising.

The way that this art work was used was extraordinary; that is, with a complete disregard for the necessary contiguity of an article and its illustrations. The latter both precede and succeed the relevant texts, in some instances at two pages or more distance, a practice yet to be found in any other magazine. However, by issue six the worst excesses seemed to be over and one gets a sense that the editor and his staff had learned a little.

By 1880, *Leslie's Monthly* had began to enjoy rising revenue from both circulation and advertising, which may have encouraged the company to use improved quality of paper. It also further increased its use of illustrations, which now ran to 579 included amongst 755.65 pages of editorial material, a density of 0.77 per page in volume 9, January to June 1880. This usage compares well with *Scribner's Monthly*, which distributed 400 illustrations among the 952 pages of volume 20, published between May and October 1880.

Leslie's degree of commitment to illustration and the regular incorporation of chromolithographs of reasonable quality was unprecedented in a major American monthly. However, perhaps even more noteworthy were two chromolithographed advertisements printed separately and inserted in the Leslie publication, the first in January 1880 on page 129. This appears to be the first full colour

Fig.14 The editor of Ladies' Home Journal, Louisa Knapp, edited the monthly from home, a point that she emphasized throughout out her years at the helm. It helped to establish a common cause with her readers. With a 5¢ cover price, she made the magazine the most popular in the United States.

advertisement published in an American magazine and may well be the first such example published anywhere in a serial.(Plate III).

Thus, by 1880 and well before the decade hitherto suggested, some of the basic patterns for the American magazine business had been established. The salesman's dollar was starting to appreciate in importance as advertising volume began to grow and had already affected the layout of *Scribner's Monthly*. Among the editorial pages, a broad range of non-literary interests were featured in the monthlies, although fiction and the related narratives of history, biography and travelogue were still very much in the ascendant.

What these publications lacked was a really substantial audience, for in that sphere, only *Youth's Companion*, with a claimed readership of about 300,000, was pointing the way forward.[18] It used an intensive and famous annual premium campaign each October, in which a vast and seductive list of goodies was paraded before youthful eyes as prizes for securing new subscribers among associates and friends. These could be anything from a toy sailing boat for one new name, to a Ruby Printing Press for eight.[19]

This success story was not lost on Cyrus Curtis, the founder of the *Ladies' Home Journal*.(Fig. 14) First published in December 1883, examination shows that this monthly used the premium system extensively, building on the technique developed by the *Companion*. But, whereas the latter confined most of its promotional efforts to one special issue, Curtis concentrated on exploiting the Christmas issue and then scattered further reminders throughout the rest of the year. When combined with an extensive and expensive advertising campaign, the effect on sales was spectacular. By the March-July period of 1888 the *Journal*'s circulation had reached 400,000 a month. By 1892 it had touched 600,000, a plateau that extended throughout the 1890s.[20] Around 1893 or 1894 *Youth's Companion*, claimed the somewhat lower circulation plateau of 500,000.[21] Also on the move was *The Delineator*, a nondescript fashion monthly which, being published by the firm of Butterick, gave away a clothing paper pattern with each annual subscription. By 1888 it was claiming a circulation of 200,000. That figure rose, apparently, to 500,000 by June 1892.[22]

Some idea of the effort expended to secure the loyalty of new readers may be gauged from Frank Munsey's account of his 1886–87 promotion of *The Argosy* (which should not be confused with other publications of that title).

I spent in the following five months ninety-five thousand dollars in advertising *The Argosy*. I put out eleven million, five hundred thousand sample copies. I covered the country with travelling men from Maine to Nebraska, and from New Orleans to St.Paul. Beyond Nebraska I used the mails. I kept fifteen to twenty men on the road, and each man employed from one to a dozen helpers in distributing these sample sheets ... I laid out routes for the men, determined just how many sample sheets should go into each town, and sent every man a daily letter designed to fill him with enthusiasm and ginger. I not only wrote to these men, but I wrote to newsdealers everywhere, and saw that they were amply supplied with the issue containing the continuation of the serial stories begun in the sample copies.

By May 1887, the circulation reached 115,000.[23]

During the 1880s, what had started as *Scribner's Monthly* used the promotion of a highly popular series to increase sales, but first it underwent a change of name. Initially, it had been owned by Scribner and Company, a separate concern from the publishing house whose name it carried. At the magazine's launch, the book company received 40% of the stock of the new company in return for the use of its name, goodwill and the subscription list of a publication it had owned, *Hours At Home*. The remaining 60%, that is 300 shares, were bought by the editor Josiah Holland and Roswell Smith, the magazine's astute business manager, for $7250 and divided equally between them.[24]

A number of developments ensued on both sides during the magazine's first decade. The death of the senior Scribner was followed by a reorganisation within his firm. Further deaths and changes in responsibility followed towards the end of the decade and, by February 1879, Charles Scribner, at 25 years old, was left in sole charge of the book publishing house. Meanwhile, Holland and Smith had developed the *Monthly* into a very valuable property. In addition, Smith's initiative had led him to develop book publishing as a profitable sideline for the magazine company. This irritated the young Scribner and within two years of the latter's assumption of power, the parties were at each others' throats.

Given Smith's resolve and his purchase of a controlling interest from an ailing Holland, the outcome was not surprising. Thus, on 4 April 1881, Smith and his wife purchased the 200 shares owned by the book publishers for $200,000. In its turn, the contract stipulated that both the magazine and its holding company must change their name within a reasonable period and that the book publishers must desist from any ventures into the magazine lists for five years. The agreement was observed by both parties, which is how *Scribner's Monthly* was transformed into the *Century Illustrated Monthly Magazine* with the November 1881 issue. Subsequently, in January 1887, Charles Scribner's Sons launched *Scribner's Magazine*.[25]

In part, the above situation was the consequence of financial success fuelled by advertising revenue. And it was not only Charles Scribner who was watching this rising star. Despite the prejudice that 'any displays other than book notices lowered the dignity of a literary monthly,'[26] Harper's could not resist the bait. So, in the June 1881 edition of their *Monthly* an insertion was made extolling the virtues of *The Sun* newspaper of New York.[27] After this toe-dipping exercise, the splash came in December later that year, when a regular number of pages of advertisements per issue for the usual variety of organs, pianos, electric hair brushes and patent medicines began to be sandwiched between the *Harper's* literary notices, like a rather nasty piece of baloney.

Once the taste had been acquired there was no holding *Harper's*. Volume 81, for June to November 1890, contained 374.55 pages of paid insertions and only 91.45 for the products of the parent company. Against a total of 990 pages of editorial text and pictures, that indicates, for the period, six issues fat with advertising. Yet, the *Century*, during the period May to October 1890, that is in volume 40, which had 952 pages of editorial material, featured 24 pages advertising the Century Company's products and 524 pages advertising everything from schools to prophylactic toothbrushes. This contradicts an assertion made by Sidney Sherman, and reiterated by John, that the advertising insertions in *Harper's* equalled those of the *Century* by this year.[28] The *Century*'s lead, selling 40% more page space than its rival, was a tribute to the foresight and drive of the company's majority shareholder and business brain, Roswell Smith. His death, on 19 April 1892, was a serious loss at a point when the magazine's status in its market came under serious threat.[29]

The 1880s have been called the golden years of *Century Illustrated*, a description which it is difficult to fault. Although Josiah Holland died, aged 62, on 12 October 1881, the editorial transition was a painless passage.[30] Richard Gilder had started with the book publishers, Scribner's, as an editor on the aforementioned *Hours At Home*. By 1869 he was editor-in-chief and was taken on to the staff of its bigger and better successor, *Scribner's Monthly*, as assistant editor to Holland. As the latter's health declined, Gilder assumed more and more of his powers.[31] So, at the moment of truth he was well prepared.

The quality of his employees appears to have been a considerable help to Gilder. It was the assistant editor, Clarence Buel, for example, who proposed the monster series on the Civil War that helped to boost their circulation in the middle of the 1880s.[32] In 1881 the magazine had claimed 125,000 subscribers.[33] Yet, at its apogee, the war extravaganza doubled that number, and even by 1890, 200,000 subscribers remained faithful.[34]

In essence, the series did not take the form that one would normally expect of an historical blockbuster, either then, before or since. Participants low and high, but usually the latter, from both sides, set down their sometimes conflicting positions and memories, frequently cheek by jowl in the same issue, forcing the readers to draw their own conclusions. Yet, despite its tendency to dominate some issues, the series was only ever part of the whole. There was still room to run Henry James' *The Bostonians* and all of the broad range of material which Holland's precedent from the previous decade had established as the magazine's normal fare, if in a reduced space.

By 1890, May to October, volume 40, the main thrust of the Civil War series was over but its mark was still apparent. (Fig. 15) Articles classifiable as history and biography were continuing to absorb over 34% of the page space, up from 28% in 1880, before the series had begun.[35] Fiction was also bullish, up to just over 22% from 15% over the same period.[36] However, that group of interests that had distinguished the *Century* under its former title in 1880, namely the arts, sciences and social concerns were waning under Gilder's regime, from its high point of 40% to a lesser 30% in 1890(see Appendix I). So, if Gilder was according to John, 'a bundle of selfless energy, forever enthusiastic about some piece of literature, work of art, or person, spending himself in civic and cultural causes,'[37] it was not always apparent in the contents of the magazine he had controlled for nine years.

Meanwhile, the old adversary was maintaining its own quite distinctive editorial profile. *Harper's* interest in fiction and articles about travel and adventure was still a dominant one, even if it had diminished from its peak of ten years before to a figure of about 54%. As it had possessed the same editor since 1869, Henry Mills Alden, such consistency is hardly surprising.[38] The regular use of Laurence Hutton to write the four pages of 'Literary Notes' each month, when combined with the similarly critical 'Editor's Study', bolstered the apparent commitment to literary analysis without any major features in the front of the magazine. The series headed 'Editor's Drawer' also bolstered the amount of page space used by 'Humour and Entertainment', a light-hearted vein that was almost entirely absent from the *Century*. Another subject that had began to appear in the older publication was the theatre; again, absent from the *Century*. Topics such as the arts, science and technology and public affairs were hardly featured, again in contrast to the *Century*. Neither bothered to describe or discuss anything to do with religion, fashion or domestic arrangements(see Appendix II). Overall, the tone of *Harper's* resembles the grip of a comfortable armchair.

As has been already indicated, advertising revenue was

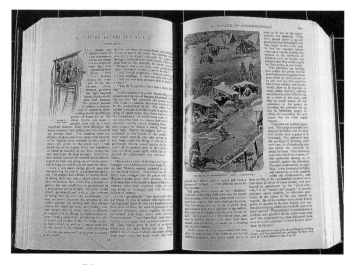

Fig. 15 The sophistication of the layouts found in the Century Illustrated by 1890 was exceptional. The text wrap enclosing the illustration on this left-hand page can be found in few magazines of the period.

flourishing and this meant that *Harper's* was, by the end of the eighties, able to use better paper throughout each issue. However, old habits died hard and the quality varied from signature to signature. Profusely illustrated articles were printed on better quality, super-calendered paper, while those that relied purely on text were printed on the signatures of the cheaper grades. Parsimony was still the watch-word. Yet, that had not halted the trend towards the greater use of illustrations. The 991 editorial pages of volume 81 were adorned with 486 reproductions, a frequency of 0.49 per page and a slight increase over the 434 in volume 61 of ten years earlier, which had used a frequency of 0.45 per page. However, given the price differential between wood blocks and halftones noted in Chapter 2, the significant numbers of halftone blocks used in this volume, that is, 97, or 20% of the total number of blocks, may have contained the cost to the publishers, who, it should be remembered, had pioneered the halftone in the monthly trade.

The visual contrast with the *Century* is particularly marked at this point for Gilder seemed resistant to the use of the new graphic arts technology. In 415 reproductions, spread among 952 pages during the May to October period of 1890, that is at a frequency of 0.44 per page, there were only eight halftones, that is slightly less than 2% of the total. In fact, this is not surprising given an editorial in this very volume which makes the magazine's stance on the matter unequivocal:

while current periodical illustration has gained much by the various mechanical or actinic processes in vogue for the reproduction of photographs from nature, and for the reproduction of original pictures, the time still seems to be far distant when wood-engraving must retire in favour of 'the process.' The process is at its best in reproducing pen drawings, though it sometimes lacks the delicacy of wood-engraving in that direction also...The process can copy outlines, but it cannot interpret tones; it cannot think.[39]

Such disdain was an expensive attitude. By 1890 it appears that the cost of drawings and engravings for each issue was about $8,000.[40] The paper used was also noticeably better in quality than that used by *Harper's*, though by this time they were indulging in their rival's practice of varying the stock with the demands of the reproductions and the text.

The way in which these changes affected a specific issue can be seen in that for September 1890. Two elements immediately catch the attention: intervals between illustrations which continue for over 10 pages on occasion; and the determination to use hand-engraved plates at whatever cost. The latter is most noticeable in 'The Autobiography of Joseph Jefferson', in which six reproductions of photographs have been engraved rather than translated into halftones, which would have been cheaper. However, at this point it is doubtful whether halftones could have matched the quality of the engravings on the printed page and attention to quality is evident throughout the issue.

Subtle rhythms are established by using different styles of engraving to reproduce the illustrations to one article, such as 'Wells Cathedral'. It fills a few centimetres short of 20 pages but is purely verbal in approach for the first three. Then a floor plan is reproduced on the right-hand page. A distant view of the building is positioned in a similar spot overleaf having been engraved by H.Wolf, who tended to cut dots rather than lines where he could, giving a relatively light result. The next spread uses two pictures: that on the left by Jo Pennel tends toward line rather than dots and features strong contrast between the silvery distance and rich, shadowy centre of the picture. That on the right, by J.H.E. Whitney, inclines toward line as much as possible but remains largely in the middle tonalities. Variations on such qualities are used throughout the article, as are changes in block size and position on the page. The typeface is also particularly attractive and composed with sufficient leading to give a satisfying balance between type colour and white paper on the page. 'How California Came into the Union' is less successful because its visual basis is less tractable, being dependent on clumsy naïve paintings for its portraits and early photographs in which the subjects would have had to remain still for an unnaturally long period in order to get a well-defined image.

Another article, 'Features of the Proposed Yosemite National Park' could also have benefited from the use of photographic illustrations rather than artwork. In fact, it seems quite probable that the blocks were engraved by hand from original photographs given the density of detail included. Most of the six spreads feature two reproductions, but the results are more homogeneous than those used to illustrate the article on Wells Cathedral. The text is very simply set in two columns of a 9 point serif face with the title in 12 point capitals, as on almost every other piece published in the issue. The only exception to this restrained approach is the illuminated drop capital used to start this and all other articles. But the way in which the two elements, text and illustrations, were used achieves considerable variations in form and no two resemble one another. Clearly the revenue from the 524 pages of advertisements came in handy when the bills for all this work were paid.

The income from paid announcements was also a growing feature of the budget of *Frank Leslie's Popular Monthly* by the end of the 1880s. Edited by the former owner's widow, Mrs Frank Leslie, it was claiming a circulation of 125,000 by 1887,[41] although, by 1890, the Rowell organisation was still only allowing that sales exceeded 75,000.[42] Unfortunately, a set of volume 29, January to June, 1890, complete with advertisements is not currently available. However, the set that does remain lacks only the month of February. As the other five months contain 110.90 pages of paid insertions, giving an average of 22.18 pages per month, it seems reasonable to assume that the missing month contains a comparable number. This would lead us to a total of approximately 133 pages for the half year, a figure greatly inferior to those already quoted for its rivals. Consequently, it is not surprising that, although the paper stock used by the magazine had improved over the decade, it was still markedly inferior to that used by *Harper's* and *Century*. Yet, if that deficiency had failed to inhibit the husband's use of illustration, it was not more daunting for the widow and, during the first half of 1890, 523 reproductions were used, including six chromolithographed frontispieces and 17 halftones. Spread over 772 pages this gives a frequency of 0.68 per page.

The editorial profile developed under the first owner was also largely maintained by his successor. The predilection for fiction was tempered from just over 39% in 1880 to 32% in 1890. The arts waxed to 13% while the sciences waned to 5.5%. Reflections on contemporary society stood at just under 15%, with the interest in foreign customs still significantly higher than its competitors at a little less than 6% (see Appendix IV). Indeed, one of the distinguishing features of the magazine was that it possessed a more cosmopolitan curiosity than its peers, particularly the *Century*, which was very insular in the matter of non-fiction. It can also claim to have provided a better balanced bill of fare for its readers than the other two.

However, the factor that distinguished *Leslie's* most clearly from its rivals was the length of each editorial item. While it led each issue with a substantial article or piece of fiction, certain pages within each issue were peppered with micro-articles. This was another editorial rhythm that the widow had inherited, but to quantify it needs care. All three publications used verse as a page filler, poems of a page or longer being comparatively rare. Such material could add up to 27 items in a mere 24.80 pages in volume 40 of the *Century*, for instance. Thus, the exclusion of all verse from any assessment of average article and story length is necessary to overcome the downward distortion of the numbers. For example, if those 27 poetry items in the *Century* are allowed to remain in the calculation, the 952 pages need to be divided among 125 editorial items, giving an average item length of 7.61 pages. If the 24.80 pages of verse are excluded, dividing 98 items among 927.20 pages, the average length comes out at 9.46 pages, which seems to be a more accurate measure of the editorial rhythm. On a similar basis, volume 81 of *Harper's Monthly* published 101 items in 960.29 pages, excluding verse; which gives an average of 9.51 pages per article. In complete contrast, volume 29 of *Leslie's* used 262 items in 758.95 pages, excluding verse, rendering an average length of only 2.90 pages per item. The difference could not be much clearer.

The 1880s had seen a number of new faces join the small group of best sellers. Charles Scribner's Sons, the book publishers, waited the five years required in their contract with Roswell Smith and then, in January 1887, set off in hot pursuit of their erstwhile stable mate. Not surprisingly, *Scribner's Magazine* was hardly a ground-breaking venture. At 227 x 158mm, it was just a fraction larger than the *Century*. At 818.91 pages of editorial material in volume 7, January-June 1890, it was shorter than the *Century's* 952. It varied its paper stock according to usage. It was comfortably adorned with illustrations without a dramatic flourish in any one direction: 393 in total, or 0.48 per page. It favoured fiction with a third of its editorial space and gave just over 16% to the arts. It ignored social problems and fashion, religion and natural history(see Appendix VIII). Items in the main editorial section were longer than was usual among its peers, at 13.47 pages each on average, excluding verse, and it tended towards a rather solid presentation. As a counterweight, it spread 32.89 pages of humour through the advertising section, which was, of course, segregated at the back. Those paid for totalled 431.86 pages, which is more than *Harper's* but less than the *Century*. Altogether, a creditable performance, perhaps, after three years of existence, by which time Rowell's credits it with monthly sales exceeding 75,000.[43] However, this substantial progress had cost the magazine's owners $500,000, according to an oblique remark in a contemporary article by a rival.[44] A rapid rise to prominence could be a very expensive ascent.

The most important innovation in the monthly market during the 1880s was the magazine which first appeared in December 1883. *Ladies' Home Journal* developed from the women's page of a weekly farm paper *Tribune and Farmer*, which measured 597 x 444 mm.[45] Perhaps it is a consequence of this genesis that the newcomer exhibited unusually large dimensions, 404 x 277 mm, for a monthly, although fashion magazines of the time were frequently of a similar size. The paper used was calendered and of a middle weight, but as each issue only used one captioned illustration on the front of each eight page issue and a couple of illuminated headings inside during the course of the first volume, the quality of the printing surface was not critical. However, it does indicate that the owner was already concerned about the monthly's appearance.

Apart from the fiction that usually filled the front page and a column on the next page, the rest of the editorial material in volume one was a matter of practical instruction in one form or another. It varied from 'The Art of Shopping' to the art of water–colours; from advice on keeping children under control to lace-work patterns. The editorial direction was provided by the wife of the publisher Cyrus Curtis, Louisa Knapp, who had developed the supplement in *Tribune and Farmer*.

By the end of the decade her editorial skill had evolved. Perhaps that was inevitable given her years of experience and the greater scope offered by the increasing size of the editions. By volume 6, which ran from December 1888 to November 1889, the last one on which she worked as the editor, issues were varying in size but averaged just over 24 pages per month. The topics discussed were now much more varied than when the *Journal* was launched and closer to those of the other publications already discussed. For example, in January 1889, the issue began with a serial. That was followed by 'Winter Ventilation of Our Homes,' another piece of fiction, 'The

Wisdom of the Ancients,' 'New Year's Calls and Receptions,' 'Hospitality, Hosts and Guests', more fiction, 'Luman Skinkle's Religion' and 'The Land of the Midnight Sun.' Perhaps such a miscellany not only reflects a particular editorial approach, but also the daily lives of the editor, her assistants and contributors, most of whom were women combining their professional life with a domestic workload in a manner that would be more usual a century later.[46] Helen Damon-Moore's analysis makes the case for their mediating influence during this transitional period in American middle-class society. Unfortunately, the argument is not as deeply embedded in the pages of the *Journal* as it might have been.[47]

Despite this increased editorial range, such changes were difficult to read from the layout as titles were merely bold type and poorly differentiated from the text. Page headings for the regular features had been designed but they were compressed into the upper left corner of the relevant page, at the top of the first column. This meant that the magazine's editorial changes were far from adequately expressed in the layout. In complete contrast, the business side of the publication had developed by leaps and bounds, setting a pattern that would profoundly influence the magazines of the following decade.

Cyrus Curtis attacked on two fronts. As already described, he used premiums extensively on the same model as *Youth's Companion*, that is he gave rewards to those who solicited subscriptions from others. Like the *Companion*, his full list of rewards was featured annually in the same issue. However, unlike his model, he used the Christmas issue rather than their choice of late October. In other words, he had no hesitation about using for commercial ends an issue usually given over to matters and sentiments of a festive and religious nature. He knew that the holiday period would create a captive audience with more leisure on its hands than normal. Curtis was nothing if not determined. For example, in the December 1887 number, thirteen pages were used to advertise everything from a tissue paper flower outfit that you received in exchange for two new subscribers, through tray cloths, books and cutlery, to a parlour organ that required 350 new subscribers to be registered before it was despatched. Also, unlike the *Companion*, the *Journal's* readers were prompted throughout the year as well, with small reminders in each issue. However, all of these benefits were available only to those who solicited full price subscriptions, that is those rated at 50¢ a year. Curtis did have a scheme whereby four or more subscribers could club together and get the 12 issues at half price but these did not count towards the premium scheme.[48]

His second important promotional thrust was also an extension of an accepted practice. He advertised the *Journal* in other publications. Yet, where others promoted themselves on a small scale, Curtis really drove the message home. His first initial investment of $400 through the leading agency of the day, N. W. Ayer, also of Philadelphia, brought in a sufficient response for him to repeat the experiment. In turn, the revenue derived from new subscriptions was reinvested in more advertising.

The effect of these promotional policies was spectacular. At a time, the mid 1880s, when a big selling magazine was one with a circulation of 100,000, he reached that figure in little more than a matter of months. Six months later he had doubled that number. He abolished cut price subscriptions but his circulation still rose.[49] Then, in November 1888 he really did take a risk. Despite having a guaranteed circulation of 400,000, one of the largest of any newspaper or periodical in the United States at that time, he told his readers that he was going to make the magazine larger and double the price.[50] As an insurance policy, he went to Wayland Ayer, the owner of his advertising agency, and asked for $200,000 credit for a massive campaign. He also obtained a $100,000 credit from Crocker, Burbank and Company, his paper makers. In the end he spent $310,000 on advertising that season, but it worked. Instead of sales falling, his circulation rose.[51]

His intention was to upgrade the *Journal*, a preoccupation that Salme Steinberg has detailed with considerable precision for the 1890s.[52] But even in the 1880s, Curtis was concerned to upgrade his paper stock and the quality of his illustrations.[53] For the cause of improved status for his publication in 1889 he appears to have put his wife on the block. It has always been accepted that Mrs Curtis quit her editorship as a result of domestic pressure, but her only daughter was thirteen years old at that time.[54] Having given herself to editorial duties through the more vulnerable years of her child's life, it seems more than a little odd that a career woman should succumb to pangs of guilt just when her child was approaching her more independent years. Could it be that there is another explanation? Could it be that this is one of those face-saving formulas so beloved of so many businessmen?

As must be clear already, Curtis was an astute and ambitious businessman. If he aspired to a situation in which the *Journal* was going to be placed on a par with the *Century* and *Harper's*, he needed to improve the appearance of his publication. If his wife had not moved beyond her current awareness of design after more than five years of editorial responsibility, then he needed someone else. That person proved to be Edward Bok.

Already, the September 1889 issue had featured a cover and some minor typographic and design improvements and a contents list for the very first time. Given the long lead-in time necessary in the 1880s for editorial preparations and printing, the decision to make these changes must have been made in the summer, well before Bok was appointed on 20 October 1889.[55] It was January before his name appeared on the editorial masthead and by the next month improvements in the layout of the pages began to appear. The page headings for the various regular departments began to escape their previous constrictions and were opened up to spread across two columns. 'Side Talks With Girls' and 'Mother's Corner' now competed with 'Literary Circles' for the reader's attention. Even more radical, the March issue led with 'Mrs Harrison in the White House', a feature about the country's first lady which was unlike anything that Louisa Knapp published. Now there was only one heading left, 'Mother's Corner', that remained compressed into one column. By May, 'Domestic Life in Egypt' faced 'Farmer Bell's Bargain' across a double spread, and 'A South African Wedding' followed 'Women's Need of Exercise'. By combining these innovations with the familiar departments, Bok could both reassure his established readers and hold those caught in the web of promotions.

Meanwhile, the weekly market was far from stagnant. *Puck*, a weekly comic publication, had appeared in the 1870s. Joseph Keppler, an immigrant artist from Vienna, tried publishing a German-language funny paper in St Louis without success in 1870. A year later he tried again, calling the magazine *Puck*, again without success. Thereafter, he moved to New York where he worked on *Leslie's Illustrated Newspaper*. In 1876 he formed a partnership with a printer called Schwarzmann and launched again. This time, with an editor, Leopold Schenck, they were successful. From September 1876 to March 1877 they produced the German-language edition of *Puck*. However, it was suggested to them that an English edition using the same lithographed reproductions, which employed English for the text on the cartoons in any case, might be successful.[56] From issue one, in March 1877, the 339 x 250mm pages employed pale, coloured tints over the monochromatic line and tone of the cartoons. The large, florid, political specimens were usually drawn by Keppler at first. President Hayes was frequently their butt, though the European royal families were also reckoned to be fair and frequent game.

In the autumn of 1881, a group of artists seceded from *Puck* as a result of personal friction and began a rival, *Judge*, whose first issue is dated 29 October 1881. Apart from a slightly larger page size, 359 x 267 mm, it was difficult to distinguish the newcomer from its older brother. Technical and artistic considerations, overall design and the victims of its satire were largely the same. So, it is really not surprising that the initial interest in the new title soon waned. New owners were found but it was not until 1884, when it joined a ferocious campaign against the Democratic presidential candidate, Grover Cleveland, that its fortunes changed. The Republican Party could see the advantage of having a combatant such as *Judge* in their corner. The following year, party supporters poured substantial funds into the empty coffers and W.J. Arkell took over the parent company. In turn, he lured further staff away from *Puck* and the battle lines were drawn between the two publications, one for each party.[57] None of this hurt circulation and by 1890 both publications were acknowledged by Rowell as selling in excess of 75,000 copies per week,[58] although Ayer set *Judge* lower at 70,000 and *Puck* much higher at 89,700.[59]

The third successful 10¢ comic weekly to appear was very different. Also New York based, *Life* appeared in the first week of January 1883. It was owned and edited by John Ames Mitchell who, according to the monograph on the magazine,

chose every illustration and spot drawing that went into the magazine for thirty five years. But he left to other men the job of choosing words to go with the pictures, and although *Life* was primarily an illustrated magazine, Mitchell's idea of illustration was decorative rather than explanatory. The words, not the pictures, supplied the humour, the opinion, the blood and bone that gave substance to the pretty face Mitchell chose for *Life*.[60]

In fact, the price was about the only similarity between this and the two other 10¢ comic weeklies. Whereas their cartoons were bold with a vigorous, reductive line that regularly filled a double spread or a single page, those of *Life* were finely detailed without any of the element of caricature so characteristic of the other two and were normally used as part of a complex page layout. With alternative captions, they might easily have been placed in the *Century* or *Harper's Monthly* and looked the part. Most of *Life's* drawings were reproduced by the still new line photoengraving process which transferred the image on to a zinc plate, where it was etched. It was probably the first American magazine to use this technology extensively.[61]

However, in the weekly market the most popular publication was undoubtedly *Youth's Companion*. Built on the back of its promotion system, its readership of 'about 400,000'[62] was held by a balanced mix of topics. Although each issue began with a solid tranche of fiction that took up over 32% of volume 63, analysis reveals a catholic spread of editorial interest. The near 6% of space devoted to travel and adventure was almost matched by 5.5% devoted to poetry. An exceptional 8% concerned the natural world, while every issue had at least one short article on matters of health(see Appendix V).

DURING THE NINETIES, the emphasis already placed on facets of contemporary society by some editors increased, with *Harper's Monthly* developing this area of its interests to over 15% of editorial space, while the *Century's* commitment grew from 16 to more than 22.5%(see Appendices I & III). From the first, *Frank Leslie's*, had been interested in social questions and had allocated 22% of its space to such matters (see Appendix IV). But, the most dramatic move came from *The Cosmopolitan* which, in the late 1880s under Edward Walker, had established its editorial persona by devoting over 36% of its space to social questions(see Appendix IX). Thus, as the 1890s began, some magazines were already demonstrating their ability to evolve with the times, building on an existing concern.

By 1900 *Cosmopolitan* was firmly established in the 10¢ a month market after an undistinguished start in March 1886. Based, initially, in Rochester, New York, its owner, Paul

J Schlicht, had pitched it at the same market as its firmly established peers: 35¢ an issue, $4 a year, although its subsequent fate only emphasizes how badly undercapitalised he was. Providing only 64 pages an issue failed to encourage the defection of readers from other titles and, after 12 months, a circulation of only 25,000 was being claimed. Yet, before John Brisben Walker bought the magazine and blandished his name on the front cover in January 1889, the circulation actually dropped further and it was only by the narrowest of margins that the title survived, despite a decrease in the cover price to 20¢. Indeed, the last volume published before Walker took over, the fifth, missed two issues. Yet, despite such erratic editorial behaviour and being possessed by three owners within an eight month period,[63] the magazine carried at least 226 pages of paid insertions. Perhaps, the rate per page sounded like a bargain to the prospective advertisers. With such a low circulation for such a periodical, the business manager would have been in a weak position and unable to charge more than the minimum rates. He may even have had to offer discounts to get advertisements. The entrepreneurial thrust of John Walker changed all that.

Born in September 1847 near Pittsburgh, his restless energy drove him on through an extraordinarily diverse career. The profits from the sale of real estate in the Denver area financed his purchase of *Cosmopolitan*.[64] There his drive, which certainly encompassed a dictatorial streak, had an immediate effect. By 1890, about a year after he took over, the *American Newspaper Directory* was prepared to credit him with a circulation exceeding 37,500,[65] although by May, Walker was claiming 50,000 a month in his advertisements.[66] Yet, the advertising published in *Cosmopolitan* did not grow in proportion to this increase in sales, quite the reverse in fact. The total number of pages paid for in volume 9, 143.75, is very substantially less than the figure quoted above for volume five. Such an uncharacteristic decline does seem to lend support to the hypothesis that, under the previous management, bargain basement page rates had been the order of the day. Now the prices were advertised quite clearly at $100 a page. The only discount mentioned related to the placing of yearly contracts.[67] By October, the management were able to publish a facsimile of a hand–written note from their printers and binders, J.J.Little and Co. of Astor Place, that certified that they were in the process of producing 75,000, copies of the current edition and that each subsequent issue would be increased by 5,000 copies, reaching 90,000 in January 1891.[68]

This turn-round was achieved through a variety of promotional ploys. In June 1890, an architectural competition, involving the design of public baths, laundries and tenement house co-operative kitchens, was announced.[69] In September a celluloid paper knife was offered.[70] In 1891, Walker hired a special railway carriage, filled it with drummers and hustled subscriptions throughout New York State. In later years he used premiums, while in 1893 he offered 1,000 college scholarships to his most successful salesmen. All-in-all, it would appear that he sank $360,000 in the venture before the corner was turned in November 1892 and the profits began to roll.[71]

In respect of the content of the magazine, Mott repeats a point made by contemporaries that Walker brought immediacy and timeliness to periodical literature.[72] Yet, while he did all that he could to promote his editorial position, there must now be some doubt as to the degree of his contribution to its editorial development. An analysis of both volumes five and nine, along lines already established above, reveals a great similarity in the editorial profile, the choices of material, encompassed by the publication both before and after John Walker bought it. Indeed, this is very noticeable as the interest in social commentary and information, prior to his purchase, is quite unprecedented in the American monthly magazine market(see Appendix IX). To devote over one-third of the page space to such matters was unheard of, even though the editors of contemporary journals were already increasing their coverage of the area as compared to ten years earlier. For example, the allocation of space to such subject matter in *Harper's* jumped from 5% to over 12% during the 1880s(see Appendices II & III). Indeed, the example of *Harper's Monthly* is not entirely irrelevant for it was from their editorial staff that Edward Dwight Walker emerged in 1888 to assume the position of editor of *The Cosmopolitan* when Ulysses Grant Jnr gained control of its publication in March of that year, the first month to be included in volume five. Even when John Walker took over, Edward Walker, who was quite unrelated, remained in the position of assistant editor. Only his death in the summer of 1890, in a drowning accident, deprived the magazine of his services.[73] So, given the editorial continuity that the analysis demonstrates, it seems not improbable that the older, more prominent John Walker has attracted some of the laurels due to his obscure namesake. Which is not to say that John did not make his own contribution.

What had been established, he persuaded the public to purchase in large and increasing numbers. Over and above that, he invested in larger editions of 128 pages each. He substantially increased the number of illustrations used, from 223 in the 534 pages of volume five to 569 in the 764 pages of volume nine, that is, from 0.42 per page to 0.74 per page, making *The Cosmopolitan* the most profusely illustrated mixed function monthly of the time.(Fig. 16) In doing this, being the astute businessman that he was, he used halftones rather than woodcuts; the cost-effective choice. Altogether he used 350 examples of the new process, that is over 60% of all the illustrations, which made him the undisputed leader in their use in the magazine trade, and maybe among all print buyers. By taking such an option he could reproduce original photographs, a choice that enriched the quality and quantity of information he was able to transmit to his readers. And what was a bold move in 1890 became established practice ten years later among all his competitors.

Another injection of energy into American sales techniques occurred in the second half of 1893 when Sam McClure founded a monthly named after him and sold it at 15¢ a copy.[74] At that time the two most prestigious 'quality' magazines, *Century* and *Harper's*, sold for 35¢ a copy. Their competitors, *Scribner's*, *Frank Leslie's Popular Monthly* and *Cosmopolitan*, cost 25¢. None had learned the lesson of the *Ladies' Home Journal*, outselling all of them at 10¢ a copy.

A month later in July, stimulated by competition, *Cosmopolitan* cut its cover price to 12.5¢, although it was forced to retreat to 15¢ six months later in January 1894. However, it was Frank Munsey who shocked the publishing

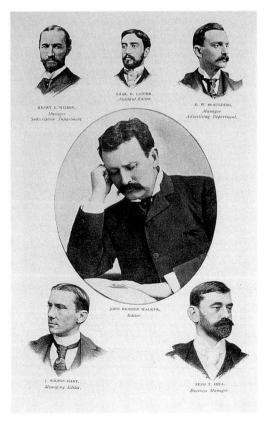

Fig.16 The spread of halftone blockmaking in the 1890s enabled the editorial staff who adopted the technology to manipulate the layout of illustrations much more freely than in the days of woodblocks. This led to designs that were sometimes a little too elaborate.

world most profoundly when in September of that year he tried to reduce his monthly from 25¢ to 10¢ a copy, or $1 per year.[75] As will be related in due course, this was largely a desperation measure, a last throw of the dice for a publisher with hitherto undistinguished results. Nevertheless, it had its effect. Since the 1860s the American News Company had completely dominated periodical distribution.[76] They refused to pay Munsey more than 4.5¢ per copy wholesale. Munsey refused to accept less than seven. On the advice of his friend Charles Dana of the *New York Sun*, Munsey formed the Red Star News Company, his own distributor. But the magazine retailers still did not buy. Then Dana offered advertising space in the *Sun* on credit. On 2 October Munsey took a four-column space, which examination reveals to be the largest display in the paper, to proclaim the virtues of his new publication. ANC immediately made an improved offer of 5.75¢ but it was ignored. The offer had been made because, in their ignorance, the retailers had sent their orders through their normal channels to ANC.[77] However, the rolling stone soon began to gather sales as the dealers realised their mistake and began to order direct from Red Star. In ten days the first printing of 20,000 had gone. Munsey printed and sold another 20,000. The October issue had cost $50,000 but Munsey retained Red Star and for many years was the only publisher independent of ANC.[78]

Of course, cheap and nasty periodicals had appeared before this time, both in the US and elsewhere. Both *Puck* and *Judge* sold for 10¢ every week, but their approach was rumbustious rather than refined, and weekly funny papers could not be considered within the same context as serious monthlies. Furthermore, Munsey was offering a great many more pages than the owners of the two weeklies. In fact, what McClure and Munsey did was to slash the price while retaining the model already established by *Century* and *Harper's*, enlarging the market for an accepted product.[79] In this they were undoubtedly aided by the new technology, in particular the new ink, the new presses and the vast reduction in the cost of illustrations that was ushered in by the halftone block. But the conceptual breakthrough, the imaginative insight that expanded this sector of the information system, beginning the process whereby this element of society's feedback mechanism penetrated whole new layers of that entity, was the realisation that if you cut the cover price of a magazine to a point below cost but subsidised it with advertising the number of potential customers would be vastly increased, simply because they could now afford to buy the publication. And as advertising rates, hence income, were related to the size of the readership, your income from this source would spiral up pro rata.[80] What you lost on the penny roundabouts, you more than made up for on the sixpenny swings. Indeed, the mathematics proved not only to be sound but very seductive. For example, calculations suggest that, in 1892, Munsey was earning about $200,000 a year from the cover price of his 100,000 circulation magazine. By 1895, his sales of 500,000 were generating about $420,000, with commensurably increased costs, of course. But his advertising revenue had risen from a miserable $12,000 to approximately $320,000. It was no wonder that the man ended his days a multi-millionaire.[81]

Not surprisingly, once the point had been made the herd followed. Ten years later Munsey himself estimated that 85% of all general interest magazines sold in the United States cost 10¢ a copy.[82] Furthermore, one has only to glance at the circulation figures of the most popular nationally distributed magazines of the first decade of the new century to realise that the aggregate audience for them had expanded enormously. And it was this substantial constituency that gave the American magazine journalists of the next decade, those known as the muckrakers, the opportunity to colour public attitudes.

The change to a 10¢ cover price helped to push *Cosmopolitan's* circulation up to approximately 300,000.[83] An advertising rate of $2 an agate line,[84] which exceeds that of the

Century, Scribner's Magazine and *Harper's Monthly*, suggests a page rate of about $350-400 per page, but at the moment it is impossible to confirm this point. Unfortunately, the volume of *Cosmopolitan* available with the advertising still extant, features some inconsistencies of pagination, which in turn strongly implies that some signatures of advertising are now missing. Nevertheless, 452 pages of paid insertions do remain for the six month period from May to October, suggesting an income from this source of approximately $300,000 per annum at least. At $1 a year subscription and total sales of 300,000, a rough balance between the two sources of income would appear to be indicated.

As at the beginning of the nineties, *Cosmopolitan*'s income was used to fund a large number of photographic reproductions, that is, they formed over 64% of all illustrations in Volume 29, May to October 1900. Already in this magazine, artwork was coming to be associated solely with fiction. The latter took about a third of the editorial space available in that volume. However, that did not stop the magazine maintaining its interest in contemporary society. As with so many other American magazines of the time, *Cosmopolitan* displayed a lot of interest during 1900 in both the Boer War and the Paris exposition.

Frank Leslie's Popular Monthly had also joined the 10¢ club during the nineties. In its case, the price change came after an unsuccessful change of editor. In 1895, the original owner's widow had leased the publication to a group of her employees headed by Frederic L. Colver, who had helped Edward Bok set up *The Brooklyn Magazine*, his first successful periodical.[85] The new management does not seem to have had any greater success than the preceding one, for *Leslie's* circulation appears to have dwindled in the face of competition.[86] So, after giving the new group their head for three years, Mrs Leslie resumed the reins, cut the price to 10¢, reduced the page size from 264 x 200 mm to 233 x 165 mm and dropped the three colour frontispieces. Immediate success was the result. By 1900 the magazine was offering advertisers a guaranteed circulation of 195,833,[87] while by 1902 the *American Newspaper Directory* was prepared to endorse an average circulation of 204,621 per month.[88]

From an editorial standpoint there was little to distinguish *Leslie's* from the *Century*. The editorial mix was similar, even if *Leslie's* showed no interest in such contemporary events as the World Exposition or the Boer War. The overall presentation was very much poorer than its rivals. With just over 42% of its reproductions coming from photographs, it used more than the *Century*, but then so did many other magazines. Its total number of reproductions, 363 in 625 pages or 0.58 per page, was only average. The one thing it did have in its favour was its price. The drop to 10¢ had an unmistakable effect on sales, which were pushed way beyond anything achieved during the magazine's earlier success in the 1880s. As might be expected, this gain attracted advertising, although again, binding of this material has been inadequate and one can only be sure of 420 pages in volume 50. Pagination suggests that at least another 100 pages have disappeared from this volume. However, in the drive towards success, that stylistic individuality that was particularly noticeable in 1890, the average length of each editorial item, 2.90 pages, had been effaced. Now, it was 9.14 pages per item, that is, it was indistinguishable from many of its contemporaries.

Although there was little to set *Leslie's* apart from its peers in terms of the subjects it used, the magazine's appearance certainly was distinctive. In the September issue, its taste for cutting a special typeface to distinguish the commencement of a particular article is evident with the very first article where the title is not merely surrounded by artwork, but becomes part of it. In addition, an explanatory sentence is set in bold type, enclosed in an engraved box and laid out to half the measure used on the rest of the page. Clearly this approach is more elaborate than that used on the *Century* and *McClure's*.

However, the art direction does not merely indulge in decoration for its own sake. Most unusually for the period, the pages are not divided into columns. This simple arrangement tends to emphasize the outlines of the blocks. To aid the effect even further, many illustrations have highly irregular forms and lack borders. Conversely, where the image is rectangular it is frequently enclosed in a two-rule border. These designs do not approach the populist rococo of *Cosmopolitan* in 1910, for instance, because the effects are not piled upon one another, while the asymmetrical layouts lack the contrived appearance that the later monthly achieved through symmetry about the vertical centre line of the page. Nevertheless, they do represent a step in that direction.

The most profusely illustrated of the articles in the issue, 'Money for Everybody', concerns the US Mint. Three photographs are reproduced on the first spread and they occupy two thirds of the printed surface. The weight is even more overwhelmingly on the visual on the second spread with 85% of the space taken up by small line drawings of government assay offices and the different branches of the mint. Reproductions of line drawings and photographs mix on the next spread. An interior of the engravers' division completes the layout, but this, in fact, is only the start of a sequence of 14 similar interiors detailing the process of dollar bill manufacture. Every spread is different and the reproductions are cropped to a highly irregular shape on three occasions. The rest sit rectangular on the page, some with a fine border line enclosing them, some without. Of the remainder of the issue, many spreads are devoid of illustrations, particularly those within a piece of fiction. The magazine never sinks to the monotonous look which was to be the mark of the *Saturday Evening Post* for close to 40 years. On the other hand, some of the self-indulgent excesses which were to be all too evident in *Cosmopolitan* in later years were here in embryo. *Frank Leslie's Popular Monthly* was one of the first to utilise the flexibility which photo-mechanical reproduction gave to designers during the 1890s.

The story of how *Munsey's Magazine* forced its attentions on the magazine sellers of America, driving its price down to 10¢, has already been told. In fact, this was only a late stage in Frank Munsey's quest for success. He had begun to produce a weekly magazine for children in December 1882 that had absorbed a great deal of effort and a similar sum of money during the decade that followed.[89] It was out of the lessons that he learned in sustaining *The Argosy* that he was moved to start the magazine that bore his name in February 1889 as a 10¢ weekly for adults. Mott reports that it was an imitation of a publication already discussed, *Life*.[90] However, it would appear that the first five volumes, that contain the weekly issues, are lost and, so far, it has proved impossible to check Mott's statement. Again, this publication produced substantial losses and Munsey changed tack again. In October 1891, his title became attached to a 25¢–a–month duplication of what was already on the market. Not surprisingly, sales remained limp. It seems almost a last ditch effort that caused him to drop his monthly price to 10¢ in October 1893, after ten years toil and, at best, a mediocre result. The consequences were spectacular. Like Curtis before him, he made a fortune and in little over two years, average circulation was about 500,000 that is, it was fast catching the *Ladies' Home Journal*.[91] By the end of the decade it had stabilised its circulation at just over 600,000.[92]

Again, one has to ask whether this was merely due to price or did Munsey bring a new editorial delicacy to tempt the jaded palate of the reading public. Examination of volume 23, for April to September 1900, suggests that while the magazine certainly possessed its own editorial personality, there was little that was particularly novel, almost the reverse in fact. Fiction adhered to the current norm of about one third of editorial space. Travel and adventure were ignored completely, while history and biography barely used 1%. Instead, the emphasis was on the arts and contemporary society: the former took a fraction under 26%, while the latter, just short of 33%. Ironically, this so-called radical devoted over 7% of its space to literary commentaries at a time when the *Century*, which is so often seen as conservative, had jettisoned such material completely. In addition, *Munsey's* managing editor, Richard Titherington,[93] demonstrated his taste for the ornate mansions of the American rich, while a section called 'The Stage', with many reproductions of the photographic portraits of attractive young actresses, consumed over 10% of each issue on average.(Fig. 17) For the first time in the magazines we have covered, religious material appeared in significant amounts. Altogether, the profile implies a different audience to that of the more expensive end of the market but a far from radical approach(see Appendix VII).

The design of the magazine incorporated a curious amalgam of paper stocks. Cheap, barely calendered paper manufactured from coarse wood pulp was used in the numerous sections that entirely lacked illustrations, while lightweight imitation art paper was used to print those sections featuring numerous photographs. Flurries of the latter, 516 in total in volume 23 out of 678 reproductions in 854 pages, were crowded round articles that were separated by sections featuring only bare text.

Fig.17 Munsey's was one of the first monthlies to realise that the stage was an unlimited source of supply of cheap, distracting photographs. Soon, regular columns were appearing in many magazines.

Only a few signatures of paper were used that were of sufficient quality to retain something approaching their original white colour after the passage of almost 90 years. The cover of each issue of *Munsey's* featured a different colour design that appears to have been created by three colour process work plus line blocks inked with individual colours, though this might well be an illusion. The overall effect exhibits lamentable draughtsmanship but, one presumes, added a note of jollity to the magazine racks of the time and attracted casual sales.

One editorial device is quite particular to *Munsey's*. The majority of articles feature a triple-lined box situated immediately below the title and preceding the main body of text, which carries an explanation, in bold type, of the nub of the subsequent text. The implication is clear that the editorial staff felt that the readership lacked the cognitive experience of the consumers of the many older journals, or at least needed enticement to try the full range of material laid out between the covers.

All of this attracted a considerable amount of advertising, considering that, by 1900, the price was $500 a page.[94] Volume 23 features 474.90 pages over a six month period. As this volume extends through the less active summer months, a total of $475,000 from advertising revenue seems a conservative sum. Added to the income from an average circulation of over 600,000 that yielded 7¢ a copy a month on casual sales[95] and $1 a year on subscriptions and a gross income of $1 million per annum from this one title is feasible.

The last of the most popular New-York-based, 10¢ monthlies, *McClure's Magazine*, has a reputation that cannot be disentangled from the muckraking era of investigative journalism, born in the opening years of the new century. Yet, a close look at volume 15, from May to October 1900, that is immediately prior to its more celebrated era, reveals a quite different animal from that usually portrayed. Of all the general magazines examined so far, none was so restricted in the range of its editorial preferences. Volume 15 used only five poems as page fillers. There was nothing else from the arts at all. Travel and adventure was also completely ignored, as were the social life and manners of the times, either at home or abroad. Discussions of social problems were, likewise, ignored for the time being. Attempts to amuse the readers were also avoided. Yet, science and technology were accorded over 8% of the page space in this volume; business and economic matters, 7.6%; public affairs, just over 7%. While in contemporary events, although most editors in 1900 focused on South Africa, McClure was more interested in the Philippines. Then there was the very substantial 41% of the page space devoted to fiction. However, perhaps the real surprise is that over 10% of the page space was spent on a serialisation of a retelling of the New Testament, 'The Life of the Master' by the Reverend John Watson, at the end of a thirty year period in which only *Munsey's*, had bothered with any aspect of religion beyond the use of a very sporadic, occasional few pages(see Appendix III).

Another surprise is revealed by an analysis of the illustrations in volume 15. Only 13.8% are photographic in origin, which is the complete opposite of the anticipated figure, and this is in a magazine that used the three-colour process to bring emphasis to the religious serial, and featured 355 reproductions in 571 pages, a frequency of 0.62 per page. This point is emphasized even further by examining one issue of volume 15 at random, that for October. There is not one photograph reproduced in this entire issue. Compared to *Frank Leslie's Popular Monthly*, which was using photography extensively to illustrate non-fiction already, *McClure's* was very conservative and the antithesis of how it has hitherto been portrayed.

Indeed, just how unadventurous Sam McClure was in the presentation of material at this time can be gauged by a more detailed look at this issue. It opens with a 13-page article on political campaigns of the previous 25 years; it being the height of the presidential campaign. All of the illustrations are sketch portraits which could easily have been supplanted with photographs. The article starts on page 482 with a full-page portrait of Theodore Roosevelt and the Republican Party chairman Marcus Hanna and continues sedately on to 494 with one picture a page, most of them rectangular. The text is in a simple two-column layout.

Two stories follow and the differences between their layouts and those of the preceding article is merely that they use fewer drawings. The cautious nature of the art direction is further emphasized by the monotonous typography. Every title is set in 14–point capitals. Most items also have a subtitle in ten–point capitals immediately inferior to it. Both are centred. Some articles, such as one from Arthur Conan Doyle on the Boer War, exhibit a complete lack of illustrations, photographic or otherwise. Most illustrations are rectangular and laid out one to a page without any artifice. Their captions usually consist of a heading set in seven–point capitals, with the remainder in tiny five–point italic. Drawing styles vary from item to item. Some exhibit a heavy, finished style, while others incline to light open lines and simple crosshatching for shadows.

Thus, the magazine that is frequently discussed as an innovator and a radical, largely, one suspects because of its contents in the following decade, can be seen to have had a singular personality. But, during its first seven years at least, it was not quite as avant-garde as some have suggested. For example, Peterson states: 'Both McClure and Munsey used photographs lavishly.'[96] Clearly, from the figures quoted above, that is just not true for the former.

Yet, none of these idiosyncrasies put off the advertisers who flocked to use the magazine's pages in such numbers by 1900 that their contributions outstripped the editorial pages. Against 571 pages of editorial were stacked at least 663 pages of paid insertions and another 55 of announcements by the McClure organisation about its own products.[97] At $384 per page with slightly greater rates for smaller sizes, and allowing for discounts, an income of over half a million dollars for the year from advertising revenue seems plausible. Coupled with their proportion of the cover price and subscriptions from their sworn circulation of 364,674,[98] which produced another $400,000,[99] it is clear that idiosyncrasy paid off. This is just as well, for McClure was a profligate editor, if a creative one, running up expenses on the magazine's production of $933,000 that year.[100]

Nothing could be a greater contrast to *McClure's* than the *Ladies' Home Journal*, now under Bok's control for a decade. Whereas the former curtailed its editorial interests exploiting only a limited range of subjects, Bok took the opposite tack, casting his net very widely, omitting only topics such as science and technology, sport and contemporary events in volume 17, that began in December 1899 and finished in November 1900. No one area dominated the others and even fiction was only allowed 13% of the editorial pages. Unlike Sam McClure, Bok devoted much space to descriptions and discussions of the social conventions of American society: 13% of editorial space(see Appendix XI). Frequently, these articles took the appearance of chatty correspondence, that is, a conceit was created rather than a documentary description. Like much women's journalism, the material was as much prescriptive as descriptive and, although he transformed the monthly from the domestic purview of the 1880s created by Louisa Knapp, the contributors, under his tutelage, still sought to provide role models, even if his tastes were more catholic than those of his predecessor.

Under his direction, his audience was given pictures and plans of modern, architect-designed houses. In August 1900, a page was devoted to a single storey, Californian residence. Under the title, the designer, owner and location were listed. Below that were situated exterior photographs, one interior shot and a ground plan. The only text was a four line caption below the leading illustration.[101] Then, in October 1900, a series began that has been the subject of frequent comments. Bok commissioned some of America's most prominent architects to prepare plans and estimates of 'model suburban houses which can be built at moderate cost.' He began with what was called a 'Georgian house' by Bruce Price.(Fig. 18)[102]

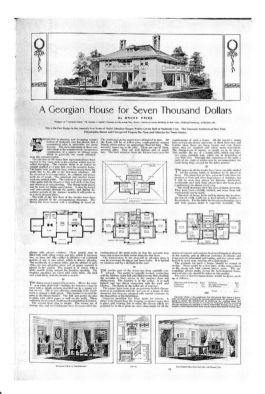

Fig.18 The Journal's series on domestic architecture has been credited with considerable influence. Stanford White, the pre-eminent American architect of his generation, who was initially opposed to Bok said: "I firmly believe that Edward Bok has more completely influenced American domestic architecture for the better than any man in his generation."

Fig.19 In the free way that Edward Bok used illustrations rather than text to present a topic in Ladies' Home Journal, he was a generation ahead of Life and Look. But the elaborate patterns, such as that used on this travel feature, were clearly related to contemporary European styles of decoration.

Yet, despite the cost of such a project to his publisher, his journalistic discipline never failed and the feature was confined to one page, just like so many of the articles, and did not seek to spread the cost of the piece over three or four pages. In fact, everything was kept very tight and in the 375.5 editorial pages he managed to squeeze in 418 items. The distinction from other monthlies could not have been more marked. However, this heady editorial pace was also a feature of other examples of the women's press at the time. *Woman's Home Companion*, for example, kept to much the same schedule of a fresh title at the top of most pages. What differentiated Bok from his rivals was the range of topics he incorporated each month and the intensity of illustrations he used to transmit information to his audience. As Damon-Moore has pointed out, Bok's intention was to seduce them into consumption.[103]

No editor ever did more than Bok to tempt his readers visually. Where a modern editor might reproduce a photograph of a select dish in a size that dominates a cookery layout and use other, much smaller photographs as accessories, Bok would fill a page with ten photographs, all of equal size, with the recipe as the caption below each. His travel features were not full of exotic tales or personalised descriptions, though a few did follow that format. Most commonly, he used his central, double-page spread for an elaborately integrated layout that crammed 10 or 12 pictures into a symmetrical design that was usually bound together by the curlicues of a derivative of art nouveau.(Fig. 19) To inform the readers of the latest fashions he did not waste his pages on text and written descriptions, the breathy superlatives of the trade. Instead he filled his page with up to 25 different drawings of the clothes in question. When the season impelled the magazine to concentrate on such matters, they would be organised so that each page had a different headline and a slightly different purpose. The pace was never allowed to flag. In total in volume 17, 1665 reproductions other than illuminated titles and letters, were used in 375.5 pages; an unprecedented 4.43 reproductions per page and over five times the density of use of any of the editors of the other 'illustrated' magazines already mentioned. Of these vast numbers, over 40% were from photographs while less than 35% originated from artwork that was reproduced via halftone blocks. The other 25% were printed from line blocks. As will be seen from Chapter Five, this was not only a radical utilisation of the new techniques of his time, such a commitment would be considered unusual for decades to come in some quarters.

How could he afford to so profligate? Because, by 1899, the magazine's average circulation was audited at 819,410 per month.[104] To gain access to this audience, the advertisers, when they were paying the $250 per page already detailed for such as *Scribner's* or *Leslie's* or even $500 per page for *Munsey's*, were prepared to pay an unprecedented $4,000 a page to a company that rigorously excluded any discount; excepting one of 5% if the bill was settled by the twenty fifth day of the month following publication. Special positions, such as the back cover, cost even more.[105] With 174 pages of paid insertions in volume 17, that suggests an advertising revenue of approximately $700,000. When added to the company's income from subscriptions and its proportion of the price of nationally distributed counter sales, it was no wonder that Bok had the resources to follow the course he chose.

In fact, the success of the Curtis organisation was such that, in the cause of both stylistic homogeneity and its own paternalistic standards of morality, it could impose its edicts on those who paid for space. In 1892 John Adams Thayer had arrived in Philadelphia after answering an advertisement in the *Boston Herald*. It said, 'Wanted. A first-class man. To take charge of the advertising pages, make up and direct artistic business, and something of an expert at devising artistic display.'[106] His job was to coerce and cajole the advertisers into relinquishing the use of heavy type and blocks that created blotches of ink on the pages. With a buoyant circulation among a readership that advertisers dream of, the space buyers could not stand aloof for long and, despite the pugnacious stand that many companies took against such unprecedented interference in how they promoted their business, the Curtis organisation soon had its way and the companies were forced to redesign their advertisements on the lines dictated by the Curtis organisation. Nothing would be allowed to disrupt the *Journal's* appearance.[107]

Then, between 1893 and 1897, the contracts with patent-medicine vendors were allowed to lapse. The publisher wished to eliminate them completely. This was a courageous decision for at this time they still constituted an important sector of the business.[108] According to Thayer, the original suggestion to follow this course came from him.[109] In 1910, the company went one stage further and issued a small book, its advertising code, stating categorically that by that stage it would allow no advertisements for instalment buying, alcohol, patent-medicines or the use of immodest texts or illustrations. In addition, it placed special restrictions on financial services, tobacco products and playing card advertising.[110] All this can be attributed to the power of numbers.

Already, by the time of Bok's appointment, as mentioned before, the *Journal* was selling about 400,000 copies a month. In 1891 a fresh campaign drew 200,000 new subscribers in just three months. Whereupon, Curtis had to call a halt. The *Ladies' Home Journal* could not print any more than 600,000 copies a month on their existing machinery. So, for three or four years, they had to mark time while a new printing plant was built and equipped. Only in 1895 and 1896 was the circulation again encouraged to expand.[111] By the latter year, the average sales per month were audited at 709,166.[112]

Collier's or *Collier's Once A Week*, as it was known at first, crept on to the publishing scene in April 1888. It was distributed with each alternate copy of the twice weekly, *Collier's Library*, which published cheap versions of popular books and novels.[113] Hence, it is hardly surprising that it took the title it did or that it put considerable emphasis on reprinted fiction during part of its first few years. It also put more emphasis on humour than was common in general periodicals at the time, featuring a central double spread of cartoons each week.

The 1890s were not a kind time for the weekly. After Richard Nugent left the editorial seat in 1892, it began to change in a way that, in the middle years of the decade, seems to have lost it readers. While Mott credits it with a 'claimed circulation of a quarter-million' in 1892,[114] the cautious *American Newspaper Directory* would only admit to one in excess of 75,000 in 1890.[115] However, by 1897 a precise figure of 19,159, quoted by Caroline Seebohm, suggests that the weekly was in a very sorry state.[116] However, as the *American Newspaper Directory* gives an average circulation of 71,296 for 1897,[117] and Ayer gives a figure of 74,500 for 1898,[118] Ms Seebohm seems to have made a serious error. What is true is that after Robert Collier became involved in 1897 and persuaded Condé Nast to join him later that same year,[119] the weekly was transformed. Sales responded accordingly, and by 1900 an average paid circulation of 225,000 per week was offered to advertisers.[120]

What Robert Collier did after he became editor in 1898,[121] was to change what was now named *Collier's Weekly* from a publication that resembled the *Harper's Weekly* of the period, itself a derivative of the *Illustrated London News* in its editorial profile. In the new format he enlarged upon and developed the use that the rival *Leslie's Illustrated Newspaper* made of photographs, particularly in dense double-page spreads, to produce a magazine that was dominated by the camera. Unfortunately, early volumes of *Collier's* are very rare and even the set possessed by the Library of Congress is incomplete, despite being the most extensive still remaining. While text can be analysed on microfilm, the quality of this latter process is so inadequate in the rendition of illustrations that it is frequently impossible to differentiate drawings of a certain sort from photographs. Nevertheless, much of the latter half of volume 25 still remains in hard copy. Thus, in the 13 issues from July 7 to September 29, 1900, which featured approximately 250 editorial pages, there were at least 697 reproductions, 680 of which were halftones, of which 575, or 82%, were photographs. This gives a density of 2.8 illustrations per page, which is not quite as many as the *Ladies' Home Journal* but far more than any of the other illustrated magazines. However, it has to be borne in mind that these figures are derived from a short run.

Yet, while Robert Collier and Edward Bok were together on the cutting edge when it came to modern magazine design, they were poles apart when it came to subject matter, overall tone and pace. Indeed, the only similarity between the two publications is in their use of fiction, which came to just over 13% in each case, a very low figure for the period. Whereas Bok, in 1900, bounced the *Journal* from page to page, usually with a different headline on each, *Collier's Weekly* featured page after page, week after week of photographs from the current wars in China, South Africa and the after-effects of the US skirmish in the Philippines. Whereas Bok speckled every issue with the broadest range of topics, Collier placed enormous weight on just two, contemporary events and public affairs. Where the *Journal* focused predominantly on American material, regarding Paris as the most exotic of subjects that it could contemplate, *Collier's* looked abroad for much of its material, perhaps the majority at this stage. Where Bok ignored sport completely, Collier gave this rising topic over 10% of editorial space and was the first successful, mixed function magazine in America to promote it in such a way(see Appendices VI & X). Whereas Bok was very positive about the world at large, stressing what could be achieved, an examination of a volume of *Collier's* can be a dampening or even depressing experience although, clearly, contemporary observers, the readership, must have seen it quite differently. If they had not they would not have been attracted to it in such numbers for its circulation increased by over 400% in the five years from 1897 to 1902.[122] Even by 1900 this increased popularity had attracted 172.21 pages of paid insertions. So, Condé Nast, who became advertising manager officially that year, was certainly giving the *Weekly* good service.[123]

THUS, IN THE FINAL DECADES OF THE NINETEENTH CENTURY, American magazines were transformed by advertising revenue and printing technology. The former had paid for the better paper which allowed the latter its head. The salesman's dollar allowed editors like Edward Bok and Robert Collier to stuff the pages of their magazines full to overflowing with illustrations, many photographic, of their chosen subjects. Layouts were becoming more elaborate as photo-mechanical reproduction allowed the staff to manipulate the sizes of illustrations at will. The increased revenue from advertising also allowed the editors to sell their magazines to the readership at less than cost. In turn, as the national magazines fell into line at 10¢ an issue, a whole segment of the American public was induced, through a variety of promotional techniques, to acquire a reading habit that broadened its perspectives.

Now, the question was what would the editors do with the national audience they had generated which would continue to expand during the years to come? So far, the income had been used to extend the audience without changing the contents. The ten cent monthlies only differed from their more expensive predecessors in price and it was the drop in the latter that had made all the difference to their circulations. Whether editors would demonstrate a more radical approach in the new century is a question for Chapter Five.

NOTES

1. Wood, James Playstead, *Magazines in the United States*, New York, 1971, p206.

2. *Frank Leslie's Popular Monthly*, New York, Vol.1, No.1, pp1-8.

3. Mott, Frank L., *A History of American Magazines*, Boston, 1938-68, Vol.2, p391.

4. Ibid., p31.

5. Ibid., p30.

6. Rowell, George P., *American Newspaper Directory*, New York, 1890, pp306, 484-497,607.

7. Mott, op.cit., vol.4, p365.

8. Ibid., vol.4, p22.

9. Sayward, Dorothy, *A Study of Comfort Magazine*, Orono, Maine, (University of Maine Studies, Second Series No.75), 1960, p15.

10. Ibid., p16.

11. Another entirely practical reason for excluding *Comfort* from further consideration is that it has been impossible to examine any copies and no microfilm exists. Sayward reports a set in good condition existed at Maine State Library in Augusta in 1960, but it has proved impossible to verify this information and no other copies appear to remain in public hands.

12. John, Arthur, *The Best Years of the Century*, Urbana, Ill. & London, 1981, pp7-21.

13. Ibid, pp43-44.

14. Ibid, pp13-16.

15. John, op.cit., pp43-45.

16. Mott, Vol.3, op.cit, p511.

17. Clair, Colin, *A Chronology of Printing*, London, 1969., p150.

18. Mott, Vol.2, op.cit., p268.

19. *Youth's Companion*, Vol.53, No.44, pp357-386.

20. Mott, op.cit., Vol.4, pp537-539.

21. Ibid, p16.

22. Ibid, Vol.3, p483.

23. Munsey, Frank A., *The Founding of the Munsey Publishing-house*, New York, 1907, pp25-30.

24. John, op.cit., p12.

25. Ibid, pp103-108.

26. Ibid, p99.

27. *Harper's Monthly*, New York, Vol.63, June 1881, p12 of the advertising section.

28. Sherman, Sidney A., *Advertising in the United States*, Publications of the American Statistical Association, Volume 7, December 1900, quoted by John, op.cit., p134.

29. John, op.cit., p137.

30. Ibid., p112.

31. Ibid., p5.

32. Ibid., pp114-120.

33. Ibid., p122.

34. Ibid., p132.

35. Ibid., p44.

36. Ibid.

37. Ibid., p3.

38. Mott, vol.2, op.cit., p383.

39. Anon., The Outlook for Wood-Engraving, *Century Illustrated Monthly Magazine*, New York, Vol.40, No.2, June 1890, p312.

40. John, op.cit., p182.

41. Mott, Vol.3, op.cit., p511.

42. Rowell, op.cit., 1890, p493.

43. Ibid., p497.

44. Anon. (but probably by John Brisben Walker, the editor), The Making of An Illustrated Magazine, *The Cosmopolitan*, New York, January 1893, Vol.14, p261. 'A gentleman familiar with the establishment of one of the four successful illustrated magazines stated in the writer's hearing recently that full half a million dollars had been made available at the start of the enterprise and the last dollar had been called for just as success came.' Mott, vol.4, op.cit., assigns this investment to Scribner's and the latter part of the *Cosmopolitan* feature appears to sustain that conclusion.

45. Measurement supplied by the librarian of the New York Historical Society, which possesses one copy for April 9, 1881. No other copy appears to exist in any public collection situated on the east coast of the United States, according to a Library of Congress computer search.

46. Damon-Moore, Helen, *Magazines for the Millions*, Albany, New York, 1994. pp30-31.

47. Ibid., pp38-58. Although the author makes out a plausible case for her view that the *Journal* under Louisa Knapp had a particular position on the situation of women in the 1880s, the argument lacks the clarity that quotations from a range of articles would have provided, especially if she had taken the opportunity to contrast the *Journal*'s approach to that of its peers.

48. Wood, James Playstead, *The Curtis Magazines*, New York, 1971, p10.

49. Ibid., pp10-13.

50. *Ladies' Home Journal*, Vol.5, No.12, 1 November 1888, p10.

51. Wood, 1971 op.cit., p13.

52. Steinberg, Salme, *Reformer in the Marketplace*, Baton Rouge and London, 1979, pp2-6.

53. *Ladies' Home Journal*, Vol.5, No.4, 1 March 1888, p8.

54. Wood, 1971, op.cit., p14.

55. Bok, Edward, *The Americanization of Edward Bok*, New York, 1920, p159.

56. Mott, op.cit, Vol.3, p521.

57. Mott, Vol.3, op.cit., pp552-553.

58. Rowell, 1890, op.cit., pp484-486.

59. N.W. Ayer and Sons, *American Newspaper Annual*, Philadelphia, 1890, pp508 & 512. The *Puck* figure is based on a sworn statement.

60. Flautz, John, *Life, the Gentle Satirist*, Bowling Green, Ohio, 1972, p2.

61. Ibid., p10.

62. Mott, Vol.2, op.cit., p268.

63. Mott, vol.4, op.cit., pp480-482.

64. *Dictionary of American Biography*, Vol.10, New York, 1936, pp347-348.

65. Rowell, 1890, op.cit., p492.

66. *The Cosmopolitan*, Vol.9, New York, May 1890, advertising supplement, p6.

67. Ibid.

68. Ibid., October 1890, advertising supplement, p26.

69. Ibid, June 1890, advertising supplement, p7.

70. Ibid., September 1890, advertising supplement, p7.

71. Mott, vol.4, op.cit., p484.

72. Ibid., p482.

73. Walker, John Brisben, In Memoriam. Edward Dwight Walker, *The Cosmopolitan*, New York, Vol.9, No.4, August 1890, p383.

74. Mott, op.cit., Vol.4, p5.

75. Ibid, p5.

76. Ibid, p18.

77. Munsey, 1907, op.cit., p45.

78. Britt, George, *Forty Years - Forty Millions*, New York, 1935, pp83-85.

79. Mott, op.cit., Vol.4, p4.

80. Peterson, Theodore, *Magazines in the Twentieth Century*, Urbana, Ill., 2nd ed., 1964, p7.

81. Mott. Vol.4, op.cit., pp608-611.

82. *Munsey's Magazine*, Vol.30, October 1903, pp151-152.

83. Rowell, 1900, op.cit., p688, gives a circulation of 300,727 for 1898. The editorial policy of this source was very stringent about precise figures and if such a report was made it follows that their editorial staff had been able to verify the data or had been given access to audited accounts.

84. *Nelson Chesman and Company's Newspaper Rate Book*, St.Louis, p123.

85. Bok, op.cit., pp78-79.

86. Mott, Vol.3, op.cit., pp511-512.

87. Chesman, op.cit., p139.

88. Rowell, 1903, op.cit., p690.

89. Mott, Vol.4, op.cit., pp417-420.

90. Ibid., p608.

91. Mott. Vol.4, op.cit., pp608-611.

92. Rowell, 1903, op.cit., pp695-696.

93. Mott, Vol.4, op.cit., p608.

94. Chesman, op.cit., p142.

95. Munsey, 1907, op.cit., p45.

96. Peterson, op.cit., p15.

97. In the volume examined, two pages of advertising were missing, according to the pagination. As this was from the front of one issue, the contents are entirely predictable and one page could be added to both paid insertions and self advertisements to give a complete figure, if so desired.

98. Chesman, op.cit., p141.

99. Wilson, Harold S., *McClure's Magazine and the Muckrakers*, Princeton, N.J., 1970, p101.

100. Ibid.

101. An Entire House on a Single Floor, *Ladies' Home Journal*, Vol.17, No.9, August 1900, Philadelphia, p21.

102. Price, Bruce, A Georgian House for Seven Thousand Dollars, *Ladies' Home Journal*, Vol.17, No.11, October 1900, Philadelphia, p15.

103. Damon-Moore, op.cit. pp98-99, 106-107.

104. Rowell, 1900, op.cit., p933.

105. Steinberg, op.cit., p25.

106. Thayer, John Adams, *Out of the Rut*, 1912, New York, p74.

107. Ibid., pp81-87.

108. Steinberg, op.cit., pp20-21. Also Reed, David, Growing Up, *Journal of Advertising History*, Vol.10, No.1, pp28-32.

109. Thayer, op.cit., pp87-89.

110. Steinberg, op.cit., p24. A copy of this publication can be found in the Parlin Papers in the collection of the University of Pennsylvania, Philadelphia.

111. Ibid. pp11-12.

112. Rowell, 1900, op.cit., p933.

113. Mott, vol.4, op.cit., p453.

114. Mott, Vol.4, op.cit., pp453-454.

115. Rowell, 1890, op.cit., p485.

116. Seebohm, Caroline, *The Man Who Was Vogue*, New York, 1892, p30.

117. Rowell, 1903, op.cit., p673.

118. Ayer, 1898, op.cit., p565.

119. Seebohm, op.cit., p29.

120. Rowell, 1900, op.cit., p708.

121. Mott, Vol.4, op.cit., p453.

122. Rowell, 1903, op.cit., pp672-673.

123. Seebohm, op.cit., p29.

The British Scene 1880–1900

I am rapidly coming to the conclusion that among our readers we number two or three hundred idiots.

Alfred Harmsworth, Editorial Chat,
Answers, Vol.4, No.9, 25 January 1890, p47.

THE BRITISH MAGAZINE underwent its own transformation at the end of the nineteen century. Here, as we shall see, an audience of some substance had already become established. But the realignment and expansion of this body of consumers, which began tentatively in the 1880s and took off in the following decade, became quite marked as a new range of periodicals was placed before it with considerable vigour. In part, the new weeklies and monthlies were financed from the growing weight of advertising that was lining the pockets of the British publishers, echoing developments in the United States. Growth in profits was also aided by technological developments, particularly in the provision of cheap paper in the case of the penny, mass-circulation weeklies, and the use of photo-mechanical reproduction in the sixpenny monthlies.

However, although the British magazine market began to develop in the 1880s and editorial innovations were increasingly visible in the subsequent decade, the penny weekly still ruled the roost. In the popularity stakes there was no rival. Whether the participants in the weekly scrimmage for customers were old-style entertainments based on serialised fiction, or the new style jigsaw format, pieced together from fragments of the foolish, the peculiar and the prodigal, the cover price among the most popular weeklies was the same: a stable situation which had existed for decades and was set to continue.

But within this growing market, establishing the scale of the success of individual titles is close to impossible in absolute terms; that is, in obtaining a reliable series of circulation figures. As has been discussed already, although directories of British serial publications did become established by the end of the nineteenth century, they did not embody the attitudes of their American peers, forming a pressure point pushing for the disclosure of information like George Rowell's *American Newspaper Directory*. They conformed to the strand of obsequiousness that runs through the history of many British institutions[1] and accepted what crumbs of information were allowed to fall from the publishers' tables.

When figures were published among their pages they were isolated numbers which were very rarely authenticated by auditors and never part of a regularly published accounting procedure. And even when a third party had verified the figures, that particular figure was frequently reiterated year after year in the pages of the directory, as we have seen. George Newnes tentatively published a few figures, while Alfred Harmsworth printed them on the front page of *Answers* every week while its sales raced ahead. But once he was established he reverted to silence.

Yet despite this statistical desert, some circulation figures do surface from time to time and enough are available to establish a group of best sellers. After all, it is not the function of this

Fig.20 Even though Britain already possessed better transport links than most countries by 1842, the creation of a railway network cut costs and journey times so dramatically that the wholesale distribution of magazines and newspapers was transformed. Soon, a range of weeklies, printed and published in London but sold throughout the country was available.

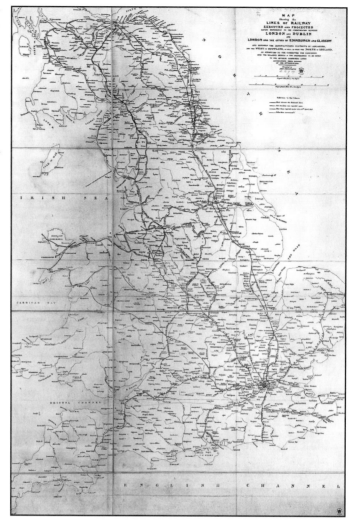

study to dwell on circulation for its own sake. The intention is to peg out a field of study by using sales to limit the publications under discussion in a way that is independent of the tastes of the investigator. It is not pertinent whether *Tit-bits* sold 300,000 or 400,000 copies a week at the end of the 1880s; merely that it sold more than any rival and that no one contested its pre-eminence either at the time or later.

Similarly, whether *The Princess's Novelettes* were selling more than *Comic Cuts* is not the point. The real issue is whether they were selling enough copies a week for them to be considered among the half dozen best sellers of the time. All of the publications examined in the following section seem to have passed the 150,000 a week mark during the decade ending 31 December 1890. Each of them, with one exception, either published a credible sales figure at the time or mentioned one in private correspondence which has subsequently been examined. The exception is *The Family Herald*. But that weekly has been endorsed by Altick as having a circulation of around 200,000 for decades and is worth discussing for its roots in the first generation of best-selling British magazines.[2]

Indeed *The Family Herald*, which had first appeared in May 1843, under the ownership of one George Biggs,[3] had stood the test of time among the best sellers. Jay has suggested that both it and the *London Journal*, which was launched in 1845, may well have taken their cue from an obscure weekly, *The Penny Story-Teller*, which began publication in August 1832.[4] Running until 1840, it seems to have enjoyed only a moderate success and no complete set appears to survive. Nevertheless, examination of what does remain neither sustains nor undermines the Jay hypothesis. There is no obvious stylistic element that emerges as a link except the devotion to fiction, but the proposition may well be true.

The years of this possible precursor's publication, the 1830s, had seen a sharp rise in serials aimed at the working class. In some measure, this can be attributed to the promotions of the Society for the Diffusion of Useful Knowledge and their success with *The Penny Magazine*. Published every Saturday, its average print order was 213,241 copies during the first nine months of its existence and very firm evidence suggests that 98% of this total were sold, giving an average weekly circulation during 1832 of about 209,000.[5] It achieved these sales, in the main, through the regular retail outlets of the already-extant book trade.[6] In this, it helped to establish a dominant pattern, that of distribution through retail outlets and vendors rather than subscription, that has lasted until the present day in Britain.

Then there was the effect, as Hollis, Berridge and others have pointed out, of the agitation for an unstamped press during the 1830s, which developed a taste for a regular read, particularly in the provinces among previously uncultivated markets.[7] The publication of novels in weekly parts costing a penny also expanded enormously in the late 1830s, as publishers, particularly Edward Lloyd, exploited the success of Dickens' *Pickwick Papers*, which was issued in that form. Working at first through plagiarism and then more original fiction, they enlarged the economic base of the publishing industry.[8] By 1840, two surveys conducted during that year revealed that, within the confines of London, 80 cheap periodicals were circulating, two thirds of which cost a penny and none of which cost more than two pence.[9] Thus, when the railway building programme of the late 1830s and early 1840s established a distribution network,(Fig. 20) that cut travelling times for freight from days to hours and costs by 80% on the trunk routes, a pre-existing demand had been established.[10] The publishers of serials of the 1840s were able to satisfy these needs without requiring the persistence of W. H. Smith Senior, for instance, who had to go to extraordinary lengths in order to promote his wholesale distribution business as late as the 1820s.[11]

The new magazines of the 1840s also came closer to the size of their readers' pockets, for no weekly newspaper during the period was able to charge less than three pence a copy for any length of time because stamp duty had to be paid on each copy. Thus, the publication which became known as *Lloyd's Weekly Newspaper* failed to match the success of *The London Journal* until after the repeal of the duty in 1855, when its price could be reduced.[12]

However, the fact that a large audience were able to afford even the pittance due for the *Journal* was helped by the increased value of their surplus disposable income that developed as a result of falling retail prices between 1842 and 1850: the first time a moment of circulation increase is linked to a rise in real income. This built on a substantial rise in real national income sustained during the first three decades of the century which eased the conditions of life for working class folk.[13]

Then there is the matter of the sustained repression of working class activities that might encourage spontaneous aggregation, such as sport, which has been itemised by Malcolmson. This developed from the middle of the eighteenth century onward, both at local and national level, because such activities might interfere with the regularity of the factory schedule.[14] The difficulty that employers had imposing the latter is further catalogued with some vivacity by Pollard.[15] Not surprisingly, any novelty that eased the workers into the industrial rhythm, such as the new magazines, met no opposition. That is, these new fictional weeklies gelled perfectly with production schedules and held the attention of the readers without encouraging the critical faculties at all. It is very noticeable that their reception by those in a position to instigate prosecutions contrasts vividly with the treatment meted out to the radical press during the previous two decades in which literally hundreds were prosecuted or imprisoned for producing or selling what was identified by those in power as a threat.[16]

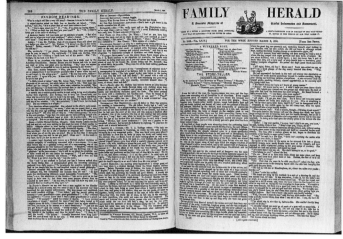

Fig.21 Despite its dreary, utterly predictable appearance, The Family Herald, which was launched in May 1843, was one of the first penny weeklies to gain national acceptance. It sold by the tens of thousands for decades.

Subsequently, once the stamp duty on newspapers was repealed, and prices reflected the economic costs of production, rather than the levels of taxation, newspaper sales rose steadily, particularly after the paper tax was also removed in 1861, when both *Reynold's Newspaper* and *Lloyd's Weekly Newspaper*, for example, could be sold for a penny.[17] Abolition also promoted the cause of the provincial press. Before the change, in 1854, Berridge counted 176 provincial dailies and weeklies in *Mitchell's Newspaper Directory*. By the end of the following decade a similar count totalled over 800. And in Manchester, by 1876, the local newspapers were selling over 120,000 copies a day where, in 1855, they had sold none.[18] As a result, despite the limited information that is available on this point, it would appear that the circulations of the largest selling magazines seem to have stalled or, in the case of the *London Journal*, begun a downward slide from this point in the 1850s. In other words, if this is true, there was an expanding but still limited market for cheap serials in Britain in the second half of the nineteenth century which was much more successfully exploited by the daily and weekly newspapers than the magazines once prices were equal. It was a dominance they have not lost to this day, unlike their trans-Atlantic counterparts.

The essential characteristic of *The Family Herald*, one of the most popular weeklies in Britain from the time of the emergence of a national distribution network in the 1840s until the rise of the new weeklies of the 1880s, was its stability. Indeed, it demonstrates this quality in an extreme form, for the layout of every issue for decades was totally predictable. Every issue was composed of 16 pages divided into two columns. By the end of the 1880s, the pages were a few millimetres larger than they had been 30 years before, at 281 x 207 mm, but the increase was only fractional. Page one always began with a short poem set in tiny six–point type. Fiction took up the rest of the page, set in eight–point, always under the heading, 'The Story Teller'.(Fig. 21) The only graphic intrusion into the columns of text which filled the following ten pages of fiction was a double line 28mm long which announced the end of one piece of fiction and preceded the next title set in 11–point capitals. No authors were credited. Sometimes very short poems were interpolated into the text as space fillers. The twelfth page was always filled with answers to correspondents set in barely readable five–point. Page 13 always deployed a 'serious topic': a sermon on a social subject. It ran on to page 14 and was followed by 'Family Matters', 'Scientific and Useful Statistics', 'Varieties' and 'The Riddler', which contained a number of puzzles, both verbal and numerical. The last page was always headed 'Random Readings'. It consisted of an undifferentiated mass of paragraphs, retailing the type of morsel that came to fill *Tit-bits* and *Answers*.

Redistributed among our familiar categories, this extraordinarily stable mixture, which survived in name at least until 1940, shows the overwhelming preponderance of fiction, using

69% of the editorial page space during period January to June 1890. Only the discussion of contemporary society, which took just over 10% and humour and entertainment at just less than 8%, used significant amounts of space outside the pages of fiction(see Appendix XIX). The only illustrations that ever invaded its pages were the occasional diagrams in 'The Riddler' and the chess problems that were a feature around 1860.

One of the characteristics common to this and a number of other magazines of the 1880s was the monthly wrapper. Each month, the publisher would gather the recent weekly editions and issue them with a coloured wrapper in an omnibus form. These wrappers carried advertising. Some publishers added an extra story or supplement. Such additions were not incorporated in *Family Herald* but they were used in *The Princess's Novelettes*, a weekly which, as far as one can judge, seems to have been the last success of Edwin Brett.

His contact with the publishing world began when he worked as an engraver on *The Pictorial Times*. He continued in that profession as one of a partnership until 1860. In that year he became the manager of The Newsagent's Company, which published a series of novels that were issued as weekly penny serials which caused a considerable volume of unfavourable comment in the monthlies and quarterlies sold to the middle classes. These serials were so extreme that when the company attempted to reissue *The Wild Boys of London* in 1871, their premises were raided by the police and publication was suppressed.[19] These were only the latest in a string of titles issued by various publishers that were known from their interest in violence as 'penny bloods'.[20]

Brett, meanwhile, moved on to produce the rumbustious rather than prurient *Boys of England*, the most successful publication for the youth market during the 1860s and 1870s. It is at this point that an entirely new phenomenon is met, one that has been entirely absent from the history of American popular serials. For the next 100 years in Britain, there was hardly a time when what came to be known by its consumers as a comic, that is an inexpensive weekly serial intended for the relatively young that might or might not be intended to be funny, did not figure at least on the periphery of the list of the best-selling serials.

Over the next 30 years, Brett produced a string of titles which were more or less successful, that stood as stable-mates to *Boys of England*. Most of these were, ostensibly, intended for youths and young men. However, in 1870, he initiated publication of *Wedding Bells*. Rather broadly subtitled, 'A Journal for the Single and Married of the United Kingdom', this penny amalgam of fiction and fashion, mainly the former, was presumably aimed at young women in the pre-maternal state. Even the stories concerned the trials and tribulations of getting a couple to the altar, that being seen as the only fate worthy of discussion. The pages were also speckled with coy verse. Fashion news was featured occasionally and paper patterns for tatting and items of clothing were used as free gifts, for Brett had used free inducements to bolster the sales of *Boys of England*. The circulation of *Wedding Bells* is completely unknown but it was published until 1879, which indicates it enjoyed moderate success.

In 1886, Brett launched *The Princess's Novelettes*. These were sold weekly for one penny or in a monthly omnibus form for four pence, whether they contained 4 or 5 issues, in a dull olive wrapper that carried advertising. Beecham's Pills and Pear's Soap took the back cover on a regular basis. A complete story was featured in each single issue. As in *Wedding Bells*, the characters were usually overcoming obstacles and adventures on the way to the altar. Their circumstances invariably left them in a position to pursue this goal without recourse to the vulgar necessities of trade. The men were frequently 'singularly handsome', while their companions sported rosebud complexions. Yet, despite this lust for respectability, the old Brett was not entirely obscured. 'Barbara's Peril', 'The Cost of Her Secret' and 'Mrs Delamotte's Lover' were all published in volume 8, which ran from September 1889 to February 1890. Needless to say, the most salacious aspect were their titles, though it would be unfair to suggest that passion was entirely unknown to the characters, even if it was fenced in. Evidently, the formula was unexceptional for the period. Yet, it did achieve exceptional sales, an average edition of 153,061 being certified by the printer.[21]

The publications which supplanted those of Brett and his rivals, the Emmett Brothers,[22] and, perhaps, exceeded them in sales, came from an unlikely source. During the 1860s and 1870s, while Brett's influence was at its height but while the older 'bloods' were still being reissued, those who saw themselves as the guardians of the nation's morals were working themselves up into a lather over what they saw as an unwholesome and corrupting influence on the minds of the young.[23] However, this is an old tune and a popular one even down unto the present. Whether it is provoked by a distaste for violence or the sight of the less respectable indulging their own inclinations without reference to their social superiors is a matter that requires further consideration. However, the pleasures of contemplating suppression are rarely foregone for the much more difficult and demanding task of creating an alternative that will oust the offenders. Yet, that was the nettle which the Religious Tract Society grasped in

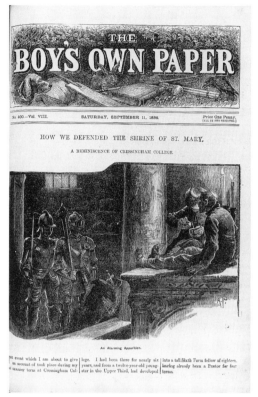

Fig.22 The launch of Boy's Own Paper was a successful attack on the less estimable working-class values by the righteous middle classes. It attempted to divert anti-authoritarian impulses into an imperial channel, to endorse the values of their 'betters' and to decry 'nervousness', that is, an interest in masturbation.

1879 when it first published the *Boy's Own Paper* (*BOP*) as a penny weekly.

Indeed, given the birth pangs evident in the Society's various committees in the year preceding the weekly's appearance, it is a wonder that it was ever published. The fact that it finally did appear is a monument to the persuasive skills of Dr. James Macaulay, who was named as its first editor. He had already successfully produced *Leisure Hour* and *Sunday At Home* for the Society, and his standing must have done much to allay the anxieties of the more inflexible members. However, the real editorial work creating the new publication, was in the hands of George Hutchinson, who had been appointed to do so but had been unable to persuade the committee to follow a realistic choice of stories and articles. Until Macaulay moved them, those who insisted on stories that were merely capsules for moral messages retained the upper hand. Ironically, the format that was finally approved had already been rejected when presented by Hutchinson.[24]

Fiction was the dominant element in *BOP*. During the 1880s, its contributors helped turn the youthful desire for adventure away from heroes who operated outside the law or on its margins, as in the 'bloods', and channelled it towards the outposts of empire, the possibilities of technology and, above all, the playing fields of minor public schools.(Fig. 22) Conan Doyle and Jules Verne began to appear. The former had been unknown hitherto, but the latter was already famous.[25] Yet, although fiction absorbed over 52% of the page space during the first six months of 1890, a broad range of other material appeared as well.

As one would expect, sport, that well known diversion from 'bad habits' or what was frequently described as 'nervousness', was given some prominence, taking over 5.5% of page space in this period, with such articles as 'The American Game of Football' by S. Fyfe,[26] or 'Cricket Hints' by Somerville Gibney.[27] Also to be expected was a similar editorial commitment to such topics as science and technology or history and biography. Humour and entertainment also exceeded 6.5% (see Appendix XVIII). Much less expected is the interest in fine art, with many engraved reproductions, and an article on Alma Tadema that included an inset chromolithographed reproduction.[28] Or, the monthly listing of domestic tasks that should be attended to, such as the needs of the garden and the poultry run. The tone of the answers to correspondents was also a little unexpected, for among the anodyne were some very tetchy replies, full of contempt for the poor suppliant for information.

That this balance was attractive to the public is beyond doubt because, for once, an impeccable source of information on the circulation is available in Britain during the late nineteenth century, even if it is very patchy. The minutes of the Religious Tract Society still exist and, occasionally, figures are given. However, the previous publication of some of this information, by Patrick Dunae, seems to contain a disastrous miscalculation of sales which, although among the highest, were not as vast as he has stated.[29] Nevertheless, a print run of an average of 153,000 per week in 1888 was impressive and, as profits from the weekly increased in 1890, the run may well have been significantly higher in that year.[30] However, it should be remembered that these are not net sales and such a figure would, almost certainly, have been several thousand copies lower at least.

The success of the Society's first significant excursion into the youth market was soon followed by a second. The *Girl's Own Paper* (GOP) first appeared exactly a year later, in January 1880. Charles Peters was named editor immediately and it is a mark of the friction that had been generated by the battles over content before *BOP* was launched, that the committee refused to award Hutchinson a similar title until Dr Macaulay retired in 1897.[31]

The contents of *GOP* exhibited a greater interest in non-fiction than the pages of Hutchinson's weekly, although serials and stories still absorbed 41% of the pages during the first six months of 1890. History and biography, at 12%, was a much more important topic than in its male counterpart. Not surprisingly, given the stereotypes of the time, verse and music were each allocated more than 20 pages out of the 415.2 used by the editor. The only other subject to take more than 5% of the space was fashion, although substantial amounts were devoted to social life and manners, decorative art, domestic matters and the answers to correspondents page (see Appendix XVIII). It is noticeable that Peters was less scornful, more mellow than Hutchinson in his replies. There is also greater flexibility in the way that articles and stories are distributed through each issue and they are much less predictable in their situation and relationship than those in *BOP*.

The consequence was that through the last two decades of the century, *Girl's Own Paper* was the more successful of the Society's two leading titles, consistently turning in larger profits, though only in 1888 is a specific figure given, a total printing of 9,853,000 for the previous year, which suggests an average of 189,481 per week.[32]

Despite the success of the Religious Tract Society, the sensation of the 1880s was, undoubtedly, George Newnes, the originator, owner and first editor of *Tit-bits*. It appeared in Manchester in late October, 1881.[33] In the very first paragraph, Newnes was quite brazen about his editorial intentions: 'It will be a production of all that is most interesting in the books, periodicals, and newspapers of this and other countries.'[34] That makes it sound like a digest but, in fact, one essential characteristic of a digest is that it acknowledges its sources. Its eclecticism is a prime virtue. Newnes was following in a much older tradition: that of the professional thief. He and his staff were paste and scissor plagiarists, an approach that has a considerable pedigree.[35] This cheap procedure was joined with that other vital characteristic of his new weekly which cut costs to the bone: its lack of illustrations, which not only avoided employing illustrators and engravers but also allowed Newnes to print on cheap newsprint. These options were a prescription for a highly profitable publication, if only he could persuade the public to purchase such a novelty in the large numbers that would turn it into a high volume operation. How could he attract enough of the curious to buy, over a long enough period, copies sufficient to induce a new habit?

The answer was intensive promotion, some of which is chronicled by his biographer.[36] Gradually, he spread out from his northern base. Two years after the launch, the circulation reached a plateau of 200,000 per week, at which it stuck. Most owners of the time would have been more than pleased with that but it is clear that, whatever the tone of his anodyne biography, Newnes must have been a singularly ambitious man. To regain the waning momentum of his circulation drive he offered a seven-room house as the prize in a competition. This was followed, some time afterwards, by £1,000 for the best serial submitted. The climax was reached with a series of treasure hunts. Caches of 500 gold sovereigns were hidden around Britain and clues to their whereabouts concealed in short stories published each week. The other major encouragement involved offering free insurance to readers.[37] In this manner, the breakthrough was made and stabilised. By the decade's end, a guaranteed circulation of 350,000 was being offered to advertisers, which gives it a substantial claim to be considered the most successful magazine of the time in Britain.[38]

Initially, Newnes resisted the opportunity to sell space in his weekly, but he was persuaded by the advertising agency T. B. Browne, which assumed control of the green wrapper and sold all four pages on behalf of the publisher. The effect on Newnes' personal fortune was spectacular and it would appear that, by the end of the 1880s, he had an income little short of £30,000 per annum at a time when only 987 people in the country had business incomes of £10,000 of more.[39] Seen another way, in terms of the amount of page space given over to selling the products of others, by the end of the decade, just short of 29% was used for this purpose. This proportion is substantially more than the *Illustrated London News* was selling in 1886, as can be seen by reference to Chapter 1. Clearly, *Tit-bits* was a commercial success and it would appear that Newnes got great satisfaction from his rewards.

Indeed, one wonders how much direct editorial effort the owner bothered to put into his publication after the first years. Even his inadequate biographer does not disguise Newnes's aversion to the daily routine his employees had to endure.[40] Furthermore, while there are certainly developments in the editorial profile that may be attributable to Newnes's evolving skills, they may also have been occasioned by a shift in the day-to-day responsibility for the pages of the magazine.

One change that did occur over the decade was the increased size of each item on the editorial pages. When Newnes began, no item, however long, exceeded one paragraph on any of the 16 303 x 235 mm pages, unless the grammatical rules of transcribing conversation interceded. On average there were 7.5 different items per page.[41] By the end of the decade there were 4.83 items per page and the contents included fiction. Yet, when that is said, one is still only emphasizing a relative shift. The initial idea still stood. Newnes set out to expand an element previously used by editors as a contrast, a diversion from the weight of fiction. By presenting information as discontiguous corpuscular fragments, its ironic contradictions, its diversionary qualities were emphasized. By eliminating the context, connections were ignored and undermined. 'Facts' were seen as random events, and such a presentation of data merges well with the way that those without the advantages of a sustained education converse and discuss. Whether by design or chance, Newnes found a formula that reflected the informality and discontinuity, the peripatetic interest span of the everyday conversation of his readers.

Yet, although he atomised his non-fiction, much of it is still amenable to categorisation in the manner already practised in Chapter 3. When considered in this way, some rather unexpected conclusions are unavoidable. The emphasis on information about the workings of contemporary society exceeds that of most American best-selling magazines of the time. A total of over 27 pages during the first six months of 1890, over 6% of the total, were allocated to public affairs. In part, this volume of material was a consequence of the weekly commitment to the publication of a page of legal information which were answers to specific enquiries. Business topics took over 7% of the editorial space. Over 13 pages in total, or just over 3% of the page space, were used to discuss health matters, again, an interest that was rare in the United States until the middle of the next century. However, to reiterate the matter once again; these totals were largely the result of adding up fragments. No attempt was made to relate these specks to one another or to broader issues: there was no context. The intention was to divert. Thus, it is hardly surprising that the largest allocation of space was to the humorous and the amusing which, in the period in question, took nearly 29% of the total over the six months (see Appendix XXI).

Yet none of these jokes were accompanied by cartoons. Indeed, the only graphic intrusion to appear regularly in the weekly was the mast-head. The remaining space was entirely given over to text set in an eight–point serif face laid out at three columns to the page. All headings were confined within columns and most were limited in size to ten–point italicised capitals. Regular features such as the 'Tit-bits Inquiry Column', 'Continental Tit-bits' and 'Answers to Correspondents' were set in sizes up to 24 point, but they still remained within the confines of the columns, each of which was divided from its neighbour by a ¼–point rule. Such a bland form of presentation, which was entirely compatible with the layout of many of *Tit-bits*'s forebears in the penny weekly market, put the emphasis entirely on the content. Other than the headings already mentioned, no attempt was made to entice the readers or direct them to one aspect rather than another. This is evident when one issue is examined, such as that of 8 March 1890.

Fig.23 The Tit-bits formula of turning information into entertainment attracted many immitators, but only two were successful: Harmsworth and Pearson. During the 1890s, even the Newnes title turned to fiction as the mainstay of the editorial pages, which was far easier to sustain on a weekly schedule.

The 24–point heading at the top of the left-hand column of the front page, 'Tit-bits General Election', is followed by an invitation to the readers to participate in a referendum being conducted by the magazine on the government of the day. The remaining two columns are filled with jokes separated by about seven or eight millimetres of space and a line of four dots.(Fig. 23) The following spread is divided into five sections by ten–point headings, while jokes fill the odd spaces, again separated by dots and white space. The fourth page is occupied by contributions drawn from European publications under the 'Continental Tit-bits' heading. Opposite is an episode of a serial. Not only does it lack any illustrations to draw the casual reader into its narrative, there is not even a brief synopsis of the story so far. The sixth page is devoted to one advertisement which is dominated by a drawing of a monkey painting a canvas. The page opposite features the final paragraphs of the current episode of the serial, a section about the trials and tribulations of the theatre, a short tale about a foolish incident in the American West, and more one-paragraph jokes. A similar pattern continues to the end of the issue with only the headings showing any variation.

Where Newnes led, others followed. Even in issue two he had the nerve, given the way that he produced *Tit-bits*, to complain of plagiarists. After six months there were 12 imitators, another half year later there were 22.[42] But it was another matter for these imitators to survive and only Harmsworth's *Answers to Correspondents* and *Pearson's Weekly* did so. Not surprisingly, both men were closely associated with their mentor, for there was more to their success than mere editorial mimicry. But, only the future owner of *The Times* and originator of the *Daily Mail* had established himself as Newnes's rival before the end of the 1880s.

As already implied, it was Harmsworth's appreciation of the Newnes method that led to the success of his own *Answers to Correspondents*, the title of which was soon shortened to *Answers*. From his mentor he learned that competitions were the key to healthy circulation growth in the British market. However, despite an ingenious diet of teasers and special offers, he could only report a circulation of 48,000 and a gross profit of £1097 3s 1d after 12 months, in June 1889.[43] It was when a competition offering £1 a week for life to the person able to guess the quantity of gold and silver coin in the Bank of England on a particular day was run that the size of the readership began to move in the direction of *Tit-bits*.[44]

As has been mentioned already, one of the more visible instances of Harmsworth's professional idiosyncrasies *vis à vis* his fellow publishers, was the way in which he not only employed chartered accountants to certify his circulation on a weekly basis, but the way he enjoyed the unabashed display of such information on the first page of every issue. The occasional employment of auditors had been practised in the past by others,[45] but, no other publisher had seen the need for a regular service and none had been either daring or vulgar enough to be so brazen in the use of the figures. For the first time, the veil of secrecy was drawn aside and the rise in sales could be followed in detail. By the end of the decade, in January 1890, average weekly sales were 133,875; by March they were 165,900; while by June they had hit 201,034.[46]

Another way in which the Harmsworth weekly differed from its main rival was the way in which Alfred's journalistic talent surfaced. At first, *Answers to Correspondents* had tried to be just that, with pages of replies to what were obviously fictitious letters. During the second year of publication, 1889, that idea was gradually abandoned and the *Tit-bits* formula was adopted. Where, in volume one the layout of the pages of *Answers* had been quite regular with two or three items to the page, clear cross-headings and legible type, volume five displayed a fragmented page, simple line-rulings between items and inadequately inked type, all of which was reminiscent of Newnes. This is not surprising as it has now come to light that Harmsworth

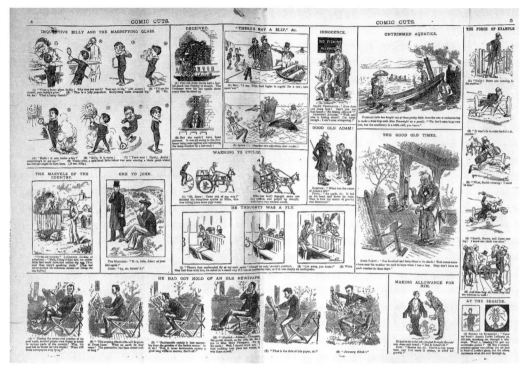

Fig.24 The instantaneous success of Comic Cuts was due to no editorial innovation. Its cover price was half that of its predecessors. This was possible because it was printed on the cheapest wood-pulp paper.

created the original dummy of *Answers* by making the paste-up on top of a copy of *Tit-bits*.[47] Yet, despite this mimicry of the pattern of success, the journalist in Harmsworth shone through in such regular features as 'Mr Answers', a 'you-are-there' series in which experiences were relayed to the reader with some vivacity. Phrenologists were visited and laughed at. The footplate of a locomotive was ridden, with Max Pemberton providing the copy.[48] Later, the clumsy name was abandoned but not the approach. 'A Night in the House of Commons', was followed by 'A Night in the Streets of London'. Appropriately, the following week 'What I Saw At Broadmoor' appeared.[49] Criminal activity, freaks, secrets and the exposé turned up again and again with a regularity never found in *Tit-bits*. Yet, despite that, the overall editorial profile and the layout of the two rivals were similar, only the emphasis differed.

Then, in May 1890, Harmsworth embarked on another venture that diverted him from the path that Newnes was taking. Nevertheless, as Gifford has point out, there was nothing original in the format that was adopted.[50] Harmsworth just chose to copy someone other than Newnes when he published *Comic Cuts*. James Henderson edited and owned *Scraps*, which he had launched in 1883. Harmsworth contributed to its pages while struggling as a teenage freelance writer and became friendly with the editor.[51] It is hardly surprising, therefore, that when he decided to publish a comic he should imitate the model that he knew so well. What he contributed was an original price. By charging only a half penny for what had previously cost a penny, he achieved enormous market penetration at a prodigious rate. The first issue sold 118,864 copies and, within weeks, the average circulation passed 300,000, easily outstripping *Answers*.[52] Such a low margin, high volume operation drew on two advantages: the continuing drop in the price of newsprint and the financial and commercial skills of Alfred's brother Harold, later to be Lord Rothermere and a publisher of enormous power and influence in his own right. One can but agree with Alfred's biographers that although he had the talent to spot a journalistic opportunity, it was Harold's business ability that kept the company afloat and functioning efficiently from a very early point.[53]

Initially, *Comic Cuts* was indistinguishable from *Scraps*, adopting the same overall design for its eight pages. Cartoons filled the first and last pages and the centre spread.(Fig. 24) Pages two and three and six and seven were given over to text. The latter's contents were very similar to that contained in *Answers* and, on occasion, were lifted directly from it. According to Gifford, many of the cartoons were stolen from foreign publications.[54]

As time progressed and the weekly became established, the cartoons, frequently comic narrative strips, expanded through more of the 380 x 280mm pages. A limited amount of advertising began to appear but the paper quality deteriorated. The latter move was undoubtedly a consequence of Harold's obsession with costs. Consequently, the pages are very difficult to handle today without damaging them, made as they were from the cheapest mechanical wood-pulp mixture.

THE LAST DECADE OF THE NINETEENTH CENTURY was one of the most vernal in the history of the British serials market. However, it would be misleading to suggest that fine new ideas flourished unhindered by the conventions of the past. More appropriate is the realisation that most of what seemed like fresh and exciting publications were regurgitated formats that had been chewed over before. The new energy arose from the intensity of the promotional skills employed, the volume of income that could now be derived from advertising, the sustained growth of the audience and the vigour of the competition between the three leading actors in the drama.

Yet despite this drive to compete, none of the participants in the race for sales seemed eager to establish an unassailable measure of their relative success by establishing a third party as an independent auditor. The Harmsworth organisation, Amalgamated Press, was prepared to issue a statement in the annual directory, *The Advertiser's ABC*, that *Answers* was selling a weekly average of 550,000 copies, audited by its own accountants.[55] Newnes followed suit and claimed 600,000 every week for *Tit-bits*.[56] But neither was willing to submit to outside assessors, not did they publish the sales figures for their other publications.

However, the situation is not entirely barren for the new century witnessed the establishment of a new organisation, the Advertisers' Protection Society, whose primary purpose was to harass the publishers into revealing more about their circulation figures. Although they did not triumph in the overwhelming manner of their American peers, they did record some successes, which were published in their own monthly circular, a hitherto untapped source. Although this information is more applicable to Chapter 5, some of it is useful in retrospective inferences.

For example, Amalgamated Press launched the *Harmsworth Popular Monthly* in 1898. By 1908 it had been renamed *The London Magazine* and in February of that year it began releasing audited sales figures to the Society. The first batch included the circulation in November 1903: 342,110 copies.[57] As the Harmsworth organisation always put considerable efforts into a launch and usually achieved very high initial sales, there is every reason to suppose that the circulation prior to the above date was even higher. However, even the above level puts it among the best-selling magazines in the last years of the nineteenth century and it seems reasonable to examine it. Similarly, as related in Chapter 5, the Society obtained information about the juvenile weeklies published by Amalgamated Press which strongly suggests that *Comic Cuts* was selling half a million a week during the first decade of the new century.[58] As we have already established that this weekly sold 300,000 in 1890, there is every reason to believe it was selling at a level somewhere between these two figures during the intervening period, which again would put it among the best sellers.

Circulation figures for other successful magazines of the period are less accessible. No record But Altick has suggested a figure of between 300,000 and 400,000, which appears reasonable considering the success of other monthlies during this decade.[59]

Although Arthur Pearson was as secretive as George Newnes, the sales of his most successful weekly emerged in an oblique way. He joined the publishing fray in July 1890 when *Pearson's Weekly* was launched, using the competitions ploy to build it to a point where it rivalled the work-horse, profit generators of Newnes and Harmsworth.[60] As he originally won a job with Newnes through a contest in *Tit-bits*,[61] the last of the successful trio must have been sensitive to this element. Being badly undercapitalised,[62] his major promotional effort had to be self-financing: that is, he charged a small entry fee for his competition that was redistributed to everyone with a correct answer. Lacking the panache of the others, this device was a slow burner. Nevertheless, before the courts declared that he was running a lottery and had to stop, his fifty third competition had drawn 473,574 entries.[63]

Thus, the evolution of the British magazine was not an apple that fell ripe from the tree but was, to the contrary, the fruit of much hard work, imagination, promotion and investment. As in America, a new habit had to be created. This should be emphasized because some commentators have assumed that the Forster Education Act of 1870 created a new but barely literate public that was waiting to devour the tasty morsels served for them by Messrs Pearson, Harmsworth and Newnes.[64] Quite apart from the exertions detailed above, such assumptions ignore recent research into the growth of literacy which suggests that the two decades subsequent to 1870 saw only a 13% growth in this attainment. Given problems regarding definitions of literacy, such figures will always be open to dispute. Yet, wherever the final tally, our best current hypotheses imply no sudden explosion of literacy, no violent expansion of the serial market potential, despite the assumptions of previous commentators.

Furthermore, recent evidence from a different quarter seriously undermines any image of the 1870 Act as the first rays of a new dawn. The clean break with the past turns out, on examination, to resemble a green-stick fracture. Vested ecclesiastical, social and industrial interests so severely hampered the implementation of the Act that the very potential readership that was supposed to be gasping for the tit-bits of titivation that were provided by our three protagonists had a hard job learning anything at all in the first years after enactment.[65] Thus, we still face the question: from whence did this new audience arise?

Doubtless some did come from the newly literate, though again the work of J.S.Hurt casts a shadow over such assumptions. The powers of compulsion of the 1870 Act were designed to coerce the very, very poor who, under the previous voluntary system had declined to send their children to school, largely for pressing financial reasons.[66] How large numbers of the children of the poor, few of whom rose beyond the most basic levels of attainment,[67] would be transformed into eager readers, particularly when few could afford even a penny magazine, let alone read it, is a question that may have eluded previous commentators.

In fact, one really needs to question the assumption that it was the barely literate that bought these magazines. Perhaps, to some they may seem like tatty little 'rags' with little to stimulate intellects made subtle by years of cultivation. Nevertheless, the journalistic skills with which the issues are composed are not entirely obscure. Indeed, their diversionary edge has not entirely diminished with time. Their true audience seems to have been a little further up the social scale according to the remarks of a contemporary observer: 'The clerks and artisans, shopgirls, dressmakers, and milliners, who pour into London every morning by the early trains, have, each and every one, a choice specimen of penny fiction with which to beguile the short journey, and perhaps the few spare minutes of a busy day.'[68]

Maybe there was another factor at work: a rise in real wages. Between the periods 1865–1874 and 1895–1904 there was a 22% growth in earnings in Britain.[69] As price changes have been allowed for, this indicates a substantial rise in overall surplus disposable income. For those families already above subsistence level, as those observed in their trains, such additional spending power might well have been expended on magazines, as well as other less vital items. At least that seems somewhat more plausible than families, for whom pawning their possessions was a weekly occurrence and survival a barely-won battle, using some of their most elusive resource to buy *Tit-bits*.

Analysis of the newspapers of the time which seem to have been bought by those situated in the less affluent parts of society, reinforces the point, for, in the late 1870s and through the 1880s, there is a pronounced rise in advertisements for consumer goods in general and saving schemes in particular, strongly suggesting an improvement in their economic position.[70] Furthermore, not only were real incomes growing, but substantial changes occurred in the composition of the work force as the modern service economy started to emerge. Between 1851 and 1911, white collar employment rose from 2.5% of the male population in work to 7.1%.[71] They were also a protected group and investigation has shown that even in the period after 1896, when inflation reasserted itself, London office workers received salary increases that kept their income ahead of price rises.[72]

Furthermore, a broader investigation of this point reveals that during the first half of the twentieth century, the period of the sharpest rise in per capita income in France, 39.74% between 1922 and 1929, coincides with one of the most dynamic periods in French magazine publishing, not unlike Britain and the United States 30 years before.[73] So, what we appear to be observing is the evolution of the serial reading market, the broadening of a weekly habit as consumption patterns changed, not a revolution built upon a change in the levels of literacy. It is a point already well discussed by Raymond Williams a generation ago, even if he offered so little supporting evidence.[74]

However, to return to the magazines, one can say that *Pearson's Weekly* was at least visibly different from the productions of its two predecessors, *Answers* and *Tit-bits*. At 376 x 273mm, as opposed to 303 x 235mm, it was bigger. Perhaps because of that, the paper used was slightly stronger and has remained a little whiter. The incorporation of chemical pulp helped give a smoother surface, which assisted in the use of illustrations, a very noticeable reintroduction by Pearson and his staff into the new penny-weekly format. Most were used in conjunction with poems, articles or fiction with a military flavour for, by 1900, the Boer War was in train. All illustrations, given the paper, were produced from line blocks and even then, close examinations reveals that the paper was too uneven to give anything more than partial contact with the broader lines on the plate. Nevertheless, 136 illustrations in just over 382 pages of editorial, or 0.36 per page, were far from insignificant, especially when five of these were used half page or larger, and such a substantial number of reproductions was new in this sector of the market.

Pearson's Weekly was also distinguished by its publication of articles on domestic matters, a topic that had been left by its competitors to the more specialised women's publications which, by the end of the century, were issued weekly by each of the competing organisations. Yet, it would be making mountains out of molehills to try to pretend that the minor differences of emphasis between these three best-selling magazines in the United Kingdom were anything other than that.

As it turned out, there were greater differences between *Answers* and *Tit-bits* at the end of the 1880s than there were between the rival weeklies during the last years of the century. That is, they had grown to look more like each other than they resembled their own early editions. Their revolutionary emphasis on dislocated information as entertainment had waned in importance over the nineties. Where, in *Answers*, during the first six months of 1890, fiction absorbed less than 10% of editorial space, by the end of the nineties it was using close to 30%(see Appendix XXII). Even *Tit-bits*, which exhibited less editorial dynamism than the other two, had increased its use of stories from 13 to 20%. The emphasis on humour and entertainment showed the reverse trend. In 1890 such material had used over 28% of editorial space during the first six months in both *Tit-bits* and *Answers*. During the nineties this was whittled down to 17.7% in the former and a mere 13.2% in the latter(see Appendices XXI and XXII). Gone was the emphasis on competitions, though they were still run. Now the promotional effort was concentrated on a serial. Indeed, this latter feature only emphasizes how closely the competitors had come to resemble one another.

On 3 March, after much loving promotion, *Answers* began serialising 'The Lion's Claw' by F. M. White, a fictional account of an invasion of Britain by the French and Russians during the approaching autumn of 1900. One week later, *Pearson's Weekly* began serialising 'The Invaders' by Louis Tracey: an account of a forthcoming German invasion of the United Kingdom. The latter story in particular drew the connection with the Boer War so that no reader could miss it. The Pearson team used their opportunity to include many illustrations and each episode incorporated most of the week's allocation. On occasion, maps of the various fictional battle grounds were used to enhance further the credibility of the presentation. Supplementary features that drew the dangers of the fictional conflict over the border into the real world were also used, such as illustrated articles on how to prepare your village against invasion.

This rivalry between the three largest magazine publishing houses is something which marked the nineties and the opening years of the new century. The three organisations competed across many of the market sectors. Where the Amalgamated Press, that is, the Harmsworth organisation, had *Forget-Me-Not*, Pearson's had *Home Notes* and Newnes had *Woman's Life*. Each had their own illustrated Boer War weekly. Each had their sixpenny monthly. Yet, they did diverge as well. Newnes scored a big success in the limited circulation but lucrative upper-middle class market with *Country Life*, while Harmsworth aimed for the large circulations possible with rock bottom prices.

Comic Cuts had been the first of the latter but, over the decade, the change in this half penny weekly was considerable. As Dennis Gifford has pointed out, the 1890s saw regular characters assuming regular positions in each issue of the funny papers.[75] In the case of *Comic Cuts*, by 1900 their front page character was Robinson Crusoe, who betrayed little resemblance to anything conceived by Defoe. Of the eight pages, the back and the centre spread were, like the front, covered with comic strips, though none of them appears to feature regular named characters. Pages 2-3 and 6-7 were given over to text; largely, in fact, serials. And the Boer War was inescapable. Robinson Crusoe was designated 'Our Own Special War Correspondent' and each week he demonstrated with unerring ease the foolishness, incompetence and stupidity of the Afrikaaner foe. Special war numbers were issued that abandoned the regular format on occasion. Another weekly feature was 'Private John Byrne of the Fighting Fifth', a serialised narrative. This concerned a character who from the title should have been insignificant and probably of humble origin. Yet every episode was preceded by an illustration which featured him leading a charge on horseback. The daring do was woven among names of battles and events which must have been familiar from the national press and it is very difficult to resist the impression that this nonsense was an attempt to exorcise the tragic farce that was being enacted 6,000 miles from the editorial offices. Or, perhaps the emotional needs behind the stereotypes were so powerful that military action could only be imagined in these degrading, trivialising terms. Maybe it was just too good an opportunity to let slip: the classic situation in which to drum up sales. Certainly, Cyril Pearson was not missing a trick. His weekly's current competition involved naming the day that the British forces would march into Pretoria. One wonders if Generals Roberts and French had entered.

Despite these cheap tricks, much that appeared in the penny weeklies was concerned with getting at the truth of the situation. *Pearson's Weekly* carried regular pages of soldiers' letters forwarded from their families in Britain that do mention the less acceptable details. *Answers* featured many pages of background material that must have proved a valuable complement to accounts of the conflict featured in the daily press. In many ways, one suspects that the contradictory responses and motives evident in the magazines may have mirrored the uncertainties of their readers.

Located at a point between these weeklies and the august reviews, the 1880s had seen a new initiative in the industry. Where the austere texts of the quarterlies were unsullied by visual displays, *The English Illustrated Magazine*, launched in October 1883, was clearly unabashed about its condition, as the first 64 page issue amply demonstrates. By the start of 1885, after the magazine had settled down, the use of artwork had stabilised into a pattern. The 384 pages of the first six issues of that year sported 31 full–page and 133 part–page illustrations, for example. By weighting their distribution towards the opening pages of each issue so that the first two articles were extensively illustrated, the impression created was particularly visual for a British monthly. As we have already seen, this form of magazine design was a feature of both *Harper's* and *Scribner's Monthly* in the United States in the 1870s. The launch of a London edition of *Scribner's* in the early 1880s and its success was hardly a coincidence and the similarities between the English magazine and its American predecessor were, surely, not fortuitous.

The text of *The English Illustrated Magazine* maintained a steady diet of picturesque anecdotes on art and architecture, light fiction, the occasional travelogue and the odd poem, sometimes illustrated. Somewhat lighter in tone than its trans-Atlantic predecessors, it was an affable mixture, not calculated to disturb the digestion. Under the editor J.W. Comyns Carr, any examination of the modern or everyday was politely excluded. However, no evidence has yet come to light of the scale of the success of this monthly.

Yet, at the beginning of the nineties, it was this formula and its use of illustration that provided the stepping off point for George Newnes and his move up-market. But first, the great crusading journalist W. T. Stead entered the field of action. It was he who came up with the idea of the *Review of Reviews*, which as its name implies, was a survey and a partial abstract of recent magazine articles. He approached Newnes, a contemporary and former fellow pupil at Silcocks, a small boarding school for the sons of Congregational clergymen in Yorkshire,[76] and asked whether he would be interested in acting as the publisher.

Their new monthly first appeared in January 1890. Not surprisingly, these two strong-willed individuals soon had a difference of opinion over editorial direction. So, Stead managed to raise £3,000 and bought out his partner, taking his magazine to another publisher. This left Newnes high and dry with a complete staff but nothing for them to work on. Undaunted, instead of throwing in the towel and sacking them all, Newnes came up with *The Strand Magazine*, editing it himself.[77] Given these shotgun circumstances, it is hardly surprising that it bears more than a passing resemblance to *The English Illustrated Magazine* and its American predecessors.

Very little appears to be known about *The English Illustrated Magazine*, not least its sales figures. But as it lasted for 30 years, until 1913, we can reasonably assume that it was a profitable concern. Fortunately, *The Strand Magazine* has retained a higher profile and we, at least, have an estimated sales figure of 300,000 to 400,000 per month through the mid-1890s, though caution and experience of the elasticity of truth in the magazines publishing world incline one towards the former figure.[78] Clearly, the chosen format did good business and the relatively fluent layout used by Carr and enhanced by Newnes became a pattern for others to mimic.

By 1895 both magazines were using substantial numbers of halftones. During the first six months of that year, *The Strand*, in a total of 712 pages, used 842 illustrative blocks, excluding, that is, illuminated titles. Thus, the frequency is 1.18 illustrations per page. Of these, 376, or 44.66% were halftones. This means that by 1895, this English example of the American tradition was much more profusely illustrated than its contemporary trans-Atlantic counterparts. Over exactly the same period, *The English Illustrated Magazine*, now edited by Clement Shorter,[79] in 568 pages, used 307 illustrations, or 0.54 illustrations per page. But, of these 237, or 77.20% were halftones, which again surpasses contemporary American efforts. However, these figures, because they do not reflect the size of the blocks used, obscure our perception of the respective editorial attitudes to illustration. By quantifying differences in dimensions a vital stylistic division between the two publications can be emphasized.

During the first six months of 1895, the 568 pages of Shorter's magazine featured 59 full-page illustrations and 132 larger than a half page but less than a full page. As these 132 were very frequently only a few lines short of a page, their average size might reasonably be said to be three quarters of the whole. Thus, if we multiply the 132 by 0.75, obtaining 99, we will get a very approximate indication of the notional number of pages used in this manner. In total, therefore, one might suggest that 158 pages out of 568 had been used for large illustrations; or 27.82% of the printed surface. Whereas, *The Strand Magazine*, in its 712 pages, used only 6 full page illustrations and 18 half a page or greater. As the latter were frequently only just half a page in length, an estimate that on average they used 0.65 of the printed surface might be considered reasonable. In other words, 11.7 pages were used for those illustrations of the smaller size. So, in total 17.7 pages were used for large illustrations in *The Strand* out of 712, or 2.49%. Or, to put it another way, Shorter used over 11 times as many large illustrations, measured by area, as Newnes. In this manner we can get some numerical indication of their different styles of layout. We can see that *The English Illustrated Magazine* used far fewer but larger illustrations. This set up a regular, stately visual rhythm through each issue, while *The Strand Magazine* used many smaller blocks peppered across each spread. Their result might be seen as more energetic or lively, calculated to stimulate rather than relax the reader. The point was reinforced by the visual disjunctions set up between the halftones and the line illustrations. Indeed, Newnes often used diagrams or cartoons during this period, a choice that enriched further the visual diet.

Of course, given what we have previously discovered regarding the cost of large halftones, that is their relative cheapness, it is not surprising that Shorter, or his art director if he had one, should use this technique. Thus, his choice of image size also led him to a particular visual texture. *The Strand*'s editorial team, by adopting an alternative tactic, left itself a freer choice. Shorter's gain was that his printers developed considerable experience with large halftone blocks and within a few years this became noticeable in the quality of their work, particularly with photographic portraits.

By the decade's end, *The Strand* was still a prolific user of illustrations at 1.28 per page. And there was still a marked balance in the use of artwork and photography reproduced through halftones, with both running at just over 43% of the total, while line-work constituted the remainder. This is not surprising, for fiction dominated the contents of every issue, absorbing over 52% of page space between January and June 1900(see Appendix XIX), and artwork was used exclusively to illustrate these pages.

Interestingly, though the Boer War dominated the weeklies, it was a peripheral preoccupation to the editor of *The Strand*, meriting little more than one article per issue on it or a related topic. This is more than a matter of production scheduling for the weeklies were equally unable to carry up-to-date news when compared to the daily press. It is more a matter of an editorial decision as to what the readers wanted to confront. More space was given to the arts, at just over 14%, than topics touching on contemporary society, which used a little less than 12%. Verse was ignored altogether, an unusual editorial choice at the end of the nineteenth century(see Appendix XIX). In part, the lack of poetry may be a consequence of the way in which each issue was organised. Whereas most editors insisted on filling each page, using a short poem to cover any white space, *The Strand's* articles were kept entirely to whole pages and if white space remained at the end of each then that was okay.

Of course, the use of the halftone block and the opportunity this gave to editorial staff to resize illustrations at will to cope with variations in the length of articles minimised the amount of white space. Where once a woodcut had to be reproduced in the same size as ordered, now illustrations could be drawn to any reasonable size and a block made or remade from them to suit. However, the staff at *The Strand* exercised this opportunity with discretion and did not plump for the populist rococo layouts which were developing in some American periodicals, such as *Leslie's Monthly*, and were to come to overripe fruition in *Cosmopolitan*.

The restraint exercised by *The Strand* can be judged by taking a glance at one particular issue. The April 1900 edition is 120 pages long, the regular size of all issues. Its 15 items are illustrated in a variety of styles, although the layouts are simple. Wash drawings are used in the leading short story, which is set in Australia. This is followed by nine pages on 'Building a Skyscraper' by Ray Stannard Baker, one of the star writers on *McClure's* and then *The American Magazine* during the next decade. Here, photographs are reproduced to describe the growth of the building from the placement of the first girders on 30 July to imminent completion on 5 November. Nine line draw-ings are used in the next 12–page story. Their open texture has encouraged the designer to set them on the page with-out a border so that the text can flow round their irregular shapes. Caricatures punctuate the pages of the political arti-cle which follows, which in

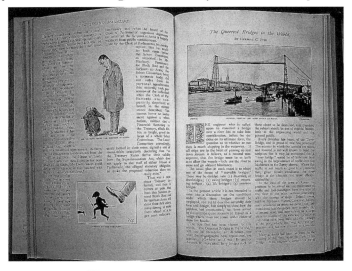

Fig.25 Newnes's promotional ma-chine made The Strand a success-ful monthly on the model of Ameri-can counterparts such as Century Illustrated. But sales flagged in the new century when sixpenny paper-backs began to appear.

turn leads on to an article on unusual bridges which again uses reproductions of photographs to furnish the descriptions.(Fig. 25) The sixth item is a story of a runaway train illustrated with line drawings. In this instance, although borders do not enclose the artwork, the earlier irregular pattern of surrounding text is also avoided. 'Chats with Transport Captains' is another opportunity to use photographic illustrations, while the last part of the serial, 'A Master of Craft', uses line work in which the outlines of characters are inked in with a heavy line, which tends to invoke the air of caricature. The latest of the series entitled 'Illustrated Interviews' uses reproductions of works by its subject, the painter Hubert Herkomer. The short story, 'Between Two Fires' reverts to wash drawings, and another article on the curious, about dolls made from shells, uses photographs to document them. Of the remaining four items, two use line-work and two photographs.

As indicated already, the layouts in which these illustrations are employed are quite straightforward. Each item starts with a title, the setting of which varies from piece to piece. Each one also starts with an illuminated drop capital. That is the extent of the typographic variation. Bold type is avoided; the pages are always split into two columns; captions are always limited to one line; no cross-heads are used in articles. It is a classically simple formula which had clearly been picked up from American practice since the publication of monthlies such as *Century Illustrated* in Britain during the 1880s, as mentioned above.

During the nineties, the example of this successful format became the model for many other, often ephemeral publications. These included the *Ludgate Magazine*, edited by Phil May, which followed *The Strand* very quickly in May 1891. It was pursued by the *Pall Mall Magazine* in 1893, while Ward, Lock and Bowden produced *The Windsor Magazine* in 1895, a very pale imitation. The same year also saw the birth of *The Minster*, another clone. In 1896 came *Pearson's Magazine*, followed two years later by *The Royal Magazine* from the same house. *The Harmsworth Popular Monthly Magazine* also began in 1898 and was followed a year later by the same publisher's *Penny Pictorial Magazine*. All these periodicals followed similar formats with similar content and even similar pages sizes, usually 238 x 161mm. To open one at random among a group would be to risk difficulties of identification. Only a look at their contents demonstrates the real differences.

By the end of the 1890s, it seems quite possible that *The Harmsworth Popular Monthly Magazine* was selling around 400,000 copies per issue and might have been the most successful of the six penny monthlies. Certainly, by 1903 it was still selling more than 350,000 in a sector in which every title seemed to be losing ground.[80] Like *The Strand*, it was emphatically visual and, like *The Strand* it tended to pepper its pages, with 1.51 illustrations on each on average between January and June 1900. Of these, over 65% were from photographs and only 25% were halftones derived from artwork. Again, this reflects the degree of emphasis placed upon fiction which, at 39%, although substantial, was a noticeably smaller amount than that published by its rival. Conversely, the Harmsworth staff were much more interested in history and biography, at 13.7% of page space, than the Newnes people at just over 2%. The former also used over 44 pages out of 569, or 7.8%, on the social life and manners of contemporary Britain, against zero. Yet, perhaps most surprising of all was the choice by Alfred's staff to use over 10% of their monthly for fine art, each issue featuring an average of 8 pages at the end reproducing paintings(see Appendix XIX). Needless to say, the subjects were largely sentimental, martial or safely historical.

THE DEVELOPMENT OF THE BRITISH MAGAZINE MARKET during the nineteenth century can be seen, from the foregoing, to split into roughly two periods: that before 1880 and the subsequent 20 years. Prior to the late 1830s and early 1840s, when the development of a railway network made an enormous difference to the ease of distribution, only the intense efforts of the Society for the Diffusion of Useful Knowledge were able to surmount the barriers to the establishment of extensive nation–wide sales of a magazine. Once the main trunk lines were in place, the demand for cheap weeklies was relatively easy to satisfy and publications such as *The London Journal* and *The Family Herald*, both dominated by fiction, sold in large numbers around the major cities.[81] Simultaneously, the sixpenny weekly, led by *The Illustrated London News*, developed a large circulation. But once this initial fertile period passed, the embryonic industry tended to stagnate.

In 1855, with the repeal of stamp duty and 1861, with the repeal of the paper tax, local and national newspapers, were given an enormous boost. Although circulation figures are virtually impossible to obtain, it may well be true that magazine sales either stabilised or diminished as the second half of the nineteenth century developed. It is certainly true that the circulations of both *The London Journal* and the *Illustrated London News* began to slide around this time.

During the 1870s, a number of new publications for the middle of the market, the sixpenny sector, appeared, though the sales of such as *Vanity Fair* were never very large. What would now be seen as juvenile weeklies, the publications of Brett, the Emmetts and, later, the Religious Tract Society also emerged around this time. Their use of small gifts as a promotional device undoubtedly helped their sales.

Then, in 1881, *Tit-bits* burst on the scene, using competitions and a variety of promotional devices to revive and expand the penny weekly market. Its transformation of information into entertainment as the mainstay of the weekly was something quite new. Among the flood of imitations, only those that realised the importance of the highly attractive competition as a circulation booster survived. In such low-profit-margin operations, only large sales could generate sufficient profits to ensure continued publication.

In the 1890s, the three empires founded on this basis, the Newnes, Harmsworth and Pearson companies, together with the Ingram family, who owned the *Illustrated London News*, diversified in different directions. The previous decade had seen the emergence of a small sixpenny monthly market derived from the 35¢ American model. Newnes used this as the basis of *The Strand Magazine*. Again, he was copied by many others but only Pearson and, much later, Harmsworth, were successful in following him and marketing the idea to a mass readership. In addition, Harmsworth had opted for the cheaper end of the market and, by cutting prices to a half penny, gained an unprecedented circulation for a 'comic' within weeks. During the 1890s, various attempts were made to develop a sixpenny illustrated weekly that was lighter in tone than the news weeklies. Eventually *The Sketch* and then *Country Life* became the market leaders, although the scale of their success never put them among the best-sellers.

These developments of the last decade of the nineteenth century in Britain were based on a steady rise in the real value of wages, that is, their convertibility into goods and services and the growth of surplus disposable income. As a result, the public were able to afford more serials, both magazines and newspapers, and the range of published material expanded. *Tit-bits* in particular promoted a new concept of information as amusement. However, fiction reasserted its value to the editor as the nineties wore on. Apart from anything else, it is simply easier to fill the weekly space with narrative than a composite of individually researched facts.

By the decade's end, the structure of the industry and the way that it promoted and produced its publications was largely established for a generation. The separation of the market into various class-defined sectors, the penny weekly on the *Tit-bits* model, the sixpenny monthlies, the illustrated society weeklies, the penny women's weeklies and the halfpenny comics, was well established. Each of the three major companies had at least one or maybe two contenders in most sectors. Sales were substantial but not enormous. With their low production and distribution costs, such circulations were quite sufficient for a steady profit. Clearly, British magazines, and the industrial framework that supported them, were developing in a very different way from their American counterparts.

NOTES

1. Thornton, Archibald Paton, *The Habit of Authority*, London, 1966.

2. Altick, R.D., *The English Common Reader*, Chicago, 1957, pp394-396. Parliament was given a circulation of 240,000 a week for *Family Herald*, *Hansard*, Series 3, CXXXVII, (1855), cols.781-783. The same source gave the circulation of *The London Journal* as 510,000 a week.

3. Jay, Frank, Peeps Into The Past, *Spare Moments*, Vol.59, No.1559, 26 Oct. 1918, p1 (London Journal Series).

4. Ibid., No.1563, 23 Nov. 1918, p17 (London Journal Series).

5. Scott, Bennett, Revolutions in Thought: Serial Publications and the Mass Market for Reading, *The Victorian Periodical Press: Samplings and Soundings*, Edited by Joanne Shattock and Michael Wolff, Leicester and Toronto, 1982, pp235-236, table 1.

6. Ibid., pp242-4.

7. Hollis, Patricia, *The Pauper Press*, Oxford, 1970, pp116-124. Berridge, Virginia S., *Popular Journalism and Working Class Attitudes, 1854-1886*, unpublished PhD thesis, London, 1976, Vol.1, pp21-25. These pages give further references.

8. James, Louis, *Fiction For The Working Man 1830-1850*, London, 1963, p30 et seq. and p65.

9. Ibid., p27.

10. Hollis, op.cit., p107.

11. Douglas, Eric Alexander, *WH Smith*, London, 1965, pp4-5. Also, Wilson, Charles, *First With The News*, London, 1985, pp43-45.

12. Berridge., op.cit., pp40-41.

13. Cole, G.D.H. and Postgate, Raymond, *The Common People 1746-1946*, London, 1938, p304 and Perkin, Harold, *The Origins of Modern English Society 1780-1880*, London, 1969, pp134-135.

14. Malcolmson, Robert W., *Popular Recreations in English Society 1700-1850*, Cambridge, 1973, p118 et seq.

15. Pollard, Sidney, Factory Discipline in the Industrial Revolution, *The Economic History Review*, Second Series, Vol.16, No.2, 1963, pp254-271.

16. Berridge, op.cit., pp20 & 23. Before 1832, over 800 people were prosecuted and in 1836 more than 400 were dealt with in a matter of months.

17. Ibid., pp39 & 41.

18. Ibid., pp112 & 138; Vol.2, p78, fig.3.3.

19. James, Louis, Tom Brown's Imperialist Sons, *Victorian Studies*, Vol.17, No.1, September, 1973, p90.

20. Medcraft, John, *A Bibliography of the Penny Bloods of Edward Lloyd*, Dundee, 1945.

21. *Advertiser's ABC*, London, 1889, p702.

22. Carpenter, Kevin, *Penny Dreadfuls and Comics*, London, 1983, p21.

23. Dunae, Patrick, Penny Dreadfuls: Late Nineteenth Century Boys' Literature and Crime, *Victorian Studies*, Vol.22, No.2, Winter 1979, pp133-150.

24. Dunae, Patrick, Boy's Own Paper: Origins and Editorial Policies, *The Private Library*, Vol.9, No.4, Winter 1976, London, pp127-132.

25. Cox, Jack, *Take A Cold Tub, Sir!*, Guildford, Surrey, 1982, pp26, 36-37.

26. *Boy's Own Paper*, Vol.12, No.582, p364.

27. Ibid, No.597, p606.

28. Ibid., No.581, pp347-350.

29. Dunae, *B.O.P.*, op.cit., pp133-134.

30. Religious Tract Society, *Minutes of Finance Sub-committee*, 19 April 1888, item 582 and 17 April 1890, item 716. These minute books are now held by the library of the School of Oriental and African Studies, University of London.

31. Cox, op.cit., p24.

32. R.T.S., op.cit., item 582. The comments on *GOP* in Kirsten Drotner's very fine study, *English Children and the Magazines, 1751-1945*, New Haven and London, 1988, because they have an entirely different purpose, complement this research.

33. Friederichs, Hulda, *The Life of Sir George Newnes*, Bart, London, 1911, p67.

34. *Tit-bits*, London, Vol.1, No.1, 22 October 1881.

35. James, *Working Man*, op.cit., p17 quotes an article in *Sharpe's London Magazine*, Vol.1, August, 1829, pp64-72, that describes the practice with equal brazenness.

36. Friederichs, op.cit., pp74-80.

37. Ibid., pp86-97.

38. *Advertiser's ABC*, op.cit., 1889, p711.

39. Pound, Reginald, *The Strand Magazine 1891-1950*, London, 1966, p25. Anon., *The British Printer*, Vol.7, No.46, July-August 1895, pp203-212, gives a full and illustrated description of the T. B. Browne office and the activities therein. The author suggests that the agency was the largest in the United Kingdom and that it serviced clients worldwide. Perkin, Harold, *The Rise of Professional Society*, London, 1989, p64, 'Between 1850 and 1880 Schedule D incomes from business and other profits of over £3,000 a year had risen from under 2,000 to over 5,000, compared with the 2,500 landowners with rentals (excluding London property) of over £3,000 in the "New Doomsday" returns of the 1870s; business incomes of over £10,000 had grown from 338 to 987,'.

40. Friederichs, op.cit., pp107-108, 112-114.

41. *Tit-bits*, op.cit., Nos.3-6. 60 pages featured 453 items. The back page of each issue was used to advertise the prize for the best tit-bit of the week submitted by a reader.

42. Pound, Reginald and Harmsworth, Geoffrey, *Northcliffe*, London, 1959, p88.

43. Ferris, Paul, *The House of Northcliffe*, London, 1971, p38.

44. Ibid, p39.

45. *Advertisers' ABC*, op.cit., 1889, p159. Entry for *The Christian Age*.

46. *Answers*, London, Vol.5, No.4, p49 and No.7, p97.

47. Hartwell, Lord, *William Camrose*, London, 1992.

48. *Answers*, London, Vol.4, No.4, Nos.8 and 9, pp122 and 132. Also Pound and Harmsworth, op.cit., p109.

49. *Answers*, London, Vol.4, Nos.17, 18, 19, pp264, 282, 298.

50. Gifford, Denis, *Happy Days. A Century of Comics*, London, 1975, p9.

51. Pound and Harmsworth, op.cit., p45.

52. Pound & Harmsworth, op.cit., p115.

53. Ibid., pp92-93.

54. Gifford, Denis, op.cit., p9.

55. *The Advertiser's ABC*, London, 1900, p301.

56. Ibid., opposite p382.

57. *The Advertiser's Protection Society Monthly Circular*, No.46, February 1908, p4.

58. Ibid., No.44, December 1907, p4.

59. Altick, op.cit., p396.

60. Ibid.

61. Friederichs, op.cit., pp104-105.

62. Dark, Sidney, *The Life of Sir Arthur Pearson*, London, 1922, p61.

63. Ibid, pp62-65.

64. White, op.cit, p59. The unthinking acceptance and dangerous diffusion of this conclusion and even its extension, can be judged from the following passage: 'Until 1870 there was no provision in England for universal schooling, and, in the eighties and nineties, the system was still far from complete, so that for many moderately prosperous people on the ill-defined frontier between the upper working class and the lower middle class, reading must have been almost as much of a novelty as reading matter.' Reader, W.J., *Bowater: a history*, Cambridge, 1981, p2. Such opinions, contradicted by every shred of available evidence, can only be attributed to unmitigated prejudice. See also Pound and Harmsworth, op.cit., p26, who allege that until the passing of the act 'only one person in seven in England could read and write.'

65. Hurt, John S., *Elementary Schooling and the Working Classes, 1860-1918*, London, Toronto and Buffalo, 1979. Although this book largely avoids the central issue of the education received by those who did benefit from the system and how it might have influenced them, it is still an extremely valuable and vivid picture of the forces that did their best to undermine and counter the act. See also Vincent, David, *Literacy and Popular Culture: England 1750-1914*, Cambridge, 1989, p53-54, which only emphasizes the point again, that almost 90 per cent of the population of England and Wales could read before the 1870 Act became law.

66. Ibid, p101 et seq., and p155.

67. Ibid, p130.

68. Vincent, David, *Literacy and Popular Culture: England 1750-1914*, Cambridge, 1989, p212, quotes from Agnes Repplier.

69. O'Brien and Keyder, *Economic Growth in Britain and France 1780-1914*, London, 1978, p70. Also Perkin, Harold, *The Rise of Professional Society*, London, 1989, p31 states that real wages rose by 34 per cent between 1880 and 1913.

70. Berridge, op.cit., pp200-201.

71. Fraser, W. Hamish, *The Coming of the Mass Market 1850-1914,* London, 1981, p17.

72. Ibid., p26.

73. Lacaillon, Jacques, Changes in the Distribution of Income in the French Economy, p44, in *The Distribution of National Income,* Edited by Jean Marchand and Bernard Ducros, London and New York, 1968.

74. Williams, Raymond, *The Long Revolution*, London, 1961, p173 et seq.

75. Gifford, op.cit., p9.

76. Pound, op.cit., pp13-14.

77. Ibid., pp28-30.

78. Altick, op.cit., p396.

79. *Dictionary of National Biography*, op.cit., p772.

80. *Newsletter of the Advertiser's Protection Society*, February 1908, No.46.

81. Altick, op.cit., p360; Downey, Edmund, *Twenty Years Ago*, London, 1905, p62; and Ellegard, Alvar, The Readership of the Periodical Press in Mid-Victorian Britain, *Gotesborg Universities Arsskrift*, 63, Gotesborg, 1957, p32. All three sources support a circulation of over 500,000 'for a considerable period' for *The London Journal*.

The Years 1901–1920

DESPITE THE TRANSFORMATION OF THE PRINTING WORLD that had taken place in the previous 20 years, technological innovation did not come to a halt in 1900. Already, the Rembrandt Intaglio Printing Company of Lancaster, England had begun using rotary photogravure, although the application of that technique to serials, on a regular basis, was still a decade away.[1]

In 1905 Ira Rubel sprang offset lithography on the world when a working press was built to his design in New York. The following year the invention spread to Britain and the year after that to Germany, according to Berry and Poole.[2] However, a memoire by a British business partner of the American inventor suggests that Rubel demonstrated his invention in London in the year of its initial appearance, that is, 1905.[3]

The speed of its acceptance was, in part, a consequence of the interest of press makers. They saw an opportunity for expansion into a new field that was not completely dominated by R. Hoe and Co.[4] But quality did not match their aspirations, as yet, and it was the 1920s before this process began to be a serious contender to letterpress in the magazine production process. None the less, that did not stop Messrs. Iliffe and Sons of Coventry, publishers of specialist journals, from acquiring one of the new machines from Harris Press of Fetter Lane, London by September 1906.[5]

One process that did have immediate consequences was the introduction of 'wet colour printing' at the *Ladies' Home Journal*, reported as occurring in 1907. Milton A. McKee, who worked for the pressmakers C. B. Cottrell, developed a system for making four-colour letterpress printing plates.[6] The blocks combined mechanical halftones and extensive retouching. All four sets of plates were placed on one press simultaneously, which was then run at the high speeds necessary for commercial magazine production.[7] The success of the process depended on using specially developed inks of differing consistencies, or degrees of tack, the most adhesive, that is the least likely to lift up, being laid down first and so on.[8] Experimental work on much the same lines was going on at the Bemrose, Dalziel Company in Britain and at the Imprimerie Crété just outside Paris. The British company had been involved in colour printing through its formerly independent constituent companies during the second half of the nineteenth century.[9] Contemporary comment suggests that they did not meet with the same degree of success as their American counterparts.[10]

However, the dates given by contemporary secondary sources regarding the Philadelphia experiment are contradicted by the primary evidence. The *Ladies' Home Journal* began using four-colour covers in October 1905, a change noted in the editorial of that issue. Examination of the material reveals no sudden change in the detailed appearance of the results during or immediately prior to 1907, so it seems reasonable to assume that the 'wet colour' process had been inaugurated some time earlier than contemporary observers reported. By 1930, such inks were standard items in the manufacturers' catalogues.[11]

The extension of the technique to the interior of the monthly took a little longer.(Plate VI) This is hardly surprising as it is easier to organise different printing for a cover on the special paper stock which would be printed separately anyway, than to integrate such a major change into the other aspects of production. Indeed, examination of other magazines of the time only reinforces this conclusion. That is, while various publications in both the US and Britain instituted colour covers on an occasional or regular basis in the decade 1895–1905, a much smaller number interpolated colour into the text.

One such was *Munsey's Magazine*, which first assigned three-colour artwork to its front cover as early as November 1899. This only became a regular feature in January 1903. It was possible because by January 1900 the company had bought sheet-fed flatbed printing presses which were used for the covers that were then added to the rest of the pages on a special covering machine.[12] More time elapsed before a clever use of two colours was introduced to create a moderately successful counterfeit of everyday appearances among the editorial pages when, in March 1905, an interleaved frontispiece on different paper stock was inserted. From the following month, three-colour reproductions were used in the same position. Nevertheless, despite this pioneer work, it is evident from the results that, even the provision of a separate printing for each colour was not overcoming registration problems with the three plates and they were frequently out of alignment. Whatever procedure they used, and it appears to have elicited no comment at the time or later, it did not measure up to the stunning quality achieved from the first by *Ladies' Home Journal*.

By way of contrast, *McClure's Magazine* of New York adopted a different strategy from its competitors. With its first colour cover in August 1906 it jumped straight in at the deep end, using a colour frontispiece and four reproductions of specially painted illustrations for a story by Jack London interspersed through the text. It was able to adopt this approach by selecting particularly high-quality imitation art paper for one of the many signatures from which the magazine was created. It was an expensive decision but not out of keeping with the personality of the owner.[13]

In Britain, a comparable delay in blending colour into the regular editorial pages could be observed in the *Illustrated London News* which had first used colour covers, printed by the Leighton Brothers, as long ago as 1855.[14] Yet, it was not until 1912 that the Ingram company managed to integrate colour blocks with the other elements of production to reproduce colour photographs and works of art regularly on the normal pagination.

During October of the same year, another augury for the future occurred when Bruce Ingram began using monochrome rotary gravure to produce weekly supplements for both the *Illustrated London News* and *The Sketch*. It had been preceded in the use of the technique by a number of newspapers in Germany, including the *Freiburg Zeitung*, the first, in 1910. In addition, a contemporary report of late 1911 locates one of the new presses in the production plant of the French weekly *L'Illustration*. By the time of the report it was alleged to be printing contributions to this profusely illustrated newsmagazine. This is corroborated by the records of the Société Alsacienne de Constructions Mécaniques, of Mulhouse, Alsace, which supplied the press in December 1910.[15]

Perhaps James Bishop in the *Dictionary of National Biography* is right in suggesting that the pressure from the increasing use of halftones in newspapers helped to prompt the editor in his decision. An emphasis on those qualities that newspapers were unable to match was important to a newsmagazine in promoting and sustaining sales.[16] However, rotary photogravure was not just a marketing device for the *Illustrated London News*. As a confidential internal memorandum prepared by an unnamed author in the Ingram organisation and dated 8 September 1913 suggests, it also had cost advantages. Ink for the process at two shillings a kilo was less than 2/3 the price of letterpress ink, which cost three shillings and six pence a kilo at the time. Both processes used similar quantities for similar jobs. Already, the German-made gravure presses could be run at 8,000 to 12,000 revolutions per hour printing one colour, while the commercial speed of rotary letterpress was about 3,500 r.p.h. There was also a considerable saving on the cost of paper. As the memo concluded, 'In the case of the *Illustrated London News* the saving in the cost of paper to the end of the current year has been sufficient to pay the cost of the license to work the process.'[17]

Clearly, the conjunction of quality and reduced costs must have prompted the publishers to use gravure in the periodicals and special publications produced to illustrate the unfolding drama during the years 1914–18.[18] Not surprisingly given this stimulus, their previous interest and the economic advantages, the *Illustrated London News* transformed the substance of its printing to gravure on 28 June 1919, after the cessation of hostilities. It did not, as was erroneously implied by Berry and Poole,[19] go over to the new process completely but retained a letterpress supplement during the twenties, which was frequently used to carry colour illustrations. *The Times Weekly Edition* began the same transition on 25 July 1919, when it produced its first eight page gravure supplement.[20] On 10 December 1931, it issued its first gravure section in colour.[21]

Another small but important change occurred during the period 1914–18. In 1915, R.Hoe and Company introduced their automatic ink pump. Henceforward, a substantial improvement in consistency and speed of operation would be easier to maintain.[22]

THE FIRST DECADE OF THE NEW CENTURY was a turning point in the American market for the magazines themselves. *The Century* had dwindled in importance as its circulation failed to match the dynamic growth of its successors to pre-eminence. By 1910, even *The Christian Herald* had a circulation of 221,082, which made the former market leader look feeble at 125,000.[23] *Harper's Monthly* was in very much the same state.

At the other end of the scale, the *Saturday Evening Post* was soaring upward with a circulation of about one and a quarter million a week.[24] It joined its stable-mate, *Ladies' Home Journal*, which by 1910 was selling 1,260,000 a month.[25] That gave the Curtis organisation such market dominance that is no wonder that they were able to issue their directives from Independence Square on what advertisements would or would not be permitted in their magazines, as outlined previously.

From a dead start, the *Saturday Evening Post* had increased in weight as the decade progressed. In 1897, when Curtis bought it, the weekly was selling 2,231 copies per issue and raised slightly less than $7,000 in advertising revenue.[26] By 1900 the circulation was claimed to be 250,000 and the page rate was $800.[27] Because this rate was disproportionately high relative to sales, advertising was slow in appearing and the magazine lost $1.25 million before it turned the corner.[28] Yet, by the decade's end, its 1576 pages plus 26 front covers for the period January to June 1910 featured a total of 788.69 pages of paid insertions. At $3,600 a page or $4,500 for the back cover, that suggests an income from advertising of about $2,800,000 for the half year, say $5.5 million gross for the whole of 1910, though it was probably more if the usual pre-Christmas boom is taken into account.[29] Even allowing for the standard 15% commission it paid to the various intermediary advertising agencies, a net income of approximately $4,675,000 from this source was very substantial. It is no wonder it managed to hold its single copy price to 5¢ a week at a time when most of those who had started the decade at 10¢ a month had succumbed to a 50% price rise. Given the price sensitivity of magazine sales already established, there can be little doubt that the low cover price boosted the *Post*'s circulation.

As discussed in chapter one, these American sales figures were produced within a system in which auditing by the Association of American Advertisers was becoming accepted practice and was to lead, in 1914, to the creation of the Audit Bureau of Circulation, which standardised all monitoring procedures. Henceforward, any doubts about US circulation figures would be unjustified. The one major magazine which tried to cheat, *McClure's*, was immediately detected by the *American Newspaper Annual* and *Nelson Chesman and Company's Newspaper Rate Book*, as will be discussed below. The only best-seller to stay outside the system, *Reader's Digest*, did so until 1955 because it ran no advertising and was extremely secretive. But even in this instance, sufficient data is available to make the judgements necessary to this study, as will be seen in due course.

A similar confidence cannot be shown in those figures which are available from British sources. As mentioned in Chapter 1, information about the different circulations is extremely patchy and would be more so were it not for the remaining records of the Incorporated Society of British Advertisers. Nevertheless, sufficient data is available to sift a group of best-sellers from the mass of titles which were sold in Britain during the first decade of the century. This information exists in the form of audited figures which came into the possession of the Society's forerunner, the Advertisers' Protection Society.[30] As this organisation was very cautious about the intelligence it published and the honesty of the publishing houses, it would seem that these net sales figures are probably reliable. Where audited figures are missing, the Society's estimates have been used, which were also leavened with considerable scepticism. In one instance a figure has been taken from Harmsworth's private correspondence, which was never intended for publication. This again tends to suggest that the information is somewhat more reliable than any published claimed figure. Information about sales is more detailed for the second decade because sudden bubbles of detailed circulation figures rose from the normally opaque depths of the industry for a very limited period. Quite why this about turn occurred at this moment is not yet known. It is unfortunate that this more open attitude did not last for any length of time.

BACK IN THE EARLY YEARS OF THE CENTURY, the *Saturday Evening Post* and the *Ladies' Home Journal* were waxing fat together in the American market, owned by the same publisher. However, that is all they had in common. It is difficult to imagine two magazines being farther apart on almost everything than these two, even in such prosaic matters as production technology. Whereas, as we have seen earlier, the *Journal* was so enthusiastic about colour that it employed its own method of printing full-colour covers of the highest quality at the highest speeds on machines that cost $800,000,[31] George Horace Lorimer, the editor of the *Post*, ignored such possibilities. The *Post* ran a second colour on its cover and that was it. Right up until the mid-twenties such gaudy extravagance was excluded from the editorial pages of his weekly. He ran a series on thrift in his magazine.

In fact, if one disentangles one's observations from the nostalgia that envelopes so many of the commentaries on the *Post* and looks at it afresh, one comes to recognise a very individual, almost strange periodical. For a weekly it assumed a very idiosyncratic editorial profile. Over 80% of its editorial page space in 1910 was given over to just three categories of information: fiction, business and public affairs, with the weight very firmly on the first. This went very much against the grain for a weekly at the time. For instance, whereas *Collier's* in 1910 was displaying an enormous interest in politics, that curiosity also extended to a whole range of material in contemporary society. Fiction in *Collier's* was contained at 14% of the

Fig. 26 George Lorimer's inflexible preference for wash drawings meant that, while he was editor, the Post ran little else as illustrations. By 1910, most other editors were using photographs in conjunction with articles and artwork with fiction.

editorial space(see Appendices VI and XVII). Comparing their graphics, 76.53% of all reproductions in *Collier's* were from photographic originals. In the *Post*, in 1910, in volume 182, the comparable figure was only 20.37%. Thus, not only was the *Post* committed to a very particular editorial profile; its appearance was also quite particular.

By 1910 most magazines used artwork to illustrate fiction and verse, with photographs linked to factual articles. This course was not followed at the *Post*. Although photographs were used to punctuate documentary writing, in many instances wash drawings were used to illustrate the various points. For example, in the edition of 12 February 1910, pages 11 and 12 of the *Post* feature a piece of fiction, 'The Boom in Spooks' by Ellis Butler, illustrated by the drawings of Mary Wilson Preston. The following pages, 13 to 15, are given over to an article entitled 'Grant - The Death Watch', subtitled, 'How the Press Reports the Death of a Great Man' by Frank Mack and illustrated with five wash drawings by H.C. Wall.(Fig. 26) The article is followed by two pages of a serial, 'A Circuit Rider's Wife', also illustrated in a similar manner.(Fig. 27) As can be realised, when leafing through the magazine it becomes very difficult to 'read' the visual syntax of the layouts, to differentiate the articles from the fiction, a refinement already used by most magazines of the period and part of the accepted syntax of magazine design by 1910.

Lorimer's approach created great visual homogeneity, which is another way of saying that the *Saturday Evening Post* of 1910 was rather dreary. As the *Post* was printed on a paper known

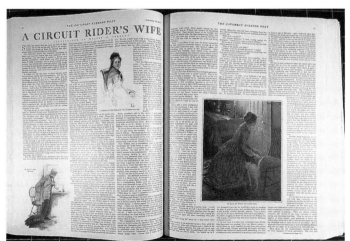

as mechanical printings, which 'is similar to newsprint but contains a higher proportion of chemical pulp,'[32] the ink colour, that is the black saturation, was poor relative to the quality achieved by a competitor such as *Collier's*, which

Fig. 27 This serial was among the most popular published by the Saturday Evening Post. But by using similar styles of illustration for every feature in every issue, articles and stories are homogenized into an indistinguishable mix.

used a much better imitation art paper. Together, these two elements, the style of illustration and the paper surface, created a grey, dull appearance in the *Post*. An alternative would have been to use more line illustrations, but these were even less popular with Lorimer than photographs. In volume 182, only 38 were used out of 869 reproductions, or 4.6%. *Collier's Weekly*, on the other hand, used 138 in volume 45, between March to September 1910, out of 980 blocks in total, or 15%. And the latter was a magazine that already possessed the advantage of a better paper.

So, one is entitled to ask, if the *Post* was so unattractive compared to such a rival, why did it sell about 2.5 times as many copies a week, 1.25 million instead of 500,000 ? For the answer to that question we have to return to a point made in Chapter 1, as well as examine further the contents of the *Post*.

The latter devoted 17% of its editorial space in 1910 to articles on business and economics(see Appendix XVII). Surprisingly, considering Lorimer's youthful success in big business, working for the giant meat packing company of P. D. Armour,[33] the *Post* did not dwell on the glories of the big companies. Many more articles were published on how to run a farm profitably. The 26 March issue, for instance, included one on the California Fruit Growers Exchange, a co-operative. The next week it was 'America's Greatest Feeding Farm'; then it was the turn of 'Does the Farmer Get His Share ?'

Now, although the farm population as a percentage of the total population was in decline, from 41.9% in 1900 to 34.9% in 1910, in absolute numbers the farm population was reaching its zenith. In 1910 the total of residents of agricultural land reached 32,077,000.[34] Thus, it was a useful constituency to cultivate, particularly as it was ignored by most of the other large circulation serials. Furthermore, although no figures are available prior to 1920 for the estimated annual movement of the farm population, it is possible to pinpoint the tides of migration from the farming states in the census data. This indicates that in the mid-west, such states as Iowa, Missouri and Indiana were experiencing some powerful tides of migration from their native white population during the period 1890–1910, particularly during the second decade. And, while numbers of these people must have moved to other less crowded rural territories, equally, a large proportion must have moved into the towns and cities, for the US population in urban areas grew from 22,106,000 in 1890 to 41,999,000 in 1910. Of these, while the giant conurbations expanded, so did the small towns. Between 1890 and 1910 the population of the United States housed in towns of between 2,500 and 50,000 population grew from 10,381,000 to 17,517,000.[35] For these first generation urbanites, such articles would have been a touchstone in an alien world. Furthermore, one does not have to read many articles in the *Post* to realise its intense conservatism.

'A New Kind of Organised Labor' by Henry Hyde in the 8 January issue in 1910 eulogised a former union boss who had been hired by the railroad owners to fight any future action by legislators. No mention was made that these 'legislators' were the democratically elected representatives of the people. 'Safety as a Good Investment' in the issue of 26 March emphasized that the best reason to take care of your workers was that it saved money. Europe also got short shrift. Under the title 'Tenderfoot Tourists' is an illustration that is captioned 'They offer you dirty oranges, faded flowers, tattered postal cards.' In other words, the text and the graphics were pulling together in one direction: a glorification of the values and bigotry of small town America.

As the readership was growing by leaps and bounds, it is clear that the large number who took up regular readership did so because they found these sentiments congenial. Again, we return to a point made in Chapter 1, a free agent will chose consonance rather than dissonance as a consequence of his or her actions, particularly if it means spending money and then reading the product every week. Thus, the readership of the *Post* seems not to have been looking for stimulation or novelty, particularly the sort offered by *Collier's* with all that aggressive challenging of authority. They were looking for reassurance and safety. They bought the *Post* in such large numbers because theirs was a large constituency. They wanted emotional balm in their rapidly changing world and George Lorimer gave it to them.

Clearly, the same could not be said of *Collier's Weekly*, which developed considerably through the first decade of the century to the point where Frank Mott could write, 'Few periodicals in America have exerted, over any decade, as strong and direct an influence on national affairs as that of *Collier's* during the Hapgood regime'.[36]

Norman Hapgood had been hired by Robert Collier in 1902,[37] primarily to add an air of culture and respectability to the editorials.[38] However, as his political position deepened in sophistication and awareness, he became more active in the conduct of the magazine. Although *Collier's* was quite definitely in Theodore Roosevelt's corner, Hapgood accused him of stirring up racial tension in the 1904 presidential campaign. Furthermore, later that year, Collier and Hapgood discovered that Roosevelt had been working in secret to undermine the campaign of another progressive but a Democrat, Joseph Folk, who was running for the post of governor in Missouri. As Hapgood was one of Folk's fans, it required a great deal of persuasion by Collier and correspondence with the President to avert what could have been a damaging attack by Hapgood in an editorial.[39]

Then, the following year, Hapgood's spine was further stiffened by a conflict with another magazine, *Town Topics*. This was a scandal sheet that was undoubtedly allowing itself to be bought off rather than run stories about New York's rich and famous. The opening salvo concerned some smutty allegations about the behaviour of the President's daughter. Despite some strong words by Hapgood, the owner of *Topics*, Colonel Mann, failed to take the bait. However, in August 1905, Hapgood linked the rag with Judge Joseph Deuel. The latter instituted criminal libel proceedings and Hapgood was arrested. The subsequent trial and acquittal put Hapgood and *Collier's* on the front page of the New York newspapers and the publicity gave the weekly an extraordinary platform from which to work in the ensuing years.[40]

In 1906 the magazine hired Mark Sullivan, who had formerly worked on campaigns for the *Ladies' Home Journal*. He contributed the column 'Comment on Congress' and was soon embroiled in a successful attack(Fig. 28) on the

Fig.28 In the first decade of the 20th century, Collier's achieved more political influence than any American magazine before or since. Their campaigns helped to curtail the power of the Speaker of the House and brought down a member of the cabinet.

Sunset

ALDRICH AND HALE: *"Come on, Joe, the day is done—it's time to go home"*

DRAWN BY F. G. COOPER

Speaker of the House of Representatives who, at that time, appointed the members of committees. This opportunity for exercising undue influence was neutralised amid cries of foul from the Speaker's supporters.[41]

Finally, in 1909–10, the Ballinger controversy broke and *Collier's* was up to its neck in a fight which brought the downfall of a government minister. Richard Ballinger was the Secretary of the Interior and amid growing rumours, *Collier's* published an editorial in August 1909 calling for his resignation. Then, on 13 November, they published an article by a former General Land Office investigator, Louis Glavis, alleging fraud. In the subsequent Congressional hearings, *Collier's*, to protect itself, employed a young lawyer, Louis Brandeis, whose skill dominated the proceedings and brought the downfall of the Secretary who, despite being vindicated by his friends on the committee, resigned.[42]

Thus, it is not surprising that *Collier's* devoted more space to public affairs than any other topic in 1910. The old preoccupation with foreign wars had long since diminished. Now, current events were allocated their own well-illustrated, usually four-page section at the front of each issue. The interest in sport was still flourishing, though the focus seemed to have moved up the social register a little. Overall, the interest in foreign stories seemed to have diminished very noticeably (see Appendix VI).

Where the magazine had made great improvements was in its art direction. Some of its covers must rank among the most elegant pieces of graphic design ever wrapped round a magazine. (Plate VII) Unlike the *Post*, they made very stylish use of colour, with a subtle employment of two, three and four-colour designs. Inside, *Collier's* was also bold enough to use a drawing full-page, as on 13 August, when one of Gibson's girls faced the editorial page, or on 7 May, when a vivid cartoon was printed to wish farewell to Joe Cannon, the Speaker of the House that they had vanquished. (Fig. 28) Not infrequently, this prime spot was filled by a full-colour reproduction of a painting by Frederic Remington, 17 September, or a Maxfield Parrish, 23 July. Altogether four-colour reproductions were used inside on 11 occasions, three-colour 29 times and two-colour 15 times in the volume which was examined.

These technical resources were also employed by the advertisers on occasion. Of particular notice were some examples featuring evocative paintings by William Hornden Foster of Oldsmobiles. Such inserts cost the manufacturer $2,200 a page. The regular price for monochrome was $1,600. So, with 383.72 pages of paid insertions in volume 48, the half year from March to September 1910 probably brought in over $600,000 of advertising, or about $1.25 million gross for the full year. It was not quite in the *Post's* class, but then it was not to be sniffed at either. At 10¢ a copy or $5.50 a year, the company's share of the cover price on a claimed circulation of 500,000 a week came to a tidy sum as well.[43]

McClure's business department was also extremely successful in soliciting advertising for the monthly, particularly in the years before the turn of the century. However, by 1910 someone had put the cake out in the rain. McClure might have been a great if neurotic editor but he was no master of finance and during the first few years of the new century the profit and loss account started to stray into the red.[44] However, by 1910, counts of the total numbers of advertisements per volume jettisoned. For that reason, for the moment at least, a reasonably accurate estimate of the magazine's advertising volume presents problems.

In two respects, the appearance of *McClure's* had changed over the decade. The three colour covers, displaying its 15¢ price, were marginally more attractive than their predecessors of 1900. In addition, photographs had come to play a far more prominent role on the magazine's pages at 49% of all reproductions used. However, the frequency of the use of illustrations had dropped over the decade, from 0.62 per page to 0.54. In part that was because the reader was getting more pages; 118.5 per issue on average, as opposed to 95 ten years previously. Yet, these statistics cannot reveal the convulsions that had hit the magazine half way through the decade; changes which had affected another of our subjects in its turn.

There can be little doubt, given the situation revealed in Peter Lyon's biography, that Sam McClure was a man of considerable nervous energy who stimulated his staff.[45] Equally, unless they knew how to put his suggestions into perspective and adopt a philosophic attitude, McClure's disposition was capable of over-exciting them. As we have seen, by 1900 *McClure's Magazine* had already achieved great success with the public and a very individual editorial profile. Always seeking novelty, the owner had also gathered on to his staff a very fine squad of journalists.[46] Then, in 1899, a catalyst in the form of John Houston Finley joined them. At 28 years old, Finley had been the youngest college president in the country, that of Knox College, McClure's alma mater. Offered the editorship of *Harper's Weekly* when McClure was involved in J. P. Morgan's first attempt to revive the old publishing house, Finley remained in the *McClure's* office after that bid collapsed. From his strong connections with charity workers throughout the country, he put the staff into contact with such reformers as Jane Addams, Albert Beveridge and Robert La Follette. Then, after attending the Trust Convention held in Chicago in September 1899, Finley proposed an article on the business combinations to McClure. Already, a less respected journalist, Maurice Low, had suggested such a series in the spring of that year. However, it was not until two years later that the idea finally crystallised in McClure's mind, while he was taking an extended rest period in Europe as a consequence of overwork. As a result, in September 1901, Ida Tarbell, a senior and respected member of the magazine's staff, began the research that led to an in-depth series on the rise of Standard Oil. The first part appeared in November 1902.

About the same time, another of the fine journalists that McClure had gathered together, Lincoln Steffens, after a tour through the mid-West, came across a story about attempts to stem political corruption in St Louis, being led among others, by the then unknown Joseph Folk, who was the circuit attorney for the St Louis area. That was published in October 1902. Then, the magazine's art director, August Jaccaci, saw a news items about political corruption in Minneapolis. The article that arose out of this lead, which was published in January 1903, 'The Shame of Minneapolis' was the first of a series, 'The Shame of the Cities'. Alongside this appeared the first of yet another series, this time written by Ray Stannard Baker, attacking the power of the unions. Thus, in January 1903, with a resounding journalistic bang and an editorial comment by McClure, one of America's largest selling magazines attacked corporate corruption, municipal corruption and the power of labour in one issue. Yet, these were not rhetorical forays. They were extensively researched articles.[47]

But, despite this editorial thunderclap, no substantial increase in circulation resulted. In 1902 sales amounted to 364,629, on average, and 371,398 in 1903.[48] Yet, such stasis is not altogether surprising. Journalistic coups may excite historians but they do not necessarily stimulate sales, unless, perhaps, the prospective readers feel a degree of curiosity or apprehension. The pump still has to be primed by promotion. So, the one magazine which did benefit from an exposé was the one that exploited its revelations to the hilt. Even more interesting, neither Chesman nor Ayer printed audited figures from McClure after 1903, but just reported a statement that the company guaranteed a circulation of 414,000 per month.[49] This is not surprising as a contemporary letter reveals that they were overprinting by forty to sixty thousand copies per month to justify their guarantee.[50]

In the three years that followed, the staff continued to churn out their indictments of American society. Then, in 1906, McClure returned energised from another European sojourn.

However, unlike his 1901 excursion, the consequences this time were destructive rather than constructive. The staff grew anxious and over-excited. In fact, in the face of a grandiose scheme, John Phillips, McClure's shrewd business partner, and Ida Tarbell, who both had stock in the magazine company, saw ruin riding energetically towards them. If McClure's scheme failed, as seemed very likely, for it was full of unrealistic expectations, their current stock, their nest eggs, might well become worthless. Unfortunately, McClure had the bit between his teeth and would not be dissuaded.[51] So, Tarbell, Baker and Steffens decamped, with Phillips and others on the magazine's staff, to buy *The American Magazine*, which was the new name of *Frank Leslie's Popular Monthly*, of which more anon.

So, with the second half of the decade well underway, *McClure's* had a steady sale, thin profits and no journalists. Though the owner managed to replace his writers, the obligations that he was forced to assume in the course of buying out his former staff seriously compromised him financially and, by 1910, the company was in trouble. He was not helped by a fall in advertising revenue consequent on the depression of 1907. Not surprisingly, in 1911 Sam McClure finally lost control of the company that bore his name.[52]

Yet, despite all these dramas, the hand of the editor was still apparent in the editorial profile of 1910. As in 1900, large areas of subject matter were excluded completely. Ironically, one of the subjects that *McClure's* had ignored in 1900 had been social problems. Now, of course, they took a fat 11%(see Appendix III). Whereas in 1900 much space had been devoted to the retelling of the life of a well known religious figure, now the biographical detail concerned the individual royal families of Europe, recounted by a member of the French *Sûreté*.

Unlike Collier and Hapgood, Sam McClure did not espouse a particular political position. Unlike their weekly, his monthly followed no politician on his regal progress. For example, page after page of volume 45 of *Collier's* was filled with stories about Theodore Roosevelt; a partisanship that McClure avoided. Instead, McClure was a brilliant editor and judge of talent who sought the latest story. He was a supernova that all too soon burned out. Yet, the afterglow was reflected in the eyes of other editors and almost all of the large circulation magazines were affected in one way or another, even the *Post*, which staunchly defended the status quo. For a decade, having a cause was believed to be good business.

In fact, only *Everybody's Magazine* successfully exploited a scandal to its own advantage. Begun in 1899 by the New York branch of the John Wannamaker department store, which had its headquarters in Philadelphia, the magazine had an audited average circulation of 159,455 per month by 1902.[53] In 1903, Robert Ogden, who oversaw the publication as Wannamaker's New York partner, was retiring and he sold the magazine to a partnership of Erman Ridgway, who had been one of the Munsey staff, and John Thayer, who had worked briefly for Munsey as well, though he had spent his time most profitably as advertising manager on the *Ladies' Home Journal* and, later, *The Delineator*. His boss in the latter organisation, George Wilder, made a number of clever suggestions for financing the venture and they were in business.[54] In fact, it was Wilder who came up with the idea that they should approach Thomas Lawson, a prominent stock market speculator from Boston, but it was John Cosgrave, the magazine's editor, who persuaded the financier to go on the record.[55] The serial, 'Frenzied Finance', began in July 1904 and was promoted to the tune of $50,000 by the owners. The effect of their skilful advertising was to unleash an intense interest on the part of the public in the scandal that was to be revealed and the circulation soared. While the serial lasted, sales moved between 750,000 and one million, and even after it finished they settled at a much higher level than hitherto.[56] By 1910, *Everybody's* was claiming a circulation of 500,000 but it is noticeable that no audited accounts were being supplied.[57] It was at this point that the original partners took their opportunity and sold out to Butterick for $3 million, which was 40 times what they had paid for the magazine in 1903.[58]

By 1910, there is nothing to really differentiate *Everybody's* from the rest of its class. Like most of the prominent mixed function monthlies of the period, a renewed interest in fiction was coupled with a continuing interest in contemporary society. With the exception of the theatre, which featured prominently during 1910 in most American magazines under discussion, any interest in the arts was purely cursory. Only its lack of interest in the past distinguished *Everybody's* from its peers(see Appendix X) Compared to material published elsewhere, critical investigative journalism was by now fairly thin on the page. An article in the February issue on Henry Flagler, the developer who changed the face of Florida, veered vaguely towards eulogy. Their article on the Insurgents, the political shock troops of their day in the Senate, lacked the force of the material in *Collier's*; in part because Hapgood and his staff had learned how to use illustrations, graphic design and cartoons to reinforce their arguments. The autobiography of Judge Ben Lindsey, 'The Beast and the Jungle', that was serialised through 1909 and 1910 in *Everybody's*, dealt with events at some distance and lacked immediacy, even if it did concern itself with the corruption of public life.

Cosmopolitan had also been affected by the mode for investigative journalism. But as it was now owned by Hearst rather than John Walker, as in 1900, its style of presentation was no longer what it was. The appearance of the magazine was entirely coloured by the extensive use of elaborate collages of photographs that frequently crossed the line that separated the eye-catching from the ridiculous. This was particularly true of their coverage of the theatre, where publicity photographs, whether portraits or views of scenes, were easily acquired without cost to the publisher. Furthermore, the editor, C. P. Narcross, was not averse to stretching a point to attract the reader's attention. In the October 1910 issue, one finds, opposite the title page of 'The Gray Brotherhood of Infamy' by 'Ex-Convict Number 7654', not itself the most restrained heading, a picture of a rather intimidating character in a boldly striped suit that extended from the top to the bottom of the page, with the text enclosing him on both sides. Inferior to the picture, a caption points out that such clothing was no longer worn. As the text claims to be an inside account of current prison life, the use of such a picture is completely inappropriate, except, that is, as an attention claimer.

A month earlier, the leading article had been entitled 'The Shame of Our Army' and subtitled, 'Why Fifty Thousand Enlisted American Soldiers Have Deserted.' Yet, beneath that was a quotation from the United States Army's Adjutant-General which stated, 'That there should have been nearly five thousand desertions from the army of the United States during the last fiscal year is simply a disgrace.' It is only as one continues reading that one discovers that the larger figure in the headline had been concocted from the totals of 12 years. So, although this is a situation worth comment, the headline does seem to be stretching a point. Furthermore, unlike the work of *Collier's* and *McClure's*, this is not a situation in which those responsible had been hiding their malign talents. It was the Adjutant-General who blew the whistle.

This issue of *Cosmopolitan* is one of the last popular representatives of the magazine format which came to prominence with the launch of *Harper's Monthly* in 1850. Although its pages include elaborate layouts of photographs which were impossible before the arrival of the half-tone plate, the overall organisation of the articles follows a pattern which had been familiar for 70 years. During the next decade, Lorimer's innovations at the *Post* influenced many of the best-selling weeklies and monthlies and the idea of running an article from start to finish on a contiguous set of pages took a back seat until the *Reader's Digest* and *Life* provided a successful

Fig.29 With a new owner and editor, Cosmopolitan looked very different in 1910. Elaborately laid out patterns of photographs were featured in every issue.

alternative to the *Post* in the 1930s. One reason why *Cosmopolitan* could still maintain the old pattern was that, like most of the other mixed function monthlies of the time, it segregated advertising from editorial, restricting it to the end of the issue, which allowed the staff to organise the contents as they wished.

As already mentioned, the first article for September opens on page 411: 'The Shame of Our Army'. However, the four pages which precede it are used for a two page homily on decadence and two tasters of things to come later in the issue. The piece on desertion and its roots in the current military culture in America is extensively illustrated with photographs. Most of them describe monotonous and uncongenial tasks typical of the peacetime establishment. The captions in five–point capitals return again and again to the theme that enlisted men are being alienated by the unsoldierly tasks which are their daily lot. Eight out of the ten pages feature two or more photographs which are frequently arranged in elaborate patterns. Those on pages 414 and 415, for example, have been cropped and laid out so that the overall shape resembles a medal.

The following ten-page short story, about 'love in the frozen north', is punctuated by three wash drawings, all on separate spreads. They are used to illustrate moments in the story and they remain unobtrusive and very unlike the layouts of reproductions of photographs. These populist rococo photo-layouts resume with the next article, which starts on page 431. The title, 'Not Enough Babies to go Around by Arno Dosch', is set in various styles and sizes of type up to 58–point and surrounded by a circle formed by the disembodied heads of 22 small children.

Two of the layouts on the following four spreads feature elaborate patterns of photographs. The next feature, a regular biographical one called 'Worth While People', is heavily dependent on photographic portraits. The two photographs used in the opening spread fill the top two thirds of the page while a biographical resumé of each of the two subjects fills the rest. Unusually for the time, the title is inset on one of the portraits and reversed out into white using a decorative serif type face of the period in 40–point. The second half of the feature is a selection of ten portraits of 'personalities' of the moment accompanied by brief captions introducing the individuals. Each picture has a three-line border which separates it from its neighbours and avoids visual confusion, particularly when the images overlap. The five photographs on each page are laid out in identical symmetrical patterns.(Fig. 29)

The following six pages are devoted to the American short story writer O' Henry, who had just died while writing a story destined for *Cosmopolitan*. Even here, a formal portrait of the author is cropped to an almost square oblong and combined with a profile of his sister in an oval frame. Beneath the pair her signature is reproduced. All three reproductions are laid out in a pattern symmetrical about the centre line of the page and slightly overlapping to combine in an odd shape. Again, this approach is abandoned at the start of the next short story on page 450. The first four spreads of the ten-page piece each feature one drawing laid out in a restrained manner. The illustrations are drawn with vertical lines which increase in number and proximity to one another to gain ink density to render shadows. The typographic design is very traditional with the text laid out in two columns. The only embellishment is an illustrated capital at the very start. At the end, the story is 70 mm shy of the bottom of page 459; so a poem is added to fill the space. Like most other American monthlies, *Cosmopolitan* had learned from *Century Illustrated* that to start a piece with a bold title at the top of a fresh page improved the clarity of the presentation.

This pattern of elaborately laid out non-fiction alternating with conservatively designed short stories continues almost up until the end of the book. The only major exception is a seven-page all picture section called 'Players at Play', which is an entirely photographic feature based on publicity shots of theatre people. The layouts all include numbers of images montaged together. This is a feature found in every issue. The minor exceptions to this visual extravagance are two two-page regulars, 'The Story-Tellers' Club' and 'Magazine Shop-Talk' which ended every issue. The former injects a touch of humour, which is enhanced by illustrating the stories with photographic caricatures: the heads of famous people montaged on to hand-drawn bodies which are far too small. The second item is little more than letters pages with nothing more elaborate than drawn enhancements to the title to enliven the layout.

These examples, when added to such articles from the October issue as 'The Theft of the Panama Canal' and the extensive serialisation of the autobiography of the malevolent Mexican President Porfirio Diaz, coupled with such enticing short stories as 'The Rape of the Beau', gave *Cosmopolitan* a rather tawdry air. Yet, with an audited average sale of 458,400 for the first six months of 1910, it clearly had a public. It was an example of one route down which investigative journalism could so easily pass: the back alley of populism.

Another path was taken by *The American Magazine*, the reborn version of *Frank Leslie's Popular Monthly*. Bought by the *McClure's* defectors in 1906, it had been edited for the six previous years by Ellery Sedgwick under the aegis of Frederic Colver, who had gained control of the Leslie empire from the widow. (Sedgwick later went on to buy and revive the *Atlantic Monthly*.) By September 1905, even the Leslie name had been expunged from the parent company and the magazine.[59] It had been retitled the *American Illustrated Magazine*. Another revision occurred in May 1906 when '*American Magazine*' appeared on the cover. The new name was found on the contents page the following month. It is interesting to note that *The Brooklyn Magazine*, which had been a joint venture between Colver and the very young Edward Bok in the 1880s had changed its name to *The American Magazine* in May 1887. In the September 1906 issue, the new ownership was announced, which, as the formes had closed at the end of July, meant that the deal had already been finalised by mid summer. A more detailed announcement led the October issue. It was couched in the usual rhetoric of such moments. Portraits of the new editorial team, known from their exploits at *McClure's* for their attacks on the rich and powerful, were prominently displayed.

Yet, for all that, the analysis of volume 70, for May to October 1910, reveals, ironically, an editorial balance broadly similar to that revealed in volume 50, of ten years earlier, when it had first come under Sedgwick's control.[60] However, within those broad strokes there were some differences. The minimal interest in the arts had diminished further during the decade, with the exception, of course, of the theatre which, as in all the other American magazines of the time, was utilising significant amounts of space; in this case over 11%. The space devoted to fiction was fairly similar in both volumes. There was no interest in science or technology at all. But the real change lay in the way that contemporary society, both at home and abroad was treated. As has been noted before, *Leslie's* had always been interested in the manners and social customs of the time, particularly in foreign parts. In its new guise as *The American Magazine*, it was not. It preferred home politics and public affairs, which is hardly unexpected(see Appendix IV). Perhaps a little more surprising is the devotion to sport, particularly baseball, which was discussed with diagrams, sophistication and in detail by Hugh Fullerton during May, June and July. As the subject had been absent from *Leslie's* and *McClure's* in the volumes examined, the interest was presumably a contribution of the new staff, at least those that remained. By 1910, Lincoln Steffens, William Allen White and Finlay Peter Dunne, all of whom had merited a large reproduction of their individual portraits and a biographic note in October 1906 when the magazine changed hands, had now left.[61] Yet, *The American* still carried a bark, even if it was heard less frequently. Ray Baker could still attack municipal corruption in Rochester, New York and show how it had been vanquished.[62] Ida Tarbell was emphasizing the inequities of trade tariffs.[63] However, perhaps most pointedly, while *Cosmopolitan* was allowing Diaz to eulogise himself, *The American* was laying bare the depravities of his regime in the series 'Barbarous Mexico.'

Yet, as with *McClure's*, none of this made too much difference to the circulation figures. The previous ownership had claimed that sales exceeded 250,000. The Phillips group immediately submitted audited accounts which substantiated sales of 280,000 for the first nine months of their control. But by 1909, the circulation was still only 285,145. During the next year it hiccuped upward a little to 315,292. This emphasizes yet again that any publisher must promote his magazine effectively to increase sales. They are rarely self-generating, no matter what the quality of the magazine and its staff.[64]

In the opening decade of the twentieth century, one successful mixed function magazine did largely ignore the fashion for the critical pursuit of those in power. Where *McClure's* had devoted a considerable amount of Ida Tarbell's time and a matching volume of editorial space to an indictment of Standard Oil, *Munsey's* eulogised the use to which the ill-gotten gains were put in an article on the Rockefeller Foundation.[65] Where most periodicals of the time, excepting the *Post*, were at least suspicious of the big corporations and their leaders, *Munsey's* ran an article on the successful sons of rich men.[66] Yet, even this monthly apologist could not avoid all mention of corporate abuses at this time and in their September number led with an article on the public service commission of New York.

Over the decade, the circulation of *Munsey's* had slipped from 625,166 in 1900,[67] to 501,580.[68] According to Mott, there was a move to counter this slow decline in 1905–1906 with better printing, a little colour and some more expensive authors, but the result was only temporary.[69] The audience had been generated by being the first general interest monthly to drop to a 10¢ cover price. With little else to recommend it, it was hardly surprising that its circulation gradually leaked away when other publishers dropped their price as well. Equally predictable was its dedication to this price at a time when most of its competitors had increased theirs to 15¢ a month, even if they had held the yearly subscription to $1.

However, something had to give somewhere in the budget and the decline in the use of illustrations in *Munsey's* is very noticeable. From a total of 678 illustrative blocks in volume 23, which gave a frequency of 0.79 per page, it fell to 0.32 per page or only 275 reproductions among 865.38 editorial pages. The number of photographs reproduced fell even more, from 516 in volume 23 to 160 in volume 43. That was where the savings were effected.

Money was not a problem for the Curtis organisation. On 1 September 1910 the *Ladies' Home Journal* began to be published twice a month. In the 15 issues produced between December 1909 and the end of November 1910, the 1239 pages available to both editorial and advertising contained 490.13 pages of paid insertions. At $5,000 per page for all those issues published on the first of the month and $4,000 per page for the three published on the fifteenth of the month, with $7,000 and $5,000 for the respective back covers, the *Journal* was generating about $2.5 million in gross advertising revenue per annum.[70]

Part of this revenue was invested in illustrations. In just over 742 editorial pages, almost 3,200 illustrative figures were used, which works out at 4.31 per page, a peak from which even the *Journal* slipped in the years to come. Of these, 42.65%, or 1366 were photographs, while 506, or 16%, were printed from line blocks, a graphic approach totally alien to its fellow publication in the Curtis stable, the *Post*. In addition, 143 full colour illustrations were used in this volume; a new high for American magazines of the time.

Yet, as the *Journal* grew fatter, Bok, still the editor after 20 years, was expanding its coverage of fashion and domestic issues, which is might be expected from an enthusiast for consumption, even if he was also keen on civic causes in the 1890s, long before others had dipped their toes in the water of confrontation. Throughout the first decade of the century he continued to promote better domestic architecture and a clean up America campaign. He attacked patent medicines for their alcoholic content and processed food for the impurities that were allowed to remain. Yet, it was fashion that grew to be the largest single topic in the monthly, at almost 22% of the editorial space in 1910. This was followed by fiction at 16% and domestic themes at close to 15% (see Appendix XI)

However, this emphasis is not immediately apparent when an issue is opened. Taking the August 1910 edition for example, the main editorial sequence starts on page four with a single page short story and a full page drawing of a young woman playing a violin facing it. The two are unrelated because the drawing by Harrison Fisher is reproduced for its own sake and presented as a fine piece of art. A patterned border frames the drawing, while the story's title is also enclosed in a box of artwork. An illuminated drop capital starts the story and the body of text is broken up by using small pieces of line-work representing an oak leaf and acorn to start different sections. The titles on both pages are set in 36–point capitals with the name of the artist and the writer in 24–point capitals. That typographic style is adhered to until page 16 and seems to be used to define the first section of the issue, which is a mixture of articles and fiction. Although the *Journal* is printed on heavy imitation art paper, the print colour is dark grey rather than the black which could have been achieved.

The second spread in the first section features two articles: 'How Long Do Animals Live?' and 'Will You Be My Husband? : How Queens Have Proposed Marriage.' The first is not illustrated, although the title is boxed in a patterned frame. The second includes a wash drawing, which purports to represent the moment after Victoria had proposed to Albert, and a view of a balcony overlooking a broad bay with a couple deep in conversation. The latter is positioned bottom left with an irregular outline around which the text is wrapped. The Victorian conversation piece is situated top right and uses just over 25% of the printed page so that the text flows between the two pieces of artwork.

The next double spread is occupied by two pieces of fiction. The oak leaf motif is used again to leaven the mass of type on both stories. The second story continues overleaf on page ten where it is faced by an article: 'Why And How Girls Should Swim'. This is enclosed in another elaborate border and illustrated by two reproductions of photographs of Annette Kellerman, the long-distance Australian swimmer who wrote the piece. In neither is she seen in the water. Instead she is posed enclosed from sole to chin in a dark one-piece garment and described as preparing to dive.

The fifth spread is composed of a story on the left and an article on the right. The former is devoid of illustrations, although the leaf motif is used again to punctuate the page. The second article, entitled 'How I Taught Flies to Do Tricks', is illustrated with macrophotographs of flies performing and photomicrographs of parts of their bodies. The next spread is less bizarre. Its only illustration is a wash drawing in a decorative oval frame which illuminates a moment in 'the love story of a country doctor'.

The first section comes to a halt overleaf on page 17 where a column of advertising accompanies 'How to be Comfortable in a Tent'; the first of a sequence of short practical articles. It is illustrated with six small line drawings, while the title is set in upper and lower case. Two similar articles follow, one of which is illustrated with photographs. But the sequence is interrupted on page 19 where drawings of two Chinese children and their different clothes have been printed in full colour on much heavier paper so that they can be cut out and used as toys.

The next section is largely photographic and shows many examples of needlework with only captions to explain the significance of the various items. Two of the three pages include advertising. Pages 25 to 27 are devoted to drawings and scale plans of three houses which the readers could build. Fourteen photographs of suburban houses around Chicago fill the centre spread. Interestingly, although a number are clearly influenced by the example of Frank Lloyd Wright, none is designed by him although, of course, much of his finest early work had been built in the area during the preceding decade.

The following 14 pages are largely about making things for the home, cookery or the tail ends of items from the opening section. They thread between more and more columns sold to advertisers and the impression is created that end of the issue is nigh. But editorial material suddenly blossoms again with three photographic features on cross-stitching, tatting and knitting. Seven pages of drawings follow illustrating clothing which can be made up from the paper patterns published by a subsidiary of the *Journal*. Then, with a half page article on fabrics, the issue does end. This last small layout is unusual for the magazine because cross-heads are used to announce different themes.

Interestingly, although photography is used extensively in this issue it does not dominate, which might have been expected given Bok's enthusiastic use of photo-mechanical reproduction in the 1890s, as seen in Chapter 3. He does not use it to introduce a wider world; to describe the role of women in other societies around the world for example. Instead it is used to illustrate domestic features. Rather than the obviously posed studio shots included in the page on swimming, a sequence demonstrating different strokes might have been used. Only the rather bizarre piece on flies demonstrates some of the potential inherent in photographic reproductions in magazines.

Overall, one almost senses from the way Bok organised each issue that he wanted to distance himself from what he was doing: purveying trivia when he knew that more substantial matters merited his attention. Perhaps this was the editorial sugar he needed to sweeten the pill of these important matters for, sometimes, they could have a very bitter centre.

In January 1907, the largest selling magazine for women in the world did something that would cause any editor today to think twice. It published an article by Judge Ben Lindsay of the juvenile court of Denver entitled 'Why Girls Go Wrong.' It discussed child sexuality, not in terms of how they were abused by adults, the handle that would be used today, but how little girls were very inquisitive and so were little boys and that if their parents did not supply them with accurate information at an early age then the children would find out by practical experiment, as they were doing already. Furthermore, the author was careful to distance his remarks from any imputation that these were street kids. They were from 'good homes of the better class.'[71]

In fact, Bok had begun this campaign in a low key in an editorial in March 1906. Then, in March 1907 he ran another article, by Margaret Delane, about a pregnant 14-year-old who 'didn't know.' Editorial followed editorial, retailing in a discrete way the indiscretions of 13 and 14-year-olds. Then, letters were printed from teachers about the knowledge of 6 and 7-year-olds. There was clearly a danger that Pandora's box would never be closed again. By his own admission, considerable pressure was exerted on Bok and the magazine in an attempt to curtail their campaign for sex education. And, eventually, they did stop, but not before one or two public figures, such as the Bishop of London, had committed themselves in print on Bok's behalf. On the debit side they appear to have lost 75,000 subscribers, a very large number of cancellations on one topic.[72] All in all, it was probably tilting at windmills, but it was a brave try and it can merit consideration as one of the most courageous attempts to utilise the soap-box of mass circulation that the American magazines had created over the previous twenty years.

AFTER THE JOURNALISTIC DRAMAS which epitomised the American magazine market during the first decade of the twentieth century, the second seems like an anti-climax. Yet, that is to focus on only one aspect of editorial life: the enjoining, or opposing of liberal causes. In another aspect, that of sales, the second decade was more successful than the first. Whereas, by 1910, the most popular mixed function magazines had sales of around half a million, their successors of 1920 were doing business that at least doubled that. In addition, the restricted function and specialised magazines were all rising with the tide. In 1910, *Literary Digest*, which was, needless to say, not a literary but a news digest, was only claiming an estimated 235,000 circulation.[73] By 1920, the weekly had a sworn average circulation of 1,200,000.[74] At the same time, the *Woman's Home Companion* was selling 1,215,069 a month, and charging advertisers $6,800 a page for black and white or $10,000 for colour.[75] Even *Popular Mechanics* was selling 450,000 a month in the period after the First World War.[76] As disposable personal income rose substantially in the United States during this period, from an average annual amount of 26.4 billion during the period 1907–11 to 61 billion per annum in the period 1917–21, such increased sales are not surprising.[77] Even allowing for a rise in the retail price index between 1911 and 1921 from 132 to 246, the rise is still significant.[78]

Yet, if some periodicals were all aglow with success, others displayed a sadder, more pallid aspect. *The Century* was now down to 69,392 a month,[79] while its former rival for the top spot,

Harper's Monthly, was doing little better at 82,770.[80] And it was not just the respectable that could fall on hard times. *Munsey's Magazine* was down to 132,835 a month, from a peak of over 600,000.[81] Even those that seemed to be going with the flow frequently concealed a turbulent existence behind an equable facade.

Yet, the economic tide of the magazine trade was not merely diverting editorial directions, a more profound structural realignment was taking place. Whereas, in the late nineteenth century successful titles usually led a solitary editorial existence in the American market, now they were forming into family groups. The Curtis Company not only published the two most successful magazines in the world, they also produced a weekly farm publication, *The Country Gentleman*, which, in 1920, had a sworn average circulation of 638,514.[82] In 1910, The Crowell Publishing Company had one best seller, the *Woman's Home Companion*. By 1920 they owned *The American Magazine* and *Collier's Weekly* as well. The International Magazine Company, alias the Hearst organisation, owned *Cosmopolitan*, selling 1,330,350 a month in 1920, *Hearst's Magazine*, with 481,967 and *Good Housekeeping*, at 682,823 sales per month, amongst others.[83] And it was only a short while now before their apotheosis, the Luce organisation, would place its first offering before the public.

And in this era of corporate competition, increasing differentiation began to pay dividends. Where, in the nineteenth century, *Frank Leslie's Illustrated Newspaper* and *Harper's Weekly* were much alike, and *Puck* and *Judge* were largely differentiated by the political colour of their targets, there was no mistaking *Collier's* for the *Saturday Evening Post* or *Literary Digest* now, even if they sometimes copied each other's artwork. The increasing skills and experience of the contributing journalists were matched by the needs of the organisations that owned the titles.

As magazine publishing grew from a gentlemanly pursuit into a capital-intensive industry, editorial careers could grow and flourish within the spreading boundaries of magazine journalism and leading practitioners could be tempted from one title to another so that the editorial persona could be revised, if and when the publisher chose to do so. For, *Cosmopolitan* under John Brisben Walker in 1900, C. P. Narcross in 1910 and Ray Long in 1920 was quite different in each instance. Furthermore, as editorial skills grew in sophistication, resources and numbers, so did those of that newcomer, the art director. Yet, both had to curtail many of their own inclinations once the super-ego of their creation was established. In the world of corporate competition, a successful persona, once settled must needs be retained. The ambitions of those journalists who created it came a poor second in most cases. The profit sheet was the prime consideration.

That was no problem for the *Post*. George Horace Lorimer was the *Post* and the *Post* was George Horace Lorimer. He initialled all layouts and every illustration in each issue.[84] All manuscripts were initialled 'OK/GHL' or 'NO/GHL' in pencil and that was the end of all discussion.[85] Yet, despite his absolute control of the throttle, he allowed others to lubricate the mechanism. Every lunchtime was spent with his authors, allowing them to talk and air ideas. Once, invariably, and usually twice a day he would walk round the editorial floor talking to his readers, asking their opinions of the latest work to be submitted.[86] All of this was essential for, by the first six months of 1920 the *Post* was averaging over 192 pages a week and, in the process, consuming material at a prodigious rate.

Filling those pages, week in, week out, was solved in a very similar way in 1920 to that which had preceded it in 1910. The overall editorial balance was approximately the same, despite a three-fold increase in the size of the average edition. The emphasis at 57.5% of editorial space, was still on fiction. There was still a substantial interest in the world at large, even if it had diminished a little over the years, from 36% to 29%. However, those general numbers conceal an editorial shift and analysis supports the contention that Lorimer was an editor who was sensitive to the need for a magazine to evolve. Gone from the *Post* were the virtually serial examinations of successful farming practice. Down from 17% to 7.5% were articles about business in general. Down also, from over 13% to a little less than 8%, was the space given to public affairs. In their stead, perhaps surprisingly, was a growing interest in life abroad and social life and problems at home. If you wanted to discover something of the aftermath of the war, the devastation of Europe, and looked in the popular magazines for it, you could only discover that sort of story in the *Post* (see Appendix XVII).

Furthermore, if you wanted to read Scott Fitzgerald or Sinclair Lewis in 1920, you could also find them in the *Post*. Indeed, the publication of Fitzgerald only emphasizes the perspicacity of the *Post*'s talent spotting facility. *This Side of Paradise* was published in March 1920 and the author soared to instant stardom.[87] 'Myra Meets His Family', his first short story to appear in the *Post*, did so on March 20 of the same year. However, the *Post*'s production schedule at that time meant that planning took place nine weeks prior to publication and the pages were closed six weeks before.[88] Thus, the Fitzgerald story would have been selected by January and probably earlier. Therefore, their perfect timing and publication of his piece was initiated before they could have known of his public reception and preceded the initiation of any band wagon effect.

Yet, if the *Saturday Evening Post*'s editorial persona was changing, albeit in a subtle fashion, that was not true of its graphic identity. In 1920 it looked all too similar to its previous issues of ten years before. True, the use of photographic illustrations was increasing, from 20.4% of all reproductions in 1910 to 32.4% in 1920. But these were all but swamped by the over one thousand drab wash drawings that crowded the *Post*'s pages during the first half of 1920. The alternative of using line work that could be printed well on the *Post*'s choice of paper stock was less acceptable to Lorimer ten years on than it had been in 1910. During the first six months of 1920, the weekly used only 13 pieces of line work out of 1606 illustrative blocks, and some of those were the tiny tail pieces that sometimes decorated the end of an article. Even more stable was the cover style, which was either a two colour rendition of a sentimental genre scene that contained little detail beyond the main figures, or a two colour rendition of an attractive woman who exposed nothing more sensational than her teeth. The two colours were always dark grey and orange-red and they always bled into an off-white, featureless picture space. Even the appearance of Norman Rockwell's first *Post* cover on 20 May 1916 made no real difference. In fact, his work is entirely homogeneous with that which precedes and succeeds it. Only his awareness of the value of gesture seems even noteworthy at this time.

Yet, Lorimer clearly knew his audience and his definition of the editorial profile for, by the first half of 1920, the *Post* was selling 2,060,987 copies per week, on average, and was charging advertisers $7,000 a page to appear between its covers.[89] With over 2,970 pages of such material in six months, the *Post* was now taking something in excess of $40 million a year in gross advertising revenue; a fabulous sum compared to those figures that have been mentioned hitherto. Not surprisingly, there was little inclination to vary the formula, for the *Post*'s only rival to such success was the other major Curtis title, the *Ladies' Home Journal*. However, their story in 1920 was quite a different one.

The words that open volume 37 of the *Journal* are a farewell address by Edward Bok. He was now 56 and he had no intention of dying in harness. The last years of his editorship had been affected by the travails of war and the *Journal*'s contribution to the home front. Yet, the sales were still progressing steadily in an upward spiral and, by the decade's end, stood at 1,906,822 per month, the fortnightly publication experiment that had been tried out in 1910 having faded away in less than a year. To gain access to this audience, advertisers were prepared to pay $8,000 for an inside page or $15,000 for the back cover in four colours.[90] That suggests a total income from that source of well over $11 million gross for the year, given that it carried over 1400 pages of paid insertions in 1920.

The real problem for the owner, Cyrus Curtis, was to find a successor to Bok who could maintain the momentum built up over 30 years under one editor. He had a tough choice: select someone compliant who would follow the established pattern and back his predecessor's manner, or find a strong journalistic personality who would echo Bok's editorial vigour but totally redefine the *Journal's* identity. From what is evident in the *Journal* in 1920, it would seem that Curtis took the first option and followed the dictates of the profit sheet. From the results, one might suggest that the choice was a monumental flop.

The name of Harry Orville Davis appeared on the mast-head for just six months, though, as it took three months to get an issue to the public from the time the printing formes closed, his stay may have been a shorter one. The contrast with Bok could not have been much greater and Peterson's comment that 'Curtis had a rare faculty for choosing capable editors'[91] was not substantiated by this experience or by the years which followed. One eccentric idea that did emerge under the Davis regime was the employment of a designer to provide exclusive fashions for the readership. Despite the very obvious limitations that such an arrangement was likely to entail, his choice, Harry Collins, lasted a little longer than his original patron, though his work did not figure so prominently towards the end of 1920 as it did in February when he started.

Another shooting star associated with this year of turmoil was John Parker, the art director whose name on the mast-head was only preceded by that of the editor. For the first half of the year, elaboration was the style, with detailed and fanciful borders individually tailored to each layout. This was a tendency that existed in embryo in Bok's day, but what had then been latent now became manifest. Many of the details were rendered in soft grey and to get this effect the designs were reproduced by a halftone screen. The expense of such work and the time it must have taken to produce them clearly took their toll on Parker's job prospects. Equally as time consuming must have been one technique employed during the year on line illustrations. The drawings were overlaid with precisely cut tints so that a lens is necessary to distinguish the result from a halftone. Such practices were unlikely to have recommended themselves to the owner or to Edward Bok, who was still an active board member. Thus, it is no surprise to discover that Mr Parker's name was consigned to oblivion almost as quickly as his editor's. By the year's end, a different, unacknowledged hand was laying out crisply outlined illustrations.

Yet, despite these stylistic follies, there was no skimping on the numbers of illustrations used in the *Journal*. Where the number of blocks used by the *Post* per page had diminished to less than one per page, the *Journal* was still averaging 2.46. Of course, part of the reason for this density of images was the magazine's interest in clothes and domestic details. These were frequently arranged in composite drawings on a single page, to compress as much information as possible into a limited space. By 1920, the skill of the layout people was such that it is very difficult to separate the individual contributions and any assessment of the numbers of separate illustrative blocks used must necessarily be tentative.

Such layout conventions were very much the current style and were also to be found in such rivals as *Woman's World*, which was published in Chicago and aimed at the mid-western woman. Yet, even with that limited constituency, it sold 1,020,007 per month, on average, during the first half of 1920. However, its advertising revenues, with 280+ inside pages at $4,000 monochrome and 12 back covers in full colour at $6,500, plus plenty of inside colour at $5,500 per page,[92] were approximately $1,200,000 gross per annum; hardly a threat to the Curtis empire and an indicator of the latter's achievement.

Yet, for all its gloss and polish, the *Journal* had something to learn from the art direction of *Woman's World*. Apart from a central signature, the latter was printed on a cheap paper stock that made black an impossible dream and turned mid-grey into a variant of speckled mud in the illustrations, although it achieved good type colour. To counter this, *Woman's World* translated a small proportion of its artwork into halftones. Instead it used line blocks to render fashion drawings with crisp outlines. Tints were applied to different areas to aid definition. In its central signature, which employed a heavier paper with a better calendered surface, colour was deployed in flat areas without any chiaroscuro to modulate saturation. The result still retains its vivacity and a certain charm.

In the issue for March 1920, the sophistication of the American designers is also confirmed as being beyond their counterparts working on the British popular periodicals of the period. After *Woman's World*'s crisply printed title page, in which the title is set in a box embedded in a line illustration surmounting a three-column editorial, a short story opens on page four. This is longer than any fiction in a contemporary popular British magazine, for it jumps from the bottom of page five to page 44 and finally ends, after sliding through the back-of-the-book section, on page 51. Its opening spread uses three monochrome wash illustrations. Two are laid out side by side at the top of page four, while the third is positioned opposite, just across the gutter, so that there is a vertical overlap of about 1 cm. The third reproduction has an irregular zigzag shape around which text is wrapped. The three together bite into the text following a path directed lower right. They are balanced by an eight-line poem, given white space and a box and placed top right on page five. The poem is unrelated to the story and its abrupt intrusion, positioned across the white-space margin between columns two and three, is eye catching. With devices such as two-line drop capitals opening sections of text and captions in 12–point italic contrasting with eight–point body type, the layouts have a sophistication unknown in the British popular magazines of the time.

Another short story opens on page seven and trails from the bottom of eight to a point two-thirds of the way down page 16, where the back-of-the-book section begins. A two-colour illustration fills the top half of page seven above the title. Another irregularly shaped reproduction is cut into the lower two-thirds of page eight. This pattern of fresh stories lasting two pages and then trailing into the back pages is repeated until page 15, where a full-page advertisement marks the break.

A second break occurs on page 20 where crochet instructions fill four columns and spill over on to two more on the facing page. These instructions thread their way between advertisements until page 27 is reached, where a full-colour advertisement for Mazola cooking oil is printed on heavier, smoother paper. This marks the start of an eight-page colour section in which editorial artwork alternates with that of advertisements. Two pages of crochet are followed by another which uses flat paintings, short on chiaroscuro, to illustrate a cooking piece.(Plate VIII)

From now on until the last page, advertisements tend to dominate with short articles on domestic matters, with the tail ends of stories threading between them. Frequently, particularly towards the end, editorial matter is squeezed into one of the four columns on each page, while advertisements occupy the other three. Only page 58, the last, uses a distinctive article, distinctly laid out to list different styles of washing machines, all of which are illustrated, some with artwork, some with photos.

This issue is typical of many American magazines of the immediate post-war period for, although its page quality does not match that of the *Ladies' Home Journal* or *Woman's Home Companion*, it makes the best of its graphic resources and deploys them with sophistication. Only the monochrome wash illustrations, which were the dominant magazine style of the time, were ill-advised because they always appear indistinct or muddy. Their use demonstrates the scale of Lorimer's influence on his fellow editors, even the successful ones.

However, it is in its content that the limitations of *Woman's World* really show up. Between January and December 1920 it relied on the standard twentieth-century mix of so many women's magazines: fiction, fashion and domestic felicity. The concentration on the home, at 32%, and fiction at 46% consumed almost four-fifths of editorial space. So, with fashion at almost 12%, that left very little room for anything else(see Appendix XII).

The same combination in the *Ladies' Home Journal*, of fiction and domestic matters, at 39% and 12% respectively, used only just over 50% of the space available to the editor during 1920. Yet, this involved a sharp change in the balance of the Curtis publication, for the burgeoning empire of tales and serials was growing during Bok's last years. In early 1917, for instance, it absorbed about 28% of editorial space. The jump in fiction's allocation, from 16% in 1910, had been largely at the expense of the fashion department and the magazine's coverage of the arts. Nevertheless, the *Journal* was still paying extensive attention to the world at large and its coverage of the potential involvement of women in politics on the brink of their immersion in the presidential election was exemplary. An increasing emphasis was also placed on social problems, as well as less pressing matters, such as life in post-war Paris(see Appendix XI).

One rather singular series that ran extensively through this decade but which terminated before its end, involved the reproduction of works of art in colour to a higher standard than had been achieved hitherto in a best-selling magazine. Each month two facing pages were given over to full-page reproductions of old masters of the stature of Vermeer, Van Dyck, Turner and Ghirlandaio. Perhaps it was Bok's last service to middle America.

If Bok had been on the cutting edge in 1890 when he expanded the horizons of the *Journal*, it was no longer alone in that situation. By 1920, the *Woman's Home Companion*, under its editor Gertrude Lane, was quite capable of running articles on the forthcoming presidential campaign, with short items by both Calvin Coolidge and Herbert Hoover leading its March issue, followed by 'Women in Politics' by Helen Taft in April. Overall, the *Companion*, if distinct from the *Journal*, followed a similarly broad agenda, balancing the arts against social commentaries, fashion against needlework and cookery, with fiction taking just less then 40% of the magazine's editorial space in the first half of 1920, as the dominating sector, which was much the same as the *Journal*(see Appendix XIII).

Yet, if the *Companion* was capable of swapping editorial punches with the *Journal*, its financial footing was not yet on a par with its rival from Philadelphia. With over 450 pages of paid insertions in the first six months of 1920, being charged at the rate of $6,800 for an inside page in monochrome, $10,000 for colour and $13,000 for the back cover, the *Companion* was probably earning in excess of $6 million gross per annum from advertising.[93] While that fell short of the probable income from such sources by the *Journal*, it was superior to the comparable earnings of *Woman's World* and many other similar publications.

The route to this strong situation had been a long one, the title and its form having gone through several metamorphoses. From 1874 to 1878 it was called *The Home*. Between 1878 and 1886 it was *Home Companion*, although it was briefly renamed *Our Young People* during the latter half of 1883. From 1886, for ten years, it was the *Ladies' Home Companion*. Only in 1897 did it finally settle on the title under which it achieved fame and fortune.[94]

Its editorial identity at the end of the century was as unstable as its name. Having begun as a mail-order monthly, that is as a publication whose primary function was to display cheap advertisements for even cheaper merchandise that could be secured by a small sum sent through the post, it graduated to a juvenile audience under the aegis of Mast, Crowell and Kirkpatrick, who bought it in 1883. After they changed its guise in 1886, it gradually developed its content, adding more sophisticated articles and authors. But it was not until 1900, when Arthur Vance took over as editor, that it really hit its stride. By the end of the following year, with Mast dead and Kirkpatrick pursuing other interests, Crowell was sole owner.[95] But he too was ageing and in 1906 he sold the company to three partners, Thomas Lamont, Samuel Untermeyer and Joseph Palmer Knapp, with the latter as the majority shareholder.

Among the major magazine publishers of the twentieth century, it would be hard to recall one as little known as Joseph Knapp, but his was the only company to challenge the hegemony of Cyrus Curtis before the Second World War. In part, that might have been because, although he controlled the company and was its driving force, his name failed to feature on the mast-head of the magazines that he published, itself an indicator of his reticence, which was very unusual among his contemporaries. Yet, the little that has been published about him indicates that he was a character as singular as Henry Luce or William Randolph Hearst.

Joseph Knapp was born on 14 May 1864 to a mother who composed hymns for the Methodist Church and a father who owned a lithographic printing business. In the spirit of responsible ownership, Joseph Fairchild Knapp started what eventually became the Metropolitan Life Insurance Company to protect his workers. When Joseph junior flunked his first year at Columbia he joined his father's firm. However, Joseph senior, being the man he was, put him to work on a press and gave him apprentice's wages. Joseph junior, being the man he was, was soon looking for something more lucrative. When he asked if he could become a salesman, his father allowed him to use his lunch hour. However, Joseph junior called one day on James Duke, also young and on the make, but very soon to be the prime mover behind the American Tobacco Company. The volume of business this contact brought to the company and the size of the commissions due to his son, proved an embarrassment to Joseph senior. To contain the problem, Joseph senior proposed paying his son, in part, in stock in the printing company. But this only postponed the problem and, eventually, magnified it, for these holdings in their turn became an embarrassment. When the father insisted that he must buy back the stock, the young Samuel Untermeyer, a friend of the son, pointed out that the latter could reverse the process and buy out his father. To the older man's horror, this is exactly what happened and he never forgave his son.

Over the next twenty years, the American Lithographic Company grew to substantial proportions and Knapp began to acquire print buying businesses to keep his presses running – which is why he bought the Crowell Publishing Company in 1906. Five years later he snapped up *The American Magazine*, though he stayed so far in the background on this deal that Mott made the mistake of ascribing the date of purchase to 1916.[96] Then, in 1919, he gained control of P. F. Collier, after Robert Collier had drained the organisation of capital to sustain the *Weekly*, only to die prematurely.[97]

Thus, by the end of the second decade of the twentieth century, Joseph Knapp had created a potential magazine empire. Interestingly, all three titles had impeccable credentials in responsible journalism. Indeed, he had acquired two of the leading crusading journals of the preceding decade and united them under one banner. Perhaps this is no coincidence, for William Chenery, who in the middle twenties became the editor of *Collier's* and was later raised to be George Lorimer's equivalent at Crowell's, ascribed to Knapp an intense desire to lift *Collier's* to the heights of its former influence and prestige.[98] In the light of such thoughts it is hardly surprising that Gertrude Lane at the *Companion* should have taken the course that she did in promoting greater responsibility for women.

Nor is it surprising that the *Companion* was so well printed. Even their use of monochrome gravure, a process usually ignored by the leading American magazines, followed from Knapp's roots in printing which, as we shall see, were to have a profound effect on the British magazine trade in an indirect way. The overall decision to avoid the crowded fashion layouts beloved by the *Journal* and *Woman's World* would tend to imply a lower density of illustration usage than these two. Yet, examination does not confirm this expectation and the density remains high at 2.26 illustrative figures per page. That just over 40% of these reproductions came from photographic originals was about the average level of the time.

The second of Joseph Knapp's acquisitions, *The American Magazine*, was transformed under the editorship of John Siddall. A former associate editor under John Phillips, who had guided *The American* after its staff had arrived following the secession from *McClure's* in 1906, Siddall illustrates one route that crusading journalism took as the first wave receded.

Here it was transformed into that type of populism which confronts the reader. Much of the tone is explicit in the titles: 'How to Use Your Mistakes,' 'Which Musical Instrument Do You Like Best ?', 'Why I Am Glad I Married a Suffragist,' 'Men I Have Had to Fire.' Yet, the quality of the writing is often much better than the headings imply. It is just that the editorial objective was to personalise everything; to make all events anthropocentric.

But that is not to deny that the emphasis of the contents had changed as well. The formerly sceptical approach was completely inverted into such eulogies as 'The Greatest Builder of Skyscrapers in the World,' a slavering portrait of Louis Horowitz, an office developer who 'has risen by grit, vision, and a really marvellous ability to overcome obstacles.' Any reader with a memory that extended back to the days of the muckrakers must have shuddered at the implications behind that gushing phrase.[99] When one looks at the editorial profile, it is to be expected that the greatest space devoted to factual material would be given over to business. In that one is not disappointed, for this topic grew to occupy over 19% of editorial space in the first half of 1920, compared to mere 1.5% just ten years before. In a mirror image, the interest in public affairs had slumped from over 11% in 1910 to less than one in 1920. And an entirely new category arose for a best-selling mixed function magazine: personal problems. At over 4% of editorial space, this interest exceeded even that of the American women's magazine examined hitherto(see Appendix V).

The graphic identity of the magazine had also shifted. The usage of illustrations had dropped from 0.56 per page in 1910 to 0.46 per page in 1920. Furthermore, as one would expect from the tenor of the articles, it is very difficult to discover any images that do not feature human features. Even the article on Horowitz does not use a photograph of one of his buildings, not even a small one. Instead we are served up a photographic portrait, printed on Joseph junior's gravure presses.

One reason for the diminution in the density of editorial illustrative content in this and other journals at this time may be ascribed to the rise of that editorial design feature known as the front-of-the-book and the back-of-the-book sections. As will be remembered from earlier passages, the weeklies, either in Britain or the United States, were never loathe to take the advertiser's money or to spread his sales pitch through their editorial pages, even if they were usually located more towards the back of each issue. The monthlies, particularly in the US, were a completely different kettle of fish. It was only in the 1870s that paid insertions began appearing in any numbers in their pages and the following decade was well underway before their volume really began to grow.

Yet, despite their increasing dependence on this revenue, the monthlies still managed to relegate the advertising to a ghetto at the back of each issue, with a few pages at the front, inside the cover. The first major title to break with this practice was *Ladies' Home Journal*, perhaps in part because its size and format were so much nearer to the weeklies than to the other, more established monthlies. Also, it would appear that such breaks with tradition were not unknown among other women's serials. However, the innovation of spreading the advertising among editorial content was accompanied by another practice, that of running a headline at the top of almost every page. Thus, although most of the attractive articles were clustered in each edition's opening pages, fresh articles appeared throughout each issue.

However, when George Lorimer took control of the *Post*, he modified this approach. After starting with an opening page or two of advertisements, the main editorial section began. Each double-page spread therein normally featured one, or sometimes two headlines. Each was the beginning of a fresh article which was completed much later in the issue, with a suitable suffix to each text, instructing the reader to turn to page x. No advertisements appeared in this part of the magazine. The end of this front-of-the-book section was announced by a full-page insertion on the right-hand side of one spread. In later years, this position in most successful American magazines was purchased by Campbell's Soup. Beyond this demarcation line, the back-of-the-book section largely intermingled advertisements and the tail ends of articles, though even the *Post* moderated this rule by introducing regular series and minor material on a limited basis.

By 1910 this practice had still to be accepted by the industry. While the most attractive editorial material was used to lead each issue, advertising was either still consigned to the rear in complete segregation or allowed to mingle in a limited way with lesser articles and stories. But editorial material still largely began and ended in one continuous sequence of pages. It was only in the following decade that the big circulation monthlies adopted the *Post's* explicit definition of the separation of the 'front' and the 'back' of each issue.

The consequence for the publisher was not only that it helped him to attract the advertiser, who liked the reassurance that the reader would have to pass by his particular insertion, but that a large proportion of the magazine could be left without editorial illustrations, allowing the frequently vivid advertisements to pick up the slack. In the *Post's* case, by 1920 more than 80% of each edition was designated as the back-of-the-book.

Under Siddall, this approach was used on *The American* and it is impossible to deny the success of such editorial tactics. From 454,517 per month in 1914, when John Phillips was still in control, circulation rose through 798,548 per month in 1917, to 1,441,080 in 1920; a rise of over 300% in six years, an impressive figure even for a new publication with a fresh momentum, let alone an established title.[100]

The contrast between Siddall's *American* and Ray Long's *Cosmopolitan* is particularly interesting because there are many parallels between the two magazines in their editorial rights of passage. By 1920, both had been transformed by a new editor, both were very successful, both were using the new front and back-of-the-book format and both seemed to be attacking the same market. But there the parallels fade for while Siddall had added an air of undeniable vulgarity to his 20¢ monthly, Ray Long had reversed the tawdry air of *Cosmopolitan* under C.P. Narcross. Though in a totally different direction, his metamorphosis of the 25¢ Hearst periodical was just as radical as that of his rival.

Ray Long had made his reputation in Chicago working for the Consolidated Magazine Corporation on their two monthly story magazines, *Red Book* and *Blue Book*, in addition to their theatre monthly, *Green Book*. So, his transformation of *Cosmopolitan* into a magazine completely dominated by fiction was hardly a surprise, even if the scale of his changes was somewhat extreme. With over 80% of the editorial space in volume 68 given over to stories and serials there could be no mistaking his purpose. Gone forever was the magazine's traditional commitment to an examination of the world at large, decimated to a vestigial 4.9%. The past, the arts, sport and even humour were trashed completely (see Appendix X).

By way of compensation, the editorial pages were laid out with a measure of elegance that outdistanced the opposition. The relatively light-weight but well-calendered paper allowed the art director to use extensively the dark, murky wash drawings that were so fashionable at the time. In the front-of-the-book section, they were used to dominate each two-page spread in large, irregular shapes enclosed by type. Frequently, the illustrations were split in two unequal parts by the gutter. However, no attempt was made to bleed them together. Instead the eyelines of the two dominant protagonists were linked so that the reader's eye bonded the two halves as it followed the drama of the illustrated moment.

The back-of-the-book, having advertisements to articulate each two-page spread, did not need editorial illustrations. Nevertheless, their enthusiastic use in the opening pages was sufficient to create an overall frequency in volume 68 of 0.68 illustrations per page, which was high for this sector of the market at the time. Another device that varied the rhythm of the layouts was the inclusion of a four-page gravure signature in each issue, which was devoted to the personalities of the entertainment industry who were very frequently female. The photographs were bled, that is, printed to the edge of the page on all four sides, a ploy that further emphasized the differentiation from the rest of the pagination.

The third of Joseph Knapp's acquisitions, *Collier's*, had only just joined the Crowell stable in 1920. Norman Hapgood, the editor of the weekly in its prime, had left in 1912. Robert Collier had taken over, but he in turn handed over in 1914 to Mark Sullivan because his mental and physical health was breaking down. But Sullivan was hog–tied by an advisory manager imposed by the bankers who were concerned about the company's debts, and the old campaigning zeal was dissipated. Sullivan resigned in 1917 and the publication was eventually sold to Knapp.[101]

Under an inexperienced editor, enduring a printer's strike that left the first half of 1920 four issues short, Mott's observation that it lacked editorial stability and purpose seems justified, though hardly surprising.[102] Its covers displayed all the mawkish sentimentality of the *Post*, as well as the same awful colour scheme. Gone were the glories of ten years before. Yet, the memories lingered, for the 5¢ weekly, although it now used the same poor quality paper as its infinitely more successful rival, had the sense to use many more line blocks than the *Post*: over 18% of all reproductions in the first six months of 1920, compared to less than 1% in the *Post*. It also retained its interest in politics and public affairs, allotting over 20% of editorial space to these topics together. Yet fiction now had the upper hand, reaching almost 50% in the 22 issues between January 1st and June 30th, 1920. In a magazine that had restricted such material to just over 14% in volume 45, it was a change that seemed to signify a further attachment to the *Post's* coat tails (see Appendix VI).

Meanwhile, one weekly that did have a definite persona and a clear head of sales steam was the *Literary Digest*. An also-ran in 1910, with an estimated circulation of 235,000,[103] by 1920 it had risen to a 1,200,000 sworn average circulation,[104] which makes it second only to the *Post* among the weeklies. Grown fat with advertising, its editorial and advertising space during the first half of 1920 amounted to 3876 pages, which must have appeared to its publishers, Funk and Wagnalls, to be within striking distance of the pre-eminent *Post's* comparable total of 4980. From this bulk they gained gross advertising receipts of $12,720,000 that year, again second only to the *Post* in dollar volume of national advertising.[105]

The digest formula was not a new one and it was common practice to publish stories clipped from other magazines before international copyright laws were agreed. More recently, an editorial formula arising from the idea of a digest of the best work of others received its biggest boost from the *Review of Reviews*, which was launched in London in January 1890. This proved to be resoundingly successful. The *Literary Digest* began weekly publication just two months later with the issue dated 1 March 1890. The appearance of an American edition of the London-based *Review* in April 1891 did not deter the New York-based weekly, probably, in part, because a digest is inherently cheap to produce and has the advantage for its publisher of a low, break-even point, particularly as it usually has limited pretensions and can be printed on cheap paper. Thus, by 1900 the *Digest* had managed to claw its way up the market to a respectable circulation of 63,000. However, it was only with the emergence of a more energetic force in the publishing company, in the person of Robert Cuddihy, that the growth in sales really accelerated. Taking a similar path to Curtis, he advertised extensively and it worked. However, the boost in sales occasioned by interest in the First World War certainly helped the pace of growth even further, establishing the magazine as an important source of news on a national stage.[106]

As the coming decades were to demonstrate, the news digest formula was a very attractive one in a country which lacked a national press and, more importantly, a national Sunday press. However, given the restricted nature of its contents, the analytical categories applied to the other titles assayed hitherto would be of limited value here.

Nevertheless, the *Literary Digest* of 1920 left a mark that not only registered among journalists but affected democracy throughout the western world in the years to come. April 1920 saw the publication of the first of the accumulating votes in its presidential poll, the first significant opinion poll. Though its margins of error were large, the fact that it and its editions in subsequent campaigns accurately predicted the presidential winner on four successive occasions was enough to bring such assessments into the public arena.[107]

DURING THE FIRST DECADE OF THE TWENTIETH CENTURY, the difference between the British and the American magazine markets became more marked than ever. Although the circulation of the penny weekly *Answers* appears to have grown during the period, the upward curve of sales growth maintained by a weekly such as the *Saturday Evening Post* was never matched by a British equivalent. Where *Tit-bits* appears to have been selling about 600,000 by the end of the nineteenth century,[108] a figure that was at least comparable to the sales of the American leader of the time, *Ladies' Home Journal*, a decade later *Tit-bits* was faltering while both Curtis publications were selling one and a quarter million per issue. In 1910, *Answers* sold an average of 716,998 per week, but it had peaked at 830,318 in 1906.[109]

This reflects the differing economic conditions current in both countries. In the US, as we have seen, the volume of disposable surplus income was rising. Between 1901 and 1914, real wages in Britain dropped by an average of 0.71% per year, reversing the trend of the previous 25 years in which they had risen by 1.85% per annum on average.[110] Under these circumstances, it is no wonder that circulation growth faltered. Yet, it was not just the size of the sales figures but their very existence that emphasized the intercontinental difference.

In the United States, accurate information had been available for many years, as will be apparent from previous pages. In Britain, such figures were very occasional, never published in a form which made comparisons easy and were frequently unreliable. It was to remedy this situation that the Advertisers' Protection Society was created in 1900.[111] Its *Monthly Circular* became a record of their efforts to extract reliable information about sales from the publishers. Although these successes were limited, the flow of facts was an improvement on the previous situation. In addition, to try to provoke the publishers into disgorging more information, the

Circular listed the Society's estimated sales figures of the more popular titles from time to time and, where subsequent revelations about specific magazines appeared, their estimates were proved to be reasonably accurate, if on the low side.

It is this hitherto unexamined source which has revealed accurate circulation figures on *Answers* and the new weekly success of the period, *John Bull*, with its eventual rise to be the first British million seller during the First World War. It revealed the fall of the six penny monthlies which developed during the final decade of the nineteenth century. The likely success of the two half penny weeklies in the Harmsworth stable, *Comic Cuts* and *Illustrated Chips* was also indicated.

In 1920, the Society changed its name to the Incorporated Society of British Advertisers but it still continued to publish its newsletter.[112] It was the *Monthly Circular* which recorded a sudden burst of frankness on the part of the magazine publishers in 1919–1920. For a short period, audited net sales figures were available on a range of magazines and gave this end-of-the-decade moment a comparative list of unprecedented completeness in Britain. It was a far cry from the comparable situation of the time in the United States.

Another area in which the British and American markets differed between 1900 to 1910 and continued to do so in the decades that followed, concerned their target audiences. Most of the best selling American magazines were monthlies and they either followed a model that had evolved from *Harper's Monthly*, that is one that had originally been aimed at a luxury-orientated clientele that could afford 35¢ a month for a magazine and who had an education to match. Or they restricted their function and went solely for a female audience. When the cover price dropped in the 1890s, the market expanded but the models only evolved gradually. In essence, their audience consisted of those with sufficient education to enjoy the formats and articles already described. There were American news weeklies that had evolved from the model provided by the *Illustrated London News* but, with the exception of *Collier's*, they remained outside the group of best sellers at the turn of the century. However, if pressed one would be hard put to suggest that their readers were not largely affluent, though one must also concede that there is, as yet, little firm information on this point.

Only with the *Saturday Evening Post* did a new model arrive that provided a new approach to magazine design and, perhaps, a different mass audience in the United States. Yet, when that is said, and even bearing in mind that the *Post* sold for 5¢ a week, it has nothing in common with the market leaders in the United Kingdom. This point is only emphasized by the two titles that appeared in Britain between 1900 and 1910 which, by the decade's end, were among the best sellers. Both *John Bull* and the British weekly known as *Woman's World* followed the price and format established in previous decades, even if *John Bull* differed in so many other ways from its peers. Thus, the penny weekly printed on poor paper, that is now on the point of disintegration, still dominated the British magazine market during that first decade of the twentieth century. Indeed, the six penny monthly that made such a mark in the previous decade, failed to sustain its previous promise and sales dwindled. Contemporary comment attributed this failure to the rise of the sixpenny paperback novel.[113] Given that we have already established that *The Strand Magazine*, for example, gave over 50% of its editorial space to fiction, it is clear that individual sixpenny publications could rival sixpenny serials that concentrated on similar fare. Thus, by the end of the decade, the British periodicals were again highly polarised between the relatively high circulation penny publications directed towards the lower end of the market and the society weeklies with tiny sales. Although the sales of the latter could only be measured in tens rather than hundreds of thousands, in following the lead of George Newnes they were able to charge premium rates for their advertising of luxury products. Indeed, comment on the Country Life Ltd company report in March 1908 suggests that, by this point, the latter was preventing the collapse of the Newnes organisation, being the only major profit centre contributing to the company's liquidity.[114]

It is, of course, possible that this suggestion was an exaggeration designed to provoke the Newnes group into releasing more information about sales. There was certainly no love lost between them and the Advertisers' Protection Society, who mounted a campaign of provocation during the later years of the decade, trying to sting the company into releasing sales figures. Certainly, by 1910, *Tit-bits*, the starting point of the Newnes group, was selling an average of over 13% more space during the January to June period of 1910, when compared to the same period in 1900 and so, apparently, remaining successful.

Despite these changes, the magazine itself still ploughed much the same editorial furrow; at least, it looked the same. Certainly, the amount of fiction used seemed to have remained stable over the decade, at just over 20% of editorial space between January and June 1910. However, even in this stagnant backwater a surprise crops up from time to time. In this case, it was the publication of a P. G. Wodehouse serial that was given considerable prominence and promotion beforehand.[115]

Some changes in other material published is also noticeable. A return to the volume of humour and entertainment, in particular competitions, employed in the early days of the weekly, is very evident, though none of the latter displayed the verve that so evidently captured the audience for *Tit-bits* in the 1880s. Page one of each issue again featured plenty of short jokes. As against that, the old reliance on tit-bits of information had diminished, almost to the level found in the contemporary *Answers*(see Appendix XXI).

One noticeable visual difference that had developed in *Tit-bits* over the decade, was the use of illustrations. At 0.76 per page, their use was quite profuse, though this was less noticeable than it might have been as they were usually small relative to the size of the page. Only in one layout in every issue did the visual dominate the verbal. At the top of the twelfth page, a two tier comic strip was located. The characters varied from week to week. Illustrated titles were also used in some profusion.

The latter option was also employed on *Answers*, though the rest of each page was much more textbound than that of its rival. This is evident from the illustration count which, at 0.22 per page, is less than a third of the frequency found in the Newnes weekly. But, when they were used it was usually to better effect for, not only was the overall ink colour more saturated throughout each edition, but *Answers* seems to have used better draughtsmen. In particular, almost every issue carried a one page comic story about a character called Harbottle, in itself a considerable departure from previous practice. Every short story incorporated two or sometimes three vivid cartoons, emphasizing a particularly farcical moment. This regular feature accounted for much of the increasing space given to humour and entertainment in *Answers*. The amount of fiction had also increased a little, from just over 29 to just over 33%. To balance that, the interest in biography and history was down, as were the number of pages given to the fragments of information, hitherto a mainstay of the weekly. Of course, the one topic that had disappeared completely from both weeklies by 1910 was the Boer War. But no all consuming topic had replaced it, although *Answers* showed an increasing interest in social problems(see Appendix XXII).

Comic Cuts had also resumed its previous eight-page pattern, sandwiching serials and short stories between the comic strips on the front, back and centre spreads. Now the comic characters were very stable, with three quarters or more continuing from week to week, usually in the same position on the same page. The Mulberry Flatites always led the front page. The

Merry Midgets, Roly-Poly and Gertie the regimental donkey were always in the centre, while Sammy Salt and Hotspur the cockerel ruled the back.

These were the golden days for this half penny weekly, but whether it really sold 'approx. 1 million copies', as Kevin Carpenter states, is open to question. This is particularly improbable as he credits *Illustrated Chips* with a one million circulation at approximately this time as well.[116] On the other hand, those cynics at the Advertisers' Protection Society estimated the net sales at 150,000 and 200,000, which seems to move to the other extreme.[117] Unfortunately, as neither carried much advertising, there was probably little contemporary interest in their circulations. However, in December 1907, it was reported in the APS newsletter that Amalgamated Press, the comics' publishers, had issued 'a chartered accountant's certificate of the circulation of their weekly periodicals of the *Comic Cuts* and the *Boy's Friend* class. Altogether, they issue twelve journals of their type and the average weekly circulation makes a very good showing, being no less than 2,176,991.' Now, if this figure can be relied upon, and there is little reason to doubt it for such figures, when issued by the Harmsworth organisation over the years, seem to have been accurate, the Carpenter figures are unrealistic, as are those of the APS. It seems much more likely that, during the first decade, the two leading comics peaked at somewhere about half a million each. Such figures seem compatible with both the certified figure above and the sort of sales achieved by the weeklies already discussed. The nature of this audience is an even more difficult question, but it seems to be false to assume that it was composed of children when the 'Grand Complete Story' series on page six of *Comic Cuts* every week was promoted as featuring 'Love, Romance, Adventure.' The *Boy's Friend*, incidentally, was a 16-page penny weekly intended for the juvenile market, that was composed almost entirely of fiction, the vast majority of it in serial form.

Illustrated Chips followed a similar format to *Comic Cuts*. Priced at a half penny, four pages of fiction were sandwiched between covers and a centre spread of cartoons, both individual and in strip form. The fiction was normally split into two short stories up to approximately 1,500 words long and the episodes of two serials. All were adventure stories and at least one always featured a heroine rather than a hero. The cartoon strip on the front page was always devoted to Weary Willie and Tired Tim, while a single picture, which used characters known collectively as Casey Court, always occupied the top of page eight. The position of the other regulars varied from week to week. The humour was broad, while most of the characters were lowly in station. The overall layout was less predictable than *Comic Cuts*.

Pearson's Weekly, now two decades old, was roughly the same page size as these comics. By 1910, it was almost as profusely illustrated. Where it had led in the 1890s in the reintroduction of illustrations among the penny weeklies, it retained that lead during the following decade. During the first six months of 1910 it used over 1.14 illustrations per page. As with its rivals, these were usually small relative to the size of the page. One innovation was in the sphere of competitions. In 1909 *Pearson's* introduced a novel competition which it called 'Picture Couplets'. A cartoon was supplied with a one-line caption. The readers had to supply a second line to complete a rhyming couplet.

Another innovation by *Pearson's* in their part of the market was a women's page. Every week, the eighteenth of the twenty pages was divided into four. One section always featured simple recipes, another household hints. The third varied between hints on health and domestic information, while the fourth took the form of an article, about 750 words long, on a contentious topic. Titles such as 'Women Who Ought Not To Marry' and 'The Man All Women Like' indicate some of the flavour. The preliminaries to matrimony were frequently the theme. Another feature that appeared in 1910 was a regular gardening column. *Tit-bits* was running a regular cycling column at the time, which helps to illuminate the difference between the two publications. *Pearson's* seems to have intended a direct appeal to more members of the family than its rivals, though such matters are largely ones of emphasis. But such differences did not inhibit the enthusiasm of the editors for good ideas, even if they had arisen in other publishing houses. Thus, in December 1909, *Answers* began 'The Life Story of Warden X'. On March 31, 1910, *Pearson's Weekly* countered with 'Seeds From a Gaol-Bird's Cage'. *Answers* then returned the complement with 'The-Ticket-of-Leave Woman'. By the end of the decade, readers of the penny weeklies had no excuse for any ignorance about the details of incarceration and its accompanying argot.

In one respect, the British and American markets did exhibit some similarity, that is in their strongly developed markets for women's magazines though again, as in the more general publications, one set was largely monthly and one weekly. Unlike their American cousins, the British periodicals, although substantial sellers, particularly over the last decades of the nineteenth century, had not made such an intrusion into the list of the most successful titles. However, by the end of that first decade, one of the productions of the Amalgamated Press was doing somewhat better than the rest. *Woman's World* was selling just below 350,000 a week.[118]

Quite why it should be so successful under its editor, Miss Perrett,[119] is not apparent at first glance, or even the second. Like so many British women's magazines but unlike its best-selling American peers, it was restricted in the range of its editorial interests. Whole areas of contemporary life escaped without comment: politics, business and sport, quite apart from any material dealing with foreign parts. Only the anticipated domestic topics, such as cookery, housework and handiwork received substantial coverage, taking almost 30% of editorial space during the first six months of 1910. Fiction, absorbed nearly half the space, while the only other topic to gain full coverage was that of personal problems. Interestingly, the latter topic does seem to be an another area in which trans-Atlantic differences do emerge for, in the United States, the 8% of editorial space accorded to this theme in *Woman's World* of London was unknown among the leading American titles(see Appendix XIX).

In fact, one suspects that the managerial skill of the Harmsworth machine was behind the success of *Woman's World*, which was launched in November 1903. Sir John Hammerton, one of the leading editors of the Amalgamated Press, gives a very clear indication of how the company encouraged its staff through the use of financial inducements to give of their best. The editor received one shilling 'for every thousand copies sold'.[120] While this seems to have encouraged circulation growth, it does not seem to have encouraged new ideas, and the only real novelty in *Woman's World* seems to have been its dedication to religion, for it is the only British publication examined so far that devoted a full page to the subject every week, taking over 3.5% of editorial space during the first half of 1910(see Appendix XIX).

A look at the 32-page edition of 2 April 1910 perhaps gives an idea of the appearance of an individual issue. Printed on uncalendered newsprint, it used few illustrations, although most titles were enhanced with simple line drawings or motifs. A 24-line, six-stanza verse with a decorative border occupies the centre of the first page, 33, surrounded by two moralistic homilies which pass for an editorial. A new serial fills the following three pages. The draughtsmanship of its sole illustration and the line work which embellishes the title are equally inept. However, some relief was needed to break up the two dense columns of eight–point type. A moderately elaborate illustrated title is used on page 38 over another prescriptive homily written by 'The Bachelor of Experience'.

One column of the opposite page is given over to the other main form of advice, that is, answers to correspondents. In this case the respondent was 'Nurse Ratchel'. Squashed into the

Fig.30 The entirely unexceptional weekly, Woman's World, is an illustration of how a well-oiled promotional machine can elevate a circulation to surprising levels. Harmsworth's staff at Amalgamated Press turned it into the best-selling women's magazine of the pre-First-World-War period in Britain.

space beside the title is a small line drawing of a seated nurse dispensing comfort to a suppliant standing mother and child. Four letters are answered in the piece. Original enquiries are set in italics and the reply is in eight–point body type. Above each is a centred subhead in capitals. The second column on the page is an advertisement.

The following spread is dedicated to the first of a two part serial. The title, 'The Mill Owner's Daughter', is centred between two line drawings: on the left a middle-aged man in a high collar is seated at his office desk; on the right a young woman is before her dressing table which is blessed with perfumes, candles and an oval mirror.(Fig. 30)

The next spread is concerned with matters domestic: one page for cookery; the second for cleaning and household renovation. Again the title is embedded in a line illustration, this time of a shelf holding plates, pots and pans. Most items on both pages are one paragraph in length and separated by white space and a 8mm long ¯–point rule. Both pages have been divided into three columns rather than two and the breaks are 5mm wide lengths of white space. The following page, 44, follows the same pattern in dealing with 'Readers Answers to Various Inquiries'.

The opposite page returns to the two-column format to deal with crochet and knitting. The detailed instructions, under another illustrated title, 'My Lady's Fancy Work', include a line drawing of hands performing a manoeuvre with a crochet needle, and two poorly reproduced halftones of photographs of finished pieces of work.

Another new serial starts on pages 46 and 47, 'My Lancashire Queen'. Again the title is sandwiched between two line drawings. This piece of fiction trails on to pages 50 and 51. Meanwhile, another page, 49, is given over to advice: 'Heart to Heart Chats', while 48 is laid out with a picture strip drama, 'The Girl Who Took the Downward Path', which is a little better drawn than most of the other illustration in the issue. 'Two grand pages of fun and frolic for the little ones' occupy a double spread covering 52 and 53. The right-hand page is filled with a simple four-cell comic strip, while the left features a poem in patterned border, the first half of a story and an invitation to join 'The Sunshine League'.

Another serial is printed on the following three pages with its usual illustrated title. Religion takes over page 57 with poems, a prayer and the usual exhortations. Another elaborate border topped by an angel surrounds one of the poems, which is positioned in the centre of the layout. A circular frame featuring two bright-eyed children and their bushy-tailed mother is attached to the page heading, 'The Way of the Cross'. The remaining seven pages feature more fiction, a 'Cheer-Up' Club, and some more domestic information, all following the pattern already described, interspersed with a little advertising. The inside and back cover is also given over to advertising, while the front always incorporates a line drawing overprinted with red enclosed in an elaborate border.

This issue illustrates the limitations that the economics of the penny weekly impose on its design, starting with very poor paper. This in turn limits the type of artwork which can be printed, that is, simple line drawings. Limited advertising revenue meant that close controls on expenses were necessary, which is why *Woman's World* used so few graphics.

After the journalistic stagnation that enveloped British periodicals at this time, *John Bull* is the proverbial breath of fresh air. While all the other titles examined for this period were the property of the three organisations that now dominated the popular market, *John Bull* was the outsider. Its first edition is dated 12 May 1906. The idea was presented by Horatio Bottomley to the Odhams organisation in the person of Julius Elias, the brains and driving force behind the company. In their relationship, one encounters one of the most extraordinary liaisons in British publishing history.

Elias was a self-effacing, quiet man who achieved a rags-to-riches climb through hard work, diligence and attention to detail. But he was also a daring gambler, though only when it came to his work. It was the chance that he took on Bottomley which propelled the Odhams company into its subsequent position as a major, dynamic force in the publishing industry of the twenties and thirties. In the pages to come it will be seen how his enthusiasm and judgement changed the face of British magazine journalism forever. The man who brought him the idea for Odhams' first magazine was his total antithesis.[121]

Horatio Bottomley was one of the most audacious, dishonest and scandalous characters to figure in British public life during the last hundred years. He made millions through outrageous frauds, was challenged in court on many occasions but was only finally sent to prison when his luck ran out in old age. In the 1880s he became involved in the promotion of a publishing company that ended in a major court case, in 1893.[122] It was during this period that he first met the notorious journalist Frank Harris.[123] Despite, or perhaps because he defended himself in court, Bottomley was acquitted, even though there is no doubt now that he defrauded his victims of at least £200,000.

In the years that followed he made a great deal of money through a series of dubious company promotions.[124] In 1902, he bought a London evening newspaper, *The Sun*, which probably came cheap as it was losing £300 a week. Through the sort of yellow journalism that had been so successful in the United States, he promoted it and in the course of two years challenged the Attorney-General and the Home Secretary in cases in which he and his staff thought miscarriages of justice had occurred. In both instances, *The Sun* carried the day. However, by 1904 he had fallen on hard times again, so he sold the paper.[125] In January 1906, his political involvement carried him to a seat in parliament, swept along on the Liberal landslide of the general election, as the member for South Hackney.[126] Later that year he approached Odhams with the idea of *John Bull*.

According to Bottomley's first serious biographer, Julian Symons, Frank Harris played a major part in the preparation of the dummy issue that was shown to Elias, as well as later acting as chief sub-editor, leader writer, as well as reviewing plays and books for a time.[127] Given Bottomley's demonstrated unreliability and erratic lifestyle, one wonders quite how much Harris contributed to the success that followed. One thing is certain. *John Bull* was quite unlike any of the other penny weeklies that had previously graced the London publishing scene. In fact, one might almost suggest that its closest ancestors could be found in the radical press that had flourished three-quarters of a century earlier. There can certainly be no doubt of its attitude to figures in public authority; those to whom the British are normally so deferential.

Thus, when Edward VII died on 6 May 1910, Bottomley immediately sent an open letter to the new king, George V,[128] while *Answers* led with a black lined page lamenting the deceased, one week later.[129] Where Bottomley emphasized the difficulties the new leader faced, *Answers* rushed to reassure everyone, emphasizing in their very first sentence about him that the new king was 'well equipped for the responsible position.'[130] In other words, while the Harmsworth weekly aligned itself with established power, Bottomley was more sceptical. It should also be noted that the Odhams production machine was able to deliver their editorial seven days before the more ponderous *Answers* set up.

Perhaps the 22 January issue for that year was typical of the magazine at this time. *John Bull* follows the *Tit-bits* formula in its opening pages, which start with number 97, but adapts it to its own purposes. Where *Tit-bits* began each issue in 1890 with a page of quick-fire jokes, just a few lines long, which were separated one from another by four large dots, *John Bull* began with single paragraphs of political comments and ironies separated by 1 cm long °–point rules (lines). This pattern continues for four pages. Each page is split into two columns and divided by a °–point rule. No cross-heads are used so that the pages appear contiguous, although the information is not.

The two columns of page 101 are quite different. That on the left is devoted to comic paragraphs and ends in a caricature of the efforts of the Evangelical Alliance to close skating rinks on Sunday. The right column is devoted to 'John Bull's Biscuits'; that is, quotations from newspapers, advertisements and recent speeches which contain mistakes which 'take the biscuit'. The quotations in these short paragraphs are set in italic, with emphasis in small capitals, while the source is listed in larger capitals. This right-hand page forms a punctuation point in the issue which separates the first section from the pages which follow.

Short articles form the second section of the issue, the longest being approximately 1,800 words. The latter also has the only title set in bold 18–point type across both columns. Cross-heads are centred and use capitals but are otherwise similar to the body type. This device aids differentiation between parts of the article without any strong emphasis which would focus attention on one element of the story. Other titles are in bold ten–point capitals and only run within the column. Right-hand pages 105, 107 and 109 are full–page advertisements. There are no illustrations other than two cartoons which end page 108.

Pages 112 and 113 are the most aggressive in the issue. The left-hand side of the spread, purely text, is composed of open letters to people or institutions in the news, either ironic or sardonic. The Mayor of High Wycombe is castigated for indulging petty corruption by the local police, while the Leicester Art Gallery Committee is pilloried for partly covering a painting of two nude bathers with fabric. The letter concludes with a complaint that the Committee is doing nothing to contain 'the corrupting and debasing influences of depravity' brought about by allowing 'dogs, cats, and other animals careering naked and unashamed through the streets of Leicester.' The right hand page is filled with a cartoon showing a group of men, each of whom represents a pressure group waiting outside a door, labelled 'General Election Court' and 'National Jury'. The caricature is in the content not the draughtsmanship, which is restrained and happy to render its illusion through the hatching and crosshatching conventions typical of the nineteenth-century wood block. But its impact on the page is considerably diminished because, following its landscape format, it was turned through 90° to fit it on the page.

The spread which follows is entirely of text devoted to financial matters. Both columns of page 114 are filled with the regular feature 'John Bull in the city'; a series of paragraphs of gossip about companies or situations. The right-hand page is filled with replies to financial enquiries set in barely readable six–point type.

Page 117 is the last full editorial page and is largely given over to an attack on church bazaars. The layout follows the style of the rest of the issue: competent, neat and dull. The last 11 pages are dominated by advertising with no one page giving more than 50% of the printed surface to editorial text. One column on page 122 is directed at women; another on 123 is filled with a series of two-line jokes. Letters take up 90% of a column on pages 124 and 125. The final editorial material in the issue is a two-thirds column of horse racing tips.

Superficially, this end of the issue section appears similar to its counterpart in the *Saturday Evening Post*. But the British weekly filled the space with fresh articles which follow one after another. The *Post* trailed continuations of articles begun earlier in each issue. Furthermore, the leading pages of this issue of *John Bull* from 1910 also provided a marked contrast to the highly illustrated American weeklies. *John Bull* was almost entirely textbound and from that point of view was very reminiscent of *Tit-bits* of the 1880s, which enjoyed such enormous success despite its lack of illustrations.

Looking at *John Bull* from another viewpoint, that of six months as a whole, brings out more emphatically its unusual profile. Only just over 1% of editorial space was allocated to fiction, and that largely consisted of the occasional short story. *Tit-bits* used about 22% and *Answers* over 33% at the same time. There were no serials. Those steady stalwarts, the natural sciences and medicine got less than a total of one page during the entire period examined. Bottomley's idea of a sporting feature was a regular column on horse racing. Yet, public affairs, with almost 30%, and business, and social problems, together took over half the editorial pages during the first half of 1910(see Appendix XXIV). *John Bull* did not run letters to the editor but letters from him. Altogether, it was a quite unprecedented way to edit a magazine, particularly in Britain. Only in the United States, in *Collier's*, at this time, do we find a magazine as interested in contemporary society as *John Bull*. And while they were sceptical, they certainly did not run a city page or encourage interest in horse racing, matters that might have alienated their constituency.

The British public lapped it up. In 1910, Bottomley organised a dinner celebrating a half million circulation.[131] But that seems to have been a little premature; one of those acts of positive embellishment to which he was so prone. When a certificate of net sales finally reached the editor of the Advertisers' Protection Society's Monthly Circular at the beginning of 1913, *John Bull* still only registered sales of 409,872 per week for December 1912.[132]

The advertisers also demonstrated their enthusiasm, despite the exaggerations about the circulation, that is, in what they were buying for their money. During the first half of 1910, *John Bull* was running 16.6 pages of paid advertisements in the 36 pages of every issue, that is 32 plus the cover. By way of comparison, the Harmsworth machine could attract only an average of 7.7 pages an issue to *Answers*, which ran to 28 pages; or *Tit-bits*, to which the Newnes staff attracted an average of 8.7 pages per week in 28 pages. The credit for this success must go to the workers at Odhams. Bottomley had just ignored the printing bills he was running up right from the first week. When his debt reached £50,000, even Elias got anxious. To overcome the problem and circumvent Bottomley's creative attitude to money, Elias suggested that Odhams take over the business management of *John Bull*, deduct their expenses and remit the remainder to Bottomley. The latter conceded the point immediately. Thus, it is to Odhams that the credit must be given for organising the most successful advertising medium amongst any of the British periodicals to this point. They achieved this without the advantage of being able to sell the front cover as all their competitors did. Their cover sported an elegant design in black on buff paper featuring an image of a rotund gentleman, whose name was, of course, encapsulated in the title.(Fig. 31) This was followed by the four lines of Byron seen above. If anything, the design was, perhaps, reminiscent of the work of the Beggarstaff Brothers. Altogether, it was an unlikely achievement, to have made such an idiosyncratic publication so successful.

WHEN WAR BROKE OUT IN AUGUST 1914, Horatio Bottomley was more interested in his horses than the forthcoming conflict. The current issue even contained an article entitled 'To Hell With Servia!'[133] Yet, as soon as he returned from the race course in Ostend and reached Victoria Station, he went straight to the *John Bull* offices in Covent Garden. There, he and his staff transformed the weekly. On 15 August it even appeared with a new cover.(Fig. 32) This was the new, improved, nationalistic Bottomley.[134]

Like many who dedicate themselves to intense sensual gratification, he was acutely aware of the moment. When Britain shook itself into a belligerent frenzy, so did Bottomley. Indeed, one act in particular seemed intended to redeem his previous distraction from the cause. At the end of the article on 'Servia', in which he had decried the idea of the British shedding their blood for what he saw as a duplicitous nation of assassins, he had quoted

Fig.31 There are a number of elements that are incorporated into the idiosyncratic Odhams's weekly that echo a much older tradition than its peers among the current penny weeklies, not least of which was the patriotic title. The other, of course, was its highly critical attitude to authority, which it shared with the radical press of the late eighteenth and early nineteenth century.

three lines from Shakespeare. He now transformed the front page with this rallying cry, seen here, discarding the previously used quotation from Byron. Alongside it stood a renewed national character, complete with a sailor's cap from HMS Victory, a cutlass in his hand, ammunition belts across his chest and a pistol pouch on his hip. At his side stood the newly alert bulldog. While it might look ludicrous now, there cannot be much doubt that the readers would have been moved to see themselves as the heirs of Nelson. Inside, the rhetoric expanded. Page four was headed 'The Dawn of Britain's Greatest Glory.' Less credibly, page six demonstrated that *John Bull* had been right all along: 'The Voice In The Wilderness - That Was Heard At Last.' When you have that much nerve, you can get away with almost anything.

Bottomley was invited to make a recruiting speech at the London Opera House in Kingsway on 14 September. By the time he began to address the audience, the building was filled with 5,000 people and such a great crowd was clamouring at the door that Kingsway was blocked and traffic had to be diverted.[135] Another rally was organised for 14 January 1915, this time by the impresario C.B. Cochran at the Royal Albert Hall. On this occasion, the crowd outside was so vast that it took Bottomley an hour just to get into the building from his carriage.[136] Under these circumstances it is hardly surprising that when the Harmsworth brothers decided to launch a Sunday paper as a companion to the *Daily Mirror*, they approached Bottomley and signed him to write a weekly article for the *Sunday Pictorial*. As they eventually paid him £7,800 a year for this, it is not remarkable that they should promote his contribution heavily. Thus, the nation–wide distribution of posters carrying the Bottomley features and paid for by the Harmsworth empire, could not help but promote the organ to which Bottomley's reputation was most clearly linked.[137] The circulation of *John Bull* soared beyond the million mark and probably stayed there for the duration of the conflict.[138] On 3 October 1914, he even had the cheek to head the front page 'Largest Circulation of Any Weekly Journal in the World.' There is no record of a complaint by George Lorrimer.

Yet, this journalistic reputation was another sleazy sleight of hand. Even the thundering attacks on the Hun of 15 August 1914 were ghosted by a member of the *John Bull* staff, a journalist called Pilley. Later, he and others wrote the *Sunday Pictorial* articles as well.[139] Maybe this ploy is no real surprise for Bottomley was rushing round the country drumming up support for King and Country. But even this activity was turned to considerable profit.[140]

Fig.32 *The nationalistic belligerence of John Bull during the First World War did not compromise its anti-authoritarian attitudes. It channelled them into publicising the grievances of the fighting men, which was illegal. Bottomley's value to the War Office, as the nation's recruiting sergeant, gave them the excuse they needed to ignore his breach of King's Regulations.*

John Bull was always over-belligerent and over-optimistic about the approaching victory. Yet, when it came in 1918, the weekly seemed to sink back exhausted. During the war, a column had published the grievances of the serving soldiers and sailors. This was quite illegal and contrary to King's Regulations, but its use as a safety valve caused the War Office to turn a Nelsonian eye to the breach of discipline. In their turn, the *John Bull* staff seem to have devoted substantial efforts to the cases of injustice brought to their attention.[141]

By the end of the decade, these causes seem to have preoccupied the staff, for the massive attention paid to politics before the war had tailed off, even if to a figure still substantial by the criteria of other editors, that is almost 14% on average during the first six months of 1920. In its place were the articles on social problems, which were almost entirely directed to particular, individual cases rather than general themes and took over 30% of editorial space(see Appendix XXIV). The only exception to this championing of particular victims during the period in question, occurred on 17 April 1920, when 'the editor' used his weekly centre-spread allocation to attack the prevalence of 'massage parlours' in London.

Given the enthusiasm of the staff for these jousts with authority, one can only assume that they had little energy left for the rest of the magazine. Not only is the range of material extremely limited for a mixed function periodical, but its layout each week was stereotyped to a considerable degree. Each week there were little more than millimetres difference in the variations and one would always expect a precise repetition of the previous week's pattern. The first three pages always contained a miscellany of critical items attacking injustice and authoritarian behaviour, all in sections no more than 5 cm long in three columns across each page. Invariably, this was followed by precisely one page of open letters to various public figures. Page ten was reserved for letters from readers. Page fourteen was always reserved for humour. The centre spread was entirely given over to a substantial statements of opinion by 'the editor'. But, by this time, it is highly unlikely that any of the articles would have been written by Bottomley, whose attention was elsewhere. His past was about to catch up with him.

This lacklustre approach seems to have had a serious effect on the circulation for, although claims were issued for a circulation of 1,300,000, when a post-war accountant's certificate was actually produced, it only substantiated an average weekly sale of 800,000+.[142] Furthermore, advertising sales had slipped as well. They now only averaged 10.45 pages in 24-pages-plus-cover editions. While both the above figures still meant that *John Bull* was the circulation and advertising volume leader in the British magazine market, there was no doubt that, relative to its own previous successes, it was in commercial decline.

Another telling indicator is the actual substance of the magazine. At the beginning of the decade, *John Bull* had been printed on paper that was noticeably more durable than that of its rivals, that is, it is still in good condition today. By the decade's end the reverse is true. The paper used to print *Answers* and *Tit-bits* had improved enormously and is still in reasonable condition. The paper used to print *John Bull* in 1920 was poor and is now brittle.

To drive the point home even further, the cover design that had been so individual for the last fourteen years was abandoned on 1 May 1920; being replaced by advertising and a banner headline. With Bottomley's expenditures as uncontrollable as ever, all revenues were crucial.

While *John Bull's* star was still in the ascendant, substantial changes in the structure of the industry had occurred elsewhere. Sir George Newnes had died on 10 June 1910.[143] He was succeeded as chairman and managing director of the company that bore his name by Sir George Riddell, an extremely capable solicitor who had become involved in the publishing world through his position as a legal adviser to a dynamic consortium that had bought the *News of the World* and turned it into Britain's best-selling weekly newspaper.[144]

In 1912, Arthur Pearson went blind and began liquidating his assets so that he could devote himself to the welfare of his fellow sufferers.[145] In 1914, the Newnes group bought the bulk of the assets in C. Arthur Pearson Ltd., thereby gaining control of a second stable of titles, largely parallel to their own.[146] In June 1920, their interests were further consolidated by the formation of the Newnes and Pearson Printing Company, which bought the assets, liabilities and goodwill of the London Colour Printing Company, proposing to build a completely new plant to service the needs of the joint company. Riddell, the son of a Brixton photographer, held by far the largest stake in both companies among their directors.[147]

Despite these changes, the editorial position of the companies' leading titles never really evolved. *Tit-bits* continued much as ever, the trends of the previous decade only strengthening, despite the cataclysms of the time. Even at the height of the war, 1916, the year of the slaughter on the Somme, the conflict barely touched *Tit-bits*. The contrast with the editorial vigour of the response to the Boer War could not be more telling. The use of fiction diminished still further during the decade, to just over 17% (see Appendix XXI). The enthusiasm for competitions increased again, though their lack of individual character made them a matter of regular volume rather than sparkling ideas. Those miscellaneous morsels that had been the hallmark of the weekly in its initial incarnation had all but disappeared. Now, information was part of a context. Where before, odd, disparate items would last a line or two, they were now consolidated into six or seven paragraphs, though their entertainment value was still emphasized. For example, the issue for 3 January 1920 carried an item headed 'Pity the Poor Pianist', which dwelt on the totalled effort of keyboard pressure during various musical performances. 'Chopin's last study in C Minor' was seen as the equivalent of three tons.

Physically, as already indicated, the paper stock used to print *Tit-bits* had improved over the decade. This may well have been a consequence of the desire to use illustrations more extensively. Over the decade there was a 60% increase in their use to 1.22 per page. Over 40% of these were now halftone reproductions of photographs, almost entirely portraits that were used to identify the subjects of various biographical paragraphs. Needless to say, despite the upgrading of the paper, the quality of these reproductions was atrocious.

Over the decade, the three successful weeklies launched before the turn of the century became increasingly convergent in their appearance and their approach. *Pearson's* had lost its early initiative with illustration and now used slightly less than *Tit-bits*. Slightly fewer of these were from photographs, just over 31%. Even more emphatically, their situation within each issue, their allocation to the different articles and serials in both publications was increasingly similar. The same comment can equally be applied to the articles. Both increasingly favoured humour and competitions at the expense of the space allocated to stories and serials. Both demonstrated an increased interest in social problems, in part one suspects, as a consequence of *John Bull's* emphasis on such material(see Appendices XX and XXI).

Pearson's only substantial claim to individuality, now that it no longer published a women's page, was its occasional use of special features in which a four-page section was devoted to one topic. On 28 February 1920 it was spiritualism, at the end of March it was the movies, on 5 June a special Derby section was produced and the end of June saw a tennis section. *Answers* did at least appear slightly more individual than its old rivals. Whereas *Pearson's* and *Tit-bits* relied on illustrations, *Answers* preferred to use a little more white space, just noticeably better paper and a better ink colour; that is, it looked 'blacker'. But, when that is said, one is only discussing matters of degree. *Answers* placed a stronger emphasis on sport at almost 6% of editorial space between January and June 1920, and 5.3% on business matters(see Appendix XXIII). It also ran its quota of competitions, of which one contained an echo of the past, that is, it featured a £2 a week for life prize. Its first page also featured that familiar miscellany of fragmentary paragraphs, a poem and jokes. In other words, everything seemed set in journalistic aspic.

This stagnation was reflected in sales, which were dwindling when compared to their pre-war heights. *Answers* was selling 412,266 per week on average during 1920,[148] while the first reliably audited figures available for *Tit-bits* covered the following year, at 473,650 per week.[149] *Pearson's Weekly* was probably selling about 400,000 a week, but no audited circulation figures for that magazine ever appear to have been published at any time.[150]

Now, these rather tired publications were being pressed by a new breed of specialist weekly. Amalgamated Press's own *Picture Show*, with its mindless puffs of long forgotten nonentities of the silent screen, was selling 442,819 a week during 1920.[151] While the equally mindless *Weldon's Ladies' Journal* sustained a circulation of 442,631 a month.[152] Out of the 366 pages published in the latter during the period from January to June 1920, only 16.38 featured genuine editorial material. The remainder was almost equally split between paid advertisements and advertisements for the company's paper pattern service.

Weldon's Ladies' Journal is a rarity among British best sellers under examination because it is a monthly, but its format is very similar to *The Delineator*, *Pictorial Review* and the early editions of *McCall's*: it claims to be a fashion magazine but is really little more than an elaborate monthly catalogue for the proprietor's paper pattern company. Perhaps it was this commercial orientation that attracted the Berry brothers, who bought the company during 1920,[153] six years before they purchased Amalgamated Press from the administrators of Lord Northcliffe's estate, so developing the base of their publishing empire to come.[154]

The layout of the *Journal* was very repetitive both from month to month and page to page, and the May 1920 issue was no exception. It is wrapped in a colour gravure cover printed with the plates out of register. Six pages of advertisements lead into the title page. However, even the magazine's title is set in type no larger than 48–point and is pushed to the corners of the layout in order to give the illustrations maximum space. The latter are three fashion drawings of garments produced from Weldon Fashion's paper patterns, or purport to be. The page paper is calendered machine printings which permits halftone reproduction of moderate quality, but it is unable to cope with a full monochrome range; what should be white is light grey and what should be black is dark grey. The text is just a number by the illustration with a paragraph at the foot of the page repeating the number at the start of a short description of possible materials and quantities necessary.

A true editorial comment on Parisian fashion follows on page eight, though even this is illustrated by a drawing of pattern no.62669: 'One of the new French models developed in foulard or soft fancy taffeta trimmed with plain soft silk.' Each spread which follows is composed of one page of advertisements facing a page of pattern illustrations. Four or five full length figures are used on each page, usually about 17 cm high on a 29 cm page. Then, between pages 26 and 27, a gravure supplement, a regular feature, has been inserted. The figures in these illustrations average 23 cm high and there is little text other than the pattern number. Details of fabrics and quantities are relegated to page 50. As might be expected, the quality of these reproductions is superior to others in the issue. The supplement is further distinguished by the use of sepia-coloured ink rather than black.(Plate IX)

The pattern established in the first half of the issue is resumed at the end of the insert with advertisements facing drawings of garments. Page 37 marks a change, with detailed instructions on crochet work. The piece is accompanied by seven reproductions of photographs of examples. Because the fabric is made from pale thread and photographed on a black background, details show up well. A rather odd combination occurs on page 38 in which a column of recipes for inexpensive cakes is accompanied by reproductions of line drawings of 'house frocks'. The remaining 14 pages are 50% advertisements with a mishmash of practical hints on making up a selection of the patterns illustrated earlier. Line drawings are used to explain details.

Although this issue is very limited editorially, it does illuminate the way in which some women's magazines were trying to upgrade the quality of their illustrations. The volume of advertising is much higher than the British *Woman's World*, for example, and the revenue would have helped offset the cost of the gravure insert. It and the publisher's portion of the sixpence cover price would have also helped Weldon's pay for the paper used for the letterpress section of the issue, which was a marked improvement on the newsprint used by the likes of *Answers* and *John Bull*. However, these changes are really quite marginal and the gap between the most popular British women's magazines and their American counterparts at this point helps emphasize the poverty of editorial culture in the British magazine trade at the time, both from the point of view of content and design.

The cover of *Picture Show* always featured the head or head and shoulders of a current player of the silver screen. But, for every portrait of a personality of some genuine prominence of the period, such as Mary Pickford, Owen Moore, Mary Miles Minter or Chaplin, there were dozens of people who have left no traceable cinematic record outside these pages and those of similar publications. Most of the text seemed to have been produced by the publicity department of the studios, although fictional serials were also used. In fact, the whole publication must have been very cheap to produce for the profusely used illustrations would also have been free publicity material. Occasionally, the readers were given a little extra when a four-page gravure section was inserted into the centre of an edition that featured more portraits and publicity stills.

THE FIRST TWO DECADES OF THE TWENTIETH CENTURY were a period of technical quiescence and adjustment for the magazine trade after the convulsions of the previous twenty years. Colour covers and a few polychromatic illustrations came to be the norm. Only the *Ladies' Home Journal* and, to lesser extent, *Collier's* in the United States, as well as *Illustrated London News* in Britain, made unequivocal commitments to new technology, which only emphasized the passivity of the rest, for they had few followers.

Collier's editorial profile for the century's opening years developed out of the weekly newsmagazine derived from *Illustrated London News* during the second half of the nineteenth century. With a much larger circulation than any found in their predecessors and a critical attitude to politicians in general, as well as splendid graphics, the magazine achieved a measure of political power unparalleled before or since in the magazine world.

The *Saturday Evening Post* was much more original in its approach, though that is not why it was bought. Its overwhelming use of fiction, which was unusual for an American weekly of the time, and its espousal of conservative values endeared it to millions. By the end of the second decade it was the dominant magazine in the United States. This led to a great deal of emulation by other editors of both weeklies and monthlies as the years passed; in particular, the organisation of each issue into clearly defined zones. A front-of-the-book limited to the opening pages of both articles and stories and devoid of advertising contrasted with the remainder of each issue which was the reverse: tail ends and advertisements, with the latter dominant. That this obviated the need for much editorial illustration in the later section had much to recommend it to the publishers in their desire to contain costs.

Of the monthlies in the American market, most took their lead from their mentors of the late nineteenth century, *Harper's* and *Century*, but flavoured the mix with spicy revelations about corrupt government and business. Only in the second decade, as Lorimer's editorial dominance became overwhelming, did they begin to acquire the practices of the *Post*. Only the monthlies with a specialised or restricted function went their own way.

As the new century opened, the specialist fashion press, which were frequently little more than house magazines for paper pattern manufacturers, together with Bok and his rivals, began to surpass the sales of the mixed function monthlies. For most, their range of topics was very limited but Bok's success was a countervailing force, and when the *Woman's Home Companion* sought to challenge his pre-eminence it also picked up his habits. Thus, social issues, politics and other topics quite unknown in the British women's popular press became embedded in the culture of the American women's press.

British magazines had no Lorimer or Bok to prod them into life and competing interests were engaging the managements of the three dominant publishing groups. Harmsworth was more interested in newspapers. After the success of the *Daily Mail*, he founded the *Daily Mirror*. In 1908 he gained control of *The Times*.[155] Pearson had launched the *Daily Express* but was making heavy weather of it.[156] Newnes was more interested in the bottle.[157] So, it is hardly surprising that the editorial staffs marked time. The only change in their leading penny weeklies was the spread of illustrations from *Pearson's Weekly* into the other two.

The only intrusion into this cosy world came when an outsider made a rude entry on to the scene. Bottomley's disinclination to tug his forelock and Odhams' managerial skill pushed *John Bull* to the top of the tree as the second decade progressed. Its trenchantly critical attitude to those in power resembled that of much earlier radical papers and was an exotic flavour at the top table; one which was never repeated.

Even the liquidation of Pearson's interest in publishing in 1914 and the merger of his company with that of the Newnes family, failed to change the industrial structure of British serials. The string of titles produced by both companies were allowed to co-exist and no significant rationalisation took place. The pattern developed by Newnes and Harmsworth in the early 1890s, of a portfolio of magazines making respectable but unsensational profits from a variety of market compartments, frequently class-related, refined from the tactics of Brett and Henderson of the previous generation and their ventures in the juvenile market, continued down the decades. As will be seen, when Odhams' became the most vigorous company in the industry, they too slotted into the industry's existing framework.

Thus, not only were the best-selling American magazines directed at an entirely different audience to the British counterparts, the industrial structure that became their context was quite different as well. The Curtis and Crowell groups sought to develop just three or four major titles that would sell in millions. Even as their income burgeoned under the weight of vast volumes of advertising, which could easily have been channelled into new projects and titles, they retained this approach. Even the Hearst chain with its swarms of newspapers never really sought to break this pattern of magazine clusters. In the following decade it even amalgamated *Cosmopolitan* with *Hearst's Magazine* in an attempt to develop a title that would match the circulations of its competitors. No British magazine publisher would ever have made such a move for such a reason at this time. Quite the reverse.

In Britain, market development meant another interest group and another set of titles. Thus, as the twenties approached and the audience for the movies flourished, the British publishers launched a gaggle of competing titles to sop up demand. They were, of course, well illustrated. After all, many of the pictures were free. The only difference from the magazines that had preceded them was the price. They cost twopence: a price change that soon affected all the best sellers. Twentieth century inflation was on the move.

Notes

1. Berry, W. Turner and Poole, H. Edmund, *Annals of Printing*, London, 1966, pp263-264.

2. Ibid., pp269-270.

3. Goodman, J., Death of I.W. Rubel, Inventor of the Rubber Offset Litho Machine, *The British Printer*, Vol.21, No.125, Oct-Nov. 1906, Leicester, p232.

4. Comparato, Frank, *Chronicles of Genius and Folly*, Culver City, California, 1979, p693. See also Harrap, Charles, The Offset Rotary Printing Press, *The British Printer*, Vol.23, No.134, April-May 1910, Leicester p68, for a list of companies that jumped on the bandwagon.

5. Anon., Trade Notes, *The British Printer*, Vol.19, No.113, Oct-Nov. 1906, p283.

6. Comparato, op.cit., p693.

7. Gamble, William, The Year's Progress in Process, in *Penrose's Pictorial Annual*, Vol.15, London, 1909-10, p11.

8. Gamble, William, The Year's Progress in Process Work, in *Penrose's Pictorial Annual*, Vol.17, London, 1911-12, p8.

9. Wakeman, Geoffrey, *The Production of Nineteenth Century Colour Illustration*, Loughborough, 1976, pp4-5 and 13.

10. Gamble, William, The Year's Progress in Process Work, in *Penrose's Pictorial Annual*, Vol.13, London, 1907-08, p3.

11. Salade, Robert F., Modern Methods of Colour Printing, *The British Printer*, Vol.43, No.253, May-June 1930, Leicester and London, p8.

12. Munsey, Frank A., The Making and Marketing of Munsey's Magazine, in *Munsey's Magazine*, Vol.22, No.4, New York and London, January 1900, pp488-491.

13. Wilson, Harold S., *McClure's Magazine and the Muckrakers*, Princeton, New Jersey, 1970, p48 et seq: 'My blood is like champagne.'

14. Wakeman, op.cit., p4. This is not the first use of printed colour in magazines, as opposed to hand-tinted prints. That honour goes to *The Art Union*, Vol.8, London, February 1846, opposite p70.

15. Jacoby, G., New Methods of Illustrating Newspapers, *The British Printer*, Vol.23, No.137, Oct-Nov. 1910, Leicester, p252. Also, Colebrook, Frank, Our Platemaking Causerie, *The British Printer*, Vol.24, No.142, Aug-Sept. 1911, Leicester and London, p178. Also, Lillien, Otto M., *History of Industrial Gravure Printing up to 1920*, London, 1972, pp129-130, 140.

16. *Dictionary of National Biography 1961-70*, Oxford, 1981, pp565-566.

17. This information, and much more, is held in the Ingram Archive, The Science Museum Library, South Kensington, London.

18. Gamble, William, Position and Prospects of Process Work, in *Penrose's Annual*, Vol.21, London, 1916, pp12-13.

19. Berry and Poole, op.cit., pp271-272.

20. Ibid.

21. Anon., Colour Gravure in Newspapers, *The British Printer*, Vol.44, No.262, Nov-Dec. 1931, Leicester and London, p204.

22. Moran, James, *Printing Presses*, London, 1973, p216.

23. Ayer and Sons, N. W., *American Newspaper Annual*, Philadelphia,, 1910, p604.

24. Ibid, pp789 and 792.

25. *Nelson Chesman and Company's Newspaper Rate Book*, St Louis, 1910-11, p174.

26. Peterson, Theodore, *Magazines in the Twentieth Century*, Urbana, Ill., 2nd ed., 1964, p12.

27. Chesman, 1900, op.cit., p178.

28. Peterson, op.cit., p12.

29. Chesman, 1910-11, op.cit., p237.

30. The collection of the *The Advertisers' Protection Society Monthly Circular* is held by the Incorporated Society of British Advertisers at 44 Hereford Street, London W1.

31. Bok, Edward, *A Man From Maine*, New York, 1923, p171.

32. Sykes, Philip, *Albert E Reed and the Creation of a Paper Business 1860-1960*, Privately Produced, 1982, p370.

33. Wood, James Playstead, *The Curtis Magazines*, New York, 1971, pp42-43.

34. US Department of Commerce, *Historical Statistics of the United States*, Colonial Times to 1970, Part 1, Washington, 1975, p457.

35. Ibid, pp11-12.

36. Mott, Frank L., *A History of American Magazines*, Boston, Mass., 1938-68, Vol.4, p59.

37. Marcaccio, Michael D., *The Hapgoods*, Charlottesville, Virginia, 1977, p73.

38. Ibid, p79.

39. Ibid, pp85-86.

40. Ibid., pp90-95.

41. Mott, Vol.4, op.cit., pp461-462.

42. Ibid, p462 and Marcaccio, op.cit., pp103-105.

43. Chesman, 1910-11, op.cit., pp162-163.

44. Wilson, op.cit., p101.

45. Lyons, Peter, *Success Story*, New York, 1963, p194, though this is only one among many examples.

46. Wilson, op.cit., pp81-103.

47. Ibid., pp130-146.

48. Ayer, 1904, op.cit., p715.

49. Ayer, 1906, op.cit., p763.

50. Wilson, op.cit., p101.

51. Ibid., pp174-182.

52. Ibid, pp186-189.

53. Ayer, 1903, op.cit., p690.

54. Thayer, John Adams, *Out of the Rut*, New York, 1912, pp227-231.

55. Ibid., pp251-255.

56. Mott, Vol.5, op.cit., p81.

57. Chesman, 1910, op.cit., p167.

58. Greene, Theodore P., *America's Heroes*, New York, 1970, p214.

59. Mott, Vol.3, op.cit., p510.

60. Ibid.

61. Ibid., p513.

62. Baker, Ray Stannard, Do it for Rochester, *The American Magazine*, Vol.70, September 1910, pp683-696.

63. Tarbell, Ida M., The Mysteries and Cruelties of the Tariff, *The American Magazine*, Vol.70, October 1910, pp735-743.

64. Chesman, op.cit: 1904 edition, p168; October 1906 to June 1907, 1907 edition, p152; 1909 in 1909-1910 edition, p163; 1910 in 1911-1912 edition, p150.

65. Casson, Herbert N., The Rockefeller Foundation, *Munsey's Magazine*, Vol.43, No.3, June 1910, pp295-304.

66. Gregory, John F., Successful Sons of Rich Men, *Munsey's Magazine*, Vol.43, No.5, August 1910, pp585-595.

67. Chesmen, 1900, op.cit., p142.

68. Ibid, 1910-11, p177.

69. Mott, Vol.4, op.cit., p616.

70. Chesman, 1910-11, op.cit, p233.

71. Bok, op.cit., p168.

72. Wood, *Curtis*, op.cit., pp29-30.

73. Chesman, 1910-11, op.cit., p174.

74. Ibid, 1921, p150.

75. Ibid, 1921, p163.

76. Ibid, p44.

77. *Historical Statistics*, Vol.1, series F9, p224.

78. Ibid., series E185, p212.

79. Chesman, 1910-11, op.cit. p140,

80. Ibid, p147.

81. Ibid., p153.

82. Ibid., p199.

83. Ibid, pp141, 146 & 147.

84. Tebbel, John, *George Horace Lorimer and The Saturday Evening Post*, New York, 1948, p208.

85. Wood, *Curtis*, op.cit., p94.

86. Tebbel, op.cit., p209.

87. Unger, Leonard (Editor-in-Chief), *American Writers*, Vol.2, New York, 1974, p77.

88. Tebbel, op.cit., p208.

89. Chesman, 1921, op.cit., p202.

90. Ibid, pp200-201.

91. Peterson, op.cit., p182.

92. Chesman, 1921, op.cit., p48.

93. Ibid., p163.

94. Mott, Vol.4, op.cit., p763.

95. Ibid., pp763-768.

96. Ibid., Vol.3, p510.

97. Chenery, William Ludlow, *So It Seemed*, New York, 1952, pp162-169; Peterson, op.cit., pp130-136; Mott, Vol.4, op.cit., pp767-768; Anon., Joseph Palmer Knapp, Magazine Publisher, 86, Dies, *New York Times*, 31 January 1951, p1, column four.

98. Chenery, op.cit., p162.

99. Bennett, Helen Christine, The Greatest Builder of Skyscrapers in the World, *The American Magazine*, Vol.89, No.4, April 1920, pp16-17, 172.

100. Chesman, op.cit., 1915-16, p275; 1917-18, p214; 1921, p135.

101. Greene, Theodore P., *America's Heroes*, New York, 1970, pp294-295.

102. Mott, Vol.4, op.cit., p468.

103. Chesman, 1910-11, op.cit., p174.

104. Ibid, 1921, p150.

105. Peterson, op.cit., p155.

106. Ibid, pp153-154; and Mott, Vol.4, op.cit., pp569-574.

107. Ibid.

108. *The Advertisers' ABC*, London ,1900, opposite p302.

109. *The Advertisers' Protection Society Monthly Circular*, No.85, May 1911, p4.

110. Wilsher, Peter, *The Pound in Your Pocket 1870-1970*, London, 1970, p94.

111. Private interview with Mr R.Best of the ISBA.

112. Private interview with Mr R. Best of the ISBA.

113. *APS Monthly Circular*, No.87, July 1911, p11.

114. Ibid., No.47, March 1908.

115. Wodehouse, P.G., The Intrusions of Jimmy, *Tit-bits*, Vol.58, No.1495, 11 June 1910, p291 et seq.

116. Carpenter, Kevin, *Penny Dreadfuls and Comics*, London, 1983, p76.

117. *APS Monthly Circular*, No.49, May 1908.

118. Letter from Alfred Harmsworth to A. E. Linforth, a director of the Amalgamated Press, dated 27 August 1911, gives the circulation of *Woman's World* as currently being 347,000. British Library Manuscript Division, File 62183-4. As this is, for all intents and purposes, an internal memo, there is no conceivable reason why it should be an exaggeration.

119. Ibid.

120. Hammerton, Sir John, *Books and Myself*, London, 1944, p180.

121. Minney, Rubeigh J., *Viscount Southwood*, London, 1954, p80.

122. Hyman, Alan, *The Rise and Fall of Horatio Bottomley*, London, 1972, pp28-51.

123. Ibid., p29.

124. Ibid., pp55-70.

125. Ibid., pp80-82.

126. Ibid., pp74-79.

127. Symons, Julian, *Horatio Bottomley*, London, 1955, pp77-79.

128. *John Bull*, Vol.8, No.206, 14 May 1910, p694.

129. *Answers*, Vol.55, No.3, 21 May 1910, p49.

130. Ibid, p58.

131. Symons, op.cit., p79.

132. *APS Monthly Circular*, No.106, February 1913, p51.

133. *John Bull*, Vol.17, No.427, 8 August 1914, p6.

134. Hyman, op.cit., pp144-149.

135. Ibid., p150 & Symons, op.cit., pp173-174.

136. Hyman, op.cit., pp151-154.

137. Symons, op.cit., pp169-170.

138. *APS Monthly Circular*, No.136, August 1915, p31. *John Bull* passed one million circulation on 3 July 1915, rising to 1,074,174; accountant's certificate.

139. Symons, op.cit., pp163 & 171.

140. Ibid., p180.

141. Hyman, op.cit., p161.

142. *Incorporated Society of British Advertisers' Monthly Circular*, No.10, March 1921, pp15-16.

143. *Dictionary of Business Biography*, London, 1985, Vol.4, p438.

144. Ibid., p911.

145. Ibid., p576.

146. Ibid., p911.

147. *Pearson's Weekly*, No.1562, 19 June 1920, pp10-11.

148. *ISBA Monthly Circular*, No.10, March 1921, pp15-16.

149. Mather and Crowther, *Practical Advertising*, London, 1922, p23.

150. *ISBA*, op.cit., pp15-16.

151. Ibid.

152. Ibid.

153. Hartwell, Lord, *William Camrose: Giant of Fleet Street*, London, 1992, 102.

154. *Dictionary of Business Biog.*, op.cit., Vol.1, p303.

155. Ibid., Vol.3, p51.

156. Ibid., Vol.4, p576.

157. Ibid., p438.

The Years 1921–1940

THE 1920S WERE NOT A PERIOD OF ABRUPT TECHNICAL CHANGE in the publishing trade, more one of steady evolution and consolidation, continuing the pattern of the two previous decades. By 1921, all of the commercially important printing processes, letterpress, gravure and offset lithography could be used to reproduce colour illustrations but not necessarily within commercial strictures or to the standards demanded by magazines. By 1930, that goal was much closer to realisation. Ten years later the British magazine scene had been transformed by gravure, both monochrome and colour, while the appearance of America's top titles had been revitalised by new technology.

To judge by the frequency of comments during the twenties, a great deal of contemporary attention seems to have been paid to rotary gravure. Although the German company of Siegburg had managed to extract single art prints from a multicolour gravure press using a web of paper in 1913, nine years elapsed before *The Chicago Tribune* tried to produce a 32-page weekly supplement in the volume required by a successful serial. To print 900,000 copies a week, a special press was built for the newspaper by the Goss Printing Press Company, also of Chicago.[1] After 'years of costly experimentation' the paper's engineers had designed a machine of double width that printed four colours on one side of the paper web and one on the other in one continuous run. It needed four days to produce each edition, running 20 hours a day. Heat had to be used to dry the inks between each roller and was necessarily so intense that the web shrank as a consequence. To compensate for this reduction, the plates for the four colours were made as a set that diminished slightly in size, by a carefully calculated amount pro rata with the paper, from the first to the last used. Only in this way could alignment, or register, be maintained between the separate colours in the final result. *The Tribune* also made its own inks.[2] Despite all this effort, even contemporary enthusiasts had to admit that the results could be described as 'somewhat crude'.[3]

Clearly such a custom-built system could not be marketed on an industry-wide basis. Despite research in Germany[4] and Britain, at the Sun Engraving Company,[5] all efforts seemed unable to push the speed of the presses beyond 3,000 to 4,000 sheets per hour before the end of the decade and still print acceptable colour work. The keenest impediment to faster production seems to have been a lack of safe, instantly dry inks. Nevertheless, these problems did not stop *L'Illustration* employing colour gravure on a regular basis by 1927 in Paris.[6]

The inadequacy of ink technology was also, doubtless, a headache for offset lithographers. However, whatever the irritations, there can be little question that, by the middle of the decade, publishers were beginning to take it seriously. Such a sober trade journal as *The British Printer* was able to report the steady expansion of the technology throughout the industry.[7] In 1925 a hagiographer of the Amalgamated Press, still owned by Harmsworth's executors, claimed that the company possessed 'the litho-offset machines which are the latest thing in colour printing' at their Sumner Street works in Southwark, London.[8] A year later, William Gamble claimed that the Elm Press, also of London, was actually using the technique to produce a number of magazines, though with the maximum number of colours set at two.[9] By way of contrast, at the same time in Berlin, Messrs Dr Selle and Company were printing at least five weekly publications on reel-fed, rotary offset presses, one of which, *Berliner Leben*, sported a four-colour cover and two-colour interior illustrations.[10]

Although letterpress had been used in conjunction with colour in the United States and Britain since 1896, there had been very little expansion in its domain since that first decade. One problem was the expense involved, both in terms of special paper stocks and the necessary plant. And, even given those resources, great care was still essential to get worthwhile results.

The other problem was common to all three major processes and that involved not the reproductions but the originals. Until the introduction of the integral tripak film in 1936, in Germany by Agfa and the United States by Kodak, the taking of colour photographs was a cumbersome and time-consuming process that was barely feasible beyond the confines of the studio environment. As late as 1928, one could still see credits for colour separation plates made direct from the original object, without the intervention of a photographer.[11] Consequently, there was a dearth of editorial material demanding page space.[12] And it must, in part, have been this lack of suitable illustrative material that led to one of the strangest of all magazines, *Colour*, which lasted from 1914 until 1924. Page after glossy page of the London-based monthly featured vivid, well printed reproductions of more-or-less modern paintings from agreeable artists. At first glance it might be taken for a publication from the art world. Yet, the contents were largely fiction, with a sprinkling of poems and a few reviews at the rear. The text was almost completely unrelated to the pictures. One is unsure which element was selling the magazine and which was its complement.

So, even when Cottrell's produced their four-colour, web perfecting press in 1926, which became the standard for the industry, there was no great colour explosion.[13] Yet, throughout the decade, the increasing finesse of the journeymen in the press shops and the platemaking departments was complemented by the manufacturers, who brought steady improvements to the colour filters, pre-sensitised plates, copy lenses and cameras for the latter and better inks and paper to the former.[14] At the Curtis plant in Philadelphia, one of the employees invented a way of avoiding 'set-off', a serious problem with presses operating at the speeds necessary to produce the huge circulations of *Saturday Evening Post* and *Ladies' Home Journal*. To avoid the still–wet ink transferring on to the back of the sheet lying upon it on the board at the end of the press, wax powder was blown on to the printed surface as it came off the impression cylinder. After drying the wax was undetectable. Known as the Gammer Process in Britain, it was used at a printing works in central London by 1926.[15] It was through small increments that technology moved forward in the 1920s.

Ink made the difference in the 1930s. Although letterpress still dominated magazine production world–wide, its continued hegemony was now in doubt. Despite their increasing use, gravure and offset remained in the wings at the beginning of the decade. But, by its end they were moving steadily nearer to the centre of the stage, particularly in Europe.

The key event for the intaglio process was the invention of the air-tight ink fountain by Adolph Weiss, who first demonstrated it to American gravure printers in 1930.[16] All the pigment solvents for gravure inks had to be highly volatile. But the most effective of these liquids were dangerous, being either highly inflammable or toxic, or both. The new design all but enclosed the printing cylinder, leaving only a narrow slit at the top through which contact with the web could be maintained. Inside, the ink was sprayed on to the plate. The excess was wiped off by a blade and drained back into the well of the box. The pressure of the gas from the volatile ink inside the box prevented air entering.[17] Speeds of 18,000 to 23,000 revolutions per hour with full colour were claimed, a three-to-four-fold increase.[18] Alco-Gravure were eventually induced to buy the process. In turn, in 1936, they sold the British rights to Odhams, who set up a company especially to exploit its potential.[19] By 1937, *The American Magazine, Woman's Home Companion, Country Home* and *Collier's*, all owned by the Crowell Publishing Company, an associate of Alco-Gravure, were all carrying signatures printed by the gravure presses fitted with the new ink fountain. Alco also printed *This Week*, a five million circulation Sunday supplement distributed in 21 major newspapers, using their Goss gravure equipment.[20] In Britain, interest in high-speed gravure developed slowly at first but by the end of the forties it was the dominant technology among the leading titles.

The Schlesinger ink system did not have quite the immediate impact of its sister process, but it was still a major advance in offset printing. By allowing stiffer inks to be used, and so avoiding the ad-hoc additions of varnish or oil so beloved by the press-minder, it promoted consistency, the use of much finer halftones at higher speeds, improved print colour and necessitated fewer printings to get a particular ink density. It achieved this by mechanical means. A system of three rollers, using a reciprocal action, beat the ink to a useable consistency and then transferred it to the main inking system of whatever machine was being used. As the device was an add-on, it could be used on a wide variety of offset presses.[21]

Such flexibility was hardly the keynote of the 'heat-set' inks which enhanced letterpress printing before the end of the decade. The patronage of Time Incorporated was crucial to their emergence. In 1932, the company, bought *Architectural Forum*. Part of the latter's publishing activities included a series of portfolios of European architects, supervised by them and printed locally. The German edition was printed in Vienna using 'heat-set' inks.[22]

Nevertheless, the company appears not to have been directly responsible for the transfer of the technology across the Atlantic, an event delayed, apparently, until about 1935. Even then the potential of the product seems to have lain largely unrealised until Time Inc. decided to publish *Life*. Their conception of a weekly, large-volume, predominantly picture magazine of the highest quality was to set a new benchmark for serials in the US. The demands of exceptionally short print deadlines necessitated by the news content and the standard of reproduction expected by Luce and his editors predicated a technological transformation in letterpress, of which new inks were an essential feature.

As implied above, these new materials required a substantial adaptation of existing presses. Two heater units, the width of the press and four feet long, were added to each machine, one on either side of the web. They were fuelled by gas, the supply of which was regulated automatically by the speed of the paper. Passing between the boxes, a heat of 1400°F was attained when the presses were running fast. The ink oxidised so rapidly that it burst into flame. Emerging from the heat chamber, the paper immediately made contact with a water-cooled cylinder, which 'set' the ink.[23]

The idea of using these inks in volume production was so novel that new press designs had to be created and constructed. Time Incorporated could not delay their new publication for the year that this would take and insisted that their printers, R. R. Donnelley of Chicago and Cuneo Press of Philadelphia, proceed on makeshift equipment. The consequences of this decision were such that the project was brought close to abortion.[24]

Another innovation in ink technology was exploited at the Curtis plant in Philadelphia when a new but secret solvent that dried very quickly, was used to replace linseed oil, hitherto the basis of letterpress inks.[25]

The other essential ingredient for this letterpress transformation was new paper: an improvement on the usual surface quality was needed that could be produced in volume, that was not prohibitively expensive. By the early thirties the American paper industry was experimenting with rollers that could coat the web in a continuous operation.[26] The result was a paper that approached the quality of art paper that did not require the detailed attention, time and skill necessary in the manufacture of the older, quality product which made it so expensive. So, when Time Inc. approached their paper suppliers, the Mead Corporation, they were offered Enameline at $98 a ton, which was well within their budgetary projections.[27] The new production process appeared in the UK in 1936 when the Star Paper Mills were granted an exclusive sub-licence.[28]

Initially, part of *Life* was printed gravure because their letterpress equipment could not handle blocks situated next to the edge of the page, that is, that were 'bled'. However, by 1940 modifications had been made to their presses and they were able to dispense with gravure altogether.[29] Such predilections emphasize an interesting difference between Europe and the United States. Gravure was never seen by the major American magazine publishers as anything more than a peripheral technology. Their pre-eminent technology remained the relief process. Indeed, as late as 1947, the Curtis organisation, which with *Saturday Evening Post* and *Ladies' Home Journal* owned two of the world's best-selling serials, made a huge investment in a brand new letterpress plant on a green-field site just outside Philadelphia. There seems little doubt that the dead weight of interest charges on an investment in what proved to be cumbersome and inappropriate plant contributed to the company's decline in the subsequent decade.[30]

Yet in Europe, the potential of the developing technologies, especially gravure, was more widely exploited during the mid-century by the magazine entrepreneurs. Nevertheless, despite this uncharacteristic American inertia, as the thirties drew to a close, innovations in platemaking materials appeared that within a generation would sound the death knell of letterpress after 500 years of dominance. But, it needed that extra generation of development before these changes could assume their place in the industry's production processes.

THE 1920s WERE A PERIOD OF SUBSTANTIAL GROWTH in the American economy. Total consumption expenditures rose by 33% between 1919 and 1929, that is, from $60,573 million to $80,761 million.[31] But, the total volume of advertising rose even more, by 50% over the same period, that is, from $2,282 million to $3,426 million.[32] In such an expansive economic situation, it is hardly surprising that the magazines were in a buoyant state as well. By the decade's end, the *Post* had pushed its circulation very close to three million, while the rest of the pack were not far behind. Again, a surge in surplus disposable income coincides with a major increase in the size of a magazine market.

Now there were four major weeklies: *Collier's*, the *Post*, a newcomer, *Liberty*, and the *Literary Digest* bringing up the rear. The latter's circulation had lagged behind the rest, a failure that seems in no small part due to the intrusion of the nascent *Time* into its sector of the market. Of the old-style mixed-function monthlies, only *The American Magazine* had raised its circulation above the two million threshold. *Cosmopolitan* had been amalgamated with *Hearst's Magazine* in the middle of the decade, but their combined circulation had not really expanded beyond the point they had achieved separately. Increasingly, the large circulations were tending to go to those magazines whose editorial profiles were either restricted in content or specialised. Among the former, *Woman's Home Companion* had taken the circulation leadership of the women's monthlies from *Ladies' Home Journal* by just a matter of about 25,000 sales per month, at 2,606,123.[33] The *Journal*, at 2,581,942,[34] was only just in front of *McCall's*, at 2,505,088,[35] and *Pictorial Review* at 2,500,000.[36] The much more specialised, *True*

Story Magazine had emerged from nowhere to gain admittance to the two million circulation club – the figure which has been used as the cut–off point during this decade. Other specialist monthlies, such as *Better Homes and Gardens*, at 1,389,990,[37] and *National Geographic*, at 1,286,808,[38] were rising steadily within the general growth in magazine sales. Such trends were only encouraged by the development and growing sophistication of market research during the 1920s. Now the media buyers in the advertising agencies had an increasingly precise tool at their command with which they could define and assess the purchasers of each publication, comparing the quality as well as the size of the readership.

Supreme in the United States, *Saturday Evening Post*, during the first six months of 1930, had a 'sworn detailed average circulation' of 2,924,363.[39] However, its popularity with the public was far exceeded by its popularity with the business community of America. While its circulation exceeded that of *Woman's Home Companion* by just over 300,000, or 12%, its advertising revenue exceeded its rival by over 460%. Whereas the monthly women's publication from the Crowell organisation took $10,187,401 in advertising revenue throughout 1930, the *Post* took $47,551,104. Of course, such comparisons are enormously affected by the frequency of publication. Yet, the *Companion's* stable mate, *Collier's*, much more comparable to the Curtis weekly, took even less: $9,525,826.[40]

In part, such dominance reflects the desire to be associated with a successful publication. It also reflects the emphasis the publisher had always placed on his advertising department, whose staff, by 1930, must have exceeded the small editorial staff many times over, having as it did seven separate offices spread across the United States from the east to the west coast.[41] The magazine's success may also have been due, in part, to the readership profile, which emerges from a contemporary report issued by the *Post's* consumer research division. By 1930, the readership had become increasingly affluent and was thus a good market for the advertisers. A detailed investigation in Schenectady, a town with a population of 95,692, revealed that 75% of homes where the head of the household was an executive took the *Post*; 65% of households whose head was a member of a profession took the *Post*; and 65% of households where its head was a wholesaler or a large retailer took the *Post*.[42] In other words, by advertising in the *Post*, a company reached a large number of people, in excess of 11 million if the research is accurate;[43] it reached a disproportionately affluent segment of the population; and it reached the majority of an executive's peers in the business community. Thus, an advertisement in the *Post* impressed through the association with success and the known cost of a page in the magazine, which in 1930 varied from $8,000 for monochrome to $23,000 for the back cover in four colours.[44] By 1930, with the depression already taking its toll, such reassurance to potential associates must have been a valuable commodity.

However, this discontiguous relationship between income and actual readership, where a magazine could become disproportionately richer than its rivals in a way that did not reflect the size of its audience but its value, or supposed value to the advertiser, was going to have enormous consequences for the future. Such a fracturing of what hitherto had normally been a reciprocal relationship between gross income and public acceptance, did not always have to work to the magazine's benefit, as was to be found to be disastrously true in the 1950s and 1960s. When so much profit depended on the notional value of a publication in the minds of a small number of media buyers in the agencies, factors that affected that notional value became much more potent in the profit and loss columns than the demand for the magazine by the paying public.

Already, the consequences of this, as advertising volume in the national media expanded and the market place for space became increasingly sophisticated, was causing significant anomalies. For example, while the total net paid circulation of *Vogue* in 1930 was 133,931, that of *Better Homes and Gardens* was 1,390,660.[45] Yet, that year the former took $3,012,593 from the advertisers, while the latter took almost half a million dollars less, at $2,515,353.[46] Thus, the survivors in the market place were increasingly likely to be those that were able to supply a closely defined and attractive readership to the media buyer.

For the moment such considerations did not trouble the *Post*; it was riding high. Now, not only did it use the advertiser's graphics to enliven the back-of-the-book, it allowed them to use four-colour illustrations as well. This transformed the appearance of a magazine whose editor used colour only once in each issue: on the cover. Without these contributions, the *Post* would have looked very drab indeed for Lorimer stuck doggedly to his wash drawings and photographs, stuffing them into the front-of-the-book section while relying on the advertisers in the back. Indeed, the magazine's use was so prodigious in that limited area, 1782 illustrative figures in just over 1927 editorial pages, that it averaged 0.92 blocks per page overall, a high figure for the time for anything outside the women's press. Yet, like 1920, only a very small proportion of these were from line blocks and many of those were, again, tiny tailpieces.

One change that the *Post* did demonstrate was in the use of photographs, which increased from 32.44% of the total number of illustrative figures in 1920, to 36.47% in the first six months of 1930. In part, this increase may be attributed to a new solution to an old problem: how to fit all the disparate elements of the magazine together without leaving awkward little white paper gaps in between. In the nineteenth century, poetry had been used by all the magazines to fill the spare spaces. It was just the right length and in plentiful supply, if you were not too bothered

Fig.33 The appearance of the Post changed slightly during the twenties, as four-colour advertising brightened its pages. The layouts also gained in fluency as Lorimer allowed the art department to spread its designs across two pages. But he forbad them the use of coloured illustrations.

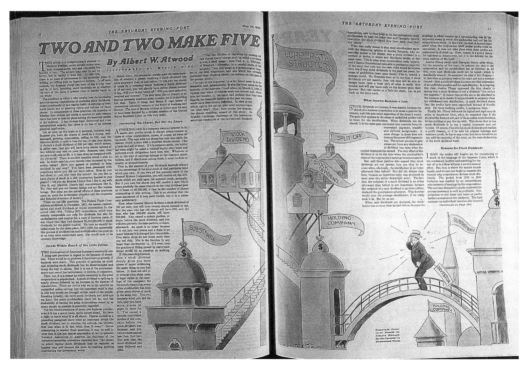

about the quality. However, as designers grew more skilful in using the facilities of photo-mechanical reproduction, they were able to enlarge or diminish the size of illustrations at will, and the need for poetry evaporated. But, if you created a magazine in which there were few illustrations in the back-of-the-book section with the advertisements confined to rigid shapes, a new problem arose. To overcome this, small photographs of the American landscape were inserted in the *Post,* for Lorimer was a man who made no secret of his passion for such scenes. Further, given the designer's increasing sophistication, these pictures were frequently moved from a position at the end of a piece and cut into the middle, thus partially avoiding the appearance of a stop gap.

Another change which was evident by the end of the 1920s was a relaxation in the rigid division between the front and back sections of the magazine. This can be seen if one issue is examined. The 24 May 1930 edition starts in much the same as the *Post* had been starting for 30 years: the magazine's title and details of its personnel were enclosed in a box at the top of page four, while the leading article began immediately underneath. In this issue it was under the by-line of the Democratic presidential candidate of the year, Alfred E. Smith. His article continued uninterrupted for three pages and then shifted to page 141. In the front section, five photographs and one drawing of past politicians on the stump, plus a shot of Smith immediately below the title, illustrated the piece. But the last page and the final third of the article in the back are purely text.

Each of the two subsequent spreads are devoted to a separate story which trails off into the back-of-the-book. Both are illustrated with two pieces of artwork, one on each page. An article on finance occupies the next spread. A caricature representing the modern corporation as a fantastic French medieval castle, redolent of a fairy tale world of make believe, is printed across the gutter and dominates the layout under the headline 'Two And Two Makes Five'.(Fig. 33) The drawing immediately establishes the tone of the piece and is no longer a decorative extra to the text in the manner of earlier decades. Even in the *Post*, the impact of a piece was a consequence of both text and graphics and the manner in which the force of their combined argument was intertwined.

This layout is followed by two more short stories covering double spreads which trail into the back. Pages 16 and 17 feature one article each, both of which are 'continued on ...'. Then the pattern of double spreads resumes until 28, where the magazine returns to single-page pieces. The right-hand page given over to Campbell's Soup is found on page 31. But instead of this marking the beginning of the end, it is immediately followed by the start of a biographical memoire written by a Russian Grand Duchess, which faces a full-page advertisement. This pattern of a fresh editorial item facing a full page advertisement continues up to page 71, where the tail ends of stories and articles from the first section start to appear.(Fig. 34) The advertising starts to close in on the editorial at this point and the space available to it rarely extends to a full page thereafter. All of these pieces, wherever they start or finish, are distinguished by titles and credit lines set in the *Post*'s own typeface; the italic, rounded-serif face which it used in 46-point for titles. It also appeared on the cover and at the top of every page, always outlined in black and filled in grey.

In terms of the contents, Lorimer was too set in his ways to change much and with such a successful formula, there must have been little pressure to do so. The proportion of space given over to fiction had drifted upward slightly from 1920 to almost 59%. History and biography, which in the twentieth century became increasingly the latter, expanded to just over 5%. Sport made a more positive appearance, increasing from 0.75% in 1920, to over 2.5% in 1930, which in absolute terms meant that it consumed over 50 pages. And while business held steady at 8%,

155

Fig.34 The classic George Lorimer formula of separating each edition of the Post rigidly into two halves began to break down as the twenties approached their end. Fresh articles started to appear at the back where continuations had formerly held sway.

public affairs slid to a little over 5% The only real surprises were the articles on fashion and children. Mere straws in the wind it is true, but unexpected ones for all that(see Appendix XVII).

What changed was not so much the *Post* or Lorimer, but the context in which they found themselves. New forces were abroad in twenties America and they produced changes that Lorimer found distasteful. His yearning for the certainties of his youth as he passed through his fifties provoked a reaction that led him to commission articles on business, as he always had, but with a strong anti-union bias, whereas once he had tried to maintain a more even-handed position.[47] His enthusiasm for thrift and his advocacy of hard work looked increasingly at variance with America's new found enthusiasm for the consumption of non-essentials. But that was being encouraged by the acres of advertising in the back of the *Post* that funded the Curtis empire. Such contradictions made Lorimer's position increasingly difficult.[48] His move further to the right was charted in his enthusiasm for Mussolini and fascism[49] as the twenties progressed. Its apotheosis was to come in the following decade with his virulent attacks on Roosevelt and the New Deal.[50]

Given their totally different backgrounds, one in big business, the other in newspapers and the social reform movement, it might be seen as ironic that George Lorimer and William Chenery should adopt not dissimilar editorial profiles in their rival weeklies. Alternatively, it might be seen as a victory for market forces, the readers getting what they wanted; voting with their nickels. Yet, the student of human behaviour might conclude that William Chenery, on inheriting in 1925 the editorial chair of a weekly whose audience was slipping away, chose to copy the most successful pattern around to staunch the bleeding. Whatever the motivation, by 1930 the overall editorial balance in both the *Post* and *Collier's* was remarkably similar. In fact, the Crowell weekly more closely resembled the overall current approach of its rival than it did its own volumes of ten years before. Now, the emphasis was heavily on fiction, at just over 59% of editorial space; which was only 0.25% different from the *Post*. History and biography at over 5% was, again, within 0.25% of its competitor's mark. The interest in the arts was vestigial in both and largely concentrated on performance, in such areas as the theatre, movies and music. Religion was also vestigial, while humour and entertainment in both were bullish as compared to 1920. They were even dipping their toes in such long disdained areas as fashion and domestic interests. Only their approaches to contemporary society demonstrated their differences, with Lorimer's continued interest in business contrasting with Chenery's editorial commitment to the repeal of prohibition and prison reform(see Appendices VII and XVII).

But, if their ends were all too similar, their means were very different. *Collier's* art direction under William Chessman[51] was much more adventurous than anything attempted at the *Post*, once inside that is. For there can be no doubt that this period is the golden one for the *Post*'s covers. When Lorimer at last released his artists from the constraints of two colours, he did them an enormous service. Norman Rockwell in particular had, by 1930, gained a stature missing ten years before. The irony and wit of his conceptions still puncture the sentimentality that was all too evident in the works of the *Post*'s other cover artists. Furthermore, if the inside pages of the Curtis weekly were printed on markedly inferior paper to their Crowell counterpart, the same is not true of the covers. Here the advantage lies with the *Post*, where the stock was marginally whiter and the inks used were better saturated than on their rival's examples. On top of that, the selection of the artists and their paintings, which was unquestionably under Lorimer's complete control,[52] demonstrates a clear conception of the *Post*'s identity, consistency and a more mature sense of humour. All too frequently, *Collier's* covers are weak in conception, whimsical in intent and poor in execution.

Yet, as already stated, once inside the latter conceded nothing to its more successful rival. While the *Post* barely varied its established graphic formula, *Collier's* had increased its already extensive use of illustrations to 1.2 per page. Of these 1163 examples, over 40% were printed from line blocks, while over 23% of both halftones and line reproductions were given a second colour to add variety to the overall design. Sensibly, given the inadequacy of their paper stock for the purpose, the use of photographs was seriously curtailed, being cut to only 17.28% of the total. Such graphic solutions to the problem of the cheap paper stock necessary for a 5¢ weekly were either resisted or never appreciated by Lorimer.

Another innovation that took root under Chenery's aegis was the development of an editorial staff whose job it was to write a substantial proportion of the magazine, unlike the *Post* with its small staff but broad circle of freelance contributors.[53] However, this editorial expansion was not limited to *Collier's*. A number of upcoming magazines started in the twenties also took this option: *Time*, *Reader's Digest* and *The New Yorker*, to name only the most prominent.

The third of the best-selling weeklies, *Liberty*, was very different from the *Post* and *Collier's* and it illustrates, in a classic way, a matter already mentioned: the disparity between successful sales to the readers and a successful pitch to the advertisers. By 1930, *Liberty* was selling 2,415,108 copies a week.[54] The longer established *Literary Digest* was selling 1,602,397.[55] Yet, despite a slightly higher page rate, *Liberty* could only generate $5,527,514 in advertising revenue, against the *Digest*'s $6,771,454.[56] Out of this lower per copy income, it had to sustain the fixed costs per copy of paper, printing and distribution. The latter, in particular, must have been high because the magazine was selling 99% of every issue on a single copy basis, that is from news–stands, not on subscription.[57] Normally, this is considered a great bonus by the media buyer for it implies that the public is buying every issue on its merits, not as a result of a cut-price promotion. In this case, the demerits of the magazines were so great they were outweighing this advantage.

For a start, probably in an attempt to minimise expenses, the paper was terrible. It was little more than calendered newsprint that has now undergone serious discoloration and is so fragile that it is impossible to handle without sustaining damage. Then there was the problem of the editorial profile. At a time when American magazines increasingly emphasized one aspect of their contents at the expense of many others, *Liberty* must have seemed rather vague with a little piece of everything to insure that it gave all its readers one topic that might interest them. Fashion got a little less than 3% of editorial space, sport got a little more. Business and economics got just over 1.25%, domestic matters got more than 1.75%. Only fiction, at almost 44% and history and biography, at nearly 12%, were given substantial amounts of space(see Appendix XVI). In other words, *Liberty* had no editorial definition.

Then there was the matter of specific articles. Quite what the editor thought he was doing in a 5¢ weekly, printed on dreadful paper, publishing articles on 'the greatest polo player in the world'[58] or 'Servantless Etiquette'[59] is open to question. At 5¢ a week for 80 pages, he could hardly go wrong with the public, but it was a different story with the media buyers who must have wondered who they were getting for their money. It is not surprising that the owners, Robert McCormick, the editor of the *Chicago Tribune*, and Joseph Patterson, the editor of the *New York Daily News*, were said to have lost $12 million on the magazine in the first seven years of its existence.[60]

The American Magazine was the last representative of that once dominant group, the traditional mixed function monthly which resembled *Harper's* and the *Century*, still to be found among the best-selling titles. John Siddall, who had edited it ten years before and turned it into a million seller, had died in 1923. He had been succeeded by Merle Crowell, who continued with the successful formula. However, bad health forced him to retire in 1929. He was succeeded by Sumner Blossom.[61]

Even as early as the first months of 1930, a change in the tone of the magazine is evident, despite Blossom's name not appearing on the mast-head until March of that year. Gone was the populism, so insistent under Siddall, the very direct, personalisation of the majority of the articles. In its place was a relaxed combination of westerns, love and detective stories, plus articles on familiar topics. In fact, it was largely the tone that had changed for there is very little difference in the overall editorial profile between 1920 and 1930. Fiction increased to almost 49% of the editorial pages, largely at the expense of articles on business. Sport reasserted itself, while social problems diminished in the editor's favour. Otherwise, the balance between the various topics remained remarkably stable (see Appendix V).

What had improved was the appearance of the magazine. Henry Quinn, the art director, used many more illustrations, 0.78 per page, as opposed to only 0.46 ten years before. As in *Collier's*, the use of photographs had diminished sharply, from 50.49% in 1920 to 27.18% in 1930. However, unlike the other Crowell publications, line blocks had not risen up to take their place. On *The American* they were used to reproduce 19% of the illustrations between January and June 1930, which was nowhere near the 40% used in their stable mate, *Collier's*. *The American* preferred halftones.

In part, the differences between the two Crowell magazines might be attributed to the differing paper stocks on which they were printed. That of *The American* was noticeably better calendered and would thus reproduce halftones better than the stock used by *Collier's*. But it was also a matter of choice. Quinn, the art director, certainly exercised his preference in the way that the illustrations related to the rest of the page. In 1920, borders were usually clearly defined by straight edges, however light the background tone. This inhibited eye movement and emphasized the parallel edges of the page. Quinn preferred his artwork and sometimes even photographs to bleed out into the white space of the unadorned page surface. This allowed the eye to move much more freely across the surface and sustained an illusion that the page was larger. He was also able to experiment with four-colour artwork for articles, as well as use the customary Crowell gravure insert.

Much the same options were open to Quinn when he wore his other hat, that of art director of *Woman's Home Companion*. The latter was noticeably richer than *The American*, attracting $10,187,101 in advertising revenue in 1930, as opposed to $5,249,378.[62] This enabled it to use a good-quality imitation art paper, which, in turn, enabled Quinn to move freely between line, halftone, two and four colours. As line blocks were used for over 40% of the illustrations and photographs were only used in 22.25%, this was clearly a matter of choice, largely unconstrained by technical parameters. Given, one presumes, a larger budget on the women's monthly, he was able to use over 70 four-colour reproductions. He tried some on fashion and home decoration articles, but concentrated them in the substantial amounts of fiction that graced each issue.

The latter had stabilised at about 40% of editorial space, which is very similar to the amount of space allocated to fiction in the *Ladies' Home Journal*. Indeed, the editorial profile was much as it had been ten years before, which is hardly surprising, given that it still retained the same editor, Gertrude Lane. And, as this formula had just knocked the *Journal* off the top spot after 40 years, there was every inducement to continue on the same path(see Appendix XIII).

A similar confident air was no longer apparent at the *Journal* which was drifting. After being pre-eminent for so long, it had been surpassed by the *Companion* and was being pressed hard by *McCall's* and *Pictorial Review*, with their very similar combination of fiction and in-house advertisements for their clothing pattern service. This drift at the *Journal* might be inferred from the decline in interest in contemporary life and affairs and the increased dependence on articles about domestic details, the commonplace patterns of so much of the women's press. The interest in the arts had also slumped to a new low, something it is hard to imagine Edward Bok tolerating(see Appendix XI). However, 1930 was the year that his obituary appeared in the *Journal*.

Despite a simplification of its graphics, as compared to 1920, the *Journal* still looked rather old-fashioned in 1930. This largely seems to be a function of its typography, with an elaborate script for its headings, which contrasted with the much simpler, serif style used by the *Companion*. However, the *Journal* did try experimenting with new graphic possibilities. In particular, it made extensive use of colour photography to illustrate its articles on garden plants. However, this was undermined by the quality of its paper. The whiter stock used by the *Companion* would always create a better impression in the mind of the reader, rendering the reproductions with greater contrast. Although the *Journal* had trimmed its page height from 401mm in 1920 to 345mm in 1930, which was very close to the size of the *Companion*, it needed more than a little nip to modernise its appearance.

By 1930, *McCall's* was becoming broader and more sophisticated in its editorial approach. Nevertheless, its primary purpose was still to publicise its clothing patterns. To that end it had used colours in a limited way as early as 1920. Ten years later, the leading designs were featured in drawings that at least avoided repeating the covers used on the pattern packets; a standard practice in 1920. There was some attempt to create a more general ambience that reflected the graphic styles in such rivals as the *Journal*. Unfortunately, there was no evading the fact that these were editorialised advertisements and not editorial fashion illustrations in the normal sense, as would be found in such rivals as the *Companion* at this time. The same situation was true of the *Pictorial Review*, which also owned a pattern service.

Over the years, between 1911 and 1927, *McCall's* changed its editor all too frequently and, although circulation moved ever upward, with one hiatus towards the end of World War One, the magazine never had the opportunity to develop a profile more sophisticated than a fiction-and-in-house-fashion formula. Then, in January 1928, the McCall Company hired Otis Wiese; at 23, probably the youngest editor of a national magazine in the US. By 1930, the monthly was showing some evidence of his touch. But it was really during the following decade that he showed his hand and mounted a direct assault on the front-of-the-book/back-of-the-book schism that guided so much magazine design at this point.

The last magazine to breach the two million circulation barrier by the end of the twenties was very much a novelty item among American monthlies: *True Story*. It was conceived and created by that great eccentric Bernarr Macfadden and his wife. According to her narrative, which certainly has a stronger ring of authenticity than the story retailed by Fulton Oursler, Mary Macfadden suggested the idea to her always impecunious husband during an evening walk in February 1918. Based upon the correspondence that was received by their *Physical Culture Magazine*, she felt that a magazine could be produced from the authentic stories of unknown individuals. So, they borrowed $1 million from a bank and engaged John Brennan, who had worked for them before, as editor, with Orr Elder as advertising manager. It was Brennan who proposed the novel idea of using photographic illustrations. This was a particularly shrewd move as one of their most serious problems was credibility and photography added an air of authenticity. The irony was, of course, that all the photographs had to be posed for the camera, that is, faked. At first the editor used his own family in his own home, but success and the necessity of variety soon dictated a more professional operation.[63] To avoid a similar slickness in the text, Macfadden engaged a team of untrained, very young men and women to read the stories and insisted that Brennan was only allowed to modify the punctuation. The material was gathered by advertising in his *Physical Culture Magazine* and running competitions for the best material.[64] Clearly, such a system was open to abuse by cunning professionals and to try to overcome this difficulty, the magazine began to insist on character affidavits by third parties.[65] Sales, to the astonishment of the publishing community, rose to unexpected heights.

Two problems remained. The first was a technical one. Having finite resources and, initially, limited credibility with the advertising agencies, as well as a small starting circulation, they could only afford very poor paper. This limited the quality of the reproductions of the photographs. To solve this problem they turned to gravure, which can give good reproduction on relatively inexpensive paper. As we have seen, other American magazines began to use small gravure inserts, and the *Illustrated London News* had used the process to print more-or-less entire issues from the summer of 1919. *True Story* began using the process to produce much of their front-of-the-book section from December 1919; a solution they were still using in 1930.

The second problem was more personal. Macfadden was not only obsessed with physical fitness, he was a life-long advocate of sexual frankness and education. When, around 1906, he published a serial, 'Wild Oats' in *Physical Culture*, that detailed the consequences of ignorance and venereal disease, he was arrested for sending obscene material through the mail. The trial had found him guilty and he was sentenced to two years in jail and a $2,000 fine. The case was appealed all the way to the US Supreme Court and confirmed on every occasion. Only a presidential pardon by Taft, demanded by the public, had saved Macfadden from incarceration. Thus, he was very cautious about giving cause for any further prosecutions.[66] To protect himself and his new publication, he engaged a pack of prominent clerics, with due publicity, to add fibre to his moral tone.[67] By implication, they also added further to the air of authenticity necessary to the stories.

By 1930, for 25¢, the readers were getting an average of 200 pages an issue. Each edition began with advertisements and a series of short, fragmented items. The main front-of-the-book gravure section opened with four bled portraits of movie stars. That was followed by a one page homily on love or happiness signed by Macfadden. The rest of the front-of-the-book was a mixture of the beginnings of first person stories and serials. The latter were concocted by professionals[68] but it is very noticeable that they share the first person format and rough style of the stories which were pronounced 'authentic'. Common sense suggests that some of the latter were written by professionals but there is, equally, no reason to believe that a proportion were not created by amateurs and participants in their dramas. More importantly, the readership clearly believed they were authentic and, for the publisher, that was what counted.

THE THIRTIES WERE A GREAT TURNING POINT for American magazines. In almost every area, technical, financial and aesthetic, the years between 1930 and 1940 marked a change. These were the years when the overwhelming strength of the Curtis organisation began to assume more mortal limits again; when a revolutionary new weekly, *Life*, erupted out of Time Incorporated; when its antithesis, *Reader's Digest*, soared from a respected if idiosyncratic, minor situation to market leadership. On the technical front, colour photography at last became a practical means of recording the world beyond the studio, and examples even graced the cover of the *Post*.

Yet, it was also a period in which the old, dead wood dropped away, shaken from its niche by a tremor at its financial base. Advertising has always been a volatile industry, servicing those who are not responsible for its welfare. Thus, when the economic collapse dictated retrenchment in 1929, advertising budgets were slashed immediately. In one year, their dollar volume dropped almost 24%.[69] This, in its turn, squeezed the magazines' receipts from this source and although the publishers withstood the first panic quite well their advertising receipts, nevertheless, declined from $318,676,144 in 1929 to $220,644,201 in 1939, a fall of over 30% for the decade.[70]

Over the years, advertising had formed an ever greater proportion of income. In 1890 it had contributed almost 50% of the newspaper and periodical industries' receipts. Ten years later, the proportion exceeded 54%, while, by 1905, it passed 56%.[71] In 1909, it touched 60% of the combined revenue of both industries. But, considered separately for the first time, the magazine industry received only 51.6% of its revenue from advertising. Yet, that proportion crept steadily upwards as well: 52.8% in 1914; 64.5% in 1919.[72] By 1929, it had stabilised at 63.7%. But after the cuts of the depression years and, by the end of the thirties, the crisis had squeezed its contribution to 55%.[73]

The consequences of this lengthy financial hiccup can be seen in the total number of magazines recorded by the Bureau of the Census. In 1929, according to their figures, the industry published 5,157 different titles. Two years later the figure was down to 4,887, but the worst was yet to come. By 1933 the total had dropped 33% from its peak of only 4 years before to 3,450.[74] Most of these failures were probably small and marginal entities, though one or two of the more successful, *Literary Digest*, *Pictorial Review* and *The Delineator*, disappeared as well. Even Curtis discontinued dividends on his common stock.[75] The effect of this cut in revenue was serious.

Yet, while the economy suffered a massive recession and promotional budgets were pared back, people still wanted to read whatever they chose, even if their preferences shifted from time to time. Of the popular weeklies, *Liberty*'s circulation slipped a little and never regained its momentum. It had been bought by Macfadden in the early thirties but his previously golden touch could not withstand the contraction in advertising budgets any more than anyone else, and by 1938 Macfadden Publications Inc. were in the red and in trouble.[76] Even *True Story* was slipping with an average circulation of 1,956,503.[77]

Among the popular monthlies, *The American* stagnated at about 2.5 million. Yet, on the whole, sales were resilient. Aggregate circulation, as recorded by the Bureau of the Census in 1933, was off its peak by only 13.5%, and by 1939 it had bounced back so well that it exceeded the 1929 total by 18.6%.[78] Thus, the graphs of magazines sales and advertising receipts, with the latter down by 30% over the same period, were describing totally different trajectories. For the first time, they had become decoupled. While one was rising, the other was falling in no uncertain manner. The American magazine was a dog with two different masters and they were now pulling in different directions.

If volume sales were anything to go by, the future seemed to belong to the weeklies and those monthlies with a restricted function. Most successful among the latter, was the *Woman's Home Companion*, which had surged ahead to 3,490,453 by 1940.[79] Not far behind was its arch-rival the *Journal*, at 3,286,560.[80] With similar page rates, advertising lineage and a cover price of 10¢, these two adversaries from the opposing Crowell and Curtis camps were evenly balanced. Not so *Collier's* and the *Post*, the two other sparring partners from these rival organisations. The Crowell weekly had made a strong circulation surge to average sales of 2,888,506, but with only 827 pages of advertising sold in the last six months of 1940, at prices that varied from $6,500 for a monochrome page to $11,750 for a back cover in four colours, it must have made somewhere between 5 and 5.5 million dollars gross for the period. By way of comparison, the *Post* had sold over 1500 pages for the first half of the year at prices that varied between $8,000 and $15,000 per page, which suggest a gross income in excess of $12 million for the period.[81] It was another case of the irrational preferences and habits of the media buyers entirely tilting the economic balance between titles, where the reading public favoured them in much more equal proportions. The condition that would prove terminal after the Second World War had already taken hold.

The one title that remained outside this tug-of-war between circulation and advertising, the exception to almost every rule, including the technical transformations of the 1930s, was the *Reader's Digest*, which first appeared in February 1922. It was the brainchild of De Witt Wallace, a previously restless young man, a few months past his 32nd birthday. His early career had been spent in the commercial departments of small mid-western publishers. In 1916 he edited and published a digest of advice for farmers in booklet form, touring the West as his own salesman. After selling 100,000, he returned to St Paul, Minnesota as the manager of the mail order department of a publisher of calendars and greetings cards. But immediately the United States declared war he enlisted. However, he was severely wounded in the neck and abdomen by shrapnel and the consequent hospitalisation for six months gave him little to do but read the plentiful supply of magazines to hand. His predilection for condensing texts found a focus in this material and his idea crystallised.

The first dummy, dated January 1920, encountered rampant apathy when Wallace touted it round the established publishers, so he gave up and went to work in the international publicity department of Westinghouse, the electrical manufacturers. However, post-war hard times soon came a-calling and Wallace was out of a job. He turned again to his notion of a digest and this time his belief in his idea was reinforced by his wife, Lila Acheson, a beautiful, imaginative and successful social worker, who joined him in the enterprise after their marriage. They determined to publish the *Digest* themselves, soliciting subscribers by circulars which Wallace's previous experience enabled him to produce with some skill. He acquired lists of teachers and nurses and combed college prospectuses for the names of faculty members. The response was sufficient, when added to their savings and a loan from his family, to float the first issue. In its turn, this drew further subscriptions, and in a matter of months, the Wallaces knew their project was self-sustaining.[82]

The concept was a very simple one: edit already published articles down to a length that averaged out at about 2,000 words by highly skilled excision. The raw material could be found in any public library. Enquiries proved that editors, provided attribution was made, did not object to this practice. For, despite what his hagiographers have said, Wallace's idea of a digest was hardly new. The *Review of Reviews* and *Literary Digest* had been successful components of the American magazine scene for 30 years. What was new was the simplicity of presentation. By eschewing any illustrations at all Wallace could have the *Digest* printed on relatively inexpensive paper that did not look cheap and nasty, as *Liberty* always did, for instance. This would contain the single largest expense any magazine publisher has to meet, that of production. In 1931, *Fortune* estimated that production plus distribution entailed almost half the cost of publishing *Cosmopolitan*.[83] So, if Wallace could contain such an important drain on revenues, he could sustain his other major novelty for 1922: no advertising. Charging 25¢ a copy or $3 a year, he needed to sell no space because his costs were relatively low. By selling on subscription, which relied on mail shots and word of mouth, he minimised any comparison with other, lower cover prices on the bookstall.

Thus during the twenties, a steady, successful business became established. Like all successful magazines, it attracted imitators, and it was one of these, *Fleet's Review*, which precipitated a change that entirely transformed the scale of the business. The interloper decided to try single-copy news stand sales in addition to subscriptions. That forced Wallace to match their move, but the dominant distributor, the American News Company, shrugged off his inquiry. He was then approached by S-M News, formed in 1919 to distribute *McCall's* and *Popular Science*. They took over this aspect of his operation and in the process Wallace was introduced to A. L. Cole, then the vice-president of the company. Cole was formally appointed business adviser to the Digest in 1932. In 1939 he was made business manager.[84]

Unfortunately most of the *Digest*'s operations have been shrouded in secrecy, but it seems very likely, given subsequent events and Cole's behaviour in later situations, that he was the catalyst that energised the circulation drive. From 1929 to 1936, the only period for which accurate circulation figures are available prior to 1955, sales bounded up from 290,000 to 1,801,400, at a time when most publishers were more than satisfied just to hold the line.[85] Given such dynamics, the statement by Wood that the *Digest* was selling 'about 4 million' a month by 1941 seems plausible.[86] In other words, it would appear that, by 1940, the *Digest* was the world's best-selling magazine.

Ironically, though it was largely created from the pages of other magazines, it resembled none of those that nurtured it. Quite apart from its small page size, 190 x 130 mm, and the clarity of its text, the editorial profile, the balance between the various topics that it published, was quite unlike those that furnished its raw material. The primary reason was its exclusion of fiction, though this was not total. In the period selected for analysis, January to June 1940, a novel formed the basis of one of the condensed books found, at this stage, at the rear of each edition. However, this was exceptional and, despite the substantial size of 'Children of God', a fictionalisation of the birth of the Mormon church, it absorbed only a little over 10% of the *Digest* during the six month period. Much more substantial and more impressive in every way was the magazine's commitment to an examination of contemporary society, to which it devoted over 47% of its page space. In particular, public affairs at over 13%, business and economics at 10%, and social life and manners at more than 7% were emphasized. By way of contrast, most of the other best-selling magazines look frivolous, even such august titles as the *Post*, which devoted the relatively modest 25% to contemporary society during the same period(see Appendices XVI and XVII).

Yet, there was one among the best-selling magazines that did take its social responsibilities as seriously as the *Digest*, perhaps even more so. And it could not have been further, physically, from the pocket-sized monthly. *Life* measured 349 x 261mm, which made the page area over 3.5 times bigger than the *Digest*. In addition, the weekly was a major innovator, being printed on a state-of-the-art coated paper created specially for it by the Mead Corporation.[87] Where the *Digest* never used even one illustration, *Life* never seemed to use anything else. *Life*, in fact, was the first popular American magazine which used photography to articulate its editorial direction. Though it did not fill every page, it did dominate. It was hardly surprising that such a vivacious, visually impressive publication took the American public by storm from its very first issue on 19 November 1936.[88]

It had been a long time gestating. Time Inc. had got started in 1922 when Henry Luce and Britton Hadden, journalistic rivals at Yale, quit their jobs on the *Baltimore News* and travelled to New York to raise the money to start their weekly newsmagazine *Time*.[89] Its first issue was dated 3 March 1923 and for years afterwards it was only one stage removed from a digest, being rewritten from items culled from the newspapers.

Yet, even before their venture was established on solid ground, these incipient tycoons (a word they introduced via the pages of *Time* from the Japanese),[90] were experimenting with new ventures. In 1924 they tried their first radio programme, 'The Time Questionnaire', as a promotional venture.[91] In 1927, Hadden took over a free monthly digest of advertising news, *Tide*, and turned it into an iconoclastic trade journal with subscriptions at $1 a year.[92] But, just over a year later, he died from a streptococcus infection of the blood and Luce was left in charge.[93] The extra responsibility did not inhibit his momentum or the launch of his own new venture, *Fortune* which, in its first decades, was a revolutionary idea in business journalism that also merits consideration as one of the most beautiful magazines ever published. Its first issue appeared in February 1930.[94] In March 1931, the radio version of 'The March of Time' was launched on the CBS. network.[95] In April 1932, the company acquired the prestigious weekly *Architectural Forum* and proceeded to transform it from an illustrated textbook into a critical journal that visualised many of the problems and buildings it discussed.[96] In February 1935, 'The March of Time' arrived on Broadway, beginning its idiosyncratic movie career.[97]

Thus, it is not really surprising that Time Inc. initiated such a radical departure in American popular journalism as *Life*. But, they were not precipitate in their commitment. Dwight Macdonald, a writer on the staff of *Fortune*, first broached the matter in 1932, when he submitted a dummy for a picture magazine to Luce. The following year he was incorporated into a small research group which worked on the project until Luce dissolved it in 1934 when he became dissatisfied with their progress.[98] Of course, there may have been a more basic reason. 'Production techniques simply were not available then to turn out illustrated pages good enough and fast enough and in the great quantity Luce and his colleagues projected for the picture magazine.'[99] Which only emphasizes how close to the cutting edge the magazine was when it finally appeared in November 1936.

There can be little doubt that the editorial team that finally brought the project to fruition were both stimulated and directly instructed by European experience. The key player appears to have been Daniel Longwell, who joined Time Inc. in 1934 from Doubleday, Doran. Of sufficient skill and reputation to have attracted previous job offers from Luce, he soon affected the volume and quality of visual material being used by *Time*. He was joined later that year by Kurt Korff, a German refugee and a former editor of *Berliner Illustrierte Zeitung* who developed the American's awareness of visual impact, of what makes a photograph exciting. Then, in the summer of 1935, Longwell visited Europe and spent time with the staff of *Paris-Soir* and *Weekly Illustrated*, the picture magazine published by Odhams Press in London.[100] In November, Luce remarried and Longwell took the opportunity occasioned by his absence on honeymoon to produce a 16-page dummy that he intended as a supplement to *Time*, which he forwarded to his absent editor-in-chief in due course. Luce returned full of enthusiasm and from that point it was a question of when, not if a completely new magazine would appear.

Through the months of 1936 they toiled, producing dummies and a promotional booklet for 'The March of Time', entitled *Four Hours a Year*, that seems, with hindsight, to have been a harbinger of what *Life* would bring. In all this, Korff appears to have played a crucial part, though there is little written record of his contribution, apart, that is, from a memo of his, quoted by Wainwright, which exposes the sort of practical wisdom that would have been invaluable to the still untested team.[101] Yet, despite all these deliberations, the overall design was still far from settled, as was the name. The former was finally knocked into shape by an outsider, Martin Hollister, who volunteered his advice to Luce after he had seen what he considered to be an appalling dummy.[102] The name was acquired by purchasing the ailing weekly begun by John Mitchell back in 1882.[103]

By the first half of 1940, the teething troubles were far behind them. Under the orderly control of the managing editor, John Shaw Billings, Henry Luce had declared war on Germany, as befitted a leading member of the Century Group.[104] Yet despite its undisguised bias, *Life* did an eloquent job reporting the war. For example, in the issue of 27 May, page 24 was laid out as a grid of maps, all precisely the same size. They described the devastating German thrust across the Low Countries of 10 to 18 May, by using each map to outline the extent of the German army's advance on one day. The transmission of information in simplified graphic form, which reads like a cartoon, could not have been clearer, yet the events themselves were only a week distant.

During this period, when each issue must have been made and remade many times as late but essential stories reached New York at moments that made a nonsense of normal deadline considerations, one of the weaknesses of *Life* was exposed: its inadequate sense of form. Prior to Germany's spring offensive, some sense of order was maintained in its pages, but it was always weak on the matter of typographic design, which is essential to the coherent understanding of

Fig.35 Until Charles Tudor arrived in 1945, the art direction of Life was inadequate. Layouts were frequently chaotic and articles often merged into one another through a proper lack of typographic distinction. Here the pictures look jumbled and the information that they carry becomes confused.

a newspaper or magazine. It is through such a subtle and transparent means that the editor and his staff guide the reader's attention to a story of importance, its ranking in their scale of values and, through subheadings, to those elements of the story that constitute its key features. In a well-ordered newspaper, such matters are so completely implicit that even though it is made every 24 hours, and frequently remade at short notice, the overall structure is maintained without any apparent effort. Unfortunately, at this point, such order was beyond *Life's* capabilities. However, to be fair to its staff, their problem was not a simple one. Most newspapers articulate their pages entirely typographically and slip photographs into the overall design. *Life* articulated its design through pictures and had too much dignity to imitate the devices employed by newspapers that are also primarily visual. That is, picture-dominated newspapers always use very large, bold type for their headlines. This is not done just because they are vulgar rags put together for vulgar people. The only way to lead a reader's attention to the essentials of a story if you use photographs that fill much of the page is via the banner headline. The size of type used and the size of the illustrations needs to be related. *Life* was too mindful of its own self-esteem to go that far. Yet, when all that is said, they still indulged in clumsy mistakes week after week that made the differentiation of stories very difficult and it frequently requires some concentration to separate the subheadings on one story from the headline of the next.(Fig. 35)

The same accusation of chaos could not be levelled at *Collier's* which, under William Chenery who was still its editor, and William Chessman, who occupied the art director's chair throughout the thirties, continued along that tasteful road that had always been its metier. Of course, *Collier's* was not trying to do the same job as *Life*. Its weekly editions were still devoted, primarily, to fiction, as they always had been under the Crowell imprint, though its volume had diminished slightly to 54% of editorial space, about 5% less than in 1930. Indeed, stability was very much the keynote here, with an editorial profile that, in 1940, varied only slightly from that described in 1930. For example, it paid some lip service to the performing arts at over 2.5%, with a little more attention to the natural sciences and medicine at 3.5%(see Appendix VII).

By way of contrast, the individual approach of the war-dominated *Life* demonstrated a devotion to the arts; using almost 15% of editorial space in the first half of 1940, frequently allotting its limited numbers of colour pages for the purpose. *Life* also covered movies more comprehensively than its rivals, with over 60 pages in six months, which is an average of over two pages a week or more than 4% of editorial space. *Collier's*, on the other hand, managed only 10 pages in a comparable six month period. In addition, *Life's* coverage concerned itself, almost entirely, with the movies themselves, rather than the stars, though it was not adverse to playing the role of Pander occasionally. It also devoted almost 3% of its editorial space to the theatre and, even more surprisingly, over 3.5% to fine art, again, using lots of expensive colour reproductions(see Appendix XV). *Collier's* did its best to avoid such dubious topics. It was more interested in baseball, with sport taking over 5% of editorial space during the six month period. Yet, no one could accuse the Crowell weekly of ignoring contemporary events, for it devoted regular amounts of space to the reports of Quentin Reynolds from London. Its affiliation to the anti-Nazi cause was as obvious as the commitment of the Luce press by 1940.

Another topic that distinguished *Collier's* was its particular interest in cartoons and humour. In the 26 issues that were produced in the latter half of 1940, it published well over 400 cartoons that together occupied over 9% of editorial space, an unprecedented level for an American mixed function magazine(see Appendix VII). By way of comparison, the *Post*, during the first six months of 1940, devoted 5.64% of its editorial space to such matters, a figure that was an apogee for that publication as well(see Appendix XVII). *Life*, on the other hand, used less than a third of 1% to make its readers laugh(see Appendix XV).

166

On the production front, *Collier's* did experience a technical transformation but nothing as radical as that promoted by Time Inc. The invention of the air-tight ink duct had transformed the industrial prospects of colour gravure and, as Crowell owned the rights, their magazines were going to take full advantage of it. Yet, the technique was never used to produce an entire issue. Instead, signatures were incorporated, which were themselves of variable length. Some weeks they were interpolated among letterpress printed pages; some weeks they formed a 12-page section at the front and back of the edition, for that was another tradition that remained at *Collier's*: the division of each issue into two zones, the back and front-of-the-book sections, the Lorimer solution that continued in the *Post* as well. The incorporation of a limited number of gravure pages into this format was the extent of Crowell's commitment to the new technology. They used it to allow greater flexibility in their art direction, for it facilitated the use of artwork and photographs 'bled' to the edge of the page.

For its part, the *Post* was too set in its ways to consider incorporating different printing processes into its production schedules. Nevertheless, even it was not immune from the cycles of change that flourished in the thirties. If the editorial profile was essentially the same in 1940 as its predecessor of 1930, or 1920 come to that, the magazine looked different and was produced by a revised team.

The first major change of the period occurred when the owner, Cyrus Curtis, died, aged 83, on 7 June 1933.[105] Although he had been remote from day-to-day management for some time, his demise made a considerable difference because the man who had encouraged his editors to transform the magazine business, wanted nothing to change after his death. His will transferred the ownership of his organisation to a trust and the board of trustees that he nominated were those of his family and colleagues who had the greatest investment in preserving the status quo ad infinitum.[106]

Meanwhile, George Lorimer was in charge. He was both editor of the *Post* and president of the Curtis organisation. But not for long. At the end of 1936 he resigned both positions and by 27 October 1937 he was dead, killed by throat cancer. From 1 January 1937, the organisation had a new president, Walter Fuller, a loyal spear carrier but not the equal of those who had preceded him, and the *Post* had a new editor, Wesley Stout, a trusted lieutenant of Lorimer's, who had nominated him

By 1940, the consequences of this forced change were very visible. Where Lorimer had totally excluded colour from the inside editorial pages, it was used extensively under Stout, particularly colour photography. In fact, at this time the *Post* seemed to be more explicitly convinced of the virtues of the use of colour in reportage than *Life*, largely, one suspects, because the Curtis organisation's printing plant was better able to adapt to the subtleties of four colour than Donnelly's of Chicago, the company which always printed the bulk of *Life*'s weekly order. Greater flexibility in graphic design encouraged such novelties as the extensive use of two-colour printing and line blocks at the *Post*, elements that *Collier's* had used for decades. In part, this change was abetted by the use of slightly better paper stock than in 1930. Although it was of similar weight to its predecessor, slightly different constituents produced a whiter surface, which accentuated the contrast achieved in the illustrations.

Of course, the *Post* in 1940 was much smaller than it had been in the 1920s, even though, as we have seen above, it had retained the loyalty of the media buyers relative to the plight of others. It had also increased circulation slightly to 3,129,168.[108] The only noticeable change in its content was the increased use of individual cartoons, already mentioned, and the increased attention it paid to contemporary events, particularly in Europe, though neither of these trends matched those in other publications. Fiction still took over half the editorial space at more than

54%. Sport was up to almost 5%, while business and economics was down to a little less than 7%(see Appendix XVII). In truth, the *Post* after Lorimer resembled the *Journal* after Bok: a well-appointed boat that lacked a helmsman, struggling to stay in a current created by others.

Among the best-selling woman's monthlies, *McCall's*, with an average circulation of 3,112,460,[109] was the one that had been the most radical in its presentation, though its contents were anything but innovative. Under the editorship of Otis Wiese the emphasis was placed wholeheartedly on fiction, which occupied nearly 63% of editorial space between January and June 1940, and domestic matters, at almost 16%. Editorial commentaries on fashion employed only 5% of the available space, but this figure does not include the 67.75 pages used to advertise the fashion patterns sold by the company, which have been classified under self-advertisements(see Appendix XIV).

In 1932, Wiese had introduced the feature with which he most radically affected American magazine design. As a consequence, he loosened the hold of the emphatic separation between an advertisement-free opening section and an advertisement-bound end to each issue. To achieve this, he split the magazine into three, with full-page colour illustrations placed to signpost each new section. In the first, fiction dominated, with the odd article thrown in for good measure. In the second, domestic features, mainly cookery and home decoration were featured, while the last concentrated on fashion. Interestingly, this is almost the same pattern as that used by Bok in the *Journal* at the turn of the century though he never emphasized matters with visual frontier markers. The opportunity to move the advertising pages forward undoubtedly helped Wiese to get the approval of his publisher. It also gave him and his staff freer rein with the way that they accommodated material.

In fact, the new format never completely obliterated the old habits, though it certainly had its effect. Fiction still trailed through the rest of the magazine, which is not surprising given the quantity that Wiese was using. To maintain the emphasis on the primary material in each section while allowing the fiction to pass through, required some sprightly footwork on the part of the art director and one does get the sense that the magazine used elaborate visual ideas with such frequency that it might be accused of being over-designed. However, that was the publication's style and it was certainly easy to differentiate from its rivals. Its commitment to illustration gave it a picture frequency of 1.43 per page, almost 50% more than the 0.97 used by the *Woman's Home Companion*. It also used a lot more monochrome photographs than the *Companion*, 217 to the latter's 86 during the same six month period. However, both were liberal in their use of colour, particularly the cheaper two colour sort, which utilised a second hue to pep up layouts in a frequently lurid way. This was used to overlay 45% of all monochrome illustrations in *McCall's* during this period. Obviously, this was a poor second to four-colour artwork or even the full colour photographs that were increasingly coming into their own. Their invariable use, both on the cover of *McCall's* and to lead the interior sections by the end of the thirties, was particularly noticeable.

At first glance, the *Companion*, in 1940, appears to have suffered little from the depredations of the thirties. Its paper stock was a noticeable improvement over that which it used when the decade began. The consequent improvement in the quality of reproduction is also noticeable. Being a Crowell publication, its use of gravure was extensive, if not comprehensive. Succulent colour illustration, bled to the page's edge, dominated the fiction section which led each issue. Now fiction occupied over 53% of editorial space, as opposed to 42.5% in 1930(see Appendix XIII). The effect of enormously improved binding machinery showed in the way that the various illustrations crossed the gutter between the pages and yet joined in perfect register time after time. One also encountered the *Companion*'s tribute to *McCall's*, a full-page colour photograph that marked out the forward boundary of 'The Companion Way', which was their designation for the domestic and fashion section. Everywhere a second colour was added, 65% of all monochrome illustrations taking this addition.

And yet there were only 314 editorial pages in six issues at a decade's end that had begun with 486 during a comparable period. Advertising pages were down from 578 to 325 pages. And these much slimmer issues used far fewer illustrations, 0.97 per page as opposed to 1.83 only ten years earlier, and 2.26 per page ten years before that. With circulation up but advertising down and the same 10¢ cover price, something had to be squeezed out. As has already been mentioned, the failure of the magazine owners and Crowell's in particular to recognise the changed reality of their revenue situation, of the shift between the relative contributions of advertising and sales revenue, which suggested an increase in the cover price, was going to drive another nail into their coffin.

Meanwhile, during the rejuvenating thirties, even the *Ladies' Home Journal* managed to get a second breath at last, though it too stuck to the 10¢ cover price. In one of his last beneficent acts for the Curtis organisation, George Lorimer sacked Loring Schuler from the editorship and brought in the husband and wife team of Bruce and Beatrice Gould. They started on 1 July 1935 and the difference that they made was enormous.[110] They introduced better paper and got better printing as a result. They encouraged the use of modern display typography and distributed stories and articles across the pages in unexpected, frequently asymmetrical layouts. They had colour photographs of food printed across a two-page, double spread, 'bled' the image to the page edge and inset the text. Hollywood stars were used to model the designs promoted on behalf of their clothing pattern service, with James Abbé, one of the West Coast's finest photographic craftsmen, shooting the pictures.

Then, in February 1940, they came up with an idea that not only stood as a landmark in the *Journal's* history, but in that of American magazine journalism as a whole. The series, 'How America Lives', took a different family every month as its example and not only reported their lives, it articulated all the traditional departments of women's journalism, food, fashion, housework, beauty, home decoration, through that family and amplified each strand from that context. It was a *tour de force*, both as an idea and as a bravura piece of journalistic execution. To take the photographs of the families *in situ*, they used the great Hungarian fashion photographer Martin Munkacsi, who succeeded in making the illustrations seem like simple snapshots. Such coverage, both in monochrome and colour, contributed substantially to the magazine's employment of photography, that is, nearly 75% of all editorial illustrations.

The effect on one issue can be seen in that for July 1940. The sixth of the series, which dealt with the Wright family of Burlington, Vermont, leads the second half of the issue, starting on page 67 out of 126. The editorial well which constitutes the front-of-the-book section, free of advertising, extends from page 11 to 28. Thereafter, continuations of articles and stories compete with advertisements for space until an apparently informal Munkacsi shot of a family picnic announces 'How American Lives'. The picture is 'bled' to the edges of the page and the text in inset into it. An acidic blue streamer encompasses the series title, which is set at 30° to the horizontal across the top of the page. A small version of the streamer becomes the series logo and is used on most spreads to help emphasize their relationship to one another. A three-paragraph introduction to the series, set in a modern serif face, bold, overlaid on the streamer, inset in a white box, also lurches at 30°. Another introduction, this time to the family in the feature, is again inset into a white box, while the title is reversed out of the photograph in white.

Although there are barely more than 200 words on the page, they are set in seven different typefaces. Such conjunctions indicate a growing sophistication in layout and typographic skill which is a mark of the 1930s. Indeed, a case can be made out for American magazines as a major conduit for such innovations, though that is beyond the scope of this work. What is undoubtedly true is that this decade is a turning point in magazine graphics and the publications of subsequent decades never returned to the simpler typography of earlier eras.

The following double spread is dominated by colour photographs which establish who is part of the extended family. Although a few shots concentrate on an individual, most are of couples and groups. Ten are used on the left page, all reproduced as 7 cm squares laid out in two columns stretching from the top to the bottom of the page. Accompanying each one is a one-paragraph description set in eight–point italic. A formal portrait, with the family set out like a championship team, reproduced 16 x 25 cm, is positioned at the top of the second page, with three more squares finishing off the job of establishing the family.(Plate X) The article is a biography of Tom Wright, the senior male member of the family. It trails through the following two spreads, accompanied by a few family snapshots from the past, but dominated by advertisements.

Page 74 is given over entirely to the Wright's holiday home, while 77 is a one-page feature on alternative holiday homes which the Wrights could have built. Between them are two full-page colour advertisements. The next double spread, pages 78 and 79, uses monochrome head shots of the five young women in the family and fills the rest of the page with 17 colour sketches of the outfits they might wear. The colour focuses the reader's attention on what might be relevant to them and away from the family.

The *Journal*'s beauty editor gets her chance on page 80. Two monochrome photographs of two of the young women in the family are used in conjunction with an article on beauty problems which appears to be a question and answer session. The questions are set in italic and the answers in regular upper and lower case, which differentiates the two clearly. However, close reading reveals that the article has nothing to do with the women in the pictures.

The next spread details the layout of the kitchen at the Wright's holiday home. It uses half of the space and is laid out across the gutter between the pages and flanked by food advertisements on either side. A cookery article, listing what are claimed as Mrs Wright Senior's favourite recipes from her collection, slides between the ads for domestic goods on the following four pages. After a 20-line introduction about Mrs Wright and the meals her family likes laid out across two columns, body type is used for the five or six-line introductions to individual recipes. The instructions themselves are set in bold type in a different face which ensures that they attract the eye. The combination of the face and cross-heads set in bold capitals also makes certain that each recipe is easy to spot on the page when trying to refer back. The six photographic illustrations are monochromatic. Four are of the food and are cropped tight to the individual dish. One, which is positioned superior to the title, is of the family at the table. The last is of Mrs Wright at her labours with a broad smile on her face.

The penultimate layout is spread across the gutter and flanked by advertising. Two articles are run side-by-side as an almost tabular comparison of the life and attitudes of Mrs Wright senior and one of her daughters. The space given to each is the same and the juxtaposition is accentuated by using similar phrases to open the paragraphs in the two articles and setting them in bold. The acid blue associated with the streamer logo which is used at the top of most pages is also used as a panel behind the title. This encourages a sense of continuity between disparate elements and variously laid out articles.

The last article in the set changes the colour of the streamer to scarlet and tries to incorporate within the group a topic which really has little to do with the family: how to make first class coffee. Again, it uses bold type to start each paragraph, thereby underlining the sense of a procedure; creating a series of steps. Clearly, typographic sophistication had reached new levels at the *Ladies' Home Journal* by the end of the 1930s.

Meanwhile, despite their new toy, the editorial team still gave 42% of editorial space to the fiction department, a slight increase over 1930. The sciences were down slightly to 2%, as were the arts. Fashion and domestic matters dropped very noticeably to a little less than 7% and 15% respectively. Of course, social life and manners rose under the stimulus of the new series to almost 12%. Yet, overall, the new feature did not really change the editorial profile enormously, it just put old feet in new socks(see Appendix XII).

BRITAIN APPEARED SLOW where the United States demonstrated considerable economic dynamism in the twenties. The UK gross national product only increased by 24% between 1921 and 1930, while that of the United States increased by 43.6%.[111] In other words, the American economy was growing at a rate that was 81% faster than the British. However, these bald statistics mask a reorientation and a renewal process within the British economy as its basis shifted from the stalwarts of the nineteenth century to the new products of the twentieth. While the Balfour Committee of 1927 bewailed the inadequacy of British research and development expenditures *vis à vis* their competitors in Germany and the United States, when compared to its own pre-war efforts, a remarkable change was in progress in British industry, a technical renewal.[112]

As far as the mass of British workers went, their income during the inter-war years largely stagnated. Between 1921 and 1930, the index of weekly real wages of fully employed workers went down and then returned to its starting point. Only in the thirties did it show a slightly steadier increase.[113] But, as Pollard has pointed out, a significant rise in the standard of living of regularly employed members of the work force came about for reasons other than an increase in real wages. The average family size diminished and thus basic expenditures on food and clothing per family unit were lower, allowing an increase in surplus disposable income that is not apparent from the bald indices. This hypothesis is supported by a 'remarkable increase in small savings' during the twenties and thirties.[114]

The British magazine scene during those years was almost a caricature of the larger world. The twenties were still dominated by the established best sellers, a tired tradition of poor paper and gaudy competitions. But, a new title based upon the unfamiliar technology of broadcasting did appear. By the end of the twenties, the highly specialised *Radio Times* was outselling all other magazines, except *John Bull*, which had itself been completely revamped. Another ten years after that, all of the old, stagnant British concepts of what a popular magazine might be and look like, which had held sway in that market for so long, had been swept away, consigned to a supporting role for publications that were now sustaining circulations that had hitherto been unattainable on this side of the Atlantic.

But the precise and authenticated size of those sales was still a matter of speculation in most cases. As has been noted in the introduction, the publication of *Press Circulations Analysed* in 1928 disseminated a list stressing comparative success in different, important market segments which needed some modification to produce a reasonable overall picture. The problem lies in the balance of the sample which is grossly over-representative of what the survey calls 'middle class' and 'lower middle class' interviewees. As noted in Chapter 1, the survey does not define its terms so it is impossible to know how close they were to those used in Routh, for instance. The latter uses occupations to anchor his terms with 'professional, employers and managers' making up 14.99% of the labour force in the 1921 census and 14.96% ten years later.

This compares to 24.93% 'middle class' interviewees of the survey. Similarly, 43.84% of the survey's respondents are 'working class', while Routh notes that 78.29% of the labour force were foremen and manual workers in 1921 and 78.07% in 1931. In between the other two, 31.23% of the respondents were 'lower middle class' while clerical workers formed 6.72% of the 1921 national census and 6.97% of that in 1931.[115] As it is impossible to show that the terms used in the two publications are compatible, it would be misleading to calculate precise coefficients which could be used to correct the imbalance of the survey in order to bring it closer to a more realistic indication of the relative success of the most popular magazines within the population at large. However, some modification is necessary because the popularity of some publications is seriously overestimated as a result of their appeal to particular sectors of the market. *Punch*, for example, was the eighth most popular magazine in the country according to the survey. But if the number of 'middle class' respondents was halved, the number of 'lower middle class' cut to one fifth and the 'working class' figures doubled - proportions which are roughly similar to those between the survey and Routh - it is only the fourteenth most popular magazine on the list. *Peg's Paper*, because its readership was overwhelmingly 'working class', moved in the other direction, from number 21 to number 9. However, the four most popular magazines were still the same: *John Bull*, *Answers*, *Tit-bits* and *Pearson's Weekly*.

Unfortunately, that is not the end of the matter. Because the survey insisted on excluding specialist publications and included *Radio Times* and *The Leader*, two of the most popular weeklies within that category, it still cannot be regarded with anything other than caution, even though it does provide a more complete comparative listing than in earlier periods.

Only in the 1930s did this parlous state of affairs really begin to improve. The Audit Bureau of Circulation was at last established in Britain late in 1931. Unfortunately, few magazines were audited by the organisation during the first decade of its existence, the only exceptions among the best sellers being *Radio Times*, *Picture Post* and *Everybody's Weekly*.

However, this tantalisingly partial situation was augmented by a study commissioned by the Incorporated Society of British Advertisers, *The Readership of Newspapers and Periodicals*, published in 1936. This publication, hitherto unused, constitutes the most precise and thoroughgoing readership survey of newspapers and magazines conducted in Britain until that time. Its statistical methodology was planned by Dr Jerzy Neyman of Warsaw and London Universities and was based on 80,000 interviews which were distributed throughout England, Wales and Scotland in a precisely controlled way.[116] The computed circulation of each publication was broken down into four different income groups on a national basis and then on a county and city basis. The results correlate well with the known audited circulations of the time. But as the magazine market was changing rapidly during these years, the relative status of the best-selling weeklies recorded in its pages is only a helpful guide to the situation at the end of the decade. As we shall see, *Weekly Illustrated* and *Passing Show*, which were separate entities when the survey was conducted, were consolidated into one publication by Odhams in March 1939. *Picture Post* was not launched until 1938, while *Woman* did not appear until 1937.

As the Odhams organisation did not join the Audit Bureau of Circulation until after the Second World War, caution in selecting magazines has to be exercised on this last decade without industry-wide circulation audits in Britain. Of those whose sales figures for 1940 remain obscure, *John Bull* had a million plus circulation in the late 1920s[117], had a computed circulation of a similar figure in the ISBA survey of 1936[118] and sold 1,098,715 a week on average at the end of the 1940s.[119] It therefore seems reasonable to assume that the magazine's circulation remained at a comparable level at the end of the 1930s and remained stable among the best sellers.

No audited figure is available for *Woman* before 1946, but White quotes a circulation of 750,000 by September 1939,[120] and this has to be taken seriously given her access during the 1960s to the staff at the International Publishing Corporation, which absorbed the three largest companies in the industry, where she was given access to confidential figures.[121] Such a sale easily establishes *Woman* among the most successful group.

The place of *Illustrated* among the best sellers is less certain. By the time of the Incorporated Society of British Advertisers' survey, *Passing Show* was computed to be the fifth most popular weekly in Britain.[122] After it was amalgamated with *Weekly Illustrated* in 1939 there can be little doubt that the Odhams publicity machine went into top gear to build on their established success. And certainly when the weekly was first audited by ABC it was almost as popular as *Picture Post*. Therefore, on balance, it seems reasonable to assume that it was among Britain's most successful magazines at the end of the 1930s and a representative of the transformation which overtook periodical publishing during that decade.

Yet, when the twenties opened, the editorial alchemy of the 1930s was still far in the distance. *Tit-Bits*, *Answers* and *Pearson's Weekly* were still being ground out 52 times a year on a conveyor belt that seemed to stretch endlessly into the past. Their seemingly unchanging appearance contributed to their apparently stagnant situation. Although illustrations were now used extensively in all three, including plenty of photographs, the average small size of these illustrations and poor ink colour undermined their impact on the layout. Thus, although changes had gradually taken place, they were far from obvious on the page.

For example, one would never guess from the editorial stability and its physical continuity that a massive upheaval had taken place in the ownership of *Answers*. When Alfred Harmsworth, alias Lord Northcliffe, died in 1922, his brother Harold, Lord Rothermere, took the reins. But, in 1926, he sold the Amalgamated Press, the company that controlled Northcliffe's magazines, to the up and coming Berry Brothers for £8 million.[123] Yet, such was the quality of incentives and organisational vitality developed in the company, that it steamed on regardless. Such momentum may well have been a consequence of the high levels of pay and system of bonuses initiated by Northcliffe which were discussed earlier. On the other hand, it also has to be noted that after Northcliffe's death his magazine empire never again launched one magazine that was outstandingly successful. The organisation demonstrated managerial skill but lacked entrepreneurial flair.

All of the three, old-established weeklies seemed to merge into one increasingly similar editorial profile during the third decade of the twentieth century. *Pearson's*, which in 1910, before the amalgamation with the Newnes group, had used 28% of its editorial space on fiction, devoted less than 16% to that topic in 1930. Where *Answers*, twenty years before, had used over a third of all its editorial space for its serials and short stories, it was now using less than 20%. *Tit-bits*, which had never been quite so devoted to fiction, had dropped its usage to a point between the other two, about 16.5% of editorial space during the period from January to June 1930(see Appendices XX, XXII and XXIII).

Of the three, *Pearson's* was the most anodyne. It rarely featured critical articles or even mentioned the troubles or injustices of the time, even in a reassuring manner. *Tit-bits* exhibited a greater awareness but was usually determinedly optimistic. In 1930 it was engaged in a series which was endeavouring to find 'Britain's Happiest Town.' It also published 'Unemployment Can Be Cured' by Ben Tillett. *Answers*, on the other hand, was using some of the writers who contributed regularly to *John Bull* and while it lacked the cutting edge of the latter, a full-page article on page three every week was usually far from comforting. Personal failings, unemployment and the dangers of coal mining were all dealt with under bold headlines in 1930.

173

During the twenties, all three titles tried to expand their appeal by developing a women's page. As might be expected, this did not develop much beyond domestic details, with recipes and advice on the ins and outs of raising children. Apart from advocating their own paper pattern services, little mention was made of clothing, though it was not entirely ignored. But, outside this format, other marginally more challenging topics did surface from time to time on family relationships, but nothing really threatening was allowed out into the open. For example, the first of Jane Doe's list of deadly sins in *Answers* were vanity and snobbery. The second article in 'this outspoken series' dealt with 'scandel-mongers'(*sic*)![124]

The trio's other innovation was the personal problem feature. *Tit-bits*, in particular, gave it a full page every week. Under the title 'The Editor Replies', roughly two-thirds of the space was allocated to responses to personal enquiries, each a short paragraph in length. The other third was given over to one specific difficulty, frequently emotional.

However, over and above all these features, the one that really dominated the trio by the end of the decade was their devotion to

Fig.36 The twenties witnessed the growth of competition fever until it appeared to reach the proportions of a mania. The Leader successfully catered to this culture by supplying the answers every week.

competitions. Pages in every issue of all three were given over to what for the period amounted almost to a mania. *Answers* offered a prize of £12 a week for life.[125] So, *Pearson's* countered with £15 a week for life a month later.[126] Even *John Bull* was not immune from the plague. Indeed, the whole situation was so intense that twopenny weeklies were published that dealt with little else but supplying answers to the competitions. One in particular, *The Leader*, was so successful that it made the top selling group among the magazines of the period. Credited with audited sales of over 500,000 a week,[127] it may well have been outselling the trio already discussed.

Although no copies of the early issues appear to have survived, it seems to have been launched as the *Racing and Football Leader* some time in 1921. In January 1929 it changed its title, obviously reflecting its enlarged information base, and though it claimed to incorporate a separate title, *The Crossword and Competition Leader*, no example of this publication has been traced either. Each issue of *The Leader*, which ran to 24 pages, followed a routine format that hardly differed from week to week. The first three pages appeared to mimic a newspaper layout, which was relatively easy given its page size, that is, 432 x 307mm. The title was set in a gothic face very similar to that used by *The Daily Telegraph* on its mast-head. Beneath it was a two-line rule, the date and price, with another two-line rule underneath. A headline in 42–point capitals was laid out across the first two columns, with sub-heads in 30–point. The four columns were separated by °–point rules. The entire typographic direction was to mimic a newspaper of the period.(Fig. 36) Yet this appearance was rather specious for much of the 'news' in this section frequently concerned *The Leader*.

Page two was always dominated by a Bert Thomas cartoon. It also normally included a column of letters, a column that aspired, rather ridiculously, to be considered a leader and a short article on a topic that usually related to competitions. Page three was dominated by one article, which was usually of more general interest than the rest. On page four the editor cast aside such window dressing. The next five pages gave the answers to the current puzzles and that apogee of twenties culture, the crossword.

The first example of the latter appeared in the Sunday edition of *The New York World*, published in that city on 21 December 1913. It was invented by Arthur Wynne, though clearly word puzzles had been a source of amusement through the centuries.[128] By 1924, a casual headcount in a New York commuter train suggested that 60% of the occupants were engrossed in their puzzles.[129] The rise of the American publishing company Simon and Schuster was founded on their publication of the first crossword book in that same year.[130] By the end of 1924, *The Times* felt sufficiently self-assured to make a snobbish and inaccurate attack on this new American fad. Unfortunately, the *Sunday Express* had already contracted the bug a few weeks earlier.[131] By the end of the decade, even *The Times* had succumbed to the epidemic, printing its first contribution in February 1930.[132] Meanwhile, of course, British erudition and perversity had made their contribution through the pages of *The Observer*, where 'Torquemade', the name of the Spanish grand inquisitor, was doing his best to torment the faithful.[133] Such intricate delicacies were not to be found in the pages of the twopenny weeklies. Their puzzles were a little more basic and it was to their pages and those of the newspapers that *The Leader* addressed itself.

Extraordinary as it may seem, not only did pages four to eight of this weekly contain the solutions of what appear to be all the current major puzzles, but Odhams Press actually paid for space so that their original competitions were reprinted on the same pages as *The Leader*'s solutions. Thus, on page four of the 8 April issue for 1930, the current *John Bull* crossword competition block, containing two puzzle blanks, the rules and an entry form was printed, using 46% of the printed page. Above it, in column two, was the solution to that very puzzle, with only nine empty squares out of 110 where the answers were uncertain because perfectly correct alternative answers were possible. These alternatives were printed below. When one considers that this competition carried a first prize of £500, the price of an attractive house at the time, one can only describe the situation as bizarre in the extreme.

The penultimate five pages of *The Leader* were devoted to forecasting football and racing results. The last page was frequently given over to advertising. The pages in between, the centre of each issue, contained a haphazard mixture of solutions to more competitions, odd attempts at a women's page, city news and gossip about competitors. The 'editorial' columns were leavened by plenty of advertising of a conventional nature plus some paid for by companies that sold their own solutions to the week's puzzles. Relative to the remaining periodicals described in these pages, one can only describe *The Leader,* and the phenomena it represents, as exotic. Without any doubt, it certainly merits a substantial study of its own.

Oddly enough, this escapist fervour seems to follow on from that whipped up by Horatio Bottomley in the preceding decades with his charismatic schemes that would somehow elude the connection between effort and reward for the participants. His story reached its climax on Monday, 29 May 1922, when he was sentenced to seven years in prison on a charge of fraudulent conversion.[134] Yet, Julius Elias, Bottomley's defender in boardroom confrontations at Odhams over the years, had seen the writing on the wall three years earlier. Elias had put together a very efficient staff and was known as a shrewd judge of men. It is, therefore, inconceivable that he did not know the general outline of Bottomley's duplicity, even if the sordid details were not flaunted under his nose. But, in 1918, even his patience was tried when *John Bull* was used to promote Bottomley's latest scheme and the one that eventually brought its author down: his very own Victory Bonds.[135] But Odhams needed the *John Bull* contract, and the strain of reconciling the need to control Bottomley without losing the magazine was so great that the health of the self-disciplined workaholic, Elias, collapsed. He had a nervous breakdown and was off work for three months. When he returned he knew the solution and how to achieve it.

Odhams was still owed very large sums for the printing of *John Bull* that had been carried since the magazine's launch. Elias had used them before to get commercial control of the weekly. Now he used them to gain full control. He pressed Bottomley on the debt and the old man could only counter with what he himself had already rejected when the suggestion had been put to him on previous occasions. A new company, Odhams Press Ltd was formed that absorbed both the existing printing concern and John Bull Ltd. That took care of the debt by the latter to the former. In return, Bottomley would still retain editorial control and a lifetime interest in the profits. At a shareholders' meeting on 17 March 1920, it was revealed that Odhams' profits for 1918 had been £35,000. Those of John Bull had been £113,000.[136]

Now, the shadow of the past slowly engulfed the charismatic figure from the Birmingham orphanage. The weekly, *Truth*, began a campaign against the Victory Bonds that continued ceaselessly for two years. Bottomley tried to staunch the flow with writs but *Truth* called his bluff. Finally, in October 1921, he agreed to a receiver being called in on the bond clubs that he had organised. It was not long before Odhams dispensed with his services, paying him £25,000 in lieu of his lifetime interest.[137] It was only then that Elias administered the *coup de grâce*. Though Bottomley's downfall was largely the consequence of the revenge fantasies of a spurned acolyte, Reuben Bigland, it was the confirmation by Elias of key points of testimony in the series of courtroom confrontations, which filled the first half of 1922, that tipped the scales against Bottomley and took him to prison.[138]

Once Odhams Press Ltd. had been formed, gaining control of its own destiny, Elias injected outside capital into the company. One contributor, Grant Morden, brought the Sunday newspaper, *The People*, with him. Elias used some of the new capital to buy a daily newspaper, *The Sporting Life*, which had a relatively small but steady circulation. When Bottomley was finally ejected from his editorship in the autumn of 1921, he was replaced by John Dunbar, who also doubled up as the editor of the daily.[139] However, the real problem erupted with Bottomley's imprisonment. The circulation of *John Bull* collapsed. But, with his hands on the prize, Elias was not going to let go now. To the astonishment of the entire industry, he fought back.

Ironically, it was Bottomley's incontinent life-style which had necessitated a competent editorial staff to keep the publication on schedule that made the successful transition possible.[140] These journalists now took the helm, while being augmented by 'names' bought in for feature articles. Many of the latter had been Bottomley's opponents. Yet despite that, much of the persona of *John Bull* survived the transition.

What changed was the appearance of the weekly. By 1930, the paper was stronger and better calendered than it had been at the beginning of the twenties. The smoother surface was needed because *John Bull* was now profusely illustrated. At 1.95 pictures per page, the number was very substantial. Many were montaged together to form rococo, decorative patterns. Such conceits were most frequent on the centre spread, which was free of advertising. Most of the photographs in the magazine were portraits and usually formal ones at that. They were used small, as adjuncts to the text. Very few illustrations were allowed to dominate a page. Out of over 1,000 used in the first six months of 1930, a mere handful had been produced beyond the walls of the photographic studio.

In fact, the editorial content had, to some extent, resumed its pre-war balance by the end of the twenties. Two pages of snippets about public affairs were followed by a full-page leading article. The topics were various. A disgraceful scheme to siphon off the wireless telegraphy function of the Post Office to private industry was apostasized.[141] The large family was eulogised.[142] The expense of the legal system was pilloried.[143] The articles were usually written by a Member of Parliament. They were followed by 'Candid Communications', Bottomley's open letters page under a new name. The pages that followed this usually attacked injustices, personal and general, maladministration and con men of every description. The centre spread was always devoted to one topic and was frequently broader in its range than other features. In 1930, its topics included the Soviet Union, the life and times of Monte Carlo, the history of the F.A. Cup Final and contemporary religious missionaries. The second half of the magazine usually began with a short story, always described as a 'real life story'. In 1930, the authors included both Evelyn Waugh and Robert Graves. The following pages featured more 'causes', perhaps a page on a sporting topic and plenty of advertising. The tail end of every issue usually contained a problem page, under the heading 'Human Documents'; a homely homily from Canon Campbell; a letters page that was normally orchestrated so that all the contributions concerned one topic; a page of crossword puzzles; an answers-to-correspondents feature called 'The Editor Replies'; there were even a few paragraphs every week on horse racing. The inside back cover was always used for a competition, which was eccentrically described as a 'bullet'.

Thus, many of the features had merely been revitalised. Patterns common to all the cheap weeklies were mixed with ideas inherited from the Bottomley era. The unrelentingly critical tone of the early years was resumed. Now, even business fell under the hammer. Altogether, the articles on public affairs, social problems and business took over 50% of every issue, just as they had 20 years before(see Appendix XXIV). This was the Elias recipe for success and it worked. During the first three months of 1930, the average net sales were audited at 1,357,237 a week and rising steadily.[144] The field was his. How he used Odhams' pre-eminence in the years to come changed the British weekly magazine forever.

The first appearance of *Radio Times* established it firmly in the penny weekly tradition which had evolved among the big three magazine publishing organisations since the 1880s. As it was originally produced for the BBC by the Newnes organisation and shared its editor, Leonard Crocombe, with *Tit-bits*, that is understandable.[145] Page seven of the first issue even featured a competition with a cash prize, jokes and entertaining snippets. Page eight, headed 'People in the Programmes', could have been taken from *Pearson's* or *Tit-bits*. Its division of the page into paragraphs on 'personalities', accompanied by their formal portraits, laid out in three columns, could have been lifted straight from pages out of the older titles. Yet, *Radio Times* was also a house publication of an extremely specialised type. Not only did it have as its core the programme details of the BBC, which through their restrained typography and lack of illustrations co-existed well with the rest of the contents, but it could draw on both programme material and station staff for articles. Yet, contributions were not allowed to get out of hand and only one in that first issue, 'Photographing Wild Animals', exceeded one page in length. Indeed, the distribution of material was very similar to the contemporary *Tit-bits*.

However, the contents of those articles were different. A number were by the BBC's engineering staff, and when combined with the advertising, which was entirely from the radio manufacturing trade, the flavour of the technically primitive broadcasts was evoked, albeit unintentionally. There was also a two-column feature on a ninth century Chinese song. This was clearly the category of material to which 'P.J. of Birmingham' was alluding in the letters column on page twelve with the indictment: 'it seems to me that the BBC are mainly catering for the "listeners" who own expensive sets and pretend to appreciate and understand only highbrow music and educational "sob stuff".'

Physically, although it shared the same typeface for its headings as *Tit-bits* and frequently used similar page layouts, the much better paper used to print *Radio Times* had a profound effect on its appearance. Super-calendered, whiter, with a high chemical pulp content, it allowed a much lighter inking to be used on the body type and, hence, a much more delicate typeface. The original cartoons that were commissioned, retained more of the original vivacity because of the better printing. Altogether, it was a modest production but a very effective one.

Leonard Crocombe's editorship of *Radio Times* ended in 1926, when the BBC assumed control of its own weekly. After a brief sojourn by Walter Fuller, Eric Maschwitz took over the following year and stayed for five. Under his control and that of his art editor, Maurice Gorham, the *Radio Times* set off in exactly the direction that 'P.J.', the correspondent in issue one had feared: towards an unabashed delight in minority culture.[146]

Picking up on the tradition so well promoted by the *Illustrated London News*, *Radio Times* began producing special Christmas issues which used colour covers, a luxury beyond the means of the routine numbers. After two over-coloured and wholly sentimental covers in 1924 and 1925, Gorham, when he took over, put the covers for 1926 and 1927 in the hands of McKauffer Knight and got a very different result. Increasingly, the graphics incorporated in the programme notes, although figurative, exhibited a sensitivity to the subtleties of picture space developed in the paintings and graphics of the previous 50 years. They also frequently exhibited a rather mannered angularity. In July 1927 a new idea was put into production, a special annual summer number which cost a penny extra, exhibited a two-colour cover and contained extra lashings of fiction.

The illustrations in this and other issues were seen to advantage for the magazine used better finished paper than the other top selling magazines. Consequently, despite being published by the Newnes organisation for the BBC and being printed at the Exmoor Street plant of the Newnes and Pearson Printing Company, it was more attractive than any of that company's twopenny weeklies. The layout was elegant, uncluttered and easy to follow. The programme notes had expanded in 1926.[147] Plenty of space surrounded the type and the graphics expanded into that space.

While the programme schedules and notes describing them used 70% of the editorial space, the editor spread a diversity of topics among the remainder. Principal among them, and not surprising given the balance of the BBC's output at the time, was music. Cartoons and humour were never forgotten and, perhaps reflecting the efforts of the other penny weeklies at the end of the twenties, there was a women's page that seemed quite unrelated to the Corporation's transmissions.

THE SUCCESS OF THIS FORMAT lost none of its momentum in the 1930s. The circulation of *John Bull* was soon surpassed and, by the middle of the decade, *Radio Times* was approaching an unprecedented two million weekly sales in the UK, or about twice the current circulation of *John Bull*.[148] By the decade's end, even this figure was surpassed as the twopenny weekly sold 2,418,612 on average during 1940.[149]

This achievement was not bought by a compromise with mediocrity, particularly in relation to its appearance. If anything, as time passed, its graphic and typographic personality matured in a way that took it further from its roots in the tradition of the popular, inexpensive weekly. In 1931, it was using about 1.2 illustrational blocks per page, balanced roughly 40/60 between artwork and photographs. By 1935, the average number of pages per issue were up and so were the number of illustration: about 1.36 per page. The emphasis was now tilted heavily in favour of the photographic, that is, about 28/72. Yet, by 1940, despite the exigencies of war, the frequency was almost exactly the same, the number of pages was down, but the balance between artwork and photographic illustration had now swung back to about 50/50. The typography had seen some changes.

By 1940 the typeface had increased in size and there were fewer lines to the column. Among the programme schedules, the page was split into two columns rather than three, there was much more white space and, consequently, the listings were much more legible. The practice of peppering these columns with small photographic portraits, in the manner developed in *Answers* and its peers in the twenties, was now largely abandoned. The illustrations in 1940 related much more closely to the content of the broadcast rather than their authors or a 'personality' featured in the presentation. Hence the resurgence of artwork as the decade closed. These layouts were the responsibility of Douglas Williams, brought in as art director when Gorham moved up to be editor in 1933.[150]

Under Gorham the idea of the special number was developed. In 1933 other special numbers began to appear on an irregular basis, though, for the time being, only the 'Summer Number' carried a colour cover. The first of that year was the 'Dance Music Number' of March 17. The innovation allowed the staff to allocate six of the 17 pages of articles that opened this 72 page edition to one topic. Such exceptional issues contained a concentration of material one–page long. Such special editions developed and increased as the thirties wore on and began sporting colour covers.

In 1936, the printing contract with the Newnes organisation came to an end. Even the editor thought that it would be renewed. 'It was not only a big printing job but a very big and intricate setting job; no other magazine was running so many pages of displayed matter, and the proportion of corrections to original setting was fantastically high. Newnes had all the experience and, though I was in no way involved in the decision, I personally did not expect a change.' The contract went to Waterlows who agreed to build a new factory especially for *Radio Times* on a new site to the west of London in which nothing but the weekly would be printed without the BBC's permission.[151] Such was the power of the best-selling magazine in Britain. According to its editor, it was probably making an annual profit of about £600,000 at this time.[152] However, this did not translate into a salary enhancement for the man in charge of it on the American or Harmsworth model. By 1940, Gorham was getting just £1600 a year as editor.[153] Edward Bok, the former editor of the *Ladies' Home Journal*, having started with nothing, left an estate valued at $16 million after his death in 1930.[154]

Interestingly, the one man in the British magazine industry who could have made his fortune, Julius Elias, seemed disinterested in personal financial gain. After his death in 1946, his estate only amounted to £100,000.[155] He seemed to measure success on a different scale. In March 1930, Odhams, under Elias, took control of and refurbished the *Daily Herald*. Their first issue sold a million. Three years later it was the first British daily to pass the two million mark.[156] The circulation of their Sunday standard bearer, *The People*, had passed that figure in 1929.[157] With *John Bull*, as the thirties began, they had the best-selling magazine in Britain. With *The Passing Show*, Odhams had another consistently successful weekly that remained on the edge of the group with the largest circulation.[158]

However, as noted already, the *Radio Times* soon passed its older rival in the circulation battle, but Elias was not one to let the grass grow under his feet. As he said to a board meeting of the period: 'At the present time *John Bull* is produced on our high-speed newspaper presses.

It is not possible to obtain better results than we are getting on our existing machines. One of my problems has been to find a process which will provide a better result enabling us to introduce colour into our publications, and at the same time printing them at high speeds and, of course, what is more important, at an economic figure.'[159]

By the mid-thirties, the Odhams' weeklies, *Picturegoer*, *Weekly Illustrated* and *The Passing Show*, were already being printed at Sun Engraving in Watford on their gravure presses, and he attempted to buy them out. As negotiations did not make much progress, he tried another tack. His works manager, W.H. Parrack, was aware of the developments at Alco-Gravure across the Atlantic. A visit to their plant fired his enthusiasm and led to the Odhams purchase of the rights to the new ink duct described earlier.

The next step was to build a factory. A site in Watford was chosen close to the Sun Engraving plant; a ruthless decision, made to capitalise on their pool of skilled, trained labour. Unfortunately for Odhams, the next stage did not proceed smoothly. For reasons that are not entirely clear, *John Bull* was not printed in the new installation for over a decade. According to Elias' biographer, this occurred because the staff would not transfer to the new location.[160] But, given the proximity of Watford to London and its location astride one of the primary railway routes out of the capital, which kept the travelling time between the company's headquarters in Long Acre and the new site to less than an hour, this does not seem particularly convincing. Furthermore, when the then current Time Inc. operation is borne in mind, in which editorial offices were located in New York and their printers in Chicago, a question mark remains. But, whatever the reason, the situation remained that Odhams had the production facilities and nothing to print on them. Which is how *Woman* came to be launched in June 1937.

The Newnes organisation had already launched *Woman's Own* in 1932 with a gravure supplement. The Amalgamated Press produced the rival *Woman's Illustrated* in 1936.[161] But, neither of them could compete with colour gravure covers and the artwork that revolutionised the twopenny women's weekly market. Furthermore, *Woman* was gravure throughout.

However, its success was not instant. Its articles displayed a degree of social awareness unfamiliar to the readership that it was wooing. The result was a 30% drop in sales after the launch. As a consequence the new staff were forced to rebuild.[162] John Gammie, who replaced the launch editor, and his assistant Mary Grieve were unable to achieve what they intended before October 1937. It was only then that the turnaround in sales occurred.[163]

Thus, by the first six months of 1940, fiction, largely romantic, used over 51% of editorial space. With domestic matters such as cookery taking another 22%, fashion over 6% and the children's section a similar volume, there was very little space for anything else(see Appendix XXVI). Odhams had been forced back, through consumer pressure, into the anodyne formula all too common in the British market over the previous decades. And while its use of colour might have been a breath of fresh air among the inexpensive women's weeklies, its art direction and utilisation of colour lacked the panache of the best-selling American monthlies like *McCall's*, *Women's Home Companion* and the *Ladies' Home Journal*. For example, the first 26 issues of 1940 used only 18 four-colour reproductions of photographs and 23 four-colour pieces of artwork inside the magazine. Even the two-colour option was only sparingly used. By way of comparison, the *Companion* ran 25 colour photographs, 37 four-colour reproductions and 161 two-colour reproductions of artwork during exactly the same period, despite that fact that it was published monthly and *Woman* was on a weekly schedule.

How this new-look weekly appeared can be seen by examining one issue, in this case that for 24 February 1940. Each page is divided into four columns, although on the first spread only one of them features editorial material – the contents column – the remainder is advertising.

Page four manages to give three columns to letters. Six examples are printed under the title 'Woman to Woman'. Each one has a bold cross-head and a simple, drawn graphic to lead. The letters are set in an eight–point serif face and the answer in seven. This does not differentiate clearly enough between the two and the result is untidy and confused.

The first full editorial page is much more clearly laid out. It is dominated by a drawing of a young woman in a slip pulling a stocking on to her right foot, which takes up 60% of the printed surface. The block is bled out into the rest of the page without any visually restraining border. The title is not, as might be expected, superior to the drawing but inferior, set in an italic script face and enclosed in rectangle with rounded corners. It is laid across the bottom of the drawing at an angle of about 25 degrees. The difference between this example and those found in *Woman's World*, published in London 40 years before, suggests a new approach; one which has been touched by American styles. The story continues on pages eight and ten purely as text, although the former is interrupted by an illustrated poem and the latter by a quiz box with multiple-choice questions and four illustrations.

The first knitting pattern is also a little unexpected because the title, in italic script, is laid out vertically alongside the monochromatic reproduction of the photograph of a model wearing the cardigan which is the product of the instructions. As the background has been retouched out, the image inhabits the same white–page space as the text.

A bold wash drawing dominates the following spread in a manner again reminiscent of American practice. However, unlike the staff on those magazines, *Woman's* editor and art director have not hesitated to use an image which is frankly sensual.(Fig. 37) The body language

Fig.37 The launch of Woman in 1937 as an all gravure weekly marked a real change in the visual appeal of the British women's market. The days of the dowdy opposition were numbered. It might also have encouraged the staff to indulge in slightly more sensuality than was normal in their sector of the market.

of the wife greeting her husband as he opens the door is unequivocal in its invitation. The effect is aided by the use of gravure because the depth of print colour which marks the woman's dress reinforces the sensual resonance. The title of the story is inset in a script face on a flowing streamer, while a bold face with square serifs is used for the author's name. The same face, set in 12–point rather than 15, is used on a brief synopsis laid out to the left of the title. Other than this, the typesetting is quite unadventurous. The second spread of the story is interrupted twice. An advertisement for the following week's issue occupies a display panel which crosses three columns at the bottom of the left-hand page. Another wash drawing of the same couple, saying a tender farewell, runs from the top to the bottom of the opposite page. It uses two and one-third columns and is bled into the surrounding space. The rich gravure tones and the bold layout mark a break with long-standing traditions among British women's weeklies.

The change is even more marked on the next page, which reproduces fashion drawings in full colour. The layout is relatively sophisticated because the separated drawings are overlaid so that one interrupts the other. However, they are also self-advertisements for each bears the number of a dressmaking paper pattern, of which more detail is given at the foot of the page. Opposite is a beauty page which reproduces four photographs of the same model side-by-side in a block across the top of the page to illustrate the effect of contrasting hair styles. The accompanying text is laid out below.

The two following spreads feature the continuation of a serial. The left-hand page of each one is completely occupied by advertisements. The right is a combination of a wash drawing and text. Although the former, in both instances, employs a style which avoids drawn outlines, the result is not the muddy image which was so common in the *Saturday Evening Post*, for example, because gravure gives a much broader tonal range than letterpress on paper such as machine printings.

The potential of colour gravure is exploited on the issue's centre spread. A painting of a romantic couple in evening dress at a tense moment in their relationship is laid out across the gutter to occupy half of the spread. The text is set in three columns per page rather than four, with two to the left of the artwork and one to the right. The art director has also taken the opportunity to use blue ink rather than black for the two-sentence synopsis. The three-line drop capital with which the story starts is reversed out of green to white.

The remainder of the issue, the second half of the edition, lacks the graphic impact and the editorial attack of the first. Although it is more flexible than Lorimer's classic back-of-the-book section, the combination of the tail-end of stories and short regular features – home hints, astrology, cookery, 'Woman Nursery Club', personal problems – and a greater weight of advertising create a coda. Yet despite this diminuendo, this issue of *Woman* demonstrates the transformation that most popular British weeklies experienced during the 1930s. The advent of gravure as a mass production technique had banished the old-style weeklies to the role of also-rans and brought new standards of presentation to an audience which had hitherto subsisted on publications which still possessed a strong family resemblance to those of 100 years before.

One weekly that Odhams had been publishing successfully since 1915 was *The Passing Show*. At the end of March 1932, the printing of this title and *Picturegoer* were changed from letterpress to gravure. This enabled the former to use a colour cover in a style reminiscent of the *Saturday Evening Post*, that is, a lively genre scene in colour against a white, featureless ground, every week. Its editorial blend of competent fiction and articles on topics beyond the narrow limits normally encountered in the British twopenny weekly market continued to hold a substantial readership: 303,055 according to the ISBA survey of 1936, which put it among the top half dozen.[164]

In 1934, Odhams launched *Weekly Illustrated* with Maurice Cowan as its editor. The idea had come from Stefan Lorant, who had edited the *Muncher Illustriete Presse* before the Nazis sent him to gaol. He worked with Cowan for a while until conflict caused him to leave.[165] The use of photographs was particularly vivid, especially on the cover. It was printed gravure from the first and, according to the legend on the inside back page, by Odhams themselves. This latter point fits ill with comments by Elias' biographer who mentions nothing of his interest in providing the company with such technology until the move to Watford. It also seems odd that a few years later, this job and that of printing *The Passing Show* were contracted out to Sun Engraving, only to be returned to Odhams in late 1939.

In its opening years *Weekly Illustrated* was a balanced mixture of photographs and articles. However, after Stefan Lorant left, the balance shifted, ironically given his commitment to photography, to the point where it was virtually all pictures with only an occasional collection of paragraphs occupying more than 25% of any one page. However, in March 1939 Odhams amalgamated *Passing Show* and *Weekly Illustrated* in an attempt to create one title that was pre-eminent and called it *Illustrated*. To promote it, Odhams used the full resources of the promotional organisation they had developed: the canvassers, the free gifts and the competitions that had been so successful in the past.[166]

Normally, when such an amalgamation takes place, the editorial approach of one title predominates while the publishers merely try to graft the residual readership of the second title on to that of the first. This amalgamation was different. The opening section of each edition was profusely illustrated with photographs of the sort that had dominated *Weekly Illustrated*. Given

Fig.38 This issue of Illustrated from 1940 demonstrates the unmistakeable influence of the German illustrated weekly press on their Anglo-Saxon counterparts. In Britain, the emigré Stefan Lorant was the conduit who transmitted the skills and knowledge that had been gained.

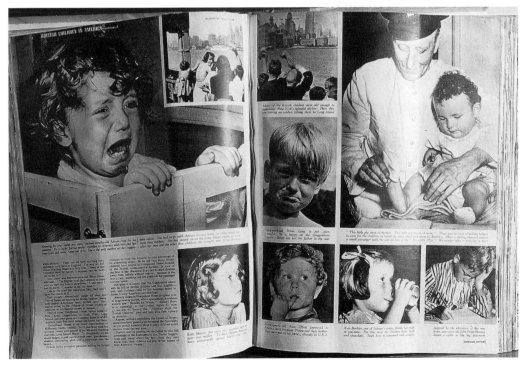

the political situation during the last months of the thirties, their content dwelt much on the war. Yet, even at a moment of maximum peril, that is June 1940, they could still run a light-hearted two page story on extravagant millinery.[167] This amalgam of pictures and captions averaged about 55% of each edition.(Fig. 38) The remaining 45% derived from *The Passing Show* and concentrated on fiction. Though each story was headed by an illustration or an illuminated title piece, very little related artwork was introduced into the body of the text. This was leavened by isolated cartoons. Again, this derived from *The Passing Show* tradition which had featured several pages of cartoons each week.

Taken together, these combined elements produced an unusual combination for the period and a successful one. Though no audited sales figures appear to have been published before the end of the war for this particular magazine, there is every reason to suppose that it was selling approximately a million a week by 1940, that is, somewhat less than its greatest rival, *Picture Post*. Certainly, throughout the period in which accurate comparisons are possible, there was little distance in sales between the two titles.

The most consistently successful of the Odhams' weeklies was still *John Bull*. Again, no audited sales figures seem to have been published in 1940 or 1941, but the ISBA survey of 1936 gave it a circulation of over a million[168] and the first audited figures published after the war indicate that it had been able to retain that number of readers.[169] Therefore, it seems probable that it was selling at least a million a week at the midpoint between these two years. As the company were unable to transform it into another of the popular illustrated weeklies because of the problem about printing, they contented themselves with placing greater emphasis on the competitions, which now occupied two complete pages at the back of every issue. *John Bull* also restricted its range of interests, ignoring the peripheral topics to which it had allocated small amounts of occasional space in the twenties. Now it no longer pretended to be interested in such things as the arts. Clearly, the war had its effect in this regard, though unlike *Illustrated*, *Picture Post* and *Everybody's*, it did not devote page after page to recent events. Instead it still directed its energies to exposing corruption and injustice, though it now preferred to deal with general situations, such as exorbitant prices, rather than individual cases. It also devoted almost 20% of its space to public affairs, while much of the close to 8% of editorial space in the first six months of 1940 that was given over to history and biography concerned itself with the lives of politicians. However, it still maintained its modest average of about 1˘ pages of fiction in every issue, or about 6.5% of editorial space, as it had done in the twenties(see Appendix XXIV).

One reason that *John Bull* was not able to give the same attention to the war that was possible in some of its rivals was, of course, a consequence of its production process. Given the presses and paper already described by Elias, *John Bull* was unable to compete with the gravure-rendered photographs of other publications. They set the standard and even the best letterpress and a machine printings grade paper could not compete. This, of course, did not stop it using illustrations. Indeed, it used one a page on average, with 60% deriving from photographs and 40% from artwork, with the last figure being split precisely in half between halftones and line blocks. However, very few of these illustrations used more than 20% of the printed area of any one page. Clearly, *John Bull* held its circulation because of the consistent way it held its pronounced critical attitude towards public figures over the decades.

Of the best-selling mixed-function weeklies that led the British market at the end of the thirties, one seems to have retained a special place in the affections of its readers. *Picture Post* is remembered today when so many of its competitors and peers have been forgotten. At the time it outsold *Everybody's* easily but *John Bull* and *Illustrated* only by a much smaller margin. So, the question as to why it should have been kept by many libraries, memorialised in anthologies and autobiographies when the other three are gathering dust in just one isolated repository is a relevant one.

Picture Post was started by Stefan Lorant, the editor whose suggestion had created *Weekly Illustrated* for Odhams. After he left them, he made his living as a freelance journalist before starting *Lilliput* in the autumn of 1937. Despite predictions to the contrary, this turned out to be a successful publication. So much so that it was bought by the Hulton Press in June 1938. The deal included Lorant's services and the young Edward Hulton had the perspicacity to give the Hungarian his head. Thus, even the page size of *Picture Post* was chosen because it related to the proportions of a 35mm format negative.

The first edition appeared in October 1938 and sold out immediately.[170] Its reception was similar to that accorded to *Life* and both were rooted in the German illustrated press of the 1920s. They exhibited other similarities as well. Their editorial profiles were broadly similar and they were certainly closer to one another than they were to their native competitors. For example, *Life* and *Picture Post* bore a much greater resemblance to each other than say *Life* and *Collier's* or the *Saturday Evening Post*. Both exhibited an interest in the arts which was entirely lacking, as we have noted already, in *John Bull*, for example.

They had their differences as well. *Life*, although lively, never bothered with direct humour during the late thirties. *Picture Post* had the cartoons of Low which it had the audacity to print full page, demonstrating a verve entirely absent in its British peers. *Life*, as we have seen, often lacked the typographic clarity necessary to lead the reader through its pages without confusion. Stories appeared to run into one another too easily. *Picture Post* never fell into that trap. Furthermore, its use of typography in its captions emphasized the information they were transmitting, whereas with *Life*, the pictures completely dominated and the caption type, which was very small, never obtruded. Lorant, and his assistant Tom Hopkinson, who was soon to take over, used capitals, white-on-black, or whatever was necessary to make their point without ever descending into the vulgar.

A particularly useful illustration of the difference between the two approaches may be seen from two issues published right at the end of the decade, which attempted to deal with the same topic. In the 17 August 1940 issue of *Picture Post*, the leading story is entitled 'Air Raid'. The cover of the issue features a head and shoulders portrait of an air raid warden, with a pensive expression, gazing upward. The story runs from pages 9 to 29 inclusive. The title is set in 96–point capitals and dominates the first pages despite being subordinate to a picture. This and the next two pages show scenes in the control and information centres monitoring the raid. The pictures dominate the page but they are used to sustain a narrative, not for their graphic impact.

The following double spread is purely artwork, explaining on the first what happens when the enemy is sighted; the second describes the response when bombs fall. Small pictures are linked by arrows to emphasize the passage of information through the network which links the observation post deep in the countryside to the citizen intent on safety. The second sequence uses the arrows to demonstrate how the emergency services act to find and care for the injured.(Fig. 39) Two pages follow on the process of taking cover. A photograph of a moment of preparation in a wardens' post is enlarged to occupy two-thirds of the page. A view of an inner city street with the occupants filing into the shelters fills the facing page. Three pages of scenes in the shelters follow with light reflected off shirts and skin; flecks of white in the dense shadows. Scenes above ground are next: the empty streets, the civil defence response, the anti-aircraft gunners, a sketch of the bombers' viewpoint printed across two pages, the ruins and, finally, opinions and comments. In other words, a narrative is laid out which leads the reader through the event with words and pictures that reinforce each other. There is a purpose: to help people

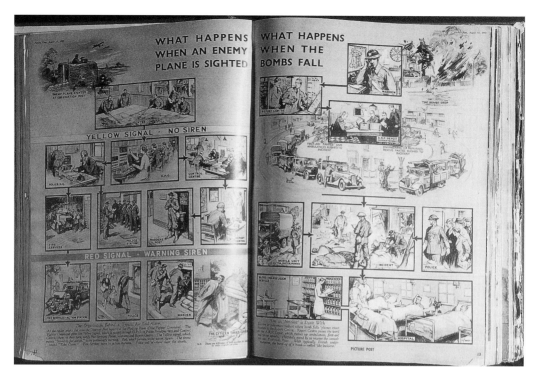

Fig.39 *The whole purpose of Picture Post was to transmit information with as much clarity as possible to its readers through its use of photographs, diagrams and typography. This is particularly obvious in its detailed explanation of how Britain's civil defence system operated in the event of an air raid.*

understand what is happening. The story fills all but five editorial pages of the issue.

In the 23 September 1940 edition of *Life*, the leading story is entitled 'Hitler Tries to Destroy London', but it only appears after 22 pages dominated by advertising have begun the issue. Letters and short pieces from overseas correspondents limp through this opening section as well. *Life*'s front cover carries a picture of a forlorn, injured child clutching a rag doll, sitting up in a hospital bed.

Inside, the story fills seven pages. The first is dominated by an impressive image of children taking cover in a slit trench. But the location is not London, as implied by the title. They are hop-pickers and, hence, must have been in the Kent farmlands when the photograph was taken. The second page features five dramatic scenes of bomb damage in London.(Fig. 40) The third page is filled by two views of shelter interiors in London which had been used by *Picture Post*. In the latter, they had been clearly labelled with simple captions, set in capitals, white-on-black and used to convey part of the whole. In *Picture Post* the effect is information. In *Life*, the story is a series of unrelated fragments that horrify, neither describing the event in its entirety nor setting it within a context. Attention is engaged and emotions are heightened to little purpose. The effect is diversion. Other details are added but there is no coherent framework in which to place the images. In the end, one can but conclude that it is an essentially meaningless but affective presentation.

The issue continues with the reproductions of photographs of shining American technology, a tennis championship and a political rally. All the headlines are set in a 24–point

Fig.40 The editors of Life *were concerned to make an impact on their readers, and in the process sometimes lost overall clarity and confused the story that they were trying to tell. The dramatic moment, and its visual encapsulation, took precedence over the need to disseminate understanding.*

condensed sans serif face which draws them together into an undifferentiated mass of information. The next story on the American Army Medical Corps fares better typographically with a 54–point headline which catches the attention. But by now the monochrome photographs are fighting the two and four-colour advertisements, and losing the battle.

The twenties, as we have seen already, were, among other things, a period during which the competition mania flourished in Britain. This preoccupation did not atrophy with the years. *The Leader* continued on its way, though its position among the best-selling magazines was assumed by *Everybody's* during the thirties. In many ways, this twopenny weekly might be described as even more curious than *The Leader*.

By the end of the thirties, each issue totalled 44 pages. Of these, the cover and a central 16-page section were printed by gravure, while the remainder were printed letterpress. This in itself was an unusual compromise in Britain where the weeklies were normally produced by one process or the other. The editorial staff used this physical arrangement as the basis of a general segregation of the contents.

The first third was a mixture not dissimilar to that found in *John Bull*. The central gravure section was emphatically pictorial, like that found in *Illustrated Weekly*. While the final letterpress section, with the exception of its first page, was entirely given over to horse racing, football pools, greyhound racing, crosswords and competitions; though the latter appear to have been far less important at this point than they had been ten years earlier in *The Leader*. Furthermore, the magazine's decidedly idiosyncratic balance did not end there.

For example, the last thing that one might expect of a two–penny weekly so devoted to horse racing was a serious interest in fine art. Yet, in the issue for 2 March 1940, one and a half well-illustrated pages were given over to Benvenuto Cellini. Two weeks later an article on Filippo Lippi used three quarters of a page. While, on 18 May, half a page was devoted to Kneller, the seventeenth century portraitist. In total, over 14 pages out of just over 737 featured fine art, or almost 2% of the editorial space between January and June 1940. Six per cent was given to sport. Yet close to 8% was given to documentary articles on life in countries as alien to the usual British interests as Indonesia and Iceland. Of course, by the decade's end, concern with the events of the war absorbed a sizeable chunk of the weekly, approaching 17%. But over 70 pages, or 9.57%, were devoted to such historical and biographical topics as Maria Gonzaga, the early seventeenth century Duchess of Monferrati , or Angus Montague, the pugnacious fourteenth-century Scottish aristocrat. Of course, the largest amount of space was devoted to humour and entertainment, the category covering the competitions(see Appendix XXIII). As in *The Leader*, the latter were mixed with advertisements placed by the publications originating the teasers. Altogether, *Everybody's* seemed to epitomise the terms 'populist'. With a circulation in 1939 of 788,292, it was clearly a very successful formula.[171]

THE THIRD DECADE OF THE TWENTIETH CENTURY was a time of sustained growth in the economy of the United States, which put more money in the pockets of the people. Even faster growth was recorded by the advertising industry, which put even more money in the pockets of the publishers. An extraordinary proportion of this for one publication passed into the coffers of the *Saturday Evening Post*, creating unprecedented profits that have yet to be equalled by any title. The grudging admission of colour into its pages helped to bolster further these revenues. However, in general this was a quiet time for print technology in both countries.

The British economy grew as well but lagged behind the Americans as it grappled with the technological renewal of many of its basic industries and the development of their replacements. The two big magazine publishers, the Harmsworth–created Amalgamated Press, and the Newnes-Pearson group seemed to lack lustre compared to their energetic performances of a generation before and were content to hold the line rather than put their resources into new products. Only two relative newcomers showed any initiative.

In the United States, the growing volume of advertising revenue and the increasing sophistication of the agencies, in particular the development of market research, gave these middlemen greater power and enhanced precision in their buying habits. Building on the basic information now available from the Audit Bureau of Circulation and the Standard Rate and Data Service, their media buyers were now able to discover the precise audience that any particular magazine was offering. This meant that magazines such as *Saturday Evening Post*, which could present a very attractive readership profile in addition to a very high aggregate number of readers, attracted a volume of advertising disproportionate to its actual sales. It also meant that magazines which restricted their functions and provided a well-defined group of readers, such as *The New Yorker* or the leaders of the women's press, the *Companion* and the *Journal*, were also able to attract large volumes of advertising. This was even more true of some of the specialist journals, such as *Vogue* which, as we have seen, had a circulation only a tenth the size of *Better Home and Garden*, but made over half a million dollars more from its sale of space. The case of *Liberty* was even more salutary, with sales of over two and a half million accompanied by serious losses. The editorial profile was such an amorphous mess that they were only able to attract readers because of the low price. Such virtues did not appeal to the media buyers.

In the United Kingdom, such information was rarely available then and it still remains obscure. Publishers were even coy about publishing their advertising rates, let alone their audited circulations. Readership surveys seem to have been regarded as arcane and an unnecessary luxury. Thus, even such a runaway success as *Radio Times* never attracted advertising on the scale of its American peers. With their low aspirations and satisfaction with steady but unspectacular profits based upon the Harmsworth formula of strictly curtailed costs, the British publishers were unable to dent the lead that the daily press had established in attracting advertising during the previous century.

Of course, even the American market had its sleepers. The Curtis organisation was unable to find a satisfactory replacement for Edward Bok and the *Journal* languished. *Collier's* was also limping along and even when it did get a new editor in the person of William Chenery, he followed the *Post's* formula with almost embarrassing faithfulness. Yet, old titles could be revived successfully, as Julius Elias proved with *John Bull*, even if he had to use the competition mania and heavy promotion to attract extra readers.

The decade that followed was a very different kettle of fish. A revolution in ink technology and big changes in paper production completely transformed the appearance of many existing magazines and made other new forms a practical reality. Pre-eminent among these new possibilities was the picture magazine.

Life would not have been possible without the advent of heat-set inks and the development of cheaper ways of coating paper. *Weekly Illustrated* and *Picture Post* would have been impossible without the steady evolution of monochrome gravure. *Woman* and all its imitators that followed, which changed the women's press in Britain completely, would have been impossible without the air-tight ink duct that accelerated colour gravure production to the speeds of the daily newspaper.

And yet the technical basis was only the start. The staff of Time Incorporated needed several years practice and the help of a German editor before they were able to realise some of the potential latent in the new technology. Odhams and then Hulton both needed the expertise and imagination of Stefan Lorant, who had also learned his trade in the German illustrated press of the 1920s, to stimulate them to success.

Talent was also at the root of changes in the American women's press. The *Ladies' Home Journal* was beginning to appear moribund before the Goulds gave it the kiss of life. Otis Wiese and his editorial team at *McCall's* made choices that challenged the hegemony of the *Post's* conception of magazine organisation into two distinct zones without basing their idea on a technical shift.

Maurice Gorham also made a difference at *Radio Times* when the idea of special issues evolved after he took over as editor in 1933. Even De Witt Wallace at the *Digest* imposed his ideas of what a monthly could be within the simplest technological framework possible in the middle of the twentieth century. Technology might be the spur, but the editor still held the reins.

NOTES

1. Brinkmann, Ernst, Multicolour Intaglio, in *Penrose's Annual*, Vol.25, London, 1923, p103.

2. Horgan, Stephen, Rotagravure in Colours in the United States, in *Penrose's Annual*, Vol.28, London, 1926, pp89-90.

3. Gamble, William, Review of Process Work, in *Penrose's Annual*, Vol.25, London, 1923, p14.

4. Gamble, William, Review of Process Work, in *Penrose's Annual*, Vol.26, London, 1924, pp5-6.

5. Gamble, William, The Editor's Review, in *Penrose's Annual*, Vol.32, London, 1930, pp8-9.

6. Gamble, William, A Review of Process Work, *Penrose's Annual*, Vol.29, London, 1927, p12.

7. Anon., A Call to Action. Steady Progress of Rotary Offset Printing, *The British Printer*, Vol.39, No.229, May-June 1926, Leicester and London. p6.

8. Dilnot, George, *The Romance of the Amalgamated Press*, London, 1925, p59.

9. Gamble, William, A Review of Process Work, *Penrose's Annual*, Vol.28, London, 1926, p11. One of the magazines involved was *The Passing Show*.

10. Goodmann, Joseph, The Triumph of Reel-fed Newspaper Offset Lithography, in *Penrose's Annual*, Vol.28, London, 1926, pp134-135.

11. *The British Printer*, Vol.40, No.240, March-April 1928, Leicester and London, opposite p292.

12. Coe, Brian, *Colour Photography*, London, 1978, p128. The type of cameras necessary prior to 1936 had to produce three separate images to give a result fit to use in a magazine. Examples of this cumbersome equipment can be seen on pages 92-93 and 109.

13. Comparato, Frank E, *Chronicles of Genius and Folly*, Culver City, Calif., 1979, p613.

14. Gamble, William, The Editor's Review, in *Penrose's Annual*, Vol.30, London, 1928, p4.

15. Colebrook, Frank, My Month in America - Some Men and Some Things, in *Penrose's Annual*, Vol. 28, London, 1926, p50. Also, Anon., The Offsetting Problem Solved. The 'Grammer' Process, *The British Printer*, Vol.42, No.250, Nov-Dec. 1929, Leicester and London, pp161-162, which is illustrated.

16. Bender, Frederick W., The Effect of the Enclosed Ink Fountain on Intaglio Printing, *The British Printer*, Vol.50, No.296, Sept. 1937, London, p101.

17. Horgan, Stephen H., Alco Gravure, in *The Penrose Annual*, Vol.38, London, 1936, pp110-111.

18. Pellissier, M. Raoul, What's New in Photogravure, *The Penrose Annual*, Vol.38, London, 1936, p107.

19. Horgan, Alco Gravure, op.cit., pp110-111.

20. Bender, op.cit., p102.

21. Montague, Noel, The Schlesinger Inking System, in *The Penrose Annual*, Vol.39, London, 1937, pp153-155.

22. Elson, Robert T., *Time Inc.*, Vol.1 1923-1941, New York, 1968, p190.

23. Wallace, N. L., 'Life' Production, in *The Penrose Annual*, Vol.42, London, 1940, pp108-109.

24. Elson, op.cit., p284 and Wallace, op.cit., p108.

25. Duhring, E.L., Quick Drying Inks on Rotary Colour Presses, *The British Printer*, Vol.50, No.296, Sept. 1937, London, p102.

26. Roehr, Walter W., Paper and the Graphic Arts, in *Printing Progress*, The International Association of Printing House Craftsmen Inc., Cincinnati, Ohio, 1959, p275, attributes the breakthrough to the Kimberly-Clark Corporation during 1932. While Franklin, A.T., A Century of Papermaking for Printing, in *Printing World*: a Century in Print, London, 1979, p32, ascribes the pre-eminent role to the Massey Roll Coater of 1933.

27. Elson, op.cit., pp283-284.

28. Anon., Paper Trend of 1936, *The British Printer*, Vol.49, No.293, March 1937, London, p225.

29. Wallace, op.cit., p110.

30. Wood, James Playstead, *The Curtis Magazines*, New York, 1971, pp195-198.

31. US Dept. of Commerce, Bureau of the Census, *Historical Statistics of the United States, Colonial Times to 1970*, Part 1, Washington, D.C., 1975, p320.

32. Ibid., Part 2, p856.

33. *Nelson Chesman and Company's Newspaper Rate Book*, St Louis, 1931, p254.

34. Ibid, p312.

35. Ibid., p241.

36. Ibid., p245.

37. Ibid., p111.

38. Ibid., p41.

39. Ibid., p314.

40. Parlin, Charles Coolidge, *National Magazines as Advertising Media*, Philadelphia, PA, 1931, p5.

41. Tebbel, John William, *George Horace Lorimer and the Saturday Evening Post*, New York, 1948, p208, without giving numbers, clearly suggests that the editorial staff was very small indeed. Parlin, op.cit., p2, lists the managers of advertising department offices in Chicago, New York, Philadelphia, Boston, Detroit, Cleveland and San Francisco.

42. Parlin, op.cit., pp12-15.

43. Ibid., p39, suggests that each copy had 3.84 readers.

44. *Standard Rate and Data Service*, Chicago, Sept. 1930, p425. Thereafter referred to as *SRDS*.

45. Ibid, pp376 & 437.

46. Parlin, op.cit., p5.

47. Cohn, Jan, *Creating America*, Pittsburgh, 1989, pp144, 147-149.

48. Ibid, pp162-164.

49. Ibid, pp180-184.

50. Ibid, pp243-246.

51. Mott, Frank L., *A History of American Magazines*, Vol.4, Boston, 1938-68, p470.

52. Tebbel, op.cit., p114; Wood, *Curtis*, op.cit., pp90-91.

53. Chenery, William L., *So It Seemed*, New York, 1952, pp174-197; Mott, Vol.4, op.cit., pp469-470.

54. *SRDS*, op.cit., p403.

55. Ibid. p404.

56. Parlin, op.cit., p5.

57. *SRDS*, op.cit., p403.

58. Vischer, Peter, Tommy Hitchcock The Polo Player, *Liberty*, New York, Vol.7, January 18, 1930, pp62-66.

59. Richardson, Anna Steese, Servantless Etiquette, *Liberty*, New York, Vol.7, January 25, 1930, pp54-57.

60. Peterson, Theodore, *Magazines in the Twentieth Century*, Urbana, Ill., 2nd ed., 1964, p80.

61. Ibid., p143.

62. Parlin, op.cit., p5.

63. Macfadden, Mary and Gauvreau, Emile, *Dumbbells and Carrot Strips*, New York, 1953, pp218-223.

64. Oursler, Fulton, *The True Story of Bernarr Macfadden*, New York, 1929, pp216-220.

65. Macfadden and Gauvreau, op.cit., p223.

66. Oursler, op.cit, pp189-196.

67. Macfadden and Gauvreau, op.cit., pp233-234.

68. Oursler, op.cit., pp223-225.

69. *Historical Statistics*, Part II, p856.

70. US Department of Commerce, Bureau of the Census, *Census of Manufactures - Newspapers, Periodicals and Books*, Washington, D.C., 1941, p20, table 4.

71. US Department of Commerce, Bureau of the Census, *Census of Manufactures: 1905. Printing and Publishing*, Washington, D.C., 1907, p29, table 23.

72. US Department of Commerce, Bureau of the Census, *14th Census of the United States taken in the Year 1920*, Volume 10, Manufactures 1919, Reports for Selected Industries, Washington, D.C., 1923, p575, table 12.

73. *16th Census*, op.cit., p20, table 6.

74. Ibid.

75. Wood, *Curtis*, op.cit., p133.

76. Peterson, op.cit., pp256-259.

77. *SRDS*, September 1940, op.cit., general magazines, p97.

78. *16th Census*, op.cit., p20, table 6.

79. *SRDS*, September 1940, op.cit., general magazines, p101.

80. Ibid., p56.

81. Ibid., p83.

82. Wood, James Playstead, *Of Lasting Interest*, New York, 1958, pp16-49. Also Garberson, John W., *A Limited Number of Pages*, Journalism Monographs, No.25, Association for Education in Journalism, Lexington, Kentucky, November 1972, p6.

83. The Cosmopolitan of Ray Long, *Fortune*, Vol.3, March 1931, p51.

84. Wood, *Lasting Interest*, op.cit., p54.

85. Reader's Digest, *Fortune*, Vol.14, No.5, November 1936, p128.

86. Wood, *Lasting Interest*, op.cit., p134.

87. Elson, Vol.1, op.cit., pp283-284.

88. Ibid., pp297-298. This issue was actually dated November 23, but it had already become standard practice in the industry, by this time, to post-date in order to give each issue longer newsstand life.

89. Swanberg, W.A., *Luce and His Empire*, New York, 1972, pp49-51.

90. Elson, Part I, op.cit., p86.

91. Kobler, John, *Luce: His Time, Life and Fortune*, New York, 1968, p63.

92. Elson, Part I, op.cit., p110.

93. Ibid., pp119-121.

94. Ibid., p141.

95. Ibid., p154.

96. Ibid., pp189-190.

97. Ibid., p225.

98. Wainwright, Loudon, *The Great American Magazine*, New York, 1986, pp8-12.

99. Ibid, p13.

100. Ibid, pp13-17.

101. Ibid, pp26-28.

102. Ibid, pp38-39.

103. Ibid, pp47-48.

104. Ibid, p106. Also Chadwin, Mark Lincoln, *The Hawks of World War II*, Chapel Hill, N.C., 1968, p63.

105. Wood, *Curtis*, op.cit., p124.

106. Ibid, pp126-127.

107. Ibid, pp143-144.

108. *SRDS*, September 1940, op.cit., general magazines, p84.

109. Ibid., p61.

110. Gould, Bruce and Beatrice Blackmar, *American Story*, New York, 1968, p156.

111. Mitchell, B.R., *European Historical Statistics*, London, 1981 (2nd Ed. rev.), p826. and *Historical Statistics*, Pt.1, p225, Series F17-30.

112. Pollard, Sidney, *The Development of the British Economy*, 2nd Ed., London, 1969, pp93-95.

113. Mitchell, B.R., *Abstract of British Historical Statistics*, Cambridge, 1962, pp344-345, tables C and D.

114. Pollard, op.cit., p293.

115. Routh, Guy, *Occupation and Pay in Great Britain 1906-79*, London, 1980, p5, table 1.1., and London Research Bureau, *Press Circulations Analysed*, London, 1928, p133.

116. Incorporated Society of British Advertisers, *The Readership of Newspapers and Periodicals*, London, 1936, ppviii-xiv.

117. *John Bull*, Vol.47, No.1244, 19 April 1930, p5.

118. ISBA, op.cit., p274.

119. ABC private ledgers.

120. White, Cynthia Leslie, *Women's Magazines 1693-1967*, London, 1970, p97, and Grieve, Mary, *Millions Made My Story*, London, 1964, p89, which is the autobiography of *Woman's* most famous editor, claims a sale of 1 million in Spring 1940 'when paper rationing hit us and reduced our size and our circulation'.

121. White, op.cit., pp8-9.

122. ISBA, 1936, op.cit.,p274.

123. *Dictionary of Business Biography*, Vol.1, London, 1984, p303.

124. *Answers*, Vol.84, No.2186, 26 April 1930.

125. Ibid., No.2170, 4 January 1930, cover.

126. *Pearson's Weekly*, No.2062, 1 February 1930, cover.

127. Ibid., No.2061, 25 January 1930, p847.

128. Arnot, Michelle, *A History of the Crossword Puzzle*, London, 1982, pp28-29.

129. Millington, Roger, *The Strange World of the Crossword*, London, 1974, p19.

130. Ibid., pp14-18.

131. Ibid., p21.

132. Arnot, op.cit., p70.

133. Ibid., p65.

134. Symons, Julian, *Horatio Bottomley*, London, 1955, pp249-255.

135. Ibid., p209.

136. Minney, Rubeigh J., *Viscount Southwood*, London, 1954, pp161-162.

137. Symons, op.cit., pp228-231.

138. Ibid., pp240-245.

139. Minney, op.cit., pp163-165.

140. Ibid., p163.

141. Middleton, George, Wireless Plot Revealed, *John Bull*, vol.47, No.1238, 8 March 1930, p7.

142. Hayday, Arthur, Back to the Big Family, *John Bull*, Vol.47, No.1239, 15 March 1930, p9.

143. Bowater, Sir Thomas V., Settled - Out of Court, *John Bull*, Vol.47, No.1241, 29 March 1930, p7.

144. *John Bull*, Vol.47, No.1244, 19 April 1930, p5.

145. *The Art of the Radio Times*, London, 1981, Brian Gearing, The Twenties, p10.

146. Gorham, Maurice, *Sound and Fury*, London, 1948, pp22-29.

147. Ibid., pp22-23.

148. ISBA, op.cit., pp272 & 274.

149. Audit Bureau of Circulation, London, private ledgers.

150. Gorham, op.cit., p50.

151. Ibid., pp72-73.

152. Ibid., p64.

153. Ibid., p101.

154. Wood, *Curtis*, op.cit., p121.

155. Minney, op.cit. p369.

156. Ibid., pp238 & 242.

157. Ibid., p192.

158. London Research Bureau, *Press Circulations Analysed, London*, 1928, p133.

159. Minney, op.cit., p271.

160. Ibid., pp271-273.

161. White, op.cit., pp96-96.

162. Ibid., p112.

163. Grieve, op.cit., p105.

164. ISBA, 1936, op.cit., p274.

165. Hopkinson, Tom, *Of This Our Time*, London, 1982, pp147-148.

166. Minney, op.cit., p274.

167. *Illustrated*, London, Vol.2, No.15, 8 June 1940, pp10-11.

168. ISBA, 1936, op.cit., p274.

169. ABC private ledgers.

170. Hopkinson, op.cit., pp161-164.

171. ABC, op.cit.

The Years 1941–1960

Wᴀʀ ɪs ꜰʀᴇǫᴜᴇɴᴛʟʏ sᴇᴇɴ ᴀs ᴀ ꜰᴏʀᴄɪɴɢ ʜᴏᴜsᴇ ꜰᴏʀ ᴛᴇᴄʜɴᴏʟᴏɢʏ. While that might be true of conflict-related fields, it seems to have applied to the printing industry in only limited ways. As in those decades after the revolutionary nineties, the years that followed the technical transformation of the thirties in the printing industry were a period of relatively slow evolution. And those changes that did occur only had a marginal bearing on the magazine industry in the period covered by these pages. It was only in the decades subsequent to our narrative here that offset lithography and electronic systems overwhelmed the old techniques.

As we have mentioned in passing, the thirties saw the emergence of polymers as an important force in materials science. At first the new plastics were used to shore up the old printing technology when they were found to be an excellent material for duplicating halftone blocks.[1] But, in the early forties, plastic began to be substituted for stone and metal by the lithographic plate makers. The Lithomat Corporation announced the production of 'Photomat', which resembled 'heavily-coated paper', came in a 52 inch wide roll and avoided many of the conventional stages of lithographic platemaking by incorporating some of the necessary chemicals into the material.[2] By the end of the fifties, the Time Inc. laboratories had introduced nylon as a material for making relief plates without resorting to metallic intermediaries.[3]

In Denmark the Aller process brought the bimetallic plate on to the lithography market and it was in use in Copenhagen for the magazine *Familie Journal* and in Berlin on *Marie Luise* by 1939.[4] The first major American title to employ the planographic process appears to have been *Time*, though, interestingly, it was not used on the main American edition. That was still produced by letterpress during the late forties.

The stimulus seems to have been the limitations of wartime air transport. To cope, a special Air Express Edition was initiated which was printed on lightweight paper. To produce it: 'Offset lithography was selected for two reasons: First, it was easy to get reproduction proofs of the pages of the regular editions which could be cut and rearranged to suit any make-up. Second, it was much quicker to cut proofs than to alter Linotype and recast stereos.'[5] By 1944, a West Coast edition of *Time* was being produced in Los Angeles by offset via cellophane proofs flown from Chicago. An Hawaiian edition, produced in the same manner appeared a little later.[6] After the War, the European edition was taken from proofs of the original pulled on to acetate. These films were then flown to Paris, where the litho plates were made directly from them.[7]

There can be little doubt, if the trade press is an accurate reflection, that the take-off period for offset occurred immediately after the Second World War. By 1948, the process was beginning to bite deep into a traditional area of letterpress hegemony, the general printer, if the contemporary trade press is to be believed.[8] However, by 1949, Pacific Press Inc., who produced the offset editions of *Time*, were still the only company in the US with the sort of large presses capable of printing magazines using this technology.[9] Then, in 1951, the first Hoe Crabtree four-colour, web-offset magazine press began production, not in the US but in Copenhagen, running at speeds of 18 to 20 thousand revolutions per hour.[10] By the end of the fifties, such technology had at last made its mark in the United States with an annual paper consumption running at 350,000 tons during 1960.[11] Nevertheless, it had yet to affect the leading titles, largely, one suspects because the investment in letterpress inhibited any radical innovations. However, in late 1957, in what might be seen as an apocryphal move, the Sun Engraving Company, that bastion of the gravure industry in Britain, started a subsidiary, Sun Litho.[12] While, in the U.S., a number of small periodicals began to use offset litho printed on a web, and at least one with a larger circulation, *Fortune*, started using the technique to produce part of an edition.[13] In other words, the trade press in the late forties were 'puffing' the process, though its use was gradually gaining adherents as time passed.

Another technology that gained ground during the fifties was photo-typesetting. Although the first machine produced by Intertype was only installed in 1946,[14] there were 120 in service in the United States nine years later, with another 30 in Europe and Australia. Significantly, none were working in Britain at all before 1956.[15] Like the electronic scanning of originals to make colour halftones, which was under development at this time, it is far from certain how far these techniques were used in magazine production before 1960, though, at least six machines in the US and one in London were producing separation negatives before the end of the decade.[16]

On a less rarefied plane, the technological upgrading of platemaking also made significant progress in the 1950s, changes that made quality printing a less time-consuming process. As with other innovations, electronics played an important part for the fifties were the years in which the press began to merge with the circuit board.[17]

If war did not seriously enhance the technological base of the printing industry, it was certainly good for business, and particularly the publishing business in America. Although the number of titles recorded by the US Bureau of the Census in 1947 was down from 1939 at 4,610, aggregate circulation of magazines was up 60% over the same period.[18] Not unexpectedly, some magazines had done better than others during the forties. *Reader's Digest* was now soaring to heights, for the time being, all its own, at least in the US. Though no audited figures are available before 1955, Wood's suggestion that the monthly had reached 8 million sales by 1946 does not appear improbable given subsequent more reliable numbers.[19] Even if it sold a million less than this by the end of the decade, it was still head and shoulders above its peers as far as volume went. *Life*, at 5,242,614 in 1950, was the next of the rest in the US, its circulation up nearly 84% over the decade.[20] It was followed by the two Curtis flag carriers, with the *Journal* at 4,429,028 per month[21] and the *Post* at 4,009,587 per week.[22], respectively exhibiting 35% and 28% higher sales over the decade.

Only these four had breached the four million barrier in the States by the end of the forties, but others were hot on their tail. *Woman's Home Companion*, at 3,999,515,[23] was only a whisker away, and *McCall's* was close at 3,936,374.[24] *Woman's Day* was a newcomer among the best-selling restricted function monthlies at 3,457,884,[25] though there was little new about its contents. This group was followed by a gaggle of titles bunched around the three million mark that included such specialist publications as *Better Homes and Gardens* and the *American Legion Magazine*. Among them was *Collier's*, which at 3,137,935 was selling more than it did in 1940 but not enough to gain it a place among the best sellers or credit among the media buyers.[26] All these figures were audited by ABC and above reproach, as were those published in Britain. Gone at last were the days of guess work by the advertisers and their agencies.

But, despite these enormous individual sales, comic books had the largest aggregate sales for any group of periodicals in America. At over 89 million in 1947, they easily surpassed the general interest publications group at just over 64.2 million or the house and gardens group at 11.8 million.[27] This is all the more remarkable when it is realised that the US Department of Commerce did not even bother to list comics separately in 1939, demand being so limited. As suggested by Peterson, their audience appears to have been predominantly juvenile at first, though the demand for them among the armed forces during the travails of the forties, suggests a broader audience.[28] Interestingly, the industry was built on the most extreme version of the concept of specialisation. In this they undoubtedly took a leaf from the pages of the pulp magazines which had preceded them in the twenties and thirties.

In that field, magazines did not merely restrict themselves to retailing tales of adventure or love, they confined themselves even more narrowly, as is indicated by such titles as *Ranch Romances*, or *Ace-High Magazine*, which excluded everything but stories of First World War aerial encounters.[29] The comic books, when they came along, frequently took this concept even further, confining their attention to just one character, such as *Hooded Horseman* or the most obvious, *Superman*. In this instance, one gets a clear insight into one of the roots of such behaviour: the need for reassurance. The repetitive format reassures its audience in the way that a mother reading or telling a story to her child over and over again reassures the infant that there is a base of reliability and predictability that can be touched in a dangerous and unstable world. In a life of mixed fortunes, the individual needs a reliable womb of conceits in which to rest its imagination and rejuvenate its will.

The anxieties of the 1940s did not end with the hot conflict in 1945, as is all too apparent in the pages of *Life* and *Reader's Digest*. It is, therefore, not surprising that the habit of stress displacement, which encouraged the sales of comic books, thrived in the greater opportunity afforded it by regular distribution arrangements and the economic buoyancy of post-war America which accompanied the Cold War. Where total personal consumption expenditures in the US had fallen by 13.5% over the decade of the thirties, expressed in dollar volume, they rose by almost 60% in the period between 1945 and 1950, despite the economic hiccup of 1948-49.[30] Even allowing for an increase in the consumer price index of almost 34% during this latter period,[31] consumer spending underwent a real increase.

Released from war-time constraints, American advertising budgets soared to previously unknown levels as well, as might be expected. For the magazines this meant a much needed boost to their flagging economies. Between 1939 and 1949, advertising receipts for all periodicals that reported to the Bureau of Census grew by 189% to $648,417,000.[32] Of course, that revenue was not distributed evenly among the various types of periodical. Comic books, although they held 23.3% of the total aggregate circulation of all periodicals notified to the Bureau of the Census, received less than 1% of the total advertising receipts accrued by the industry. Periodicals in the 'general interest' category, however, possessing 16.7% of the total aggregate circulation, took 34.0% of the total advertising receipts.[33]

Among the most popular magazines, though the disparities were not so obvious, anomalies in the sale of space were evident. As we have seen above, *Life* was now easily the best-selling weekly, yet the *Post* still sold 13% more advertising pages during the first half of 1950. In part, that would have been a direct consequence of price differentials. The *Post*'s rates ran from the one time use of one page in monochrome at $11,200, to $20,900 for the back cover in colour.[34] Comparable figures for Life were $16,100 and $30,800 respectively.[35] Yet, there was also a sense of loyalty to the *Post* among media buyers which *Life* spent a great deal of time and energy during the late forties trying to undermine.

In the immediate post-war era, Time Inc. launched a sales-training programme for recently demobilised men that offered applicants a year's employment as a 'retail representative'. This involved travelling the country trying to persuade shopkeepers to display red labels and posters proclaiming that the goods were 'Advertised in Life'.[36] A completely different tactic, aimed as much at television as the *Post*, led to the report commissioned from the Alfred Politz Research organisation, which, when it was boiled down, was a very sophisticated way of inflating *Life*'s readership figures through the concept of an 'accumulating audience', that is, a pass–on readership.[37]

A third, less direct ploy involved *Life*'s pricing structure. By the late forties, both the weeklies under discussion charged a 15¢ cover price. By increasing *Life*'s price to 20¢, it was reasoned that the magazine would be able to diminish its dependence on advertising while, at the same time, portray its audience as a superior group to the media buyers because they were prepared to pay more per copy than those of the *Post*. However, the price rise had a second facet. The subscription price would also be raised but not pro rata, so that regular readers would increasingly be wooed into that method of purchase. Such readers were, at the time, felt to carry more weight with the advertisers.

This move to increase subscription sales was already well underway. In 1940, single copy news–stand sales accounted for 61.6% of *Life*'s circulation.[38] By 1950, they accounted for only 35.3%.[39] While, by the end of our period, 1960, *Life* sold a bare 10% of each edition in this manner.[40] This change, however, was a two-edged sword for, although it allowed the publisher to penetrate the growing tentacles of suburbia, where much purchasing power resided but the single sales infrastructure was weak, it also made the companies very dependent on the postal system.[41] In 1948, when the policy was initiated, the commitment looked like a sensible decision. By 1960, it began to look like a serious mistake for reasons that were entirely beyond the control of the executives of Time Inc., as will be seen in due course.

What the readership got for their money by the end of the forties was a publication considerably larger, 33%, than when the decade began. However, the quality of both the paper and the printing of *Life* was noticeably inferior to the issues produced 10 years before. The paper now in use lacked the finish of Enameline, Time Inc.'s original choice, and it left blacks degraded to a dark grey in the illustrations. This was a serious problem for a magazine that used 2.76 pictures per editorial page, of which over 90% were reproductions of photographs. Lack of quality undermined the visual impact made by the images, which were still the primary carriers of the magazine's stories, its main transmitters of information. Despite an improvement in the vital area of typographic design since the appointment of Charles Tudor as art director in 1945,[42] the physical quality of the product had diminished during the forties. Today, despite being 10 years younger, issues from the end of the forties already show greater paper discoloration than their predecessors of the earlier decade.

As for what was printed on that paper, the hot conflict of the first half of the decade gave way to the cold conflict of the years after 1945. Henry Luce, however, did not wait for the half-time whistle to be blown. He changed ends before the rest of the US team. This is best documented by Shirley Keddie, who has itemised with mathematical precision the subtle shifts of editorial policy on *Time* and how it was easing towards an accommodation with Germany even before Hitler was dead; an alliance that would be directed against the Soviet Union.[43] On a broader, perhaps more rhetorical front, W. A. Swanberg has attacked the way that Luce used his magazines to promote his viewpoint over many decades. In particular, in 1944 *Life* published a long article entitled 'The World From Rome' by William Bullitt, which looked towards the post-war world. 'It is an old picture of western Europe and Western civilisation threatened by hordes of invaders from the East.' So much for the ally of whom 81% of the American public at that time thought could be accommodated on friendly terms after the war.[44]

Thus, it is not surprising that, by the decade's end, *Life* was prepared to attack any measure that smacked of public intervention in private woes.[45] Yet, two weeks after the editorial page assailed the pink tendencies of the welfare state, it turned on Joseph McCarthy with even greater ferocity: 'we deplore the wild and irresponsible behaviour of Senator Joseph McCarthy. We deplore the aid and comfort which he has received from Senator Taft and some others.'[46] From a publication that had always stood in the Republican corner, those were strong words. Thus, however much one might resent the power of Henry Luce, as Swanberg clearly does, the position Luce assumed was a complicated one and the same goes for his magazines.[47] This was particularly true on matters other than politics.

For example, during the course of the first half of the twentieth century, popular American magazines paid less and less attention to the arts, particularly the fine arts. *Life* stood like a rock against this trend. In the first half of 1940 it had devoted over 3.5% of its editorial space to the topic. A decade later it used more than 5.5% for the same ends, that is, 92 pages in six months (see Appendix XV). However, in the intervening period, editorial attitudes had changed. At the end of the thirties, modern art largely meant American figurative painting, most of which had little durability. But, some time during the mid-forties, according to Nelson Rockefeller, a friend and fellow member of the board of trustees of the Museum of Modern Art in New York, Luce, on the urging of Rockefeller, had a long meeting with other trustees and museum officials. He emerged from the evening completely convinced of the indissoluble union of democracy and freedom of expression in modern art. Subsequently, *Life* gave modern painting a fair crack of the whip. By 1949, even the avant–garde Jackson Pollock was allowed three pages in the 8 August issue.[48]

Nothing even closely comparable appeared in the pages of the *Post*, even under its new editor, Ben Hibbs. He had been offered the job in April 1942 after Wesley Stout resigned following a furore over an article entitled 'The Case Against the Jews' by Martin Meyer, who was, of course, a Jew, in the issue of 28 March of that year. The article was not anti-Semitic but the truth counted for little once tempers had become inflamed.[49]

The new editor had joined the Curtis organisation in 1929 from the newspaper world of the mid-west, initially as a writer on *Country Gentleman*, for whom he travelled for 11 years. In September 1940 Hibbs was made the editor of the farm publication, which was selling over two million a month at the time.[50] His rebuilding of its editorial position undoubtedly recommended him to Walter Fuller, the company chairman, when Stout had to be replaced.[51]

As the Goulds had done for the *Journal*, so did Hibbs for the *Post*. Over a three–month period he chipped away, week after week, at the sterile conventions that had seemed to be more enduring than the substance of the magazine. Each week a key element was changed without a fanfare: typography, page design and even the cover.[52] Under Stout, the old graphic constrictions imposed by Lorimer had been loosened. Reproductions of photographs, both monochrome and colour, had increased to the point where they contributed 43% of all illustrations, slightly more than those rolling acres of wash drawings. Now even that measure looked timid as the typical *Post* artwork was jettisoned completely.

By the end of the forties, the new *Post* had been transformed, both visually and editorially, as can be seen by taking a look at the issue for 15 April 1950. Lorimer had always opened his lead story immediately after a short advertising section. Hibbs had the contents on page three and strung letters and editorials among the advertisements before opening the main editorial well on page 19 with a serial. Richly–coloured artwork dominates this right-hand page and occupies the top two-thirds. The story continues on to the next spread, which is again dominated by full–colour illustrations. Following the Lorimer model, the serial then continues in the back-of-the-book, allowing the next spread to carry an article on public schools, which

is again fully illustrated, this time with photographs. The text uses only a quarter of the printed page, while the illustrations are bled to the edge. 'A Post novelette complete in this issue' starts on the following spread. Like the *Ladies' Home Journal* in 1940, the *Post* appears to have picked up this editorial idea from the *Reader's Digest*.

The feature on pages 26 and 27 could have been taken from *Life*, being a picture feature on the forties film star Betty Grable shot on the set of her latest movie. Lorimer never used such features, which are little more than undiluted publicity material, and never ran photo-stories. More to his taste might have been the article on Germany's future, but again, the text occupies less than half of the double spread with the majority of the space being given to photography.

The next layout reverts to full–colour artwork because it features another story.(Fig. 41) The picture now completely occupies the left-hand page and announces the theme of the story, conflict at sea, together with the title on the right-hand page, 'Northeast Fury'. The message is reinforced by a second painting which is reproduced to fill the bottom of the second of three columns of text: an image of a small wooden boat with a lone occupant. The integration of text and pictures to sell a piece to the readers, which had begun under Lorimer, continued under his successor.

And so the pattern continues up to page 48, where a comic spread marks the end of this section of the magazine. The remaining three–quarters of the issue is all advertisements and continuations in the classic Lorimer tradition. Very occasionally an illustration appears but text is primarily fitted to the available space by interpolating one-cell cartoons.

Hibbs loved cartoons. He must have, for all those little oblongs of humour and entertainment added up to over 184 pages between January and June 1950, or over 11% of editorial space, which was three times more than the appropriation received by either sport or business topics. Down, to make way for these increases, went the fiction department's allocation which, by the first half of 1950, stood at less than 40%, from a high point of almost 60% under Lorimer in 1930. Up as well was interest in the social life of America(see Appendix XVIII). The successful series that Hibbs had launched despite the opposition of his staff, 'The Cities of America', ploughed on. On 21 January, a series on divorce by David Wittel began with a large, dramatic picture facing headlines that promised to deliver 'the full, sordid story of America's broken homes'. Good old George must have been spinning in his grave. It is no wonder that his *Post* is remembered in a golden glow of nostalgia while that of Ben Hibbs, which attracted many more readers, is never discussed with the same approbation.

Yet, with the investigative reporting went a repetitive, carping paranoia in the editorials. On 7 January the headline said 'Wartime Policy Towards Reds is in for Beating'. Next week the complaint was that the communists were pursuing czarist policies in Asia. On 4 February, the leading article on Alaska was entitled 'The Reds are Rapping at Our Arctic Door.' Page 30, the following week was graced with the headline 'How Our Commies Defame America Abroad.' In this context Senator McCarthy's behaviour appears unexceptional.

The same odour clung to the *Reader's Digest*. February 1950 saw an article on the 'pink fringe' of Methodism. March saw the appearance of another in a continuing series written especially for the *Digest* on the evils of British socialised medicine and how it was failing completely. April witnessed an attack on old age pensions, as well as another indictment of the National Health Service in the UK. A magazine that had presented a balanced viewpoint at the end of the thirties was unequivocal in its inclinations by the end of the forties. Fortunately, that is not the whole story.

The *Reader's Digest* had another obsession that distinguished it from its peers in a positive way: its preoccupation with the health of the nation – 7.6% of editorial space during the first half of 1950 was devoted to the topic(see Appendix XVI). Appropriately, the leading article in the January issue, which had been prepared exclusively for the *Digest* was entitled 'How Harmful are Cigarettes?' It was the opening salvo in a campaign that the monthly conducted in isolation for many years. In the time to come it was a very important channel of information for penetrating the American consciousness, linking the habit indelibly to cancer. On that count alone, it did an incalculable service to the American people.

Over the years, the appearance of the *Digest* had changed as well as its contents. Now the cover featured a pretty landscape or city scene, printed in four glowing colours on a heavy art paper, in addition to the list of contents. Inside, illustrations had made their appearance, though there were few of them and they were usually taken from simple line blocks with additional colours added on occasion by overprinting from matching blocks. Headlines also strayed into different colours from time to time. The paper stock was still the same cheap material which is now starting to discolour quite noticeably.[53]

In complete contrast, the unexceptional appearance of the three mixed function magazines of the forties discussed so far in no way prepares the reader for what could be found in the top women's magazines of the late forties. This was their glory day. Each month, *McCall's* led with an elegant, photographic cover on heavy art paper. The subject was usually a model showing only her head and shoulders and the image was bled to all four edges of the page, which meant that on the 333 x 262 mm sheet, her features were frequently three-quarters life size. From March 1950, the magazine's name was printed so that it filled the width of the sheet. It was normally situated on a pale or white background element in the photograph to maximise its impact. As can be imagined, the overall effect could be stunning.

McCall's also participated in the move away from fiction already seen in the *Post*, which had been led by *Life* and the *Digest*, and the former vehicle for clothing patterns had now grown in sophistication and breadth, though each month still featured an average of something over seven pages of such promotional material. The quota of fiction had dropped over the decade, from nearly 63% of editorial space in the first half of 1940 to just under 37% during a similar period ten years later, to make way for its new interest in society and public issues. The domestic department had also grown and now consumed over 21% of the editor's quota(see Appendix XIV). In its graphics, *McCall's* developed the interest in photography that it had shown in the thirties. After another decade, its use had risen from 47.26% of all illustrations to a completely dominating 80.88%.

Physically, the old division between the classic front and back-of-the-book sections had reasserted itself, with, of course, Campbell's Soup guarding the frontier. The ideas of Otis Wiese and his team had been unable to prevail against the advantages, commercial and editorial of the Lorimer pattern. Now there was more advertising before the front-of-the-book section, but little else was new. Given the material that *McCall's* and its peers used, such a format seemed inevitable. Indeed, it is noticeable that, at this stage, only two of those magazines under observation here that evaded this classic Lorimer format were the *Reader's Digest* and *Life*. They both had one other thing in common: their lack of interest in fiction. It needed space and if the editor wanted to hold the readers' interest and introduce them to a range of such material quickly, the Lorimer pattern was difficult to avoid.

Among the opposition, the *Woman's Home Companion* usually had a more subdued cover than *McCall's* but it made up for this in the art direction of its contents. Each issue began with lush pages of fiction; the rich colours of the gravure pages were bled to the edge as the images almost overwhelmed the text. These were no longer mere illustrations of incidents in the narrative. They announced the situation and social context of each story. Consequently, styles frequently varied from page to page, reinforcing the message. Sometimes a little fashion was interpolated into this signature, a double-spread or two of straightforward oblongs of colour, the photographs crisply outlined and featuring simply posed shots in unexceptional circumstances. These were printed gravure as well.

The front-of-the-book section usually ended with three articles, one of which touched on a matter of health, frequently mental health. Altogether, medical material consumed over 5% of editorial space in the first half of 1950(see Appendix XIII). Titles such as 'Why Not a Caesarian ?,' 'Is Cancer a Danger to Your Child ?' or 'The Truth About Nervous Breakdown' were laid out in superb layouts using some of the finest typographic ideas ever employed in a best-selling magazine. One high point came in May 1950 when 'Women in Strait Jackets' by Albert Deutsch appeared on pages 32 and 33. The left page presented an unadorned text surrounded by plenty of white space. The right page featured one photograph at its centre with a very wide, blue border. The picture displayed a woman, trussed up and sitting on a bare wooden bench. The effect was and remains very disturbing. The headline caption, reversed out of the blue, asked, 'Is the torture of a strait jacket really necessary for this woman..?'

A long back-of-the-book mixture of advertisements, the tails of stories and articles interposed before what was known as 'The Home Service Centre' appeared. By the end of the forties, cookery dominated these domestic details. Such topics used over 20% of editorial space in the *Companion* at this time, easily outstripping fashion, at less than 9%, and second only to fiction which, at just over 39% had dropped noticeably under the new editor(see Appendix XIII).

Gertrude Lane had died in harness at the *Companion* in 1941, after nearly 30 years in charge. She was succeeded by her managing editor, Willa Roberts, who lasted barely two years. William Birnie, after learning his trade in newspapers, had moved on to *The American* and then the *Companion*, taking over as managing editor under Roberts. It was under his editorship that the *Companion* took its new aggressive stance on social issues. For the time being, the approach brought success with the public and the media buyers.[54] Advertising lineage for the first half of 1950 was up almost 45% over the comparable period of 1940.

Like *McCall's*, the *Companion* had used a great deal more photography over the last decade. It had risen from 36.39% of all illustrations in the first half of 1940 to 84.22% in the first half of 1950. Such changes which, as we shall see, were paralleled in the *Ladies' Home Journal* as well, seem to be the consequence of a number of converging stimuli.

The most important must be the success of *Life* and, to a lesser extent, *Look*. In their total commitment to photography and the visualisation of information, they changed the concept of what a modern magazine looked like. But, more important than their provision of a handy example of a new format for American magazine editors to follow, they achieved enormous success with that model. Where in the 1920s, the *Post*'s format came to dominate the internal organisation of most of the popular magazines, apart from the *Digest*, not only because it solved a design problem, but also because it was immensely successful, so, in the forties, the overwhelming success of *Life* must have dazzled the other editors and publishers.

Another element which may have contributed to the change in the appearance of the top women's magazines was the nature of the information which was crucial to their existence. Fashion, food and home decoration are all visual topics, that is, they are concerned with the physical presence of objects. Photography provides very precise information that is particularly conducive to comparative judgements. That is, it encourages differentiation in a way that words never can and artwork can only partially attempt. Thus, as the editors of these publications were increasingly drawn to non-fiction, the use of photography burgeoned.

The appearance of the *Ladies' Home Journal* changed in other ways. It developed a predilection for cartoons which was very unusual in a woman's magazine. For example, during the same period of analysis, not one cartoon was recorded in 440 pages of *McCall's*. At the same time, the *Companion* published a total of only 3.11 pages of humour. The *Journal* published just over 12 pages.

Another major change in presentation occurred because the forties finally saw the acceptance of colour photography as a reasonably practical way of recording the world at large. Thus, by the end of the decade, all three of the top women's magazines were using it extensively. In fact, close to 20% of all illustrations in all three were reproductions of colour photographs. The cost of acquiring the originals and, more importantly, the cost of making plates and printing from them would have been more expensive than the monochromatic alternative. However, such costs could not be avoided, caught as they were in a fierce three-way struggle. That it told on the resources of the *Companion* might be inferred from the fact that it was using a slightly poorer quality paper at the decade's end than at its beginning. Nevertheless, for a moment at least, such calls on their resources did not worry them too much for they were still waxing fat on the advertiser's dollar.

The *Ladies' Home Journal* in particular was open handed with its revenues, pushing its use of illustrations up to 2.01 per editorial page, with 1121 used in six issues. Furthermore, the *Journal*'s page displayed much greater stylistic diversity than could be found in its two major rivals. One gets the sense that the Goulds actually enjoyed surprising their readers. And if the circulation figures are any criterion, their audience liked it as well. Thus, with the confluence of these factors, women's magazines shifted radically in their appearance in the forties and create what can only be described as their golden age of graphic design.

The contents of the *Journal* had also shifted noticeably over the decade and the editorial profile was not balanced in the usual way of twentieth–century women's magazines, that is, overwhelmingly towards a fashion/domestic dominance in the articles coupled with a preponderance of lush, romantic fiction. In fact, the balance under the Goulds was, in many ways but not all, reminiscent of that established by Bok in his last year on the *Journal*. Like him they were ready to commit many pages every month to articles on varying aspects of contemporary society. In 1950 they totalled almost 17% of the editorial space during the first six months of the year; in 1920, at the end of the Bok years, similar material had absorbed 16.5% of the full twelve months of the *Journal*. Such an appropriation was singular even in 1950(see Appendix XII). For example, this percentage was twice that deployed by the *Woman's Home Companion* in respect of the same topics during the same period(see Appendix XIII). At the end of the fifth decade of the twentieth century that meant that the *Journal* was running a regular page entitled 'Making

Marriage Work'. It had a regular Public Affairs Department which in April 1950, for instance, was promoting the League of Women Voters, a non-party pressure group dedicated to the discussion by women of current political topics. It ran a series, 'Profile of Youth', that delivered its information in a photo-journalistic form, describing the social life and times of a young person every month from a wide variety of backgrounds. For example, the normally four–page spread featured an 18–year–old boy from Wyoming one month, who 'pays more attention to horses' legs than he does to any girl's', and the next a black schoolgirl from Chicago's South Side.

To accommodate such topics, the use of fiction was curtailed. At just over 32%, it had dropped noticeably from the 42.6% of ten years before. The Goulds also kept a tight rein on the traditional 'women's topics', fashion, cookery, homemaking and children, at 27%. Where they did let go, starting a tendency that lasted through the subsequent decade, was in their enthusiasm for biography(see Appendix XII).

In January 1950, the *Journal* launched 'The Little Princesses' with a great fanfare. This voyeuristic peek into the British royal closet was, as we shall see, bought by *Woman's Own* for home consumption and, one has to say, was more attractively laid out there than in its original form. Nevertheless, the commercial success of the series was such that for many years the *Journal* ran a continual stream of biographical material.

The last of the best-selling women's magazines serves as a reminder that there was another audience in the US and a large one that the big three were neglecting. That audience was not interested in mental health or other tendentious topics. It just wanted more of what they had always enjoyed in the past and it wanted it cheaply. *Woman's Day* sold for 5¢ a month when the cover price of the *Journal* was 25¢. Its information was very basic. It concerned itself with giving very clear instructions on how to cook fish or make dolls clothes. Every month, one section of eight to ten pages called 'The How To Section' was filled with detailed instructions and illustrated with line drawings. The fiction used four–colour gravure for its artwork, just as in the *Companion*, though at 264 x 217 mm the pages were very much smaller. It clearly served very simple needs, but it must have served them well given the size of its circulation. With just over 12% of its articles, mainly those on fashion, illustrated with colour photographs, it did not look as out of step with current graphic trends as some publications that have tried to fill such a niche. Clearly, it was doing its job well. Things were very different on the other side of the Atlantic.

APOLOGISTS FOR BRITISH WOMEN'S WEEKLIES, in particular Mary Grieve, the editor of *Woman* during the forties and fifties, have claimed that the readers did not want anything more than 'practical skills, personal relationships, and increased self-confidence'[55] and, presumably, romantic fiction, which was supplied in bulk. She claims only to have sinned by omission, but such assertions do not stand up under examination or analysis.

During the war years, close cooperation between various government ministries and the editors of the British women's magazines was translated into regular meetings in the offices of the Periodical Publishers Association. By late 1943, the *World's Press News* could say of the women's press that 'it has won a dominant and very adult place in the periodical field, and is rivalled in sales and social influence only by the newspapers.'[56] And in 1941, Mary Grieve herself had said, 'we feel that the women's press is above all other media best fitted to translate to women the role they must fill in increasing numbers.'[57]

Yet, once peace had broken out in Europe, those running these publications committed themselves to re-establishing the pre-war *status quo*. As Marjorie Ferguson's analysis has pointed out, considerable and continuous pressure was exerted to deny women their own role outside the home.[58] Those who had risen under the pre-war system were keen to re–establish it, despite its massive rejection by the voters in the 1945 British elections.

In America, before the nineteenth century closed, the *Ladies' Home Journal*, in Edward Bok's hands, had been campaigning on civic issues. Thus, when Gertrude Lane took over *Women's Home Companion* she saw nothing amiss in running articles on the involvement of women in the presidential election of 1920. The *Journal* had spoken out and the *Journal* was an overwhelming success. In later years, the heirs to these two pioneers continued the tradition, as we have already seen. In other words, a cultural context was established within the most successful American women's magazines which incorporated serious social commentary alongside practical domestic information, fashion and large volumes of fiction. In Britain, that option was never exercised, though there can be no doubt that, for instance, James Drawbell at *Woman's Own* knew exactly what was going on in the American market.[59]

During the war, although paper supplies were severely restricted in Britain and advertising space had to be curtailed, the elimination of promotional expenses and the sale of all available copies, avoiding the expense of returns, the cost of printing and then transporting them to and fro, meant that profits increased substantially.[60] Thus, when at the end of the war, James Drawbell was appointed as managing editor of *Woman's Own*, he determined to use these accumulated profits on behalf of Newnes to pep up the magazine.[61] To that end he not only assisted his editor, Jean Lorimer, by expanding the staff, he also visited the United States. There he developed his relationship with the Goulds, the husband and wife team who edited the *Journal*, and through them contracted many American illustrators to work on *Woman's Own* to enhance its appearance.[62] Thus, there can be no claim of ignorance of possibilities. Choices were made for which the staff were responsible. Within that structure, Marjorie Ferguson has isolated a number of themes that recur again and again during the late forties and fifties. Pre-eminent among them was 'Getting and Keeping Your Man'.[63]

Fiction dominated every issue of *Woman's Own* with over 41% of editorial space for the first half of 1950. Cookery, knitting and the other domestic hints used another 12% (see Appendix XXVII). But the staff were not as besotted with these two areas as other magazines. In fact, in 1950 they opened another seam that was to be enormously productive and one that infected much of British journalism in the years to come. In the spring of 1950, *Woman's Own* and *Ladies' Home Journal* turned the British royal family into show business.

The Goulds, through a British journalist, Dorothy Black, had acquired the rights to a book on the Princesses Elizabeth and Margaret by their ex-governess Marion Crawford, as we have seen already. Having just married a bank official, the latter managed to exact a high price for the world rights. In their turn, the Curtis organisation wanted to recoup as much of their original outlay as possible.[64] The price for the British rights went so high that some rival publishers had difficulty believing it.[65] So that Newnes in their turn could retrieve some of their costs, the series was heavily promoted. Indeed, *Woman's Own* held fire on publication until paper restrictions were rescinded so that they could respond freely to the anticipated rise in sales. In the event, their circulation jumped by half a million.[66]

Not surprisingly, the rival publishing houses responded vigorously. The very same week, the first in March 1950, *Woman* inaugurated its own series 'The Real Princess Elizabeth'. Even *Woman's Weekly* feigned a riposte with 'When the Royal Family Travels By Air' on May 13, 'Nanny To A Baby Prince' the following weekend, 'The Story of Clarence House' the week after that. From now on the royal family were just another promotional device. Meanwhile, *Woman's Own* tried to build on their lead with biographical series on other show business 'personalities':

Ingrid Bergman, Jean Simmons, Jean Kent and the radio comedienne Joy Nichols. It was not really surprising that historical and biographical articles absorbed over 10% of editorial space during the period(see Appendix XXVII).

So, by 1950, with *Woman's Own* selling an average of 1,605,500 a week,[67] a ratio of editorial to paid advertising pages of 178:100, a page rate of £940,[68] and an income of approximately £340,000 gross for the first half of the year, the magazine could be said to be thriving. With Joanna Chase as editor, it had taken over the second spot in the women's market from *Women's Weekly*, more than doubling its circulation since the war.

Yet, whatever James Drawbell might think about 'the quality of the editorial' making the difference in developing sales,[69] the fact remains that all of the three major women's weeklies more than doubled their circulation during the last four years of the forties, irrespective of their approach. The war, as we will see, had stimulated a great demand for reading material and the British women's press exploited that need with great determination.

Woman was somewhat more home–orientated than their rival from Newnes. They published more knitting patterns and encouraged their readers to be more adventurous and colourful in redecorating their rooms. They were also increasingly interested in giving fashion and beauty advice, particularly the latter. No longer were cosmetics ignored as being tantamount to harlotry. (The *Ladies' Home Journal* ignored cosmetics almost completely at this time.) As in the other two British circulation leaders, *Woman* showed a strong interest in personal difficulties, something that has never been in evidence in the American market. Indeed, it would be hard to imagine any of these British weeklies without their problem page, and very frequently other sections on health or children followed the same format of answers to correspondents, itself a very British element.

Woman at the end of the 1940s showed only minor differences from its issue of 10 years before. The organisation of the edition of 1 April 1950 was basically the same as that of 24 February 1940. The contents page and 'Woman to Woman' still preceded the first story. Their layouts were a little more fluent ten years on but the typographic differentiation between letters and the editorial response was still not clear.

Using a colour illustration with the first story opens the main editorial sequence with a flourish. But the story only continues halfway across the subsequent page before encountering a fashion feature on hats which used nine portraits of models in a checker board pattern alternating with short descriptions in bold type centred in white space.(Fig. 42) To lay out a feature like this indicates how better binding machines increasingly allowed designers to think in terms of a spread as a coherent space rather than two pages. More romantic fiction followed over the page. The second colour used to pep up the wash drawing of a couple kissing was also used to

Fig.42 The passing of the forties made little difference to Woman. Although design elements might evolve to some extent, the content stayed much the same.

print the script typeface of the title. And so the pattern continued with much the same features and much the same designs as the issues of the pre-war years.

Amalgamated Press Ltd's contender in the circulation race was *Woman's Weekly*. Its sales rose too in the post-war period. Yet, it had nothing new to offer, having been around since 1911. Its distinctively awful pink and blue covers enclosed speckled reproductions of photographs of seemingly endless knitted cardigans. If any periodical ever offered security through repetition, this is the one. Even the model in the photographs was normally the same young woman week after week. With fiction absorbing over 55% of editorial space and those acres of wool taking another 22%, there was not too much room for other topics. Only the problem page and, interestingly, some early articles on holiday travel, took noticeable amounts of space(see Appendix XXVII).

Of the three competitors, this was easily the most dreary in appearance, lacking colour other than on the cover. The illustrations it did use were predominantly, 63%, monochromatic drawings printed letterpress. *Woman* and *Woman's Own* were in a completely different class graphically. Drawbell's contacts with New York put the emphasis in the latter on four–colour artwork, which comprised 18% of all illustrations inside, as well as all the covers. Without question its graphics were bolder and more aggressively stylized than those of *Woman*. The latter opted for colour photography which it used on most covers and increasingly between them. Despite using four-colour artworks to open its stories and on its occasional home decoration features, they only contributed 7.7% of all illustrations by 1950.

As will be seen, the *Radio Times* had a completely different heritage to that of America's *TV Guide*. Although, it suffered the same restrictions on paper supply experienced by all the British serials during the forties, both newspapers and magazines,[70] it still attempted to retain an integrated magazine format. While the programme schedules, in 1943 for example, ran from pages six to nineteen in every twenty–page issue, they were always preceded by short articles commenting on the broadcasts. Page three was always devoted to the miscellany 'Both Sides Of The Microphone', which had its roots in the introductory miscellanies of the penny weeklies developed by Newnes, Pearson and Harmsworth decades ago. Through both sections, the pages were linked by a stream of small, column-wide illustrations, many of which were still reproduced from original artwork which displayed a range of graphic styles far removed from the flatulent illusionism found, for instance, in the women's press.

By 1947, the paper shortage had eased sufficiently for issues of 28 pages to be the norm, with some of 32 being not unknown. The clear sans-serif typography hitherto mandatory for the schedules had been abandoned for a conservative and less legible serif face. Interpolated among the listings were occasional articles which again had the effect of drawing issues into a coherent whole. Occasionally, the opening articles were omitted, which immediately gave the impression that the weekly was little more than a list. However, the illustrations, both drawn and photographic, were on the increase, which helped to vitiate the austere appearance of those years. Meanwhile, another of the magazine's roots appeared to have atrophied with the abandonment of the opening miscellany.

By January 1950, the regular size had risen to 48 pages and the *Radio Times* did not exhibit the sudden increase in mass evident on 1 March of that year in all the other popular magazines when the restrictions on magazine paper supply were finally lifted.[71] The balance of each issue had shifted again. 'Both Sides Of The Microphone' had returned but not to its page three slot. With more space available, the articles expanded and the listings absorbed only about 60% of each issue instead of the 70% prevalent in 1943. The transmissions now included three nationally broadcast radio services and the renascent television service that had been

Fig.43 By 1950, Radio Times was the most popular weekly magazine in the world with regular sales of more than 8 million. But the articles that surrounded the listings were overwhelmingly elitist and reflected little of the predominant interests of the listeners.

interrupted by the war but now functioned for three or four hours every day.

The subjects of the articles were weighted disproportionately towards minority culture. For example, in an issue taken at random, that of 14 April 1950, the cover of the 'Television Edition' features a photograph of the English Lake District in springtime and a caption linking it to Wordsworth. The 151 x 223mm image is an awkward format for a landscape, but the column of programmes listed on the right balances the image, alternating bold 12–point capitals which are used for programme titles, with italic ten–point for a one-sentence comment or a listing of the participants.(Fig. 43)

A full page of advertisements on the inside cover leads to another selection of radio programmes on page three which isolates about 50 and groups them under headings such as 'Plays', 'Talks' and 'Features'. This is enclosed in a box created from a half–point rule. Also within the box is a 6 x 6 cm reproduction of a shot of Dove Cottage, Grasmere, again pushing the Wordsworth connection. The third plug for the poet comes with a 300–word piece under the title 'The Wordsworth Centenary'. The page is completed by a piece promoting a series on art in England between 1700 and 1840.

Another full-page advertisement leads on to a one-page article on a successful quiz of the period between competing pairs of schools, 'Top of the Form'. A jigsaw of four photographs is reproduced at the top of the page showing the contest in progress and a portrait of the producer, while the text is laid out below in three columns, interrupted by two centred cross-heads in bold. Forty per cent of page six is given over to Mozart's Idomeneo, with the rest is devoted to 'Michael Tippett: the Man and his Music'. A small portrait of the composer and a conductor is centred at the bottom of the page. The facing page is entirely given over to the Wordsworth binge. His portrait is sandwiched between two more Lakeland scenes while about 900 words are used to try to establish his significance.

'Both Sides of the Microphone' is not so emphatically elitist and manages to get Marcel Proust and Billy the Kid on to the same double spread. It gathers short items on a variety of programmes and surrounds them with photographs of the subjects of the broadcasts. An article on Christopher Fry's 'The Lady's Not For Burning' dominates page 11. Quotations from and a description of the play are accompanied by a photograph of a scene from a recent television production, although the article has been provoked by a radio version. The final article before the listings is one puffing Puffney, a new comedy series being introduced that week. The page–long article is laid out across the gutter so that it can be flanked on both sides by advertisements.

The radio listings are given considerable space with four pages devoted to each day. Type sizes vary enormously in the attempt to cram in as much information as possible while allowing

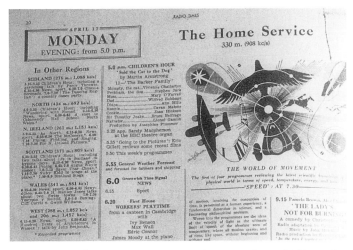

plenty of white space round each programme. Each spread has at least two illustrations, usually photographic but sometimes uses an original artwork.(Fig. 44) The television listings are all compressed into just one two-page spread, with another digest promoting them overleaf. Listeners letters and an article on Tallyrand completes the issue.

Amazingly, this was the most popular magazine ever published in Britain. Already, by 1945, *Radio Times* was selling an average of four million a week. A year later, sales had grown by over 25%. By the decade's end, it was selling 8,108,431 per week on average, a circulation unparalleled in Britain before or since by any other title.[72] In fact, at this point it had the largest audited sale of any magazine in the world, weekly or monthly.

Yet, when that is said, it would be foolish to suggest that these articles induced the public to part with two pence every week. By the late forties, the relative popularity of the competing BBC transmissions, as monitored by their Listener Research Unit, revealed that the Light Programme, which allotted over 50% of its broadcasting time to 'Light and Dance Music', had an audience almost 50% larger than that for the Home Service, which tended to be rather more sober.[73] The audience for the Third Programme, which was transmitting the programmes that related to most of the articles published in *Radio Times* that we have listed, got only 4% of the audience at best.[74] No other editors attempted to proselytise their readership in this way.

As usual in Britain, the most successful magazines in the forties were the cheap weeklies. Apart from the *Radio Times*, they can be divided easily into two distinct groups: the 'illustrated weeklies' and the women's press, which we have discussed already, with *John Bull* somewhere in between. Of the group of seven with a million plus circulation, five were printed by gravure in Watford, just north of London. *Illustrated*, *John Bull* and *Woman* were all owned and printed by Odhams Press. *Picture Post*, owned by Hulton, and *Woman's Own*, owned by Newnes, were printed by Sun Engraving.

Although no audited circulation figures are available for the war years, the 'illustrated' sector of the market seems to have held a stable audience through the forties, with *Picture Post* still selling 1,381,809 in 1950, as opposed to 1,185,915 in 1940.[75] By way of contrast, the women's weeklies and the *Radio Times*, experienced an enormous readership surge during the decade. Fortunately, the latter half of this rise is documented for, at last, the publishers stopped trying to pretend that the Audit Bureau of Circulation did not exist, and there was a large growth in membership of that organisation immediately after the war.[76]

Clearly, this change in the volume of readers cannot be attributed to the 1870 Education Act. (See page 90 and the associated footnotes 64 and 65.) As one might expect, there was a steady rise in real wages during the period 1938 to 1950 of about 7%.[77] However, when analysed in more detail, it can be shown that the mass of the lower paid in Britain did disproportionately well in respect of pay increases during the forties and their purchasing power had increased by about 30% by 1949.[78] By way of contrast, 'the administrative class civil servants' salary index, which stood at 100 in 1938, was only 108 in 1945.[79]

Therefore, it is not surprising, when one compares the Hulton Readership Surveys for the years 1947 and 1950, to find an increase of approximately 58% in those readers in the lowest sociological categories, DE, taking *Woman*. An only slightly smaller increase, 46%, for those readers in the same category, during the same short period, took *Woman's Own*.[80] In other words, yet again there is a positive correlation between substantial circulation increases and growth in surplus disposable income, though this time it applied primarily to one section of British society. However, the growth in the sales of women's weeklies in Britain was affected by a choice that the publisher had to make.

The amount of paper available to each company was limited throughout the forties. But, if the size of each page and each edition was cut, circulation could be allowed to rise with demand. That is, if the size of each issue was halved, the number of copies could be more or less doubled while still using a comparable amount of paper. On the other hand, if page sizes and their number per edition were retained at the pre-war level, then circulation would stagnate. *Woman* and *Woman's Own* took the first option, *Picture Post* the second.

The 'illustrated' group of weeklies were deeply affected by the division of the decade into two by the end of the hostilities. However, the war had an even earlier effect on *Picture Post* when Stefan Lorant, its editor, seeing the obvious and imminent collapse of British resistance, departed for the United States in July 1940 in an attempt to avoid further German hospitality.[81] He was succeeded by his deputy, Tom Hopkinson, who had absorbed his former boss's style so well that *Picture Post* did not deviate from its existing editorial path.

The early forties were the years in which there was a 50% increase in per capita sales of books in Britain; when even poetry sold in editions of thousands rather than hundreds.[82] In January 1941, *Picture Post* ran a special issue on the post-war world that provoked enormous interest and may well be described as the first of the many discussions and reports on what peace would bring.[83] Perhaps repeating a well-thumbed adage about fear concentrating the mind wonderfully might not be inappropriate, for the examination of these pages and those of *Illustrated* also disclose the fear and anxiety consequent on being isolated in front of a war machine that had crushed all resistance in its path hitherto.

Yet, the post–war *Picture Post* exhibited an unexpected change: the virtual elimination of interest in matters defined purely as contemporary events. In the throes of wartime such an allocation would, understandably, be high. However, one might have anticipated a diminished but continuing interest once the conflict was at an end. Not so. From an editorial profile in 1940 that devoted 20% of editorial space to such matters, the first six months of 1950 included just one page out of 900(see Appendix XXV). By way of comparison, contemporary events in *Life* dropped from 17.5% of editorial space in the first six months of 1940, to a little over 4% during the first six months of 1950(see Appendix XV). Even public affairs in *Picture Post*, in a period covering a general election, were down when compared to the similar period in 1940: 8% as opposed to 14%(see Appendix XXV).

In their place was a broader interest in the world at large. That displayed in the arts was up from 9.7% to 15.8%. The allocation for fashion doubled to 4.6%, while the documentation of foreign social life and manners soared from 5.3% in 1940 to 13% ten years later(see Appendix XXV). Of all the changes, the latter is the least expected, for few British editors of popular periodicals had hitherto been inquisitive about life beyond the Dover Straits. Clearly Tom Hopkinson was an exception.

He has described the second half of the forties as 'years of consolidation';[84] when 'we could again tackle subjects needing to be treated at some length, the sort of subjects around which television documentaries would be made but which in the 1940s were not handled by the media at all, being considered too controversial and distressing.'[85] As we have seen, *John Bull* had been built on the foundation of criticism and controversy. But it was very much on its own at the time and Hopkinson is quite right to assert the exceptional nature of the editorial choices made at *Picture Post*, even if they were not unique. It was certainly a clear stream in a dry land.

Perhaps this is the answer to the question posed towards the end of the last chapter, that is, why *Picture Post* should be remembered while others have drifted from view. From the very first, it had presented its features with simple graphic lucidity. It structured its material so that understanding could be gained, not mere stimulation. Now, in the post-war years, the objective was to present at least one topic every week 'which was going to be argued over in the pub or around the breakfast table.'[86] Perhaps the answer is simply a matter of respect. By the end of the forties, there were over a million people in Britain who were prepared to pay three pence a week to be treated as though they were intelligent, compassionate men and women who appreciated the evocative power, majesty and humanity of great monochrome photography. In that respect, the trail of this weekly is still marked in the dust, for none who have come after have followed the same route with any success. Many of its finest journalists moved over into television in the fifties. Perhaps that is why the topics with which they concerned themselves in print reappeared on the box in subsequent years.

Unfortunately, the respect accorded by its readers to its editorial policy was not shared by *Picture Post*'s owner, Edward Hulton. He had twice married the daughters of Russian emigrés, the children of czarist officials. It is, therefore, not entirely surprising that as the forties drew to a close and the Cold War grew colder, that he should start seeing reds under the bed. Furthermore, his wife, who had no qualifications or experience in journalism, tried to interfere in the running of the magazine.[87] The end came in October 1950 when Hulton tried to suppress a story critical of the South Korean regime and its 12–year–old victims. Hopkinson refused to comply and forced Hulton to sack him rather than resign.[88] From there on, the way forward for *Picture Post* was all downhill.

The war also had a catalytic effect on *Illustrated*. By 1943, the link to *The Passing Show* through the compromise instituted in the new magazine's opening years had disappeared. The picture stories of *Weekly Illustrated* and the fiction from *Passing Show*, had now been subsumed in a fresh editorial profile. The dialectic between the evocative picture stories from the war and the essentially escapist fiction had been synthesized into an approach that largely avoided direct description and images of the fighting. *Illustrated* concentrated on the home front, the social life of the war. It ran stories on American nurses at a field station in Tunisia but only showed them off duty. It showed Aldershot rather than El Alamein. Without ignoring the war, it tried to raise spirits by being determinedly light in tone. In this it was undoubtedly helped by its use of colour photography, which was used on every cover and on at least one, usually two inside pages. Relative to the quality achieved post-war, the results were not of the best. Yet, given that colour film was virtually impossible to obtain after the war, let alone during it, the efforts of the magazine's staff were extraordinary.

Even after the war, there was little improvement in quality at first. However, by 1950 the paper stock and the end result had been upgraded in a noticeable way. While the covers were frequently used to exploit discreetly the charms of young women, they were also used to feature the leading protagonists of the British election of 1950. Where else could one discover that Churchill had dark blue eyes? Inside, the reproduction of colour photography was used with a variety of subjects: from a feature on Leger's mosaic at Notre Dame de Toute Grâce on 4 February, to one on an Irish bloodstock farm on 6 May. In this they reflected the range of *Illustrated* by the end of the forties.

In many ways, the editorial profiles of both *Illustrated* and *Picture Post* were similar. For popular British magazines, they both placed surprising emphasis on the arts; that is, 14.8% of the editorial space during the first six months of 1950 by the former. But, where *Picture Post* took a particular interest in the theatre and movies, *Illustrated* was more devoted to fine art and the movies. In the case of both magazines, painting meant Matisse and Picasso, in addition to the mosaics already mentioned. That indeed was a revolution, though it might be seen as a continuance of the serious wartime interest in the arts.

Illustrated also paralleled its competitor in its interest in life abroad at 13%. It devoted over 4.5% of editorial space to fashion(see Appendix XXV). Interestingly, these emphases were common to more than the two British publications. They were also a feature of *Life* at the time. As Tom Hopkinson has made no bones about acknowledging his use of other magazines as stimulants,[89] the realisation that such topics were unusually amenable to visualisation could well be said to have been something the picture magazine staffs had learned both separately and together.

By the end of the forties, *John Bull* was selling 1,098,715 a week on average,[90] which was roughly the same level that it had maintained for the last 20 years. Only the rising sales of other publications had eclipsed its pre-eminence. By 1947 it was printed by gravure, the consequence being that its appearance had improved immeasurably, particularly when compared to its mid-war editions. Like the other Odhams' publications, it featured a colour cover. But its stylistic choices were very much its own, signalling an editorial profile very different to the two 'illustrated' weeklies. In fact, the balance between fiction, the critical articles that had always been its metier, and some radical proposals, was quite singular. For example, its 30 August 1947 edition used a banner on the cover to draw attention to its leading article: an attack on the current abortion laws as unfair to women. Such an article could never have been found in the women's press of the time.

The forties were a buoyant time for American magazines, which was hardly surprising given the state of both the economy and the even more prosperous advertising industry. The changes of the thirties, with the rise of novel market leaders like *Life* and *Reader's Digest* and the emergence of new inks which initiated fundamental changes of appearance, were consolidated in the subsequent decade. However, although the leading titles at the end of the decade were largely those that were dominant at its beginning, the stuffing that filled the wrapper was of a different texture as paranoia colorised American society. Only the comic books provided a mass of new titles. But their extreme specialisation was intended to cultivate a form of reader loyalty that would generate a low profit margin from a low cost operation, produced by a publisher with a host of other, similar titles. None of the producers were looking for another *Reader's Digest*.

Time Incorporated's *Life* and the Cowles Brothers' *Look* provided new and highly successful role models for other editorial teams to emulate. As Lorimer's concept of a fiction-dominated weekly hiccuped and spluttered to a halt in the *Post* itself, the only vigorous alternative to the Luce creation was the *Digest*, which had always been overwhelmingly inclined towards fact rather than fiction. The drama of the current mass conflict must also have been a stimulant to the move away from stories and serials. This affected not only the mixed function market, but the more restricted mix of the women's monthlies as well.

The Goulds in Philadelphia and Birney and Wiese in New York all drew on the Bok tradition to enlarge the understanding that American women had of themselves and their society. This was reinforced by the move towards documentation created by the picture magazines in their use of photography. And, as photographic materials developed, so the magazines used more and more colour. Ironically, as the women's monthlies strove to generate understanding and compassion in the post-war years, the *Post*, *Digest* and *Life* were all playing on ignorance and fear to whip up hatred of such qualities when exercised in the political arena. Interestingly, these roles were almost reversed in Britain.

The London-based weeklies and the choices available to their editors in the forties were conditioned by the constrictions in the paper supply occasioned by the war. The publishers of the women's magazines chose to cut the number of pages and their size and allowed their circulations to rise, when that was possible. The 'illustrated weeklies' retained their pre-war dimensions and had to restrain their sales, given the limits on the supply of paper.

As the war continued, the women's press was given increasing credit for its influence and was used as an important channel of information from government ministries. But, with the coming of peace they tried to use that power to stifle the changes in the situation of British women which had been developing for decades. *Picture Post* and *Illustrated*, in retrospect, seem to have been better attuned to the society of which they were a part. They were less afraid to confront the world around them than the women's weeklies. Meanwhile, *John Bull* was as pugnacious as it had ever been, still ploughing a solitary furrow. Only the *Radio Times*, with its astounding sales and odd concept of what those who bought it wanted to read, stood outside this pattern. It, in fact, reflected an attitude endemic to its owner, the BBC. Don't give them what they want, give them what they should want.

WHEN DAWN BROKE ON THE OPENING OF THE FIFTIES, the three dominant American magazine publishing houses, Time Inc., the Curtis Publishing Company and the Crowell-Collier Publishing Company were still weaving the thread of success. Circulations were on the up and up and, for the time being, advertising revenues were flowing. On 14 December 1956 the thread broke and a shudder of impending doom quivered through the industry. On that day, the demise of both *Collier's* and *Woman's Home Companion* was announced. With *The American* already axed the previous summer, the publisher of some of America's greatest magazines had abdicated its role. Yet, its audience was still in place. Both magazines were selling over 4 million when they 'failed'.[91] To understand such a contradiction and how such a dramatic collapse took place is to understand how the undercurrents of the times welled up to submerge and carry off the great weeklies, the giants of their times, leaving the magazine landscape forever changed.

Yet, as long as one remembers that magazines had two masters, the reader and the advertiser, the reasons are not that obscure. The fifties were a time of escalating costs. According to one estimate, 'the cost of printing rose by 44 per cent, paper by 31 per cent, salaries by 41 per cent, postage by 89 per cent.'[92] Most of the best-selling titles had invested time, effort and a lot of money in selling subscriptions. For example, by the decade's end, the *Post* sold 6,227,075 copies per week, of which about 78% were on subscription.[93] Thus, an increase of 89% in the postal charges had serious implications. Moreover, it was not just a matter of distributing copies: there was also the matter of soliciting renewals and other promotions. By 1960, *Life*, according to the official history of Time Inc., sent out 82 million pieces of mail in one year.[94]

Against this upward movement in costs, the increase in receipts was sluggish, gaining just less than 25% for the industry as a whole between 1951 and 1958.[95] Yet, the economy was moving solidly ahead, total personal expenditures increasing 56% over the complete decade to 1960.[96] Advertising, as an industry, was even more buoyant with its dollar volume expanding by 86% during the fifties.[97] Significantly, the magazines' advertising revenues grew only 64% during the same time, while those for television grew 378%.[98] Furthermore, the effect of this intruder tended to be selective. As *Life*'s advertising director, Clay Buckhout pointed out in January 1959, his magazine's strongest business was in food, toiletries, tobacco and drugs, which were exactly the same industries that chose to use television. The weeklies offered advertisers large audiences at low unit cost, which was precisely the intention of the television networks.[99] Yet, as the total sales of all ABC registered general and farm magazines in the United States rose by 25% during the fifties,[100] the decade when television sales boomed, magazine reading was clearly still a growing occupation. However, the extraordinary growth of television advertising diverted media buyers, constraining income from advertisers for the magazines at a time of rapidly rising costs. It was a formula for disaster.

To some extent, the quality of the managements of the best-selling magazines and the resources at their disposal can be measured by the time that elapsed before they succumbed to the pressure just described. *Collier's* as we have seen, died in 1956. The *Post* survived to the end of the sixties. *Life* struggled on until the early seventies, as did the fortnightly *Look*. But, whatever they did, the writing was on the wall.

The Crowell organisation was certainly not its own best helper, though it did lose many important executives in a short time for reasons that were not always within its control. William Chenery, who edited *Collier's* so successfully from 1925 to 1943, moved on to be its publisher in the latter year and retired from that position in 1949, though he remained as executive vice-president of the parent company.[101] In 1951, both Joseph Knapp and Thomas Beck, two key figures in the company, died.[102] *Collier's* managed to go through 7 different editors in twelve years. This seemed to worry the media buyers and even before the forties were over, advertising revenue had dropped 25% in two years.[103] Under the pressure of rising costs and dropping revenue, any changes began to look like measures of desperation, which only further discouraged the advertisers and their intermediaries.

Woman's Home Companion was caught up in the same web of failure, even if it was serving a different market. In 1953, one major advertiser, on checking the company's financial statements, cancelled one million dollars worth of advertising in one go.[104] In such circumstances, a lack of confidence is infectious.

The *Post* was in a stronger position than *Collier's*. It had a stable but dynamic editorial team led by Ben Hibbs and where *Collier's* circulation figures had largely stagnated in the late forties, those of the *Post* had moved steadily ahead. But as the fifties wore on and all the best-selling magazines came under pressure as their costs rose faster than their revenue, a circulation war broke out in which numbers became the be-all and end-all of the game. The *Post* held its own in this war, increasing its sales by about 35% between 1954 and 1960. Advertising revenue increased by a similar amount for the same period, to $105,049,136 in 1960.[105] But this occurred because the rate per page that the *Post* could charge was rising with the circulation increase. The number of pages sold actually dropped just over 24% during the same period. As an advertising executive working for the *Post* at the time explained, the rate increases excluded many companies that traditionally advertised in the magazine. They were simply priced out of the market. But those companies that could afford the new rates were either *Life* or *Look* users, or were already turning to television.[106]

Additional circulation also meant increased print and distribution expenses. In 1947, the Curtis company had invested a large amount of capital in one giant, brand new printing plant outside Philadelphia at Sharon Hill. Eventually, the plant held 12 giant presses, each of which could disgorge 18 million pages in up to five colours every 24 hours. Unfortunately, such impressive figures involved impressive over–capacity at first.[107] Later, towards the end of the fifties, the increased circulation necessitated round the clock production that impeded proper maintenance schedules that led to breakdowns. This led to top overtime rates being paid to printers to overcome the backlog.[108] In addition, the plant's location on the east coast created delays in distribution that other companies avoided by using more than one plant or locating their production in the mid-west. The consequence of this and severe overmanning problems in areas of the company outside the editorial floor, meant that the Curtis Publishing Company increased its revenue during the fifties by 66% over the decade but watched its profits dwindle from $5.3 million to just $1 million. By 1961 they were in the red.[109]

Yet, for all this trouble and strife back stage, the audience saw a smooth performance up front. Paper quality at the *Post*, by the end of the fifties, showed a marked improvement over previous stock; there was much less show-through and the surface was more highly glazed. This gave much better reproduction of photographs in particular. Ironically, considering Lorimer's attitude, the *Post* even experimented with the use of colour photographs to illustrate a story, 'The Hands of Cormac Joyce' by Leonard Wibberley, in the issue for 16 January 1960. But, generally speaking, fiction was normally illustrated with colour artwork, though it was now frequently enlarged so that it filled the right-hand page and part of the left-hand page of the double spread on which it began. As in the women's magazines at the end of the previous decade, the image was used to set the tone and not merely to illustrate an incident. In the back-of-the-book section, a division still rigidly adhered to in the *Post*, line reproductions of panel cartoons or pithy little *bons mots* broke up the text as it slid between the advertisements. As for the editorial profile, it was very close to that created by Hibbs and his team at the end of the forties, with only the smallest variations between the decades, even though the details of the topics differed(see Appendix XVIII).

Life was a little more responsive to the passage of time and its reflection in the editorial profile, but not much. Its enthusiasm for biography had waned and sport had waxed. Otherwise, it was still not interested in cartoons even if it did like pictures of animals in ridiculous situations. Its coverage of the arts was still exceptional and, in that respect, it may have influenced *Look* (see Appendix XV). In particular, the fifties were the years of the big series, 'The World We Live In' and another in 1955 on the great religions. Then, in 1959, *Life* secured the exclusive rights to the private stories of the first seven astronauts, amidst some controversy. Overall, its outlook remained cosmopolitan.

One thing that had improved was the paper stock and, hence, the magazine's ability to reproduce photographs. Though monochrome did not quite regain the standard achieved at the end of the thirties, colour showed an enormous improvement over anything in the earlier volumes. It was also infinitely better than anything achieved by the *Post*, which reproduced colour photographs to much the same standard as was found in daily newspapers in the 1980s. In *Life*, monochrome still predominated in news stories but some colour was appearing. But, for travelogues, fashion, theatre and the magazine's rather peculiar manifestation of an interest in gardening, colour was much more frequently employed.

With Charles Tudor still in charge of the art department, the typographic cues to the audience were still as clear as they had been since his arrival. In the issue of 1 February 1960, for example, the title on page eight, 'Classic Photo of Launching', competes with the reproduction of a very powerful image, which fills almost the entire double spread. But, by being set in a 48–point serif face isolated on white space at the bottom of the left-hand page, the type catches

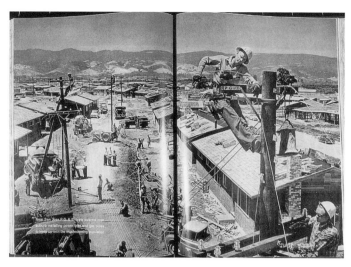

the eye and retains its function of establishing the context for the image. Most other titles in the issue are set in a sans serif face. The letters page which follows overleaf is the most clearly designed of any discussed here with headings in eight–point sans serif easily differentiated from the eight–point serif body text.

The first half of the issue is given over to events of the week, most of which are gathered into articles covering a double spread. Photographs dominate and usually take about 75% of the page space. All the pictures are reproduced in monochrome. The second half is largely given over to much larger sequences: a ten-page feature on an electricity generation company in California; the fourth in a series on world crime which focuses on the Mafia in Sicily; and, on a lighter note, the actress Dinah Shore at work and play. The first of the three uses colour throughout and many shots are reproduced so large that they cross the gutter, while one fills an entire double spread.(Fig. 45) The other two are black-and-white features. Mug shots make up many of the illustrations to the article on crime but the Shore feature involves a lot of posing and playing to the camera.(Fig. 46)

In fact, the camera dominates the issue. Most articles are inconceivable without it and no article appears which would retain an equal impact in its absence. This roots *Life* in the here and now because photography is a very specific medium. It does not generalise. It records a paradigm of a particular moment in a particular place. This means that any magazine which derives its editorial direction from the camera must tackle any topic through detailed moments past. It was very difficult for *Life* to deal with general trends, as Lorimer tried to do, or be prescriptive, like most women's magazines.

Decisions about such matters were in the hands of Ed Thompson, the managing editor, during the fifties. His approach encouraged the scrap-

Fig.46 Life found the entertainment world was full of co-operative stars who would put on a show for the camera to promote their careers. The publisher liked it because it was cheap and popular.

ping of stories so that last minute items could be included. This progressed to the point where, on occasion, a small editorial team would fly to the R. R. Donnelly printing plant in Chicago to supervise changes up to the very last minute.[110] Yet, despite such legends of extravagance that have clustered round the memories of the magazine, at 7% of revenue these expenses were proportionally lower than those at *Time*.[111] In fact, from the very beginning senior management at Time Inc. had known what it had on its hands. In August 1938, one of the most important executives in the first 50 years of the organisation, Roy Larsen, made a report to the company that evaluated progress to date. 'In *Life* we have our first big-volume, small-profit-margin operation. A large profit for *Life* must come with a tremendous volume of advertising.'[112]

Look began in a very different way to its more famous fellow. For the first 10 months it did not even accept advertising. In fact, as it was conceived, its origins were as far from *Life* as any picture magazine could be from another begun in the same period. It evolved from the Sunday gravure section of the *Des Moines Register and Tribune*, which was owned by the Cowles family. This freebie was so successful that the family syndicated it to other newspapers.[113] This prompted the idea of a separate publication. John and Gardner Cowles were stockholders in Time Inc. and friends of Henry Luce, so they knew of the impending publication of *Life*. They were sufficiently confident that their upcoming periodical was different from that of Time Inc. that they discussed it with Larsen and Luce and showed their dummy to them. It was intended to be a monthly, printed by gravure on cheap paper that would be profitable on single copy sales on account of its low production costs, even without taking advertising. The executives at Time Inc. were so impressed that the company invested $90,000 in shares. In July 1937, the Cowles brothers bought back the stock at a substantial profit to Time Inc.[114]

Look first appeared as a monthly in January 1937, selling 700,000 of that first issue. After four months it was changed into a fortnightly, which was how it stayed. Before the end of 1937, circulation reached 1.7 million and the first advertising was accepted. It was on this basis, somewhat more distant from the hurly burly of the moment than *Life* but accepting the advertiser's dollar, that the magazine evolved its own niche in the market.

By the end of the fifties, with the circulation at 5,881,787[115] and chasing that of the *Post*, its stories at 3.09 pages per item, were longer and more detailed than those of *Life*. In *Look*, the Lorimer-inspired segregation of advertising into front and back sections was avoided, as it was in *Life*. Each issue began with about 8 to 10 pages of advertising amongst which were just the contents listing and the reader's letters. The first story was usually left undiluted but advertising pages were soon interpolated into the rest of the magazine. No stories were trailed into the back pages. All ran continuously, interrupted by, at the most, a four–page advertising section. Long items which were a balanced mixture of words and pictures on topics such as 'Our New Hospital Crisis' or 'Psychiatry: the Troubled Science' contributed to an emphasis on medical matters unusual outside the pages of the *Reader's Digest*. Much of their material was approached through an individual experience. Hence, the large amount of space given over to historical and biographical articles: 17%. The other major emphasis was on sport, at just over 10%. But overall, *Look*'s editorial profile was not that of a dominating preoccupation with a limited range of topics, more the broad coverage of many(see Appendix XV).

Ironically, the same was true of *McCall's*, which underwent a palace revolution in the late 1950s. Only 20 years before, under Otis Wiese, the magazine had been utterly dominated by fiction, which had taken over 60% of editorial space. Now, in the first six months of 1960, it took less than 20%, a surprisingly low figure in the women's market(see Appendix XIV).

The new editor, Herbert Mayes, had been appointed in 1958 by the new owners, a financial group headed by Norton Simon, who had gained control of a number of companies already.

Wiese had obviously felt threatened by the new management and had flounced out in the company of others.[116] Mayes, who had taken *Good Housekeeping* to its current circulation of 4,673,416,[117] had himself only just left Hearst after a management disagreement. Contrary to many predictions in the industry, Simon did not fold the magazine and concentrate on *McCall's* lucrative printing contracts, quite the reverse. He poured money into the magazine in a spectacular attempt to dethrone the *Ladies' Home Journal* from the top spot. Much of this fresh capital funded the large-scale mailing of bargain subscription offers.[118] In less than two years, *McCall's* was already closing fast on the *Journal* with a circulation of 5,726,103,[119] as opposed to the latter's 5,986,727.[120] *McCall's* page rate was already edging ahead of the *Journal*'s as was their number of advertising pages sold, 517 as opposed to about 480 in the *Journal* during the first six months of 1960. By 1963 *McCall's* had achieved its goal with a circulation of over 8 million and advertising revenues that had climbed from $18,391,000 in 1958 to $41,868,000 in 1963. At the end of 1962, Mayes announced that the monthly had shown its first quarter's profits since the Second World War.[121]

However, it was not just a matter of a bought circulation. *McCall's* at the end of the fifties was a beautiful magazine that published some of the finest editorial photography and layouts of the time. Under the art director, Otto Storch, fine covers and fashion sections by Diane and Allan Arbus competed month after month for the reader's attention with the superb food photography of Paul Dome. The witty, elegant typography that opened each article vied with the vivid artwork that announced the start of every piece of fiction. And all of it was splendidly printed for such a large circulation publication, particularly as the publishers did not indulge in the luxury of the best paper.

Yet, even though the *Journal* had been eclipsed in the commercial race, the Goulds still had enough life in them to keep producing a magazine that conceded nothing editorially to its rival. Where Mayes put his greatest emphasis on domestic matters, as might be expected from a former editor of *Good Housekeeping*, the Goulds stayed with fiction and the condensed novel complete in one issue, even though they had now reduced their allocation of space to narratives to just over 30%. They also sustained their interest in contemporary society, which was given over 17%(see Appendix XII). Unfortunately, the *Journal*'s art direction was not in quite such capable hands as those of Otto Storch at *McCall's* and the layouts, particularly in the back-of-the-book section, were frequently somewhat fussy, even if the illustrations that accompanied the fiction exhibited considerable elegance. Both publications used the Lorimer formula for the overall design of each issue.

Meanwhile, over in Pleasantville, even the *Digest* was feeling the pinch. Rising costs, after 30 years, forced it to consider other sources of revenue than subscriptions and single copy sales. As Albert Cole, the company's business manager explained in 1970 when interviewed, 'It was a matter of economics. We either had to start taking ads or the magazine would lose a million dollars a year. It was that simple. There may have been a possibility of getting readers to pay more for the magazine, postponing the necessity of advertising revenue for a while, but we did some research that certainly didn't give us any encouragement in that direction.'[122]

Unfortunately, mistakes were made when the policy was announced which irritated the media buyers. De Witt Wallace did not wish to go the way of others and allow his carefully crafted digests to be engulfed in the competing claims of advertisers. So, it was announced that a maximum of 32 pages would be permitted in each issue and that no advertiser could have more than 12 pages in one year.[123] The media buyers were affronted and the *Digest* was not always able to fill that quota. Only in the succeeding years did the policy change in a way that encouraged the agencies into using the *Digest*.[124] By the decade's end, 1960, revenue from this source exceeded $27 million[125] which was not a large amount compared to some of its competitors, but then that was the way Wallace wanted it to be. By the first half of 1960, the ratio of editorial to advertising pages was 247:100, a very low one compared to that needed by most of the other magazines. For example, *McCall's* ratio over the same period was a much higher 121:100.

From the point of view of the editorial profile, advertising seems to have had very little effect on the balance that Wallace employed year after year. The only noticeable increase was in the use of humour which, as with most magazines of the period, was growing, in the *Digest's* case to just over 9% of the editorial space(see Appendix XVI). Of course, advertising did have a profound effect on the appearance of the monthly. Not only did it violate those discrete little pages with its strident, usually visual message, it forced the *Digest* to use better paper stocks on which to reproduce the advertisements. This spilled over on to some editorial space but not much. Overall, it stuck to the same cheap paper that it had always used. It had few reasons to change when only one other magazine was selling more than 7 million copies per issue at a time when the *Digest's* average net circulation was 12,011,389.[126]

The magazine built on the Lorimer model when it came to positioning the advertisements in each issue. It had an opening section which combined regular features and editorial listing with plenty of paid insertions. An uninterrupted editorial well followed and then a back-of-the-book section ended the issue.

How this worked can be seen by running through one issue. In that for May 1960, for example, the opening section lasts until page 36. Most of the advertisements are printed in four colours and the stock used is super-calendered imitation art paper. The features include 'It Pays to Increase Your Word Power' and 'Personal Glimpses' amongst others. No editorial graphics are used in this section, apart from a little line work around titles. The advertisements are all full-page. The editorial core of the issue is announced by a mast-head on page 37. It is also marked by a change to a much cheaper machine printings paper. The first six-page article, on the American armed forces, is not illustrated. The second, 'Murder by Airplane', features a dark, atmospheric line block, tinted with a second colour, light blue, on page 45. The text of both is set in an 11–point serif face laid out in two columns with white space between them. No cross-heads are used but attention is focused on a specific aspect of an article through the use of a brief introductory paragraph next to each title. Every article starts on a fresh page, while any space remaining at the end is filled by brief jokes and amusing asides.

This pattern is followed for the two subsequent articles 'How to Get Along with a Man' and 'What I Saw in Khruschev's Uneasy Empire', neither of which is illustrated. 'Is Your Family Safe From Death by Fire' marks a change by using an illustration beside the title. The image is coloured by overprinting with pale inks on top of the black line image. A similar tactic is used to start the next article, 'The Bitter Author of Mother's Day'(Fig. 47). A rather more elaborate image is used on page 67 but the technique is the same: colour printed from line

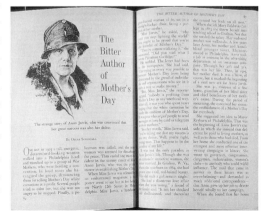

Fig.47 In its appearance, Reader's Digest is not very different from the 35¢ monthlies of the 19th century.But in its use of selling techniques, it is pure 20th century.

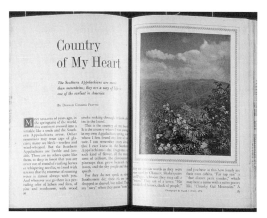

Fig.48 Once the American edition of Reader's Digest started taking advertising in 1955, it had to use better paper for at least part of each issue, allowing the editorial staff to use colour as well.

blocks. Such a technique is a sensible tactic given the poor quality of the paper. A colour photograph is reproduced with some success on page 87(Fig. 48), but only one other is used before the Campbell Soup advertisement announces the back-of-the-book section on page 144. This is printed on super-calendered imitation art like the opening section of the issue.

Although advertising dominates most spreads between page 144 and the last, 312, articles are still run as continuous text and the reader is never asked to turn to another part of the issue. This means that a piece such as 'Life with Grandfather' starts on page 152 and ends on 162, even though it only occupies seven editorial pages. Unlike Lorimer, Wallace used as many illustrations in this section as the core editorial well. He had clearly tried to change the Digest as little as possible as a result of the advertisers' presence, even if he was forced to include their material through economic necessity. The illustrations concentrated on incidents within the feature. They were not used in the manner typical of the *Post* or the *Ladies' Home Journal*, for example, to establish the mood or theme of an article.

The *Digest*'s nearest competitor was very much an intruder among the best-selling magazines, the first specialist magazine to reach those rarefied heights in the US, and it was a weekly. *TV Guide* may not seem much compared to the glories of *Life* or *McCall's*. It was printed on poorer paper than the *Digest* and had the same pocket-sized dimensions. Yet, when it was first published by Triangle Publications on April 3, 1953, it was an augury for the future in many ways. Perhaps most important, it appears to have been the first magazine conceived from the beginning as a national title that would be produced in a myriad of regional editions. In the late forties, one or two publishers seem to have been producing regional editions of some already existing periodicals. The stimulus was the growing economic power of regions such as Southern California or Greater New York. That usually meant that a regional edition would concentrate on soliciting advertisements from local firms and incorporating them in the copies distributed locally at a special rate. *TV Guide* was something different. It intended to vary its editorial content from area to area as well, for programme listings varied from city to city.[127]

The idea arose when Walter Annenberg of Triangle purchased *TV Digest* of Philadelphia, *TV Guide* of New York and *TV Forecast* of Chicago with the intention of creating the multi-edition magazine. Circulation started at 1,560,000 and was split among 10 different editions. But it was autumn before the idea really took off.[128] By the end of the decade *TV Digest* sold 7,307,436 copies a week. That total was split among 18 major editions and 42 minor editions with local sections reproduced by offset lithography, the first significant appearance of the process in a major American magazine. Its cover and the feature articles were the only elements common to all editions.[129] Clearly, the latter must have weighed with some of its purchasers but it seems more that it was the package that the information came in: a small, handy size that was easy to locate and view days in advance of transmission, which was not true of the listings in newspapers.

BRITISH WOMEN'S WEEKLIES witnessed an apparently unstoppable continuation of the post–war boom during the fifties. As they had in the late forties, all three of the leading titles rose together and peaked together, though their subsequent decline was not obvious before the sixties. Again, this parallel buoyancy tends to undermine the personal claims of the editors as to their undeniable contribution to the process. As will be expected, this growth in circulation was matched by economic activity. Average real weekly earnings in Britain rose by over 28% during the period 1950 to 1960.[130]

Woman was still the market leader. By 1954 it had passed the three million marker but the pace eased off and although it approached 3.5 million in 1957, it never quite made it and by the end of the decade the circulation was sliding a little.[131] The editorial profile shifted quite considerably over the decade as the process which was noticeable in the forties, that of the decline in the space devoted to fiction, continued. From a point at the end of the thirties in which over half of all editorial space was given over to stories and serials, they took just over 41% by the end of the forties. By the end of the fifties, they took about 31%. Part of their allocation had been redistributed to history and biography, largely the latter, under the thrust of the initiative instigated by *Woman's Own* ten years before. Travel articles had also increased a little. Interest in the arts had broadened to included popular music and radio at the expense of the movies. Contemporary society was given much the same weight as before. In absolute terms, cookery, knitting, home decoration and all the other domestic hints had doubled the number of pages devoted to them. But as the size of *Woman* had increased by nearly 50% over the decade, the increase in percentage terms was not so large: a rise from 17.8% to 22.6%, comparing the first six months of 1950 and 1960. Unexpectedly, the magazine was much less concerned with children by the end of the fifties. Conversely, where between January and June 1950 no articles on medical topics or matters of health were published at all, ten years later they absorbed 3% of the magazine(see Appendix XXVI).

This performance has been defended in strong terms by Cynthia White, endorsing Mary Grieve's claim that as editor she 'strenuously resisted' the encroachment of pressure from advertising.[132] This claim seems difficult to support when one encounters short features in every issue endorsing various products. Then, one cannot but notice the coincidence that the articles on travel were all bunched at the start of the year in the issues in which travel advertising was concentrated. Then again, one has to note the amount of merchandising that *Woman* itself was doing, like all its competitors; the paper clothing patterns, the special offers. But, above all, one has to ask what was Mary Grieve defending against the ravages of the advertisers? There was nothing controversial in *Woman* to begin with that needed defending. For over 20 years it had a pleasant but anodyne mixture of soporific fiction, prescriptive advice and encouragement to consume. If Mary Grieve had a more radical track record, one might be able to take this defence of the editor a little more seriously.

As the fifties passed, it was increasingly difficult to distinguish between *Woman* and *Woman's Own,* despite being owned by rival publishers. By the end of the decade, the latter had abandoned the vivid artwork used ten years earlier on its cover. Now it used the same rather vapid colour photography as *Woman* to catch the potential reader's eye on the bookstalls. Only its continuing preoccupation with biography stood out. Now they tackled somewhat more daring topics: John Osborne by the only marginally older George Scott;[133] or the autobiography of a nun who had been decommissioned.[134] In other respects the Newnes weekly was much the same as its rival from Odhams. It too had decreased the volume of fiction it carried. It too had a weekly feature on health. It too discussed popular music and television in a glib, uncritical manner. And, like virtually all British women's magazines and most American, it contained

Fig.49 Clarity of presentation, both verbal and visual, helped turn Woman's Realm into a best-seller after it had been launched purely as a cost/effective way to take the circulation pressure off Woman.

little humour(see Appendix XXVII).

Woman's Realm was launched in February 1958 to utilise some spare printing capacity at Odhams, as well as relieve the circulation pressure on *Woman*, which by exceeding 3 million sales was passing the point at which gravure could be used economically to print it. According to its editor, Joyce Ward, the intention was to produce a modern version of the old formula of fiction plus domestic hints and information.[135] In fact, by 1960, the latter exceeded the former in the number of pages used(see Appendix XXIII). Apart from the fifties contributions to the formula of a medical page, plus another on personal problems, a little fashion and a couple of regular spots for kids, that was it. What took it into the million plus circulation bracket immediately was the publicity fanfare of the Odhams machine. What helped it retain those readers was the crystal clarity of its helpful hints on domestic matters, particularly those devoted to cookery.

Its art direction was also a model of clarity. Coming from the Odhams stable, it is not surprising that it started each issue like *Woman*, with letters and moralising editorials. It even started with colour artwork to illustrate the first story. But thereafter, particularly on the domestic front, photography was used in close up without fussy backgrounds and cropped tight so that attention was focused on the subject without any distractions. A four-page feature on slimming was broken down into topics which were isolated in white space and headed with ten-point capitals printed in mid grey rather than black.(Fig. 49) The page is further divided with simple patterns and drawings of people. A knitting spread is split horizontally with a jagged grey line to direct the eye from the pattern to the colour photograph of the result reproduced on the right. Clarity is, in fact, the essence of *Woman's Realm* and its art direction is really only a variant of that developed in the British women's weeklies during the previous 20 years.

However, this success had an effect on *Woman's Weekly*, which is not surprising as the latter had an almost identical editorial profile. After years of stagnation it underwent radical renovation in early 1960. Although it was still printed letterpress and remained entirely monochromatic, apart from its deathly pink and blue cover, the art direction suddenly changed gear. After years of utter predictability, asymmetrical, dynamic artwork began to invade the pages. And while the print colour was still a desaturated, dreary grey, one had a sense that at least the staff had woken up. Even the descriptions of domestic redecoration showed the effect of the clear instructions of its rival. Presumably the management thought that their sales of 1,459,600, already down from 1,858,400 in the mid-fifties, might drop even further under pressure from the new Odhams' weekly.[136] Ironically, within a few years every one of these 'competitors' would be owned by the same company.

The two weeklies that outsold even these highly successful restricted function weeklies by the end of the fifties were specialist publications: *Radio Times* and *TV Times*. The former changed as the listings expanded during the fifties. By separating the daytime and evening radio programmes, with the television section laid out completely separately, the listings used many more pages of an enlarged weekly: something like 44 pages out of 52, while some of the remainder were given over to advertisements. So, what had begun in the 1920s as a magazine that discretely incorporated the listings, was now an elaborate list that tacked on a few introductory pages. And while original artwork was used throughout every issue, the television pages were predominantly illustrated with formal portrait photographs; a return to the tradition of the two–penny weeklies of the twenties. This pattern was very stable throughout the fifties and seems to have been little affected by the appearance of *TV Times* in September 1955. This, one presumes, was largely due to the presence of Douglas Williams as editor through the fifties and sixties.[137] Although he worked as the art editor under Gorham, producing stylish, elegant typography, his post–war editions became increasingly turgid and it would be hard to fault an assessment that apostatized this period as the weekly's nadir.

As the transmissions of the BBC and its commercial alternative were rival services, so were their programme digests. Consequently, although the interloper used a slightly smaller page size at 292 x 220 mm, as against 303 x 244 mm, *TV Times* needed to be seen to be approaching the substance of its competitor, particularly as it too was charging four pence a copy by the decade's end. Ironically, this meant that *TV Times* would always be essentially different from the BBC's publication. Without the mass of radio listings, the emphasis would always remain on the articles, that is, if it needed to mimic the size of its rival.

During the first years, it was printed letterpress on calendered newsprint by the Amalgamated Press. Not surprisingly, it looked cheap and nasty. Thus, given that it could not rely on the listings for bulk, it had to make a stab at promoting itself as a moderately attractive magazine. In these circumstances, it made graphic sense to change over to gravure and use Sun Engraving at Watford to do the job. It also made economic sense, because by 1960 *TV Times* was selling 3,945,214 copies a week on average. Interestingly, *Radio Times* was still selling 7,002,914. Subsequently, they both declined in tandem to the point in the 1980s where their circulations both stood just above 3 million.[138] One did not take the other's readers. Weeklies dependent on bookstall purchase, without the inertial weight of subscriptions, are extremely price sensitive in respect of circulation. As the inflationary pressures of the sixties and seventies raised cover prices with unprecedented speed, so the circulation of all the best-selling British weeklies declined.[139]

Despite the need for *TV Times* to develop its articles as it established itself in the late fifties, it declined to stake out more general territory, relying wholly on programmes or those taking part in them as subject matter. As the network was a mixture of bought-in American dramas and series, leavened by their British counterparts and home–grown variety shows in the late fifties, there was every incentive for *TV Times* to concentrate on 'personalities'. As one might expect, it was illustrated overwhelmingly with formal portraits of the protagonists with occasional *in situ* shots of actors. Original artwork was extremely rare.

Thus, by the end of the fifties the best–sellers of the British magazine market were dominated, as ever, by weeklies, all of which were sold overwhelmingly through retail outlets. Even more so than in the United States, the restricted function periodical for women and the specialist magazines were outselling everything else. In America, some of the great titles and even companies had fallen, not because of a drop in circulation but because of the flight of the advertiser's dollar. In Britain the situation was entirely different.

223

The end of the forties was a time of considerable buoyancy for the British periodical. Yet, in less than ten years that market changed quite radically. The bottom of the market, the DE sector, between 1948 and 1955, began to lose interest in *Picture Post*, for instance. As these groups formed over 70% of the British population over the age of 16, that was a serious problem for Hulton Press. But they had others. As we have seen already, Tom Hopkinson, had been sacked as editor in 1950 after a decade's service. Once he had gone, the large editorial turnover completely destabilised the weekly, which lacked any editorial consistency whatsoever. Sales diminished in the following two years by 32%, to 935,000, probably as a result of a 50% price increase during 1951 to sixpence a week. But, when the company retraced its steps and cut the cover price to fourpence, sales did not bounce back and circulation remained doggedly below one million until 1956 when it nose-dived.[140]

Thus, for *Picture Post*, readers were actually lost. This occurred at a time before television ownership was significant. However, the final sudden drop in circulation did occur at a moment of substantial penetration by the new medium, just after the commercial network had been launched in late 1955. Thus, it may well be that in this particular instance, a price hike alienated readers, who were not recovered by a magazine that was unable to re-establish a consistent editorial personality. It only required a drop of a few hundred thousand in *Picture Post*'s circulation to kill it off, and this may well have arisen from the competition for attention created by commercial television. It is very noticeable that *Illustrated* also died at this time and for the same reason, a loss of readers. In fact, during 1956 and 1957, magazine circulations peaked in the UK, and have gradually eroded ever since. By the 1980s, with the exception of the two TV weeklies, individual circulations of the best-selling magazines were back to the levels of the 1930s . In the United States, the picture was completely different, with the circulation of the *Reader's Digest*, for instance, being four or five times what it was 50 years before.

Indeed, we have come full circle. In the 1840s in Britain and a decade later in the United States, the establishment of the railway networks was the basis upon which mass magazine sales were founded. At the end of the twentieth century, the distribution systems of both countries, in a very different way, predicate certain consequences. The enormous infrastructure behind magazine subscriptions in America has sustained circulation levels and enabled steady growth for successful titles. But the cost of maintaining that sales infrastructure has been so high that profit margins have been squeezed, leaving the magazines totally exposed to the whims of the media buyers of the major advertising agencies.

In Britain, the dominance of retail distribution and the single copy sales system was unable to withstand the combined pressure of price inflation and the more pluralistic culture that gradually developed after World War Two as a consequence of higher levels of surplus disposable income and shorter working hours.

Magazine publishers in both countries came under increasing pressure during the fifties from television but in different ways. In the US the burgeoning networks constrained the growth of magazine advertising revenue but never actually pushed sales into a decline. The big volume, low profit margin operations that topped the best-selling magazine league were unable to contain their costs to match their only slowly rising revenue. They were, therefore, squeezed out of the market and succeeded by highly specialised titles that focused on a readership profile beyond the grasp of the TV networks, such as the *National Geographic*, or *Modern Maturity*. But the titles of earlier decades that were relatively low cost operations, such as *Reader's Digest* and *TV Guide*, were able to withstand the tide.

In Britain a relative squeeze on the less affluent sectors of the population during the fifties combined with a new television network that seemed to be specifically targeted at them, actually took readers from the 'illustrated weeklies' during 1956–7. This drop in incomes from sales and the subsequent drop in page rates that would have resulted from the loss of circulation, was sufficient to finish them off. The subsequent growth in the British leisure industries and the pressures of price rises on publications that have had a practically non–existent cushion of subscriptions, has drained the top of the British magazine market of its readers. Although *Woman* and *Woman's Own* have survived, their circulations are only a third of what they were a generation ago. *Radio Times'* circulation in the late 1980s was just 40% of its peak.

ADVERTISING REVENUE HAS DEFINED THE CREATION OF THE POPULAR MAGAZINE. *Scribner's* grew rich during the 1870s because it was the first 35¢ monthly to pursue the selling of space in a serious way, enabling it to use better paper; which gave the editor and his staff greater flexibility in the way that they organised each issue and where they placed the illustrations. In the following decade, advertising spread to all the 35¢ monthlies. It sustained *Ladies' Home Journal* during the owner's successful attempt to make it the most valuable magazine in the American market while only charging 10¢ a copy. In the nineties, Munsey, in a last desperate attempt to sustain a flagging magazine, dropped his cover price to match the *Journal*, a change which he advertised aggressively. He survived and prospered because the extra circulation attracted a larger volume of advertising for which he could charge much higher rates. Over the years, the other ambitious American monthlies that followed his lead also experienced sustained circulation growth and prosperity. *Century* and *Harper's* did not change their price and soon slipped from the group of best-sellers. Because the increased revenue from advertising allowed the publishers to sell their magazines at less than cost, a whole segment of the American public was induced, through a variety of promotional techniques, to acquire a reading habit that broadened its perspectives.

However, the editorial model that the older 35¢ monthlies had provided did survive and, despite what previous authors have alleged, the increases in circulation which occurred at the end of the nineteenth century did not flow from changes in the contents of the various titles. Simple statistical analysis has revealed that *Munsey's*, for instance, was conservative in its editorial approach, yet was one of the first to sell more than half a million copies a month. On the other hand, *Century* and *Harper's* were already showing increasing interest in developing a more varied editorial profile before the end of the 1880s, but their adherence to the old cover price ensured that sales stagnated. A new editor at *Cosmopolitan* shaped it to feature relatively large amounts of lively material on contemporary society, yet sales dropped. Only when a new proprietor bought the ailing monthly and used his entrepreneurial flair and capital to promote the magazine did circulation rise. Sales were much more sensitive to price and promotion than to content.

Mistakes have also been made by previous authors on the nature of the influx of illustrations that occurred in the American magazines of this era. Some publications have been credited with a profuse use of photographic reproductions where even the most cursory examination reveals that few exist. What did happen was that the editorial staffs were able to transform layouts at will, if they chose, by remaking and resizing the blocks from which the illustrations were printed. Some did use large numbers of reproductions of photographs, particularly if they were concerned with documenting the contemporary world. Such choices were made because, as time passed, artwork came to be associated with fiction and photography with reportage. The decisions as to which should be employed came to be seen as the province of a new post in the editorial department, that of art director, which made its appearance during the 1890s. Such flexibility was possible because the second half of the nineteenth century had seen a complete transformation of the printing trade.

Paper manufacturers had moved from a rag to a wood base, precipitating a price collapse which transformed the economic structure of publishing, particularly for serials. The industrialisation of the etching of metal plates allowed the use of line work and then halftones to spread as the prices for blocks dropped. Colour was transformed from a luxury item in the 1850s to a regular decoration by 1900. Mechanical composition also moved from the inventor's workshop into the production cycle. This enabled vast stores of type to be scraped and permitted a much wider range of faces to be employed on the page, further liberating the art department. Thus, in the final decades of the nineteenth century, American magazines were transformed by advertising revenue, some of which was invested in printing technology.

Meanwhile, advertising revenue in Britain was being channelled in a different direction. The national daily newspapers dominated the selling of space, diverting potential revenue from both provincial dailies and magazines. In part, this occurred because the best-selling magazines were not particularly attractive to the advertisers, for they possessed readerships built on different foundations to their trans-Atlantic peers. Penny weeklies, aimed at wage earners at the lower end of the socio-economic scale, sold the most copies and such a market only attracted a limited amount of advertising until, that is, George Newnes joined forces with the agency T.B.Browne.

Newnes success attracted many would-be emulators of *Tit-bits*, but only two, Arthur Pearson and Alfred Harmsworth, used their ingenuity successfully to develop promotional schemes that caught the public's fancy, for clever competitions were the key to public loyalty in the British magazine market. None of these three demonstrated any great talent for journalistic innovation in the popular magazine market once *Tit-bits* had become established; their abilities were of a promotional nature. They were content to exploit the innovations of others in their pursuit of greater profits. Newnes's staff became adept at cultivating advertising in the weekly for the luxury market, while Harmsworth moved downmarket and expanded the sales of comic papers by dropping the price from a penny to a halfpenny. But as the nineties passed, the publishing empires looked increasingly similar. The separation of the market into various class-defined sectors, the penny weekly on the *Tit-bits* model, the sixpenny monthlies, the illustrated society weeklies, the penny women's weeklies and the halfpenny comics, was well established and based on patterns that had existed in embryo for decades. Each of the three major companies had at least one or maybe two contenders in most sectors. Sales were substantial but not enormous. These developments of the last decade of the nineteenth century in Britain were based on a steady rise in the real value of wages. As a result, the public were able to afford more serials, both magazines and newspapers, and the amount of published material expanded. *Tit-bits* in particular promoted a new concept of information as amusement. However, fiction reasserted its value to the editor as the nineties wore on. With their low production and distribution costs, the circulations achieved were quite sufficient for a steady profit. Clearly, British magazines, and the industrial framework that supported them, were developing in a very different way from their American counterparts. The owners of the latter looked to maximise sales, and hence advertising revenue, on a portfolio of just one or two publications.

The market structure established during the closing decades of the nineteenth century in the British magazine industry dominated it for the next half century. When Odhams entered the fray in 1906 they adapted existing formulae and, as they grew, they produced titles that were comparable to those of their more established competitors. The amalgamation of Pearson and

Newnes, did little to affect the situation. Even when Odhams managed to get control of *John Bull* as the twenties began, and initiated an expansion programme that, by the following decade, had transformed the company into the dominant force in the industry, they followed the established patterns in developing magazines which competed with their rivals on a narrow front. At the core of their operation was an extremely effective space–selling department.

The opening of the twentieth century saw a number of major innovations on the other side of the Atlantic. The weekly, in the form of the *Saturday Evening Post* and *Collier's*, rose in importance. The extraordinary success of the *Post* in selling space in particular, initiated a new way of organising magazines into two, very distinct sections which dominated the industry in the States for decades. The *Post*'s concept turned on attracting high–volumes of advertising. The other major, turn-of-the-century change first appeared in the other Curtis publication. Edward Bok at the *Ladies' Home Journal* began to campaign for various civic causes during the 1890s, using the platform of his enormous circulation. When Robert Collier took over his father's weekly he brought with him the same critical energy. Over the next decade, with varying degrees of cynicism, others followed suit.

While there was a steady increase in the sales of American magazines over the early years of the century, those of their British peers faltered as the real value of wages slipped and the budgets of the largest group of British magazine consumers were squeezed. The British sixpenny monthly, after the successes of the 1890s, lost favour and sales went into a serious decline, probably as a consequence of competition from sixpenny paperback books. Comics retained their hold on the British that they lacked in the United States.

As the American industry grew in sophistication, so editors became more mobile, taking editorial approaches with them on their travels. Mark Sullivan learned the art of fighting for civic causes at the *Journal* under Edward Bok and then applied it when he moved on to *Collier's*. Ray Long transposed his devotion to fiction from *Red Book* to *Cosmopolitan*, totally changing the latter in the process.

Neither market witnessed major technological innovation among the most popular magazines during the first three decades of the century. Colour increased in importance in the United States, although its use on editorial pages was still far from extensive, but made no impression at all in Britain because all the best selling weeklies were printed on the cheapest paper possible. More important were general shifts in editorial approaches. American editors supported civic causes before 1910 but appeared to have gained little financial advantage from their activities. Only when they followed the *Post*'s example did sales rise in a sustained way. This growing wealth may have encouraged the restructuring of the industry into a series of publishing groups, each with two or three highly successful titles. With the *Journal* still the leading woman's title, those who tried to emulate its success, like the *Woman's Home Companion*, responded to its concerns about civic matters. There was no comparable developments in the UK, where little changed until the thirties.

The twenties were great days for the American industry as personal affluence grew and advertising revenues increased even faster. Yet a hole was growing beneath it, even at this apogee of its success. Marketing research was developing new analytical tools that would have serious consequences for the magazines of the future. Agencies could direct campaigns at a specific audience with greater accuracy. This meant that the mere size of circulation was not enough, as *Liberty* found to its cost. Now the magazines had to sell to the right people, that is those that the agencies wanted. Such choices became even more critical after the stock market crash of 1929. Advertising spending crashed as well and even the *Post* suffered. Magazines which restricted their audience and provided a well-defined group of readers, such as *The*

New Yorker, attracted disproportionate volumes of advertising. This aided the really specialist journals, such as *Vogue* which, as we have seen, had a circulation only a tenth the size of *Better Home and Garden*, but made over half a million dollars more from its sale of space. This created serious problems for the future as an increase in circulation swelled costs such as paper and printing which could not be recouped from diminished advertising revenues among those publications which did not appeal to the media buyers.

Although the twenties were not a time of upheaval, certain editorial shifts were underway that would have consequences in the decades to come. Extreme specialisation made its first appearance among the best-sellers when *Radio Times* was launched in Britain and began the climb that would establish it as the leading weekly for decades. Weeklies also increased in importance in the United States, with four titles among the best-sellers. The old approach to content, through a compact editorial staff commissioning and accepting contributions from outsiders, changed as *Collier's*, *Time*, *Reader's Digest* and *The New Yorker* employed relatively larger editorial teams to write the text and commissioned far less. For the time being, fiction dominated the contents.

The thirties gave the editors and publishers in both the British and American markets new options. Heat-set inks and new paper gave letterpress one last shot in the arm. Gravure made the difference in Britain, enabling the public to buy well-illustrated, attractive weeklies for two or three pence. The three dominant publishing houses, Odhams, Pearson-Newnes and Amalgamated Press, were able to keep their hold on the market by merely adding such innovations to their already existing strings of titles. The only newcomer to make an impact was Edward Hulton with *Picture Post*, but he never developed his magazine business as extensively as the others before his momentum faltered in the fifties.

The publishing scene was more flexible in the States and more fertile, as Time Inc. and the *Reader's Digest* moved up to challenge the Curtis, Crowell and Hearst machines. The success of *Life* provided a new editorial model as the *Post*'s absolute pre-eminence began to fade. By the end of the thirties, not only were the advertisers allowed to use colour in its pages, the editor was even using colour photography on the cover. And when, in the early forties, a new editorial team took over the *Post*, the old formulae cherished by the weekly were soon swept aside. The interest in contemporary society which had proved such a successful topic for the *Digest* and *Life*, became the order of the day in Philadelphia as well. This was equally true at the *Ladies' Home Journal* where a new husband and wife team filled the editorial chair and launched a radically new way to deal with many of the old topics. Despite nostalgic elegies for the earlier forms of these two publications, their renovated formats sold more widely than their predecessors. A new approach was also tried at *McCall's*. But that magazine's insistence on using large amounts of fiction undermined its sustained attempt to impose its will on the monthly editorial structure.

As the thirties progressed, the trend that had emerged in the twenties, of a separation between advertising revenue and circulation in the US, was accentuated. By the end of the decade, sales had picked up and were more than matching their pre-Wall-Street-crash levels. But advertising had not. Publishers had not adjusted their cover prices or subscriptions to take this change into account, and profits on even the previously wealthy *Post* dwindled. The *Digest* stayed with its no-advertising policy and had no problem with soaring sales, for its cover price and subscriptions covered increased costs from that quarter on a *pro rata* basis. Because the British market was less reliant on advertising, it experienced fewer problems of this nature.

One area in which there was a marked similarity between the two markets at this time, was in the launch of illustrated weeklies. Both took their cue from the German market and used the expertise of exiles fleeing from the Nazi experiment. The Second World War had no particular impact on the American market, with the exception of the temporary rise of the comic book, whose sales flourished before withering in the fifties. Unable to attract advertising, and confronting the changing distribution set-up that affected all American magazines, they died almost as quickly as they had risen.

The growth of the suburbs, with their weak sales and distribution infrastructure, encouraged all American serials to develop their subscription base. But the considerable increase in postal charges during the fifties compromised the position of the best-sellers, which had been operating on narrow profit margins since the thirties. Simultaneously, cost inflation on other fronts contributed to the increasingly unfavourable balance sheets. Although circulations climbed steadily, allowing higher page rates to be charged, the media buyers of fifties America were enthralled by television, which received a disproportionate allocation of the growing national advertising budgets. When combined with the existing disjunction between circulation and the sales of space, the profits of the best-selling magazines were squeezed. This resulted in catastrophic, high-profile failures as publications read by millions disappeared for reasons that left their public mystified. Even the American edition of *Reader's Digest* was obliged to sell advertising space after over 30 years abstinence.

All British serials were profoundly affected by the war, for the country was dependent on paper imports that were difficult to sustain through the U-boat blockade. Individual titles were pegged to a defined allocation. They could choose whether to cut the size of their editions and let sales rise, or retain their established form and limit their circulation. Because the former course was chosen by the women's weeklies, their importance on the Home Front increased as the war progressed. Their involvement with Whitehall encouraged their editors to view their position in society in a new light and, after the conflict ceased, they tried to bring their influence to bear to re-establish the pre-war, domestic *status quo*.

The traditions of their trans-Atlantic peers, of civic responsibility and an openness to more innovative solutions to social problems, encouraged a different attitude on the part of their editors. While the *Woman's Home Companion* and the *Ladies' Home Journal* could publish sympathetic leading articles on mental illness and social tensions, their equivalents in London stuck to the tried and trusted formulae. Ironically, that position was largely reversed among publications like *Reader's Digest* and the *Saturday Evening Post*, which apostatised anything that smacked of a sympathetically humane attitude as red filth, while *Picture Post* and *John Bull* criticised existing institutions and looked for a new way forward. In both markets, many editors were affected in their editorial choices by the success of the illustrated weeklies. Photography increasingly ruled the roost and the use of art work became more and more circumscribed.

Where Britain differed was in the effect of inflation on the industry. Cover price inflation during the fifties hit circulations and, without the cushion of a substantial subscription base, brought down some of the leading weeklies. Over the coming decades, this was to have a profoundly depressing effect on sales, and where those of American titles in general grew, those published in Britain frequently fell back. To this day, a subscription-based circulation is the exception in the UK.

This is one characteristic that has remained remarkably consistent for over 150 years. By adopting the decennial cross-section to investigate both industries, other, more variable currents have been exposed: the dominance of fiction in the American market during the 1920s; its diminution in importance during the forties and fifties. The subtle shifts in the London-based penny weeklies during the 1890s have also been exposed for the first time. We have given the lie to established opinion on the changes in the contents of the newly popular American magazines of the same period.

We have seen how colour illustrations, although introduced into a major British magazine on an experimental basis in 1855, and on a regular basis into *Frank Leslie's Popular Monthly* in 1876, were still the exception until the late 1930s. In fact, technological changes went in fits and starts. The greatest happened during the final two decades of the nineteenth century, which was a real revolution in the printing industry. The next major upheaval took place in the thirties. But the American magazine industry has been technologically conservative throughout the twentieth century, never wholly accepting gravure in the manner of its European peers. It was also very slow to accept offset lithography, which was already being used to print multi-colour editions of some German periodicals in the 1920s. Indeed, it is the acceptance of this process since 1960, and the way in which it has transformed the publishing industry, that necessitates our cut-off date. In the years since that time, the magazine world has undergone another major transformation. The familiar combination of new technology with fresh attitudes in advertising has thrust the highly specialised monthly to new prominence and success. The cynosures which were mentioned in our introduction have grown. Also familiar is the key element of surplus disposable income. Where the American economy continues to thrive, five publications sell more than 10 million copies per issue. As the British economy falters and what politicians describe as the way forward increasingly looks like the way back, magazine circulations over one million are now rare.

This is to be expected as magazines are just another sector in an integrated industrialised economy. What we have attempted to map over eight decades are the macroscopic changes in the product of that industry as it is pressed by many forces: technology, geography and finance among them. Individuals have been mentioned but few of them have made any lasting impression. For every George Lorimer or Julius Elias, thousands of the faceless shuffle by and remain anonymous. Publication patterns arise and subside, seemingly beyond the reach of all but the most exceptional individual intervention. Perhaps academia is much the same.

NOTES

1. Fishenden, R.B., Editor's Review, in *The Penrose Annual*, Vol.42, London, 1940, p9.

2. Anon., Lithomat - a Plastic Mat, *The British Printer*, Vol.55, No.327, Nov. 1942, London, p83.

3. Anon., New Developments in Nylon Letterpress Plates, *The British Printer*, Vol.70, No.426, Sept. 1957, London, p42.

4. Fishenden, 1940, op.cit., p12.

5. Anon., Offset Lithography + Air Transport = Time, *The British Printer*, Vol.55, No.329, March 1943, London, p157.

6. Mitchell, R V., Past, Present and Future, Elements of Post-War Lithographic Expansion and Advancement, *The British Printer*, Vol.57, Nov. 1944, London, p78.

7. Chapman, B.D., Co-ordinated Production and Research at Time Incorporated, in *The Penrose Annual*, Vol.45 London, 1951, p90.

8. Mennell, P. B., Litho's Impact on Letterpress, *The British Printer*, Vol.61, Jan-Feb. 1949, London, p28.

9. Anon., Printing, *Fortune*, October 1949, p109.

10. Fishenden, R.B., Editorial Review, in *The Penrose Annual*, Vol.45, London, 1951, p11.

11. Delafons, Allan, Editorial Notes, in *The Penrose Annual*, Vol.54, London, 1960, p(xxvi).

12. Anon., Process Engravers in a New Venture: Sun Litho, *The British Printer*, Vol.73, No.455, February 1960, p90.

13. Safran, Hy, American Progress in Web-fed Offset, *The British Printer*, Vol.73, No.463, October 1960, p82.

14. Wallis, L.W., *A Concise Chronology of Typesetting Developments 1886-1986*, London, 1988, p24.

15. Fishenden, R.B., Editorial Review, in *The Penrose Annual*, Vol.50, London, 1956, p11.

16. Anon., Progress Report on Electronic Colour Scanners, *The British Printer*, Vol.72, No.446, May 1959, pp66-73.

17. Canon, R.V., Methods and Techniques of Process Engraving in the Nineteen Sixties, *The British Printer*, Vol.73, No.464, Nov. 1960, pp88-89.

18. US Department of Commerce, *United States Census of Manufactures 1954*, Volume II Industry Statistics, p27A-16, table 6D.

19. Wood, James Playstead, *Of Lasting Interest*, New York, 1958, op.cit., p134.

20. SRDS, *Consumer Magazines*, Smokie, Ill., Vol.32, No.22, Part II, 11 September 1950, p115.

21. Ibid., p114.

22. Ibid., p171.

23. Ibid., p209.

24. Ibid., p121.

25. Ibid., p209.

26. Ibid., p65.

27. *Census*, 1954, op.cit., p27A-18, table 6F.

28. Peterson, Theodore, *Magazines in the Twentieth Century*, Urbana, Ill., 2nd ed., 1964, p357.

29. Hersey, Harold Brainerd, *Pulpwood Editor*, Westport, Conn., 1974, (originally New York, 1937) p157 et seq.

30. US Bureau of the Census, *Historical Statistics of the United States*, Washington, DC, 1975,, Part I, pp318-319, series G 416.

31. Ibid., p210, series E 135.

32. *Census*, 1954, op.cit., p27A-16, table 6C.

33. Ibid., p27A-18, table 6F.

34. SRDS, September 1950, op.cit., p170.

35. Ibid., p115.

36. Elson, Robert T., *The World of Time Inc., 1941-1960*, New York, 1973, pp255-256.

37. Politz (Alfred) Research, Inc., *A Study of the Accumulative Audience of Life*, New York, 1950.

38. SRDS, September 1940, op.cit., general magazines, p58.

39. SRDS, September 1950, op.cit., p115.

40. SRDS, *Consumer Magazine and Farm Publication Rates and Data*, Smokie, Illinois, September 1960, p120.

41. Elson, op.cit., pp256-257.

42. Ibid., pp417-418. It is not surprising that Tudor was able to overcome *Life*'s typographic uncertainty. He had learned his trade on newspapers and knew how to control the elements affected by last minute changes.

43. Keddie, Shirley M., *Naming and Renaming: Time Magazine's Coverage of Germany and the Soviet Union During the 1940s*, Ann Arbor, Michigan, 1985.

44. Swanberg, W.A., *Luce and His Empire*, New York, 1972, pp217-218.

45. There is Another Way, *Life*, Vol.28, No.13, 27 March 1950, p34.

46. McCarthy And the Past, *Life*, Vol.28, No.15, 10 April 1950, p32.

47. There can be little doubt that Luce did oversee the contents of his magazine. There are far too many memos on record for that to be denied. In particular, in this instance, see the memo quoted in Swanberg, op.cit, p215, that was written by Luce during the forties, that leaves the matter in no doubt whatsoever.

48. Elson, op.cit., pp420-422.

49. Wood, James Playstead, *The Curtis Magazines*, New York, 1971, p153.

50. SRDS, September 1940, op.cit., farm magazines, p124.

51. Goulden, Joseph C., *The Curtis Caper*, New York, 1965, pp56-57.

52. Ibid., p55.

53. Wood, *Lasting Interest*, op.cit, pp159-160.

54. Mott, Frank L., *A History of American Magazines*, Boston, Mass., 1938-68, Vol.4, pp770-771.

55. Quoted in White, Cynthia Leslie, *Women's Magazines 1693-1967*, London, 1970, p129.

56. Ferguson, Marjorie, *Forever Feminine*, London, 1983, p20.

57. Ibid., p19.

58. Ibid., pp39-77.

59. Drawbell, James, *Time On My Hands*, London, 1968, pp39-40.

60. Minney, Rubeigh J, *Viscount Southwood*, London, 1954, p322, and Drawbell, op.cit., pp39-40.

61. Drawbell, ibid.

62. Ibid., p62.

63. Ferguson, op.cit., p44.

64. Drawbell, op.cit., pp80-81.

65. Grieve, Mary, *Millions Made My Story*, London, 1964, p157.

66. Drawbell, op.cit., p93.

67. White, op.cit., Appendix 4.

68. *The Newspaper Press Directory and Advertisers' Guide 1951*, London, p297.

69. Drawbell, op.cit., pp53.

70. Gerald, J. Edward, *The British Press Under Government Economic Controls*, Minneapolis, 1956, pp26-27.

71. Ibid., p102.

72. Briggs, Asa, *The History of Broadcasting in the United Kingdom*, Vol.4, Sound and Vision, Oxford, 1979, p569.

73. Ibid., pp61-62.

74. Ibid., p65.

75. Audit Bureau of Circulation, private ledgers.

76. Ibid.

77. Pollard, Sidney and Crossley, David W., *The Wealth of Britain 1085-1966*, London, 1968, p260.

78. Wilsher, Peter, *The Pound in Your Pocket 1870-1970*, London, 1970, p161.

79. Burnett, John, *A History of the Cost of Living*, London, 1969, p313.

80. *The Hulton Readership Survey*, London, 1947 & 1950, compiled by Hobson, J.W. and Henry, H., tables 7, 8 and 9 (1947) and table 3 (1950).

81. Hopkinson, Tom, *Of This Our Time*, London, 1982, p171.

82. Calder, Angus, *The People's War*, London, 1969, pp512-523.

83. Hopkinson, op.cit., p171.

84. Ibid., p248.

85. Ibid., p243.

86. Ibid.

87. Ibid., pp261, 272-277.

88. Ibid., pp282-289.

89. *The Art of Radio Times*, London, 1981, p262.

90. ABC private ledgers.

91. Peterson, op.cit., p128. Also c.f. the prologue of *Gotterdammerung* by Richard Wagner.

92. Ibid, p78.

93. SRDS., September 1960, op.cit., p133.

94. Prendergast, Curtis, with Colvin, Geoffrey, *The World of Time Inc.*, Vol.3, New York, 1986, p41. Van Zuilen also points out, very effectively, that during the 1950s the magazines did everything that they could to hold on to market share. This included selling cut-price subscriptions at the moment when their costs were rising. Thus

60% of *Collier's* subscriptions in 1956, the year that it collapsed, were less than the standard price. The same strategy was pursued at *Look*, *Life* and the *Post*. van Zuilen, Antoon J., *The Life Cycle of Magazines*, Uithoorn, Holland, 1977, p88.

95. US Department of Commerce, *United States Census of Manufactures: 1958*, Vol.II Industry Statistics, Part 1, p27A-26, Table 6C.

96. *Historical Statistics*, Part 1, op.cit., p317, series 416.

97. Ibid, Part 2, p855, series 444.

98. Ibid, series 450 and 455.

99. Prendergast, op.cit., p39.

100. Magazine Publishers Association, New York, statistical information sheet, F.S.310.1, May 1986.

101. Peterson, op.cit, p138.

102. Ibid, p136.

103. Ibid, pp138-140.

104. Ibid, p142.

105. Goulden, op.cit., p91.

106. Ibid, p92.

107. Wood, *Curtis Magazines*, op.cit., p197.

108. Goulden, op.cit., p97.

109. Ibid, p98.

110. Wainwright, Loudon, *The Great American Magazine*, New York, 1986, pp186-188.

111. Prendergast, op.cit., p40.

112. Elson, Robert T., *Time Inc.*, Vol.1 1923-1941, New York, 1968, p344.

113. Peterson, op.cit., p351.

114. Elson, Vol 1, op.cit., pp292-293.

115. SRDS, September 1960, op.cit., p124.

116. Peterson, op.cit., pp204-205.

117. SRDS, September 1960, op.cit., p337.

118. Peterson, op.cit., pp205-206.

119. SRDS, September 1960, op.cit., p341.

120. Ibid, p339.

121. Peterson, op.cit., p206.

122. Garberson, John W., *A Limited Number of Pages*, Lexington, Kentucky, Nov. 1972, p9.

123. Ibid., p18.

124. Ibid, pp21-22.

125. Ibid, p27.

126. SRDS, September 1960, op.cit., p129.

127. Peterson, op.cit., pp113-114.

128. Harris, Jay S., *TV Guide*, the First 25 Years, New York, 1978, pp16-17.

129. Ibid.

130. Pollard, Sidney, *The Development of the British Economy*, 3rd Edition, 1914-1980, London, 1983, p322, table 7.29.

131. White, op.cit., Appendix 4.

132. Ibid., pp156-157.

133. *Woman's Own*, 13 February 1960, p14 et seq.

134. *Woman's Own*, 27 February 1960, p32 et seq.

135. White, op.cit., p170.

136. ABC private ledgers.

137. *The Art of Radio Times*, op.cit., pp102 & 136.

138. ABC private ledgers.

139. Recent events have only confirmed these conclusions beyond any doubt. In March 1991, both *Radio* and *TV Times* lost a legal challenge to their hitherto claimed exclusive rights to the advance publication of programme listings. The immediate result was the publication of this information in newspapers, sometimes in weekly supplements, or in much cheaper listing weeklies. Both *Radio* and *TV Times* continued at their existing cover prices and their circulations suffered a catastrophic loss to the one million level. After 60 years' pre-eminence, *Radio Times* has lost its number one slot to the British edition of *Reader's Digest*.

140. Hopkinson, op.cit., pp293-297.

Appendices

The figures which form the tables displayed on the following pages were assembled in Washington during the summer of 1987 and in London during the spring of 1988. Each column represents an analysis of all issues of the particular magazine during a six month period, normally the first six months of the year named. The exceptions to this rule occurred during the early decades of the publication of the *Ladies' Home Journal*, where entire years were analysed because it was felt that the number of pages published within a six month period were too few to be statistically legitimate, and *Collier's*, where some of the volumes during the first decade of publication have been lost, leaving only three month continuous selections available from any source.

The basic unit of measurement in this study was the page. Subdivisions and fragments of a page were expressed as a percentage of the unit by measuring the area and calculating it in square millimetres. This was then divided by the area of the printed page and multiplied by 100 to record the result as a percentage of the unit. Each page or fragment was then allotted to a topic. An entire volume could be analysed in this way and then the whole numbers and percentages could be totalled to give the breakdown for that volume. The number of pages allocated to each topic in the volume was then divided by the total number of editorial pages that constituted that volume and multiplied by 100 to express the totals for each topic as percentages of the whole. This approach gives a uniform result which is independent of page size, type size, leading and the number of pages in each volume and allows the reader to concentrate on the emphasis placed on each topic by each editor at the end of each decade. Given the volume of calculations made during the course of the analysis and normal human fallibility, an error level of up to 0.05% was allowed in the figures.

As stated before, these figures should not be taken as cast in stone. They were created to give greater precision to the discussion of cross-title comparisons over an eighty year period. It is obvious that fiction published in Tit-bits is dissimilar to that published in *The Cosmopolitan*. The purpose here was not to make such comparisons; the purpose was to plot the gradual shifts that have taken place over 80 years in two countries; to make a sketch map.

Content Analysis
Percentage Allocation to Various topics

(i)

Scribner's Monthly/Century Illustrated

Topic	1871	1880	1890	1900
Fiction	26	15	22.40	28.09
	26	15	22.40	28.09
Travel and adventure	13	6	13.29	11.63
	13	6	13.29	11.63
History and biography	3	28	34.24	20.13
	3	28	34.24	20.13
Fine art	6	8	4.19	4.00
Decorative art	—	2	1.66	1.70
Literary comments	5	10	2.79	—
Verse	3	2	2.60	3.04
Theatre	—	2	—	0.66
Music	—	—	—	—
Movies	—	—	—	—
Radio and tv	—	—	—	—
Dance	—	—	—	—
	14	24	11.24	9.40
Science and technology	9	4	0.98	3.78
Nature	2	1	1.30	—
Health	—	—	—	0.63
	11	5	2.28	4.41
Social life and manners	3	6	0.92	0.66
Sport	—	—	1.00	1.29
Foreign life	—	—	0.83	8.28
Public affairs	11	5	10.57	6.91
Business and economics	—	—	1.50	1.05
Social problems	2	—	1.66	0.60
Personal problems	—	—	—	—
Contemporary events	—	—	—	3.88
	16	11	16.48	22.67
Religion	4	2	—	0.63
	4	4	—	0.63
Fashion	—	—	—	—
Domestic	3	—	—	—
Children	—	—	—	—
	3	—	—	—
Humour and entertainment	1	3	0.07	2.38
	1	3	0.07	2.38
Miscellaneous	9	6	—	0.66
	9	6	—	0.66

(ii)

Harper's Monthly

Topic	1850		1860		1871		1880	
Fiction	41.81		28.40		33		34	
		41.81		28.40		33		34
Travel and adventure	6.96		23.34		19		27	
		6.96		23.34		19		27
History and biography	16.00		14.38		13		6	
		16.00		14.38		13		6
Fine art	0.02		—		2		11	
Decorative art	—		—		—		—	
Literary comments	7.23		1.66		4		5	
Verse	1.57		3.59		1		2	
Theatre	—		—		—		—	
Music	—		—		—		—	
Movies	—		—		—		—	
Radio and tv	—		—		—		—	
Dance	—		—		—		—	
		8.8		25.25		7		18
Science and technology	5.41		—		10		—	
Nature	1.91		6.25		—		3	
Health	—		—		—		—	
		7.32		6.25		10		3
Social life and manners	2.51		0.83		—		1	
Sport	—		—		—		—	
Foreign life	—		—		—		—	
Public affairs	8.38		5.33		5.5		4	
Business and economics	2.44		—		—		—	
Social problems	2.28		1.93		—		—	
Personal problems	—		—		—		—	
Contemporary events	—		—		—		—	
		15.61		8.09		5.5		5
Religion	1.29		—		1		—	
		1.29		—		1		—
Fashion	1.28		1.39		—		—	
Domestic	—		—		—		—	
Children	—		—		—		—	
		1.28		1.39		—		—
Humour and entertainment	—		10.27		5.5		2	
		—		10.27		5.5		2
Miscellaneous	0.91		2.63		6		5	
		0.91		2.63		6		5

(iii)

Topic	Harper's Monthly 1890		Harper's Monthly 1900		McClure's Magazine 1900		McClure's Magazine 1910	
Fiction	38.21		60.85		41.63		39.44	
		38.21		60.85		41.63		39.44
Travel and adventure	16.06		3.49		—		—	
		16.06		3.49		—		—
History and biography	7.49		3.94		8.95		15.33	
		7.49		3.94		8.95		15.33
Fine art	1.24		1.41		—		—	
Decorative art	0.37		—		—		—	
Literary comments	7.81		—		—		—	
Verse	3.11		3.88		1.17		1.41	
Theatre	3.55		—		—		—	
Music	—		—		—		—	
Movies	—		—		—		—	
Radio and tv	—		—		—		—	
Dance	—		—		—		—	
		16.08		5.29		1.17		1.41
Science and technology	0.56		7.08		8.28		2.11	
Nature	1.96		—		3.19		2.89	
Health	—		0.88		—		2.95	
		2.52		7.96		11.47		7.95
Social life and manners	1.79		1.45		—		—	
Sport	2.39		0.20		—		—	
Foreign life	3.00		1.34		—		8.29	
Public affairs	5.02		2.13		7.29		11.71	
Business and economics	0.57		1.03		7.63		2.11	
Social problems	—		0.87		—		11.15	
Personal problems	—		—		—		—	
Contemporary events	—		6.28		8.37		—	
		12.72		13.30		23.29		33.26
Religion	—		2.32		10.99		1.97	
		—		2.32		10.99		1.97
Fashion	—		—		—		—	
Domestic	—		—		—		—	
Children	—		—		—		—	
Humour and entertainment	3.55		2.85		—		—	
		3.55		2.85		—		—
Miscellaneous	3.32		—		2.50		0.64	
		3.32		—		2.50		0.64

(iv)

Frank Leslie's Popular Monthly/The American Magazine

Topic	1880		1890		1900		1910	
Fiction	39.61		32.00		38.13		34.04	
		39.61		32.00		38.13		34.04
Travel and adventure	14.06		16.27		8.90		3.39	
		14.06		16.27		8.90		3.39
History and biography	11.90		15.68		14.77		16.75	
		11.90		15.68		14.77		16.75
Fine art	3.52		8.37		—		—	
Decorative art	0.05		1.65		2.56		—	
Literary comments	0.13		1.40		0.61		—	
Verse	2.60		1.69		3.43		1.05	
Theatre	—		0.17		1.66		11.29	
Music	—		—		—		—	
Movies	—		—		—		—	
Radio and tv	—		—		—		—	
Dance	—		—		—		—	
		6.30		13.28		8.26		12.34
Science and technology	5.35		3.33		3.84		—	
Nature	5.45		2.23		1.92		1.52	
Health	—		—		—		0.70	
		10.80		5.56		5.76		2.22
Social life and manners	1.05		5.82		5.16		1.00	
Sport	0.71		—		—		6.19	
Foreign life	6.14		5.94		10.70		1.78	
Public affairs	2.76		3.18		0.64		11.63	
Business and economics	2.61		—		3.40		1.58	
Social problems	3.32		0.02		1.99		5.72	
Personal problems	—		—		—		—	
Contemporary events	—		—		—		—	
		16.59		14.96		21.89		27.90
Religion	—		—		—		0.70	
		—		—		—		0.70
Fashion	—		—		—		—	
Domestic	—		—		—		—	
Children	—		—		—		—	
		—		—		—		—
Humour and entertainment	0.74		1.50		0.93		1.19	
		0.74		1.50		0.93		1.19
Miscellaneous	—		0.75		1.36		1.47	
	—			0.75		1.36		1.47

(v)

Topic	The American Magazine				Youth's Companion		The Delineator	
	1920		1930		1890		1890	
Fiction	40.07		48.94		32.74		0.38	
		40.07		48.94		32.74		0.38
Travel and adventure	0.63		3.36		5.91		—	
		0.63		3.36		5.91		
History and biography	9.14		6.44		7.74		—	
		9.14		6.44		7.74		
Fine art	—		0.78		—		0.64	
Decorative art	—		0.26		0.39		0.45	
Literary comments	—		—		—		1.19	
Verse	—		—		5.50		—	
Theatre	3.84		1.59		—		—	
Music	0.54		0.86		0.76		—	
Movies	—		0.60		—		—	
Radio and tv	—		0.65		—		—	
Dance	—		—		—		—	
		4.38		4.74		6.65		2.28
Science and technology	0.67		2.98		1.84		—	
Nature	3.64		3.10		8.35		—	
Health	2.60		0.64		1.32		3.62	
		6.91		6.72		11.51		3.62
Social life and manners	4.35		4.99		1.35		0.82	
Sport	0.57		3.17		0.44		—	
Foreign life	—		—		5.40		—	
Public affairs	0.15		3.62		2.09		—	
Business and economics	19.30		8.60		2.61		—	
Social problems	4.74		0.74		0.82		—	
Personal problems	4.46		4.23		0.39		1.22	
Contemporary events	—		0.16		0.30		—	
		33.47		25.51		13.40		2.04
Religion	1.47		0.55		0.68		—	
		1.47		0.55		0.68		—
Fashion	—		—		—		75.01	
Domestic	0.51		—		2.49		13.47	
Children	—		0.16		—		0.24	
		0.51		0.16		2.49		88.72
Humour and entertainment	1.40		1.30		16.94		—	
		1.40		1.30		16.94		—
Miscellaneous	2.02		2.28		1.94		2.96	
		2.02		2.28		1.94		2.96

(vi)

Collier's

Topic	1889		1900		1910		1920	
Fiction	15.28	15.28	13.20	13.20	14.10	14.10	49.76	49.76
Travel and adventure	1.20	1.20	2.08	2.08	3.92	3.92	—	—
History and biography	8.32	8.32	0.76	0.76	2.02	2.02	6.47	6.47
Fine art	2.39		4.29		1.94		—	
Decorative art	0.36		—		1.67		0.08	
Literary comments	1.51		—		1.02		0.56	
Verse	1.75		1.22		0.68		0.29	
Theatre	1.28		0.86		1.27		0.46	
Music	—		—		0.10		—	
Movies	—		—		—		0.76	
Radio and tv	—		—		—		—	
Dance	—	7.29	—	6.37	—	6.68	—	2.15
Science and technology	0.62		2.53		1.34		1.05	
Nature	0.92		—		0.39		0.86	
Health	0.36	1.90	0.43	2.96	0.40	2.13	0.59	2.50
Social life and manners	11.68		3.44		7.48		1.67	
Sport	2.31		10.52		5.30		1.76	
Foreign life	2.05		6.12		2.30		0.97	
Public affairs	13.04		18.43		24.01		20.37	
Business and economics	1.84		1.77		7.25		7.65	
Social problems	7.18		2.26		0.41		4.62	
Personal problems	—		—		—		0.35	
Contemporary events	4.60	42.70	27.66	68.20	18.93	65.68	—	37.39
Religion	—	—	—	—	1.27	1.27	0.51	0.51
Fashion	1.40		0.20		—		—	
Domestic	0.27		2.06		—		—	
Children	3.27	4.94	0.20	2.46	—	—	—	—
Humour and entertainment	10.90	10.90	1.58	1.58	1.55	1.55	0.90	0.90
Miscellaneous	7.47	7.47	0.39	0.39	2.65	2.65	0.30	0.30

(vii)

Topic	Collier's		Munsey's	
	1930	1940	1900	1910
Fiction	59.22	54.42	34.62	46.57
	59.22	54.42	34.62	46.57
Travel and adventure	0.28	—	—	—
	0.28	—	—	—
History and biography	5.31	1.20	1.17	15.91
	5.31	1.20	1.17	15.91
Fine art	—	—	0.53	0.58
Decorative art	—	—	6.89	1.74
Literary comments	—	—	7.34	—
Verse	—	0.05	0.92	2.96
Theatre	1.78	0.73	10.31	9.19
Music	0.18	0.91	—	0.51
Movies	0.47	1.14	—	—
Radio and tv	—	—	—	—
Dance	—	—	—	—
	2.43	2.83	25.99	14.98
Science and technology	0.55	1.58	2.45	3.71
Nature	0.47	0.90	—	1.17
Health	0.63	1.09	—	0.79
	1.65	3.57	2.45	5.67
Social life and manners	1.08	1.50	2.91	2.79
Sport	5.81	5.67	2.29	1.16
Foreign life	—	3.10	5.23	0.93
Public affairs	4.66	4.26	11.36	1.64
Business and economics	3.85	0.76	6.00	8.28
Social problems	4.46	1.87	1.41	2.07
Personal problems	—	—	—	—
Contemporary events	—	3.85	2.93	—
	19.86	21.01	32.13	16.87
Religion	0.19	—	3.64	—
	0.19	—	3.64	—
Fashion	1.61	0.77	—	—
Domestic	1.12	1.34	—	—
Children	—	—	—	—
	2.73	2.11	—	—
Humour and entertainment	5.24	9.15	—	—
	5.24	9.15	—	—
Miscellaneous	3.09	5.70	—	—
	3.09	5.70	—	—

(viii)

Scribner's Magazine

Topic	1890	1900	1910
Fiction	33.19	35.91	40.19
	33.19	35.91	40.19
Travel and adventure	12.28	1.39	22.96
	12.28	1.39	22.96
History and biography	12.35	22.28	2.66
	12.35	22.28	2.66
Fine art	6.96	2.86	8.42
Decorative art	2.51	1.89	4.00
Literary comments	1.88	—	1.28
Verse	2.73	1.59	3.04
Theatre	2.14	—	0.46
Music	—	—	3.58
Movies	—	—	—
Radio and tv	—	—	—
Dance	—	—	—
	16.22	6.34	20.78
Science and technology	5.72	2.36	—
Nature	—	1.19	—
Health	—	—	—
	5.72	3.55	—
Social life and manners	1.77	3.41	—
Sport	0.98	—	0.44
Foreign life	2.44	6.18	—
Public affairs	4.36	3.66	4.44
Business and economics	—	1.70	5.06
Social problems	—	—	—
Personal problems	—	—	—
Contemporary events	2.20	9.60	—
	11.75	24.55	9.94
Religion	—	—	—
	—	—	—
Fashion	—	—	—
Domestic	—	—	—
Children	—	—	—
	—	—	—
Humour and entertainment	4.02	3.60	*
	4.02	3.60	
Miscellaneous	4.47	2.38	3.47
	4.47	2.38	3.47

* All cartoons were distributed among the advertisement and a change in binding policy has meant that all advertisements, and consequently all cartoons, have been lost, making an assessment impossible.

(ix)

The Cosmopolitan

Topic	1888		1890		1900		1910	
Fiction	26.91		23.74		32.32		46.30	
		26.91		23.74		32.32		46.30
Travel and adventure	9.02		13.46		3.18		—	
		9.02		13.46		3.18		—
History and biography	10.91		11.82		3.40		7.08	
		10.91		11.82		3.40		7.08
Fine art	5.43		3.16		3.43		0.99	
Decorative art	—		3.05		3.57		0.37	
Literary comments	4.31		3.14		—		—	
Verse	2.92		2.44		0.88		1.15	
Theatre	2.81		—		0.86		5.72	
Music	—		—		—		—	
Movies	—		—		—		—	
Radio and tv	—		—		—		—	
Dance	—		—		—		—	
		15.47		11.79		8.74		8.23
Science and technology	—		1.00		3.14		—	
Nature	1.43		1.47		—		—	
Health	—		—		2.25		0.62	
		1.43		2.47		5.39		0.62
Social life and manners	10.22		7.12		3.29		2.11	
Sport	5.43		3.75		—		—	
Foreign life	13.48		8.69		14.39		—	
Public affairs	1.31		7.84		6.43		5.94	
Business and economics	3.47		2.62		4.00		5.72	
Social problems	0.94		4.15		0.86		13.56	
Personal problems	—		—		—		—	
Contemporary events	1.41		—		9.00		—	
		36.26		34.17		34.77		27.33
Religion	—		0.65		—		2.61	
		—		0.65		—		2.61
Fashion	—		0.46		—		—	
Domestic	—		—		—		—	
Children	—		—		—		—	
		—		0.46		—		—
Humour and entertainment	—		—		8.29		2.86	
		—		—		8.29		2.86
Miscellaneous	—		1.44		0.71		4.97	
		—		1.44		0.71		4.97

	The Cosmopolitan		Everybody's Magazine(US)		Ladies' HomeJournal	
Topic	1920		1910		1890	
Fiction	81.31		46.85		22.53	
		81.31		46.85		22.53
Travel and adventure	—		2.92		0.35	
		—		2.92		0.35
History and biography	—		—		2.56	
		—		—		2.56
Fine art	—		0.90		—	
Decorative art	—		0.56		0.55	
Literary comments	—		1.91		3.28	
Verse	1.96		1.79		4.50	
Theatre	3.73		5.62		—	
Music	—		—		0.18	
Movies	0.20		—		—	
Radio and tv	—		—		—	
Dance	—		—		—	
		5.89		11.07		8.51
Science and technology	0.72		—		0.29	
Nature	—		3.15		—	
Health	3.64		0.79		1.05	
		4.36		3.94		1.34
Social life and manners	0.91		2.81		4.05	
Sport	—		—		0.39	
Foreign life	—		—		0.77	
Public affairs	0.91		4.72		0.71	
Business and economics	1.98		12.02		0.39	
Social problems	1.11		9.07		0.28	
Personal problems	—		—		10.08	
Contemporary events	—		—		—	
		4.91		28.62		16.67
Religion	1.24		—		1.86	
		1.24		—		1.86
Fashion	—		1.23		9.89	
Domestic	—		—		22.02	
Children	—		—		6.24	
		—		1.23		38.15
Humour and entertainment	—		1.35		0.09	
		—		1.35		0.09
Miscellaneous	2.29		2.02		7.93	
		2.29		2.02		7.93

(x)

(xi)

Ladies' Home Journal

Topic	1900		1910		1920		1930	
Fiction	13.40		16.28		39.76		38.89	
		13.40		16.28		39.76		38.89
Travel and adventure	5.61		0.64		0.88		1.29	
		5.61		0.64		0.88		1.29
History and biography	7.65		2.22		2.93		2.62	
		7.65		2.22		2.93		2.62
Fine art	2.93		2.49		0.79		0.19	
Decorative art	8.04		2.63		2.41		3.14	
Literary comments	0.33		1.01		—		—	
Verse	0.68		1.72		1.45		0.28	
Theatre	4.05		2.06		0.52		—	
Music	1.59		3.12		0.51		0.62	
Movies	—		—		0.46		—	
Radio and tv	—		—		—		—	
Dance	—		—		—		—	
		17.62		13.03		6.14		4.23
Science and technology	—		0.10		—		—	
Nature	—		0.13		0.49		1.12	
Health	1.00		1.57		2.19		3.35	
		1.00		1.80		2.68		4.47
Social life and manners	13.08		7.75		3.60		2.72	
Sport	—		0.13		—		0.83	
Foreign life	0.92		—		3.20		—	
Public affairs	1.53		3.13		5.63		1.60	
Business and economics	1.33		0.79		1.59		2.26	
Social problems	0.66		1.67		2.36		2.36	
Personal problems	1.87		0.88		0.14		0.29	
		19.39		14.35		16.52		10.06
Religion	4.79		2.63		0.56		—	
		4.79		2.63		0.56		
Fashion	9.65		21.77		9.31		14.10	
Domestic	13.44		14.90		12.60		19.16	
Children	4.28		7.49		3.76		2.94	
		27.37		44.16		25.67		36.20
Humour and entertainment	3.17		1.31		1.26		0.13	
		3.17		1.31		1.26		0.13
Miscellaneous	—		3.58		3.60		2.12	
		—		3.58		3.60		2.12

(xii)

	Ladies' Home Journal			Woman's World(U.S.)
Topic	1940	1950	1960	1920
Fiction	42.58	32.41	30.46	46.38
	42.58	32.41	30.46	46.38
Travel and adventure	—	—	—	—
	—	—	—	—
History and biography	10.02	11.14	12.59	—
	10.02	11.14	12.59	—
Fine art	—	0.20	0.38	—
Decorative art	0.83	2.01	2.50	0.71
Literary comments	—	0.79	0.52	—
Verse	0.88	0.97	1.90	0.47
Theatre	—	—	—	—
Music	—	—	—	—
Movies	0.73	—	—	—
Radio and tv	—	—	—	—
Dance	—	—	—	—
	2.44	3.97	5.30	1.18
Science and technology	0.43	—	—	—
Nature	—	—	—	—
Health	1.76	1.83	3.16	0.65
	2.19	1.83	3.16	0.65
Social life and manners	11.13	11.74	5.51	—
Sport	—	—	—	—
Foreign life	0.53	—	—	—
Public affairs	1.79	2.24	3.17	0.15
Business and economics	—	1.08	0.31	—
Social problems	—	0.50	3.32	—
Personal problems	2.41	1.27	5.03	—
Contemporary events	—	—	—	—
	15.86	16.83	17.44	0.15
Religion	—	0.31	0.11	—
	—	0.31	0.11	—
Fashion	6.91	7.83	8.98	11.93
Domestic	14.84	14.49	11.02	32.25
Children	2.53	4.74	5.58	3.29
	24.28	27.06	25.58	47.47
Humour and entertainment	0.38	3.78	2.33	0.20
	0.38	3.78	2.33	0.20
Miscellaneous	2.27	2.65	3.12	3.97
	2.27	2.65	3.12	3.97

(xiii)

Woman's Home Companion

Topic	1920	1930	1940	1950
Fiction	39.35	42.45	53.68	39.17
	39.35	42.45	53.68	39.17
Travel and adventure	—	5.68	2.01	0.21
	—	5.68	2.01	0.21
History and biography	0.75	0.93	1.72	1.73
	0.75	0.93	1.72	1.73
Fine art	2.10	1.02	—	—
Decorative art	0.78	1.94	1.27	2.09
Literary comments	0.36	0.61	0.29	—
Verse	0.42	0.12	0.02	0.17
Theatre	2.52	—	—	—
Music	1.28	—	0.54	—
Movies	2.55	0.21	2.22	1.57
Radio and tv	—	—	—	—
Dance	—	—	—	—
	10.02	3.90	4.34	3.83
Science and technology	—	—	—	—
Nature	—	3.22	0.25	0.27
Health	1.15	2.23	1.50	5.40
	1.15	5.45	1.75	5.67
Social life and manners	2.01	3.14	2.50	3.43
Sport	—	0.36	—	—
Foreign life	0.34	—	—	—
Public affairs	2.94	2.30	0.32	1.97
Business and economics	2.74	1.21	—	—
Social problems	2.04	1.02	—	2.05
Personal problems	2.02	0.83	1.64	1.27
Contemporary events	—	—	—	—
	12.09	8.86	4.46	8.62
Religion	0.92	—	—	0.23
	0.92	—	—	0.23
Fashion	12.89	13.71	4.95	8.99
Domestic	12.02	10.89	20.63	21.69
Children	8.07	3.63	2.71	6.92
	32.98	28.23	28.29	37.60
Humour and entertainment	0.39	—	0.15	0.65
	0.39	—	0.15	0.65
Miscellaneous	2.35	4.50	3.61	2.19
	2.35	4.50	3.61	2.19

(xiv)

McCall's

Topic	1940		1950		1960	
Fiction	62.88		36.77		19.89	
		62.88		36.77		19.89
Travel and adventure	—		0.34		1.07	
		—		0.34		1.07
History and biography	—		8.80		13.52	
		—		8.80		13.52
Fine art	—		—		—	
Decorative art	0.53		0.90		0.80	
Literary comments	—		—		0.59	
Verse	0.24		—		1.26	
Theatre	—		—		—	
Music	—		—		0.46	
Movies	5.33		1.59		0.84	
Radio and tv	0.54		—		1.45	
Dance	—		—		—	
		6.64		2.49		5.40
Science and technology	—		—		—	
Nature	—		—		—	
Health	2.72		1.82		0.96	
		2.72		1.82		0.96
Social life and manners	0.81		4.04		0.99	
Sport	—		—		—	
Foreign life	—		—		0.96	
Public affairs	0.12		3.61		0.88	
Business and economics	0.24		—		1.24	
Social problems	0.24		2.87		—	
Personal problems	0.27		0.30		4.95	
Contemporary events	—		—		—	
		1.65		10.82		9.02
Religion	—		0.61		1.92	
		—		0.61		1.92
Fashion	5.67		7.95		8.45	
Domestic	15.80		21.64		31.31	
Children	3.30		4.92		2.46	
		24.77		34.51		42.22
Humour and entertainment	0.08		—		1.13	
		0.08		—		1.13
Miscellaneous	1.22		3.84		4.86	
		1.22		3.84		4.86

(xv)

Topic	Life 1940		Life 1950		Life 1960		Look 1960	
Fiction	—		—		—		—	
		—		—		—		—
Travel and adventure	4.05		0.91		3.23		0.67	
		4.05		0.91		3.23		0.67
History and biography	9.49		14.23		8.16		17.00	
		9.49		14.23		8.16		17.00
Fine art	3.71		5.61		2.87		1.20	
Decorative art	2.81		2.04		2.03		2.20	
Literary comments	0.07		0.06		0.36		—	
Verse	—		—		0.66		—	
Theatre	2.96		2.88		3.16		—	
Music	0.67		1.71		1.98		0.60	
Movies	4.28		3.46		3.53		3.26	
Radio and tv	0.23		0.84		1.92		3.86	
Dance	0.21		—		—		—	
		14.94		16.00		16.51		11.12
Science and technology	2.84		5.47		4.51		1.13	
Nature	3.19		5.06		3.51		2.13	
Health	1.18		2.29		1.67		7.83	
		7.21		12.82		9.69		11.09
Social life and manners	9.34		9.67		5.30		7.87	
Sport	4.69		4.85		7.33		10.15	
Foreign life	11.18		12.47		12.98		2.46	
Public affairs	9.41		6.79		10.97		9.52	
Business and economics	2.75		2.76		0.77		0.91	
Social problems	1.06		4.19		5.39		4.59	
Personal problems	—		—		0.72		1.22	
Contemporary events	17.53		4.16		7.43		—	
		55.96		44.89		50.89		36.72
Religion	1.10		1.18		0.62		2.40	
		1.10		1.18		0.62		2.40
Fashion	1.48		3.01		3.60		5.46	
Domestic	0.59		0.12		1.76		3.73	
Children	0.38		1.00		0.77		2.40	
		2.45		4.13		6.13		11.59
Humour and entertainment	0.32		0.69		0.89		6.04	
		0.32		0.69		0.89		6.04
Miscellaneous	4.47		4.57		3.90		3.36	
		4.47		4.57		3.90		3.36

(xvi)

	Liberty		Reader's Digest	
Topic	1930	1940	1950	1960
Fiction	43.93	10.71	6.46	0.99
	43.93	10.71	6.46	0.99
Travel and adventure	2.43	3.41	2.96	3.30
	2.43	3.41	2.96	3.30
History and biography	11.73	16.23	20.21	19.61
	11.73	16.23	20.21	19.61
Fine art	0.34	—	—	1.09
Decorative art	—	0.28	—	0.24
Literary Comments	0.21	0.53	—	—
Verse	0.03	—	0.07	0.06
Theatre	—	—	0.28	—
Music	—	1.51	0.32	0.72
Movies	5.62	0.72	—	0.35
Radio and tv	0.20	2.12	0.26	0.49
Dance	—	—	—	—
	6.20	5.16	0.93	2.95
Science and technology	1.65	3.41	4.73	5.37
Nature	—	3.06	2.57	3.26
Health	1.10	3.88	7.63	5.17
	2.75	10.35	14.93	13.80
Social life and manners	3.67	7.34	9.72	4.73
Sport	3.28	0.54	0.95	2.83
Foreign life	2.42	6.91	7.08	8.67
Public Affairs	0.86	13.47	11.28	11.26
Business and economics	1.28	10.00	7.34	1.40
Social problems	3.18	3.61	6.06	8.32
Personal problems	0.34	1.13	0.89	1.66
Contemporary events	—	4.32	0.54	2.14
	15.03	47.32	43.86	41.01
Religion	0.10	2.54	3.13	2.36
	0.10	2.54	3.13	2.36
Fashion	2.84	—	—	—
Domestic	1.76	0.07	0.58	1.58
Children	0.38	—	0.54	2.08
	4.98	0.07	1.12	3.66
Humour and entertainment	8.03	1.59	4.43	9.06
	8.03	1.59	4.43	9.06
Miscellaneous	4.62	2.61	1.97	3.24
	4.62	2.61	1.97	3.24

(xvii)

Saturday Evening Post

Topic	1910		1920		1930		1940	
Fiction	51.21		57.53		58.97		54.68	
		51.21		57.53		58.97		54.68
Travel and adventure	1.29		2.51		1.01		0.41	
		1.29		2.51		1.01		0.41
History and biography	1.56		3.61		5.11		7.27	
		1.56		3.61		5.11		7.27
Fine art	0.09		—		0.30		—	
Decorative art	—		0.20		0.80		—	
Literary comments	—		0.10		—		0.22	
Verse	0.36		0.26		0.24		0.88	
Theatre	1.99		1.10		0.36		—	
Music	—		—		0.37		—	
Movies	—		0.25		0.66		0.22	
Radio and tv	—		—		—		0.31	
Dance	—		—		—		—	
		2.44		1.91		2.73		1.63
Science and technology	1.66		0.42		0.74		0.57	
Nature	—		1.33		2.38		0.53	
Health	0.43		0.99		0.29		0.64	
		2.09		2.74		3.41		1.74
Social life and manners	1.55		3.53		2.63		2.37	
Sport	1.84		0.75		2.74		4.77	
Foreign life	0.96		3.89		3.35		2.33	
Public affairs	13.60		7.88		5.33		5.29	
Business and economics	17.04		7.56		8.38		6.87	
Social problems	1.35		4.46		1.80		0.80	
Personal problems	—		0.02		—		—	
Contemporary events	—		1.10		—		2.63	
		36.34		29.19		24.23		25.06
Religion	—		0.18		0.14		0.60	
		—		0.18		0.14		0.60
Fashion	—		—		0.59		—	
Domestic	0.25		0.15		—		0.28	
Children	—		—		0.18		—	
		0.25		0.15		0.77		0.28
Humour and entertainment	1.44		1.82		3.13		5.64	
		1.44		1.82		3.13		5.64
Miscellaneous	3.38		0.36		0.50		2.69	
		3.38		0.36		0.50		2.69

(xviii)

Topic	Saturday Evening Post 1950	Saturday Evening Post 1960	BOP 1890	GOP 1890
Fiction	38.79	38.51	52.44	41.09
	38.79	38.51	52.44	41.09
Travel and adventure	2.20	1.63	4.19	0.81
	2.20	1.63	4.19	0.81
History and biography	4.87	6.37	5.70	12.11
	4.87	6.37	5.70	12.11
Fine art	—	—	4.33	2.06
Decorative art	0.39	—	0.94	3.86
Literary comments	—	0.53	—	1.05
Verse	0.97	0.66	1.71	6.07
Theatre	0.47	0.38	—	—
Music	0.33	—	1.09	5.40
Movies	0.96	0.92	—	—
Radio and tv	—	0.57	—	—
Dance	—	—	—	—
	3.12	3.06	8.07	18.44
Science and technology	2.42	3.77	5.11	0.39
Nature	0.87	0.81	0.91	1.63
Health	2.19	1.82	—	1.00
	5.48	6.40	6.02	3.02
Social life and manners	5.92	1.43	2.43	2.92
Sport	3.71	4.11	5.56	1.04
Foreign life	5.32	6.61	1.73	2.68
Public affairs	4.89	6.40	—	—
Business and economics	3.23	3.23	0.38	0.38
Social problems	5.80	5.82	—	—
Personal problems	0.12	—	0.83	0.54
Contemporary events	0.21	—	—	—
	29.20	27.60	10.93	7.56
Religion	0.45	—	0.15	0.91
	0.45	—	0.15	0.91
Fashion	—	0.56	—	5.37
Domestic	—	—	1.17	3.84
Children	—	0.27	—	—
	—	0.83	1.17	9.21
Humour and entertainment	11.32	10.58	6.62	1.94
	11.32	10.58	6.62	1.94
Miscellaneous	4.59	5.00	4.70	4.92
	4.59	5.00	4.70	4.92

(xix)

Topic	Family Herald 1890	Harmsworth Popular M 1900	The Strand 1900	Woman's World(UK) 1910
Fiction	69.21	39.02	52.17	48.03
	69.21	39.02	52.17	48.03
Travel and adventure	—	0.70	1.12	—
	—	0.70	1.12	—
History and biography	1.02	13.70	2.24	—
	1.02	13.70	2.24	—
Fine art	0.02	10.71	3.09	—
Decorative art	0.07	—	5.89	—
Literary comments	0.26	—	—	—
Verse	0.96	0.74	—	1.07
Theatre	0.02	2.28	3.93	—
Music	—	2.11	1.26	0.44
Movies	—	—	—	—
Radio and tv	—	—	—	—
Dance	—	—	—	—
	1.33	15.84	14.17	1.51
Science and technology	1.28	4.31	6.45	—
Nature	1.38	1.76	2.66	—
Health	0.89	—	0.42	0.80
	3.55	6.07	9.53	0.80
Social life and manners	4.81	7.82	—	4.42
Sport	—	2.99	2.52	—
Foreign life	1.03	3.95	0.84	—
Public affairs	0.29	1.05	5.89	—
Business and economics	2.23	2.11	1.96	—
Social problems	1.31	—	—	0.18
Personal problems	0.50	—	—	8.07
Contemporary events	—	3.84	0.70	—
	10.17	21.76	11.91	12.67
Religion	—	—	—	3.55
	—	—	—	3.55
Fashion	—	—	1.26	1.83
Domestic	1.23	1.23	2.24	18.70
Children	0.25	1.58	—	8.99
	1.48	2.81	3.50	29.52
Humour and entertainment	7.84	0.09	0.98	0.23
	7.84	0.09	0.98	0.23
Miscellaneous	5.39	—	4.35	3.70
	5.39	—	4.35	3.70

(xx)

Pearson's Weekly

Topic	1900	1910	1920	1930
Fiction	25.43	28.06	23.15	15.75
	25.43	28.06	23.15	15.75
Travel and adventure	—	1.87	0.17	1.74
	—	1.87	0.17	1.74
History and biography	7.74	2.30	4.18	6.13
	7.74	2.30	4.18	6.13
Fine art	—	—	—	—
Decorative art	—	—	0.02	—
Literary comments	0.09	—	—	—
Verse	2.11	0.71	0.60	0.14
Theatre	0.48	0.84	0.40	2.86
Music	0.62	0.23	0.34	0.06
Movies	—	—	2.18	1.61
Radio and tv	—	—	—	0.18
Dance	—	—	—	0.42
	3.30	1.78	3.54	5.27
Science and technology	2.39	2.45	1.03	2.34
Nature	0.77	1.08	1.18	1.13
Health	0.73	0.39	1.32	1.94
	3.89	3.92	3.53	5.41
Social life and manners	1.87	2.31	2.60	5.41
Sport	1.97	4.07	4.39	4.95
Foreign life	1.97	1.05	0.74	1.79
Public affairs	4.90	3.02	1.24	3.61
Business and economics	4.31	1.79	2.36	2.09
Social problems	1.52	3.11	6.98	3.42
Personal problems	—	—	0.31	2.10
Contemporary events	4.88	0.53	—	—
	21.42	15.88	18.62	23.37
Religion	—	0.10	1.79	0.56
	—	0.10	1.79	0.56
Fashion	0.38	0.48	0.20	0.59
Domestic	4.63	5.57	0.62	3.31
Children	0.14	0.42	2.96	0.86
	5.15	6.47	3.78	4.76
Humour and entertainment	21.47	32.35	36.49	29.40
	21.47	32.35	36.49	29.40
Miscellaneous	11.63	7.29	4.74	7.61
	11.63	7.29	4.74	7.61

(xxi)

Tit-bits

Topic	1890		1900		1910		1920	
Fiction	13.30		20.77		22.50		17.40	
		13.30		20.77		22.50		17.40
Travel and adventure	—		0.47		3.00		0.42	
		—		0.47		3.00		0.42
History and biography	7.38		17.47		11.30		12.31	
		7.38		17.47		11.30		12.31
Fine art	0.55		0.11		0.20		—	
Decorative art	—		0.20		—		0.12	
Literary comments	0.38		0.09		—		0.14	
Verse	0.40		0.65		2.10		0.34	
Theatre	0.84		0.66		1.80		0.79	
Music	0.04		0.27		0.30		0.09	
Movies	—		—		0.10		3.47	
Radio and tv	—		—		—		—	
Dance	—		—		—		—	
		2.21		1.98		4.30		4.95
Science and technology	1.52		1.13		0.90		0.90	
Nature	0.87		0.28		0.50		1.24	
Health	3.21		0.95		0.50		1.57	
		5.60		2.36		1.90		3.71
Social life and manners	5.60		2.77		2.10		1.25	
Sport	0.10		3.68		3.90		3.69	
Foreign life	2.81		0.92		0.80		0.26	
Public affairs	6.35		2.61		3.70		1.18	
Business and economics	7.14		3.23		2.40		4.15	
Social problems	1.05		0.97		2.80		5.54	
Personal problems	—		—		0.20		0.11	
Contemporary events	—		4.02		1.20		—	
		23.05		18.20		15.10		16.18
Religion	0.57		—		—		0.20	
		0.57		—		—		0.20
Fashion	0.16		0.14		0.50		0.29	
Domestic	—		0.12		1.50		2.41	
Children	—		—		—		0.16	
		0.16		0.26		2.00		2.86
Humour and entertainment	28.72		17.70		29.70		34.65	
		28.72		17.70		29.70		34.65
Miscellaneous	19.02		20.78		8.20		7.33	
		19.02		20.78		8.20		7.33

(xxii)

	Tit-bits	Answers		
Topic	1930	1890	1900	1910
Fiction	16.49	9.88	29.31	33.26
	16.49	9.88	29.31	33.26
Travel and adventure	1.65	2.32	0.74	2.61
	1.65	2.32	0.74	2.61
History and biography	6.29	12.35	14.03	6.12
	6.29	12.35	14.03	6.12
Fine art	0.17	—	—	0.18
Decorative art	0.12	0.06	0.03	0.17
Literary comments	—	0.56	0.53	—
Verse	0.63	0.46	0.88	0.08
Theatre	—	1.74	0.09	1.12
Music	0.22	0.10	—	1.19
Movies	0.70	—	—	0.19
Radio and tv	—	—	—	—
Dance	0.17	—	—	—
	2.01	2.92	1.53	1.93
Science and technology	4.51	2.13	2.46	0.64
Nature	2.49	1.57	2.53	0.70
Health	1.97	1.50	1.79	0.73
	8.97	5.20	6.78	2.07
Social life and manners	4.84	4.81	4.48	3.03
Sport	3.46	1.12	1.56	2.71
Foreign life	1.22	2.35	1.46	1.76
Public affairs	3.30	2.34	6.50	4.62
Business and economics	2.89	5.54	2.87	5.26
Social problems	6.04	4.35	1.45	5.72
Personal problems	5.12	0.35	1.12	0.47
Contemporary events	—	—	3.78	0.09
	26.87	21.06	23.22	23.66
Religion	0.30	0.41	—	—
	0.30	0.41	—	—
Fashion	0.33	0.65	0.23	0.61
Domestic	2.71	0.10	0.73	0.81
Children	1.39	—	0.19	0.07
	4.43	0.75	1.15	1.49
Humour and entertainment	29.64	28.54	13.22	22.02
	29.64	28.54	13.22	22.02
Miscellaneous	3.33	16.56	10.02	6.82
	3.33	16.56	10.02	6.82

(xxiii)

Topic	Answers				Everybody's (UK)		Woman's Realm	
	1920		1930		1940		1960	
Fiction	22.79		19.27		1.60		32.17	
		22.79		19.27		1.60		32.17
Travel and adventure	1.09		2.04		0.97		3.52	
		1.09		2.04		0.97		3.52
History and biography	7.37		1.28		9.57		—	
		7.37		1.28		9.57		—
Fine art	0.11		—		1.98		0.10	
Decorative art	—		0.45		0.83		—	
Literary comments	0.32		—		—		—	
Verse	1.22		1.68		0.03		0.93	
Theatre	0.23		0.91		1.31		—	
Music	0.40		0.25		0.08		—	
Movies	1.42		1.26		2.74		—	
Radio and tv	—		0.18		0.11		—	
Dance	—		—		0.98		—	
		3.70		4.33		8.06		1.03
Science and technology	0.29		2.42		4.61		0.11	
Nature	2.14		2.14		2.34		0.27	
Health	1.08		1.45		1.34		3.07	
		3.51		6.01		8.29		3.45
Social life and manners	7.72		4.41		1.42		2.14	
Sport	5.90		3.97		6.00		0.52	
Foreign life	1.58		0.50		7.79		—	
Public affairs	3.15		4.99		3.28		—	
Business and economics	5.28		4.63		2.92		0.83	
Social problems	3.35		3.85		1.17		—	
Personal problems	0.62		3.34		0.27		3.32	
Contemporary events	0.26		—		16.83		0.11	
		27.86		25.69		39.68		6.92
Religion	1.00		0.34		0.41		1.87	
		1.00		0.34		0.41		1.87
Fashion	0.44		1.63		1.82		3.11	
Domestic	2.45		2.62		0.08		37.76	
Children	0.70		0.78		0.58		5.05	
		3.59		5.03		2.48		45.92
Humour and entertainment	20.37		28.29		21.71		1.23	
		20.37		28.29		21.71		1.23
Miscellaneous	8.71		7.30		7.22		3.89	
		8.71		7.30		7.22		3.89

(xxiv)

John Bull

Topic	1910		1920		1930		1940	
Fiction	1.39		—		6.95		6.53	
		1.39		—		6.95		6.53
Travel and adventure	0.20		—		1.06		0.17	
		0.20		—		1.06		0.17
History and biography	0.66		0.82		1.02		7.73	
		0.66		0.82		1.02		7.73
Fine art	—		—		0.03		—	
Decorative art	—		—		—		—	
Literary comments	0.52		—		—		—	
Verse	1.44		—		0.04		—	
Theatre	2.24		—		0.32		—	
Music	0.09		—		0.43		—	
Movies	—		—		0.16		0.14	
Radio and tv	—		—		—		—	
Dance	—		—		—		—	
		4.29		—		0.98		0.14
Science and technology	0.06		—		2.09		1.13	
Nature	—		—		0.14		—	
Health	0.09		—		1.68		—	
		0.15		—		3.91		1.13
Social life and manners	3.35		—		2.39		1.43	
Sport	1.59		6.17		4.51		4.47	
Foreign life	0.86		0.57		1.72		2.73	
Public affairs	29.86		13.83		24.51		19.86	
Business and economics	12.86		5.25		5.67		1.45	
Social problems	13.17		30.71		20.94		9.93	
Personal problems	0.32		—		3.42		4.67	
Contemporary events	1.05		—		0.13		11.80	
		63.06		56.54		63.29		56.34
Religion	1.21		0.08		1.48		1.44	
		1.21		0.08		1.48		1.44
Fashion	0.96		—		—		—	
Domestic	0.60		—		0.59		0.76	
Children	—		—		0.73		—	
		1.56		—		1.32		0.76
Humour and entertainment	17.18		17.40		11.12		18.77	
		17.18		17.40		11.12		18.77
Miscellaneous	10.28		25.40		8.85		6.98	
		10.28		25.40		8.85		6.98

(xxv)

Topic	Illustrated		Picture Post	
	1940	1950	1940	1950
Fiction	15.05	0.45	0.72	0.08
	15.05	0.45	0.72	0.08
Travel and adventure	1.40	3.63	0.98	2.26
	1.40	3.63	0.98	2.26
History and biography	7.44	4.86	14.29	11.13
	7.44	4.86	14.29	11.13
Fine art	0.22	5.37	1.20	3.11
Decorative art	0.43	0.91	0.77	1.65
Literary comments	—	—	—	—
Verse	—	—	—	0.58
Theatre	1.19	1.89	4.53	4.76
Music	0.22	0.30	0.87	0.88
Movies	4.66	4.24	0.55	4.49
Radio and tv	0.76	0.38	1.04	0.33
Dance	0.54	1.74	0.76	—
	8.02	14.83	5.69	15.80
Science and technology	1.10	1.44	3.82	3.80
Nature	0.97	6.21	0.78	7.85
Health	0.86	2.95	1.09	1.54
	3.14	10.60	5.69	13.19
Social life and manners	10.63	10.79	9.50	6.61
Sport	0.86	7.16	1.64	10.11
Foreign life	11.80	13.42	5.35	13.12
Public affairs	6.12	9.05	14.07	8.46
Business and economics	2.78	2.57	3.82	3.69
Social problems	—	6.63	—	2.15
Personal problems	—	—	—	—
Contemporary events	19.34	1.21	20.50	0.11
	51.53	50.83	54.88	44.25
Religion	0.54	2.42	0.33	—
	0.54	2.42	0.33	—
Fashion	1.62	4.79	2.33	4.60
Domestic	0.14	—	0.66	0.61
Children	0.97	1.66	0.66	1.07
	2.73	6.45	3.65	6.28
Humour and entertainment	8.93	2.44	3.19	2.29
	8.93	2.44	3.19	2.29
Miscellaneous	1.45	3.48	6.55	4.72
	1.45	3.48	6.55	4.72

(xxvi)

Woman

Topic	1940		1950		1960	
Fiction	51.49		41.66		31.24	
		51.49		41.66		31.24
Travel and adventure	—		0.64		1.17	
		—		0.64		1.17
History and biography	—		2.20		4.72	
		—		2.20		4.72
Fine art	—		1.00		—	
Decorative art	—		0.48		0.37	
Literary comments	0.36		—		—	
Verse	0.89		0.35		0.52	
Theatre	—		—		0.04	
Music	—		—		1.09	
Movies	0.12		2.19		0.67	
Radio and tv	—		—			0.31
Dance	—		—		0.11	
		1.37		3.02		3.11
Science and technology	—		—		—	
Nature	—		—		0.18	
Health	—		—		3.26	
		—		—		3.44
Social life and manners	0.63		3.10		4.68	
Sport	—		0.63		0.88	
Foreign life	—		0.28		0.05	
Public affairs	—		—		0.11	
Business and economics	—		0.39		0.96	
Social problems	—		0.24		0.19	
Personal problems	3.57		5.07		3.27	
Contemporary events	—		—		—	
		4.20		9.71		10.14
Religion	1.56		1.00		1.38	
		1.56		1.00		1.38
Fashion	6.74		10.27		11.92	
Domestic	22.67		17.82		22.63	
Children	6.27		3.51		0.92	
		35.68		31.60		35.47
Humour and entertainment	2.31		2.34		1.45	
		2.31		2.34		1.45
Miscellaneous	4.00		6.82		7.87	
		4.00		6.82		7.87

(xxvii)

	Woman's Weekly				Woman's Own			
Topic	1950		1960		1950		1960	
Fiction	55.25		43.25		41.70		33.47	
		55.25		43.25		41.70		33.47
Travel and adventure	3.12		2.16		0.21		0.56	
		3.12		2.16		0.21		0.56
History and biography	1.03		1.83		10.40		12.94	
		1.03		1.83		10.40		12.94
Fine art	1.05		—		0.31		—	
Decorative art	1.33		—		—		0.06	
Literary comments	—		—		0.14		—	
Verse	0.27		0.10		0.17		0.13	
Theatre	—		—		0.29		0.45	
Music	—		—		0.11		0.46	
Movies	0.31		—		2.21		0.87	
Radio and tv	—		—		—		0.28	
Dance	—		—		—		—	
		2.96		0.10		3.23		2.25
Science and technology	0.36		—		—		0.06	
Nature	0.07		0.27		—		—	
Health	—		0.85		2.27		2.69	
		0.43		1.12		2.27		2.75
Social life and manners	1.25		2.63		3.59		3.31	
Sport	—		—		—		—	
Foreign life	—		—		0.23		—	
Public affairs	—		—		—		0.59	
Business and economics	—		—		0.52		0.32	
Social problems	—		0.71		0.11		0.43	
Personal problems	3.17		2.98		4.62		3.70	
Contemporary events	—		1.47		—		—	
		4.42		7.79		9.07		8.35
Religion	2.23		1.98		1.69		2.17	
		2.23		1.98		1.69		2.17
Fashion	2.98		7.58		9.59		9.60	
Domestic	22.41		29.49		12.47		16.47	
Children	1.61		3.21		3.06		1.51	
		27.00		40.28		25.12		27.58
Humour and entertainment	0.06		0.40		0.56		0.90	
		0.06		0.40		0.56		0.90
Miscellaneous	3.50		1.09		5.75		9.03	
		3.50		1.09		5.75		9.03

Bibliography

Abrams, M. H., *The Mirror and the Lamp: romantic theory and the critical tradition*, New York, 1953.

Ackerman, Martin S., *The Curtis Affair*, Los Angeles, 1970.

Albert, Pierre and Terrou, F., *Histoire de la Presse*, Paris, 1979.

Aldcroft, Derek, The Efficiency and Enterprise of British Railways, 1870-1914, *Explorations in Entrepreneurial History*, Vol.5, 1968, pp158-174.

Aldcroft, Derek H. and Freeman, Michael J. (Eds.), *Transport in the Industrial Revolution*, Manchester, Eng. and Dover, New Hampshire, 1983.

Allen, Frederick Lewis, Fifty Years of Scribner's Magazine, *Scribner's*, Vol.101, Jan.1937, pp20-21.

Allen, Frederick Lewis, The American Magazine Grows Up, *The Atlantic Monthly*, Nov. 1947.

Allen, Irving L., Community Size, Population Composition, and Cultural Activity in Smaller Communities, *Rural Sociology*, Vol,33, Sept.1968, pp328-338.

Altick, R. D., *The English Common Reader*, Chicago, 1957.

Amalgamated Press, *Souvenir of Banquet Held at Fleetway House 7th November 1912*, London, 1912.

Anderson R. L. and Bancroft, T. A., *Statistical Theory in Research*, New York, 1952.

Annuaire-almanach du Commerce de l'Industrie, Paris, 1857 et seq.

Anon., Answers: Our Sixtieth Birthday, *Answers*, London, June 5, 1948.

Anon., A Call to Action. The Steady Progress of Rotary Offset Printing, *The British Printer*, Vol.39, No.229, Leicester And London, May-June 1926.

Anon., Automatic Engraving Processes, *The Printing Times And Lithographer*, October 15, 1874, London.

Anon., Colour Gravure in Newspapers, *The British Printer*, Vol.44, No.262, Nov-Dec.1931, Leicester And London.

Anon., Death of Max Levy, *The British Printer*, Vol.39, No.230, Jul-Aug. 1926, Leicester And London.

Anon., F.A.Ringler Company, *The Inland Printer*, Vol.11, No.2, May 1893, Chicago.

Anon., Joseph Firms and his Inventions, *Frank Leslie's Popular Monthly*, Vol.9, p758, New York.

Anon., Joseph Palmer Knapp, Magazine Publisher, 86, Dies, *New York Times*, January 31, 1951, p1.

Anon., Life with Time, *Forbes*, Vol.72, 15 Aug.1953, pp12-13.

Anon., Lithomat - A Plastic Mat, *The British Printer*, Vol.55, No.327, November 1942, London.

Anon., New Developments in Nylon Letterpress Plates, *The British Printer*, Vol.70, No.426, Sept.1957, London.

Anon., Offset Lithography + Air Transport = Time, *The British Printer*, Vol.55, No.329, Mar.1943, London.

Anon., Paper Trends Of 1936, *The British Printer*, Vol.39, No.293, March 1937, London.

Anon., Photo-Mechanical Colour Printing, *The British Printer*, Vol.6, No.35, Sept-Oct.1893, Leicester.

Anon., Printing, *Fortune*, Vol.40, Oct.1949.

Anon., Process Engravers in a New Venture: Sun Litho, *The British Printer*, Vol.73, No.455, Feb.1960, London.

Anon., Progress Report on Electronic Colour Scanners, *The British Printer*, Vol.72, No.446, May 1959, London.

Anon., The August 'Scribner' Poster, *The Inland Printer*, Vol.17, No.3, June 1896, Chicago.

Anon., The Commercial History of a Penny Magazine, *Monthly Supplement of The Penny Magazine*, Vol.2, Nos.96, 101, 107 & 112, Sept-Dec. 1833.

Anon., The Cosmopolitan of Ray Long, *Fortune*, Vol.1, No.3, March 1931.

Anon., The Making of an Illustrated Magazine, *The Cosmopolitan*, Vol.14, June 1893, New York.

Anon., The Offsetting Problem Solved. The 'Gammer' Process, *The British Printer*, Vol.42, No.250, Nov-Dec.1929.

Anon., The Outlook for Wood-engraving, *The Century Illustrated Monthly Magazine*, Vol.40, No.2, June 1890, New York.

Anon., The Reader's Digest, *Fortune*, 14 November 1936, p131.

Anon., Three-Color Process, *The Inland Printer*, Vol.19, No.2, May 1897, Chicago.

Arnott, Michelle, *A History of the Crossword*, London, 1982.

Aspinall, A., *Politics and the Press 1780-1850*, London, 1949.

Association of National Advertisers, *Magazine Circulation and Rate Trends*, New York, 1953.

Auerbach, Carl F. and Zinnes, Joseph L., *Psychological Statistics: a case approach*, Philadelphia, 1978.

Ayer And Sons, N.W., *American Newspaper Annual*, Philadelphia, 1877 et seq.

Badger, Reid, *The Great American Fair*, Chicago, 1979.

Bainbridge, John, *Little Wonder, or The Reader's Digest and How It Grew*, New York, 1946.

Bakeless, John, *Magazine making*, New York, 1931.

Baker, T. Thorne, High Speed Rotary Intaglio Printing, *Penrose's Pictorial Annual*, Vol.14, 1913-14, London, pp55-56.

Baldasty. Gerald J., *The Commercialization of News in the Nineteenth Century*, Madison, Wisconsin, 1992.

Balle, Francis, *Institution et Publics des Moyens de l'Information*, Paris, 1973.

Bannion, Sherilyn Cox, Reform Agitation in the American Periodical Press, 1920-1929, *Journalism Quarterly*, XLVIII (Winter 1971), pp562-659.

Beak, Dr Julius, Coated and Uncoated Papers for Half-tone Printing, *The Penrose Annual*, Vol.38, London, 1936, pp99-102.

Bell, Daniel, *The End of Ideology*, New York, 1962.

Bellanger, Claude (Ed.), *Histoire Générale de la Presse Française*, Paris, 1972.

Bender, Frederick, The Effect of the Enclosed Ink Fountain on Intaglio Printing, *The British Printer*, Vol.50, No.296, Sept.1937, London.

Benjamin, Walter, *Illuminations*, New York, 1968.

Bennett, Charles O., *Facts Without Opinions*, Chicago, 1965.

Berelson, Bernard, In the Presence of Culture, *Public Opinion Quarterly*, Vol.28, 1964.

Berlo, David K., *The Process of Communication*, New York, 1960.

Baldasty, Gerald J., *The Commercialization of News in the Nineteenth Century*, Madison, WI., 1992.

Berridge, Virginia S., *Popular Journalism and Working Class Attitutdes 1834-1886*, Unpublished University of London PhD thesis, 1976.

Berry, W.Turner, Evolution of the pictorial press, *Printing*, Vol.XX, 1959, pp19-23.

Berry, W.Turner and Poole, H. Edmund, *Annals of Printing*, London, 1966.

Besant, Walter, An American Magazine, *The Author*, Vol.5, No.2, July 1894, London.

Bezzant,R., *Newspaper Carriage and Parcels Traffic on British Railways*, London, 1949.

Blum,E., *Basic Books in the Mass Media*, Urbana, Ill., 1972.

Blumenfeld,R.D., *The Press in My Time*, London, 1933.

Bok, Edward, *The Americanization of Edward Bok*, New York, 1920.

Bok, Edward, *A Man From Maine*, New York, 1923.

Bone, Frederick Dorling, The Birth of the Picture Paper: Early Days of the Illustrated London News, *World's Press News*, July 25, 1929, London.

Borden, Neil H., *The Economic Effects of Advertising*, Homewood, Illinois, 1944.

Bourdieu, Pierre and Passeron, Jean Claude, *La Reproduction*, Paris, 1970.

Bowley, A L, *The Change in the Distribution of the National Income, 1880-1913*, Oxford, 1920.

Braithwaite, Brian and Barrell, Joan, *The Business of Women's Magazines*, London, 1979.

Brake, Laurel, Jones, Aled and Madden, Lionel, *Investigating Victorian Journalism*, London, 1990.

Bray, Howard, *The Pillars of the Post: the Making of a News Empire in Washington*, New York, 1980.

Briggs, Asa, *The History of Broadcasting in the United Kingdom*, Vol.4, Oxford, 1979.

Brinkman, Ernst, Multicolour Intaglio, *Penrose's Pictorial Annual*, Vol.25, London, 1923, pp102-104.

Brinton, James F., Bush, Chilton R and Newell, Thomas M, *The Newspaper and its Public*, Stanford, California, 1958.

Britt, George, *40 years - 40 millions: the career of Frank A Munsey*, New York, 1935.

Brocki, Mary D., *A Study of Cosmopolitan Magazine*, Ann Arbor, Mi., 1959.

Brown, Bruce W., Family Intimacy in Magazine Advertising 1920-1977, *Journal of Communications*, 32, Summer 1982, pp73-83.

Brown, Dorothy M., The Quality Magazines in the Progressive Era, *Mid-America*, LIII (July 1971) pp139-159.

Brown, M. Lamont, Engraved Half-tones, *The Process Year Book for 1897*, Vol.3, London, pp33-37.

Brown, M. Lamont, Process Work in the States, *The Process Year Book*, Vol.7, London, 1901, pp101-103.

Brown, T. W., Rotary Web Offset Printing, *Penrose's Pictorial Annual*, Vol.33, London, 1931, pp109-113.

Browne, T. B., *The Advertisers' ABC*, London, 1886 et seq.

Burch, Robert, *Colour Printing and Colour Printers*, London, 1910 and New York, 1911.

Bureau International du Travail, *Les Conditions de Travail et de Vie des Journalists*, Geneva, 1928.

Burnett, John, *A History of the Cost of Living*, London, 1969.

Burt, Sir Cyril, *A Psychological Study of Typography*, Cambridge, 1959.

Cable, W. Cable, *A Memory of Roswell Smith*, New York, 1892.

Calder, Angus, *The People's War*, London, 1969.

Camrose, Lord, *British Newspapers and Their Controllers*, London, 1947.

Canfield, Cass, *Up and Down and Around*, New York, 1971.

Cannon, Derek F., *The Strategy and Structure of British Enterprise*, Boston, 1973.

Canon, R. V., Methods And Techniques Of Process Engraving In The Nineteen Sixties, *The British Printer*, Vol.73, No.464, Nov.1960, London.

Caron, Francois, *An Economic History of Modern France*, London, 1979.

Carpenter, Kevin, *Penny Dreadfuls and Comics*, London, 1983.

Carre, J. J., Dubois, P and Malinvaud, E, *French Economic Growth*, Berkeley, 1975.

Cate, Phillip Dennis, *The Color Revolution, Lithography In France 1890-1900*, Santa Barbara and Salt Lake City, 1978.

Chadwin, Mark Lincoln, *The Hawks Of World War II*, Chapel Hill, North Carolina, 1968.

Chambers, Eric, *Camera and Process Work*, London, 1964.

Chambers, Frank P., *The History of Taste*, New York, 1932.

Chambure, A. de, *A Travers La Presse*, Paris, 1914.

Chandler, Alfred D., *The Visible Hand*, Cambridge, Mass., 1977.

Chandler, Alfred D., and Daems, Herman, *Managerial Hierarchies*, Cambridge, Mass. and London, 1980.

Chapman, B. D., Co-ordinated Production and Research at Time Incorporated, *The Penrose Annual*, Vol.45, London, 1951, pp 89-91.

Chase, Edna Woolman & Ilka, *Always in Vogue*, New York, 1954.

Chauvet, Paul, *Les Ouvriers du Livre et du Journal*, Paris, 1971.

Checkland, S. G., *The Rise of Industrial Society in England 1815-1885*, London, 1964.

Chenery, William L., *So It Seemed*, New York, 1952.

Chunn, Calvin Ellsworth, *History of News Magazines*, Unpublished PhD thesis, University of Missouri, 1950.

Cipolla, Carlo, *Literacy and Development in the West*, Harmondsworth, Middx., 1969.

Clair, Colin, *A Chronology Of Printing*, London, 1969.

Clair, Colin, *A History of European Printing*, London and New York, 1976.

Clapperton, Robert H., *The Paper-making Machine*, Oxford, 1967.

Clapperton, Robert H., *Modern Paper Making*, Oxford, 3rd Ed, 1952.

Coe, Brian, *Colour Photography*, London, 1978.

Cohn, Martin, Three-color Process: Its History And Adaptability To Printing Methods, *The Process Year Book For 1896*, Vol.2, London.

Cole, G. D. H. and Postgate, Raymond, *The Common People 1746-1946*, London, 1938.

Colebrook, Frank, My Month in America - Some Men and Some Things, *Penrose's Pictorial Annual*, Vol.28, London, 1926, pp48-51.

Colebrook, Frank, Our Platemaking Causerie, *The British Printer*, Vol.24, No.142, Aug-Sept.1911, Leicester And London.

Coleman, D. C., Gentlemen and Players, *Economic History Review*, Series 2, Vol.26, 1973, pp92-116.

Coleman, D. C., *The British Paper Industry 1495-1860*, Oxford, 1958.

Coltham, S., The British Working Class Press in 1867, *Bulletin of the Society for the Study of Labour History*, No.15, Autumn 1967.

Comparato, Frank E., *Chronicles of Genius and Folly*, Culver City, California, 1979.

Connolly, Robert D., Yesterday's Magazines, *American Collector*, Dec.1975, pp12-29.

Cook, Michael L., *Mystery, Dectective, and Espionage Magazines*, Wesport, Conn., 1983.

Courmont, E., *Histoire et Technique de la Photogravure*, Paris, 1947.

Courtney, Janet E., *Making of an editor: W L Courtney 1850-1928*, London, 1930.

Cox, Jack, *Take A Cold Tub, Sir !*, Guildford, 1982.

Craig, Robert Leo, *The Changing Communicative Structure of Advertisements 1850-1930*, Ann Arbor, Mi., 1986.

Cramer, R. S., *The British Magazine and the United States 1815-1848*, Dissertation Abstracts, 21, 1968.

Crowell Publishing Company, *National Markets and National Advertising 1922*, New York, 1923.

Curran, James and Seaton, Jean, *Power Without Responsibility*, London, 1988, 3rd Ed.

Cutler, T. H., The Effectiveness of Page Size in Magazine Advertising, *Journal of Applied Psychology*, Vol,14, No.5, 1930, pp465-469.

Cyganowski, Carol Klimick, *Magazine Editors and Professional Authors in Nineteenth-Century America*, New York & London, 1988.

Damon-Moore, Helen, *Magazines for the Millions*, Albany, New York, 1994.

Dark, Sidney, *The Life of Sir Arthur Pearson*, London, 1922.

Davis, Alec, The Trade and Technical Press, *The Penrose Annual*, 1950, London, pp58-61.

De Clark, William E., *The Relationship Between Periodical Fiction and the Rise of Realism in the United States, 1887-1939*, Ann Arbor, Mi., 1952.

Delafons, Alan, Editorial notes, *The Penrose Annual*, London, 1959, ppxv-xxxviii.

Delafons, Alan, Editorial notes, *The Penrose Annual*, London, 1960, ppxv-xl.

Delafons, Alan, Editorial notes, *The Penrose Annual*, London, 1961, ppxv-lviii.

Deutschmann, Paul J., *News-page Content of 12 Metropolitan dailies*, Cincinnati, 1959.

Dictionary of American Biography, New York and London, 1928.

Dictionary of Business Biography, London, 1984.

Dictionary of National Biography, Oxford, 1917.

Dictionnaire de Biographie Française, Paris, 1933.

Dilnot, George, *The Romance of the Amalgamated Press*, London, 1925.

Dinsmore and Company's New and Complete Map of the Railway Systems of the United States and Canada, 1850.

Directory Of Paper Makers Of The United Kingdom, London, 1885 et seq.

Dolmetsch, Carl Richard, *The Smart Set*, New York, 1966.

Douglas, Eric Alexander, *W H Smith*, London, 1965.

Downey, Edmund, *Twenty Years Ago*, London, 1905.

Drawbell, James, *Time on my Hands*, London, 1968.

Drotner, Kirsten, *English Children and their Magazines, 1751-1945*, New Haven & London, 1988.

Duhring, E. L., Quick Drying Inks on Rotary Colour Presses, *The British Printer*, Vol.50, No.296, Sept.1937, London.

Dumazedier, Joffre and Hassendorfer, Jean, *Elements pour une Sociologie Comparée de la Production, de la Diffusion et de l'Utilisation du Livre*, 1962.

Dunae, Patrick, Boy's Own Paper. Origins and Editorial Policies, *The Private Library*, Vol.9, No.4, Winter 1976, London.

Dunae, Patrick, Penny Dreadfuls: Late Nineteenth Century Boys' Literature and Crime, *Victorian Studies*, Vol.22, No.2, Winter, 1979.

Durrant, W. R., Look Back on 100 Years of Machine Printing, *Printing World: a century in print*, London, 1979, pp19-24.

Eade, W. G., The Standardisation of Trichromatic Inks, *Penrose's Pictorial Annual*, Vol.32, London, 1930, pp33-38.

Eder, Josef Maria, *History of Photography*, New York, 1945.

Egoff, Sheila A., *Children's Periodicals of the Nineteenth Century*, Library Association Pamphlet No.8, London, 1951.

Einzig, Hettie, *Verve 1937-1960*, Cambridge, unpublished BA thesis, 1976.

Ellegård, Alvar, The Readership of the Periodical Press in Mid-Victorian Britain, *Gotesborgs Universities Arsskrift*, 63, Goteborg, 1957.

Elson, Robert T., *Time Inc., 1923-1941*, Vol.1, New York, 1968.

Elson, Robert T., *The world of Time Inc., 1941-1960*, New York, 1973.

Emery, F. E. and Oeser, O. A., *Information, Decision and Action*, Melbourne, 1958.

Enzensberger, Hans Magnus, *The Consciousness Industry*, New York, 1974.

Epstean, Edward, The Beginnings of the Three-Color Process in the United States, *The Photo-Engravers' Bulletin*, Sept.1940.

Evans, Bertram, Design in Continental Magazines, *The Penrose Annual*, Vol.42, London, 1940, pp42-44.

Evans, J., *The Endless Web - John Dickinson and Co. Ltd., 1804-1954*, London, 1955.

Ewen, Stuart, *Captains of Consciousness: advertising and the social roots of the consumer culture*, New York, 1976.

Exman, Eugene, *The House of Harper*, New York, 1967.

Felbermann, Heinrich, *The Memoirs of a Cosmopolitan*, London, 1936.

Ferguson, Marjorie, *forever feminine*, London, 1983.

Ferris, Paul, *The House of Northcliffe*, London, 1971.

Ferry, John William, *A History of the Department Store*, New York, 1960.

Festinger, Leon, *A Theory of Cognitive Dissonance*, Evanston, Ill., 1957.

Fischer, David Hackett, *Historians' Fallacies*, New York, 1970.

Fishbein, Meyer H., *The Censuses of Manufacture 1810-1890*, Washington, 1973.

Fishenden, R. B., Editor's review, *The Penrose Annual*, Vol.38, London, 1936, pp1-16.

Fishenden, R. B., Editor's review, *The Penrose Annual*, Vol.40, London, 1938, pp1-16.

Fishenden, R. B., Editor's review, *The Penrose Annual*, Vol.42, London, 1940, pp1-16.

Fishenden, R. B., Editorial review, *The Penrose Annual*, Vol.43, London, 1949, pp1-12.

Fishenden, R. B., Editorial review, *The Penrose Annual*, Vol.45, London, 1951, pp1-12.

Fishenden, R. B., Editorial commentary, *The Penrose Annual*, Vol.50, London, 1956, pp1-20.

Fisher, Charles H., Half-tone (screen) Blocks: their nature and treatment in printing, *Penrose's Annual for 1895*, Vol.1, London.

Flader, Louis, The Passing Show, *Penrose's Pictorial Annual*, Vol.17, London, 1911-12, pp41-44.

Flader, Louis, The Passing Show, *Penrose's Pictorial Annual*, Vol.19, London, 1913-14, pp21-24.

Flautz, John, *Life. The Gentle Satirist*, Bowling Green, Ohio, 1972.

Fleury, M. and Valmary, P., Le Progrès de l'Instruction Elementaire de Louis XIV à Napoleon 111, *Population*, 12, 1957, pp71-92.

Forcey, Charles, *The Crossroads of Libralism: Croly, Weyl, Lippman and the Progressive Era, 1900-1925*, New York, 1961.

Ford, James C. L., *Magazines for Millions*, Carbondale, Illinois, 1969.

Forrester, Wendy, *Great-Grandma's Weekly*, Guildford and London, 1981.

Fox, Stephen, *The Mirror Makers: a history of American advertising and its creators*, New York, 1984.

Fox Bourne, H. R., *English Newspapers*, London, 1887.

Franklyn, A. T., A Century of Papermaking for Printing, *Printing World: a century in print*, London, 1979, pp32-33.

Fraser, W. Hamish, *The Coming of the Mass Market 1850-1914*, London, 1981.

Freiberg, J. W., *The French Press*, New York, 1981.

Freund, Gisèle, *Photographs and Society*, London, 1980.

Friederichs, Hulda, *The Life of Sir George Newnes*, London, 1911.

Fuller, Walter Deane, *The Life and Times of Cyrus H. K. Curtis, 1850-1933*, Philadelphia, 1948. (Other editions 1953 & 1957)

Furet, Francois and Ozouf, Jacques, Literacy and Industrialization: the case of the Department du Nord en France, *Journal of European Economic History*, 5, 1976, pp 5-44.

Gamble, William, *Line Photo-engraving*, London, 1909.

Gamble, William, *Modern Illustration Processes*, London, 1933.

Gamble, William, Process in Magazine and Book Illustration, *The Process Year Book for 1897*, Vol.3, London, pp3-16.

Gamble, William, The Editor's Forewords, *Penrose's Pictorial Annual*, Vol.11, London, 1905-6, ppxv-xvi.

Gamble, William, Progress in Process Work, *Penrose's Pictorial Annual*, Vol.12, London, 1906-7, pp1-4.

Gamble, William, The Year's Progress in Process Work, *Penrose's Pictorial Annual*, Vol.13, London, 1907-8, pp1-7.

Gamble, William, The Year's Progress in Process Work, *Penrose's Pictorial Annual*, Vol.14, London, 1908-9, pp1-8.

Gamble, William, The Year's Progress in Process Work, *Penrose's Pictorial Annual*, Vol.15, London, 1909-10, pp9-16.

Gamble, William, The Year's Progress in Process Work, *Penrose's Pictorial Annual*, Vol.17, London, 1911-12, pp1-11.

Gamble, William, The Year's Progress in Process Work, *Penrose's Pictorial Annual*, Vol.18, London, 1912-13, pp1-12.

Gamble, William, The Year's Progress in Process Work, *Penrose's Pictorial Annual*, Vol.19, London, 1913-14, pp1-9.

Gamble, William, The Year's Progress in Process Work, *Penrose's Pictorial Annual*, Vol.20, London, 1915, pp1-12.

Gamble, William, Position and Prospects of Process Work, *Penrose's Pictorial Annual*, Vol.21, London, 1916, pp11-16.

Gamble, William, The Editor's Forewords, *Penrose's Pictorial Annual*, Vol.23, London, 1921, pp1-12.

Gamble, William, A Review of Process Work, *Penrose's Pictorial Annual*, Vol.24, London, 1922, pp1-16.

Gamble, William, Review of Process Work, *Penrose's Pictorial Annual*, Vol.25, London, 1923, pp1-16.

Gamble, William, Review of Process Work, *Penrose's Pictorial Annual*, Vol.26, London, 1924, pp1-13.

Gamble, William, A Review of Process Work, *Penrose's Pictorial Annual*, Vol.28, London, 1926, pp1-21.

Gamble, William, A Review of Process Work, *Penrose's Pictorial Annual*, Vol.29, London, 1927, pp1-16.

Gamble, William, The Editor's Review, *Penrose's Pictorial Annual*, Vol.30, London, 1928, pp1-16.

Gamble, William, The Editor's Note Book, *Penrose's Pictorial Annual*, Vol.31, London, 1929, pp1-16.

Gamble, William, The Editor's Review, *Penrose's Pictorial Annual*, Vol.32, London, 1930, pp1-16.

Gamble, William, The Editor's Review, *Penrose's Pictorial Annual*, Vol.34, London, 1932, pp1-14.

Gamble, William, The Editor's Review, *Penrose's Pictorial Annual*, Vol.35, London, 1933, pp1-15.

Garberson, John W., A Limited Number Of Pages, *Journalism Monographs No.25*, Association For Education In Journalism, Lexington, Kentucky, Nov.1972.

Garlin, Sender, *The Truth About Reader's Digest*, New York, 1943.

Gaunt, W., The Studio, an International Art Magazine: its origins and development, *Creative Art*, ii, 1-10.

Gerald, J. Edward, *The British Press Under Government Economic Controls*, Minneapolis, 1956.

Getzels, J. W., The Question-answer Process, *Public Opinion Quarterly*, Vol.XVIII, 1954, pp80-91.

Gifford, Denis, *Happy Days*, London, 1975.

Gifford, Denis, *Victorian Comics*, London, 1976.

Goldman, Irwin, *Communication and Culture: a Q-methodological study of psycho-social meanings from photographs in Time Magazine*, Ann Arbor, Mi., 1984.

Goldstein, Cynthia, *The Press and the Beginning of the Birth Control Movement in the United States*, Ann Arbor, Mi., 1985.

Goodman, J., Death of I. W. Rubel, Inventor of the Rubber Offset Litho Machine, *The British Printer*, Vol.21, No.125, Leicester, Oct-Nov.1908.

Goodman, Joseph, The Triumph of Reel-fed Newspaper Offset Lithography, *Penrose's Pictorial Annual*, Vol.28, London, 1926, pp132-136.

Gorham, Maurice, *Sound and Fury*, London, 1948.

Gould, Bruce & Beatrice, *American Story*, New York, 1968.

Goulden, Joseph C., *The Curtis Caper*, New York, 1965.

Gourmont, Remy de, *Les Petites Revues*, Paris, 1900.

Graff, Harvey J., *The Literacy Myth*, New York and London, 1979.

Graff, Harvey J., *Literacy in History: an interdisciplinary research bibliography*, New York and London, 1981.

Graff, Harvey J., *Literary and Social Development in the West: a reader*, Cambridge, 1981.

Graff, Harvey J., The New Maths: quantification, the new history and the history of Education, *Urban Education*, Vol.11, 1977, pp 403-440.

Grant, Dr J. and Battle, S., The Nature and Uses of Paper and Board, *Board Manufacture*, Various Editors, London, 1978.

Greene, Theodore P, *America's Heroes*, New York, 1970.

Greiman, Liela Rumbaugh, William Ernest Henley and 'The Magazine of Art', *Victorian Periodicals Review*, Vol.XVI, No.2, 1983, pp53-64.

Gress, Edmund G,. The Printing Business in America, *Penrose's Pictorial Annual*, Vol.18, London, 1912-13, pp117-120.

Grieve, Mary, *Millions Made My Story*, London, 1964.

Gross, John, *The Rise and Fall of the Man of Letters*, London, 1969.

Halliwell, Betty May, *A Method for the Content Analysis of Cartoons*, Ann Arbor, Mi., 1972.

Halsey, Alfred H., *Change in British Society*, London, 1986.

Hamblin, Dora Jane, *That was the Life*, New York, 1977.

Hamilton, Alan, All the Pictures Fit to Print, *The Times*, London, October 22, 1981.

Hammerton, Sir John, *Books and Myself*, London, 1944.

Handover, P M, *Printing in London from 1476 to Modern Times*, Cambridge, Mass., 1960.

Hannah, Leslie, *The Rise of the Corporate Economy: the British experience*, Baltimore, 1976.

Hannah, Leslie, Ed., *Management Strategy and Business Organization in Britain: a historical and comparative view*, London, 1976.

Harmsworth, Alfred, The Future of Magazines, *The Independent*, London, 19 November 1908.

Harper, J. Henry, *The House of Harper*, New York, 1912.

Harrap, Charles, The Offset Rotary Printing Press, *The British Printer*, Vol.23, No.134, April-May 1910, Leicester.

Harris, Jay S., *TV Guide: the First 25 Years*, New York, 1978.

Harris, Louise, *Nothing But the Best or The Story of Three Pioneers, The Youth's Companion, Daniel Sharp Ford, C A Stephens*, Providence, Rhode Island, 1966.

Hartwell, Lord, *William Camrose*, London, 1992.

Hasler, Charles, Mid-nineteenth Century Colour Printing, *The Penrose Annual*, Vol.45, London, 1951, pp66-68.

Hatton, Joseph, *Journalistic London*, London, 1882.

Hazzlewood, John W., The Growth of the House Magazine, *The Penrose Annual*, Vol.47, London, 1953, p67.

Heilbroner, Robert L. and Singer, Aaron, *The Economic Transformation Of America*, New York, 1977.

Hendrick, Burton J., *The Life and Letters of Walter H Page*, Garden City, New York, 1922.

Herd, Harold, *The March of Journalism*, London, 1952.

Hersey, Harold Brainerd, *Pulpwood Editor*, Westport, Conn., 1974 (originally New York, 1937).

Hershey, Lenore, *Between the Covers*, New York, 1983.

Hibbert, Christopher, *The Illustrated London News Social History of Victorian Britain*, London, 1975.

Hitchman, T., The Penny Press, *Macmillan's Magazine*, Vol.43, London, 1881.

Hodson, J. S., Modern Processes Of Automatic Engraving, *The Art Journal*, London, 1885.

Hogarth, Paul, *The Artist as Reporter*, London, 1986.

Hollis, Patricia, *The Pauper Press*, Oxford, 1970.

Hopkins, Mark W., *Mass Media in the Soviet Union*, New York, 1970.

Hopkinson, Tom, *Of This Our Time*, London, 1982.

Horgan, Stephen H., *Horgan's Half-tone and Photomechanical Processes*, Chicago, 1913.

Horgan, Stephen H., Inventor of Rotary Photogravure, *Penrose's Pictorial Annual*, Vol.19, London, 1913-14, pp110-112.

Horgan, Stephen H., What Process Work Owes to New York, *Penrose's Pictorial Annual*, Vol.26, London, 1924, pp98-100.

Horgan, Stephen H., Rotagravure in colours in the United States, *Penrose's Pictorial Annual*, Vol.28, London, 1926, pp89-90.

Horgan, Stephen H., Alco gravure, *The Penrose Annual*, Vol.38, London, 1936, pp110-111.

Hower, Ralph M., *The History of an Advertising Agency*, Cambridge, Mass., 1949.

Hughes, Helen MacGill, *News and the Human Interest Story*, Chicago, 1940.

Hulton, Edward, The future of Picture Post, *Penrose Annual*, Vol.42, London, 1940, pp21-24.

Hulton Readership Survey, London, 1947 et seq.

Humphreys, Nancy K., *American Women's Magazines*, New York, 1989.

Hunter, Dard, *Papermaking*, London, 1947, 2nd Ed.

Hurt, John S., *Elementary Schooling and the Working Classes, 1860-1918*, London, 1979.

Hyman, Alan, *The Rise and Fall of Horatio Bottomley*, London, 1972.

Hynes, Terry, *Magazine Portrayals of Woman 1911-1930*, Journalism Monographs No.72, Association For Education In Journalism, Lexington, Kentucky, May 1981.

Hyslop, W. H., Three-Color Half-tones, *The Inland Printer*, Vol.14, No.1, October 1894, Chicago.

Incorporated Society of British Advertisers, *The Readership of Newspapers and Periodicals in Great Britain*, London, 1936.

Incorporated Society of British Advertisers, *The Radio Times And The ISBA Report*, London, 1937.

Innis, Harold Adams, *The Press. A Neglected Factor in the Economic History of the Twentieth Century*, London and New York, 1949.

Innis, Harold Adams, *Empire and Communications*, Oxford, 1950.

Innis, Harold Adam, *The Bias of Communication*, Toronto, 1951.

Ives, Frederic E., The Progress of Three-colour Printing, *The Process Year Book*, Vol.7, London, 1901, pp85-86.

Jackson, Mason, *The Pictorial Press*, London, 1885.

Jacoby, G., New Methods Of Illustrating Newspapers, *The British Printer*, Vol.23, No.137, Oct-Nov.1910, Leicester.

James, Louis, *Fiction for the Working Man 1830-1850*, London, 1963.

James, Louis, Tom Brown's Imperialist Sons, *Victorian Studies*, Vol.17, No.1, Sept.1973.

Jay, F., Peeps Into the Past, *Spare Moments*, London, Oct.26,1918 to Feb.19, 1921.

Jeffreys, James B., *Retail Trading in Britain, 1850-1950*, Cambridge, 1954.

Jessup, John K., *The Ideas of Henry Luce*, New York, 1969.

John, Arthur, *The Best Years Of The Century*, Urbana, Ill. and London, 1981.

Johns-Heine, Patricke and Gerth, Hans, Values in mass periodical fiction 1921-40, *Public Opinion Quarterly*, Vol.13, Spring 1949, p105-13.

Jones, H. L., The Trend of Letterpress Printing, *The Penrose Annual*, Vol.41, London, 1939, pp152-154.

Kainen, Jacob, The Development of the Halftone Screen, *The Smithsonian Report For 1951*, Washington, D.C.

Kaldor, N. and Silverman, Rodney, *A Statistical Analysis of Advertising Expenditure and the Revenue of the Press*, London, 1948.

Katz, Elihu and Lazarsfeld, Paul F., *Personal Influence*, Glencoe, Ill., 1955.

Keddie, Shirley M., *Naming and Renaming: Time Magazine's Coverage of Germany and the Soviet Union during the 1940s*, Ann Arbor, Mi., 1985.

Kerst, Otto, Printing in Germany Today, *Penrose's Pictorial Annual*, Vol.28, London, 1926, pp22-24.

Kery, Patricia Frantz, *Great Magazine Covers of the World*, New York, 1982.

Kielbowicz, Richard Burket, *Origins of the Second-Class mail Category and the Business of Policymaking, 1863-1879*, Columbia, South Carolina, Journalism Monographs No.96, 1986.

Kielbowicz, Richard B., *News in the Mail*, New York, 1989.

Kimball, Richard B., Frank Leslie, *Frank Leslie's Popular Monthly*, Vol.9, No.3, New York, March 1880.

Kindleberger, Charles P., *Economic Growth in France and Britain 1851-1950*, Cambridge, Mass.,1964.

Kinter, Charles V., How Much Income is Available to Support Communications?, *Journalism Quarterly*, XXV (March 1948, p38

Kirsten Drotner, *English Children and the Magazines, 1751-1945*, New Haven and London, 1988.

Klapper, Joseph T., *The Effects of Mass Communication*, Glencoe, Ill., 1960.

Klein, H. O., A Glimpse at Some Continental Schools and Studios, *Penrose's Pictorial Annual*, Vol.6, London, 1900, pp79-93.

Kobler, John, *Luce: His Time, Life and Fortune*, New York, 1968.

Korper, P., *Apollo: a literary and artistic journal 1909-1917*, Unpublished PhD, New York University, 1972.

Kramer, Dale, *Ross and The New Yorker*, New York, 1951.

Kuznets, Simon, *Economic Growth of Nations*, Cambridge, Mass., 1971.

Landes, David S., *The Unbound Prometheus*, New York, 1969.

Larken, H. W., A Century of Compositors, *Printing World: a century in print*, London, 1979, pp31.

Lascault, Gilbert, La Gazette des Beaux-Arts en 1913: le discours de l'ordre, *L'Année 1913*, Paris, 1971, pp1093-96.

Lazarsfeld, Paul F., Berelson, Bernard and Gaudet, Hazel, *The People's Choice*, New York, 1944.

Lazarsfeld, Paul F. and Wyant, Rowena, Magazines in 90 cities - who reads what ?, *Public Opinion Quarterly*, Vol.I, Oct. 1937, pp29-41.

Lazell, David, *Flora Klickmann and her Flower Patch*, Bristol, 1976.

Lee, Alan J., *The Origins of the Popular Press in England*, London and Totowa, N J, 1976.

Leech, Russ B., Ballard Plating Process for Photogravure, *The Penrose Annual*, Vol.40, London, 1938, pp148-150.

Leekley, Robert M., Nylon Printing Plates, *The Penrose Annual*, Vol.52, London, 1958, pp127-130.

Legros, Lucien Alphonse, *A Note on the Legibility of Printed Matter*, London, 1922.

Lehnus, Donald J., *Who's On Time ? A Study of Time's Covers from March 3, 1923 to January 3, 1977*, New York, 1980.

Leigh, J. G., What do the Masses Read ?, *Economic Review*, Vol.14, London, 1904.

Levy, Max, A New Method of Etching, *The Process Year Book for 1899*, Vol.5, London, p104.

Levy, Max, The Levy Acid Blast and the New Process of Etching, *Penrose's Pictorial Annual*, Vol.6, London, 1900, pp101-103.

Levy, Max, The New Home of the Levy Screen and Some New Developments in Screen Making, *Penrose's Pictorial Annual*, Vol.9, London, 1903-4, pp53-56.

Lillien, Otto M., *History Of Industrial Gravure Printing up to 1920*, London, 1972.

Linton, David and Boston, Ray, *The Newspaper Press in Britain*, London and New York, 1987.

Liu, Alan P. L., *The Press and Journals in Communist China*, Cambridge, Mass., 1966.

Lofts, William and Adley, Derek, *The Men Behind Boy's Fiction*, London, 1970.

London Research and Information Bureau, *Press Circulations Analysed*, London, 1928.

Lyons, Peter, *Success Story: the Life and Times of S S McClure*, New York, 1963.

MacDonald, Dwight, Fortune Magazine, *Nation*, Vol.144, 8 May. 1937, p527.

Macfadden, Mary & Gaurvreau, Emile, *Dumbbells and Carrot Strips*, New York, 1953.

Mackay, Charles, *Through the Long Day*, London, 1887.

MacLuhan, Marshall, *The Gutenberg Galaxy*, London, 1962.

Magazine Publishers Association, *Some Indicators of National Growth*, No.10-D, New York, no date.

Malcolmson, Robert, *Popular Recreations in English Society 1700-1850*, Cambridge, 1973.

Maraccio, Michael D., *The Hapgoods*, Charlottesville, Virginia, 1977.

Marchal, Jean and Ducros, Bernard (Eds.), *The Distribution of National Income*, London and New York, 1968.

Marcosson, Isaac F., *Whenever Men Trade*, New York, 1945.

Marczewski, J., The Take-off Hypothesis and French Experience, *The Economics of Take-off into Sustained Growth,*, W W Rostow, (Ed.), London, 1963.

Marquette, Arthur, *Brands, Trademarks and Good Will*, New York, 1967.

Martin, Richard Owen, *The Nonverbal Language of Typographic Layout*, Ann Arbor, Mi., 1963.

Marzio, Peter, *The Democratic Art*, London, 1980.

Maschwitz, Eric, *No Chip on my Shoulder*, London, 1957.

Mason, Robert George, *Information Source Use in the Adoption Process*, Ann Arbor, Mi., 1962.

Masson, Thomas Lancing, *Our American Humorists*, New York, 1922.

Mather And Crowther, *Practical Advertising*, London, 1895-1923.

Mathias, Peter, *Retailing Revolution*, London, 1967.

Matthews, Roy T. and Mellini, Peter, *In Vanity Fair*, London and Berkeley, 1982.

Matthews, Thomas Stanley, *Name and Address*, New York, 1960.

Mayes, Herbert R., *The Magazine Maze*, New York, 1981.

Mayne, Fanny, *The Perilous Nature of the Penny Periodical Press*, London, 1851.

McBride, Sarah Elizabeth, *Women in the Popular Magazines for Women in America 1830-1956*, Ann Arbor, Mi., 1967.

McCall Corporation, *A Qualitative Study of Magazines*, New York, 1939-1946.

McClure, S. S., *My autobiography*, New York, 1914.

McNemar, Quinn, *Psychological Statistics*, New York and London, 1969, (4th Ed.).

McQuitty, Louis L., Elementary Linkage Analysis for Isolating Orthogonal and Oblique Types and Typal Relevancies, *Educational and Psychological Measurement*, Vol.17, No.2, Aug.1957, pp207-229.

Medcraft, John, *Bibliography of the Penny Bloods Of Edward Lloyd*, Dundee, 1945.

Medill School of Journalism, *Magazine Profiles*, Evanston, Ill., Dec.1974.

Meier, Richard L., *A Communication Theory of Urban Growth*, Cambridge, Mass., 1962.

Melot, Michel, *L'Illustration*, Geneva, 1984.

Mengel, Willi, *Ottman Mergenthaler and the Printing Revolution*, New York, 1954.

Mennell, P. B., Litho's Impact on Letterpress, *The British Printer*, Vol.61, London, Jan-Feb.1949.

Menz, Gerhard M. H., *Die Zeitschrift: ihre Entwicklung und ihre Lebensbedingungen; eine wirtshaftsgeschichtliche Studie*, Stuttgart, 1928.

Merriman, John M., *French Cities in the Nineteenth Century*, London, 1982.

Meuriot, Paul, *Des Agglomerations Urbaines dans l'Europe Contemporaine*, Paris, 1897.

Meyer, Josef Bernhard, *The Coated Paper Industry*, New York, 1931 (trans. S. E. Fox).

Miller, M. B., *The Department Store and Social Change in Modern France. The case of Bon Marché 1860-1920*, Unpublished PhD, University of Pennsylania, 1976.

Millington, Roger, *The Strange World of the Crossword*, London, 1974.

Minney, Rubeigh J., *Viscount Southwood*, London, 1954.

Mistler, J., *Le Librairie Hachette de 1826 à Nos Jours*, Paris, 1964.

Mitchell, B. R., *Abstract Of British Historical Statistics*, Cambridge, 1962.

Mitchell, B. R., *European Historical Statistics 1750-1975*, London, 1981. (2nd Ed.)

Mitchell, R. V., Past, Present and Future. Elements Of Post-war Lithographic Expansion and Advancement, *The British Printer*, Vol.57, London, Nov.1944.

Mogel, L., *The Magazine*, New York, 1980.

Montagu, Irving, *Wanderings of a War Artist*, London, 1889.

Montague, Noel, The Schlesinger Inking System, *The Penrose Annual*, Vol.39, London, 1937, pp153-155.

Montaron, Marcel, *Tout Ce Joli Monde*, Paris, 1965.

Moran, James, *Printing in the 20th Century*, London, 1974.

Moran, James, *Printing Presses*, London, 1973.

Mott, Frank L., *A History of American Magazines*, Cambridge, Mass., 1938-68.

Munsey, Frank A., *The Founding of the Munsey Publishing House*, New York, 1907.

Munsey, Frank A., The Making and Marketing of Munsey's Magazine, *Munsey's Magazine*, Vol.22, No.4, New York, January 1900.

Munson, Fred C., *History of the Lithographers' Union*, Cambridge, Mass., 1963.

Myers, Kenneth H., *SRDS*, Evanston, Ill., 1968.

Myers, Robin and Harris, Michael, *Serials and Their Readers 1620-1914*, Winchester, 1993.

National Advertising Company, *America's Advertisers*, New York, 1976 (originally 1893).

Nattier-Natanson, Evelyn, *Les Amitiés de la Revue Blanche et Quelques Autres*, Vincennes, 1959.

Naylor, Leonard E., *The Irrepressible Victorian*, London, 1965

Nebehay, C. M., *Ver Sacrum 1893-1903*, Vienna, 1975.

Nelson Chesman And Company's Newspaper Rate Book, St.Louis, 1898 et seq.

Nevett, Terence R., *Advertising in Britain*, London, 1982.

Newspaper World, *The Press, 1898-1948*, London, 1948.

Noble, Frederick, *The Principles and Practice of Colour Printing*, London, 1881.

O'Brien, Patrick (Ed.), *Railways and the Economic Development of Western Europe*, London, 1983.

O'Brien, Patrick and Keyder, C., *Economic growth in Britain and France 1780-1914*, London, 1978.

O'Day, Alan, *The Edwardian Age: Conflict and Stability*, London, 1979.

Odhams, W. J. B., *The Business and I*, London, 1935.

Ousler, Fulton, *The True Story of Bernarr Macfadden*, New York, 1929.

Ovink, Gerrit Willem, *Legibility, Atmosphere-value and Forms of Printing*, Leiden, 1938.

Pariat, Maurice, *Le Marché Français des Papiers Cartons*, Paris, 1959.

Parlin, Charles Coolidge, *National Magazines as Advertising Media*, Philadelphia, 1931.

Peirce, Carol Majorie, *Cosmopolitan: the Democratization of American Beauty Culture*, Ann Arbor, Mi., 1986.

Pellissier, M. Raoul, What's New in Photogravure, *The Penrose Annual*, Vol.38, London, 1936, pp107-109.

Perkin, H., The Origins of the Popular Press, *History Today*, No.7, July 1957.

Perkin, Harold, *The Origins of Modern English Society 1780-1880*, London, 1969.

Perkin, Harold, *The Rise of Professional Society*, London, 1989.

Perry, George, Pioneer of the Picture Scoop, *The Sunday Times Magazine*, London, May 7, 1967.

Peterson, Theodore, *Magazines in the twentieth century*, Urbana, Ill., 1956. (2nd Ed, 1964.)

Peterson, Theodore, Jensen, Jay W and Rivers W L, *The Mass Media and Modern Society*, New York and London, 1965.

Pickett, Calder, *Six New York Newspapers and Their Response to Technology in the Nineteenth Century*, Ann Arbor, Mi., 1959.

Pierce, Robert N., Lord Northcliffe: Trans-Atlantic Influences, *Journalism Monographs*, Lexington, Kentucky, Aug.1975.

Poindexter, Philip, The Making of Illustrated Weeklies, *Frank Leslie's Illustrated Weekly*, New York, 22 Feb.1894.

Politz (Alfred) Research, Inc. *A Study Of The Accumulative Audience Of Life*, New York, 1950.

Pollard, Sidney, Factory Discipline in the Industrial Revolution, *The Economic History Review*, Second Series, Vol.16, No.2, 1963, pp254-271.

Pollard, Sidney, *The Development Of The British Economy*, London, 1969, (2nd Ed.).

Pollard, Sidney and Crossley, David W., *The Wealth Of Britain 1085-1966*, London, 1968.

Pool, Ithiel de S., *Trends in Content Analysis*, Urbana, Ill., 1959.

Pope, Daniel, *The Making of Modern Advertising*, New York, 1983.

Porter, Glenn and Liversay, Harold C., *Merchants and Manufacturers: studies in the changing structure of nineteenth century marketing*, Baltimore and London, 1971.

Pound, Reginald, *The Strand Magazine 1891-1950*, London, 1966.

Pound, Reginald And Harmsworth, Geoffrey, *Northcliffe*, London, 1959.

Powell, Hickman, Collier's, *Scribner's*, Vol.105, New York, May 1939, p20.

Pred, Allan R., *Urban Growth and the Circulation of Information: the US system of cities, 1790-1840*, Cambridge, Mass., 1973.

Prendergarst, Curtis with Geoffrey Colvin, *The World of Time Inc., 1960-1980*, New York, 1986.

Presbrey, Frank S., *The History and Development of Advertising*, New York, 1929.

Prior, Melton, *Campaigns of a War Correspondent*, London, 1912.

Quinlan, Roy, The Story of Magazine Distribution, *Magazine Week*, Vol.1, 19 Oct.1953, pp4-5.

Rankin, William Parkman, *The Evolution of the Business Management of Selected Magazines in the US from 1900 through 1975*, Ann Arbor, Mi., 1979.

Raub, Patricia, *Popularizing the City: Urban Imagery in the National Geographic Magazine 1950-1984*, Ann Arbor, Mi., 1986.

Reader, W. J., *Bowater: a history*, Cambridge, 1981.

Reader's Digest Association, *Inside Test City*, Pleasantville, New York, 1959.

Reed, David, Growing Up, *Journal of Advertising History*, Vol.10, No.1, 1987.

Reed, David, The Use of Photography as a Research Tool in Sociology, *British Journal of Photography*, Vol.123, Nos.6051-2, London, July 9 & 16, 1976.

Reid, A., How A Provincial Newspaper Is Managed, *Nineteenth Century*, Vol.XX, London, 1886.

Reynolds, Quentin, *The Fiction Factory, or From Pulp Row to Quality Street*, New York, 1955.

Riegel, Robert Edgar, *The Story of the Western Railroads*, London and Lincoln, Nebraska, 1964.

Riley, John T., *A History of the American Soft Drink Industry,* Washington, D. C., 1958. (American Bottlers of Carbonated Beverages)

Roehr, Walter W., Paper and the Graphic Arts, *Printing Progress: a mid-century report*, Helbert, Clifford, Ed., The International Assoc. of Printing House Craftsmen Inc., 1959, Cincinnati, Ohio, pp2-75.

Rogers, Alva, *A Requiem for Astounding*, Chicago, 1964.

Rosner, Charles, *Printer's Progress*, London, 1951.

Rosner, Charles, *Printing for Pleasure and Profit in France*, Reading, 1959.

Rowell, George P., *Forty Years an Advertising Agent 1865-1905*, New York, 1906.

Rowell, George P., *American Newspaper Directory*, New York, 1869 et seq.

Rumbaugh, Liela M., *The Magazine of Art*, Northwestern University, PhD, Dissertation Abs. XXX, 1969-70, 2979a.

Saathoff, Roger C., *Some Effects of the Repetition of Environmental News Stories: an experiment*, Ann Arbor, Mi., 1984.

Safran, Hy, American Progress in Web-fed Offset, *The British Printer*, Vol.73, No.463, London, Oct.1960.

Salade, Robert E., Modern Methods of Colour Printing, *The British Printer*, Vol.43, No.253, Leicester And London, May-June 1930.

Sales, Hubert, *Les Relations Industrielles dans l'Imprimerie Française*, Paris, 1967.

Sandage, C. H., The Role of Advertising in Modern Society, *Journalism Quarterly*, Vol.28, Winter 1951, pp31-38.

Saul, Samuel B. (Ed.), *Technological Change*, London, 1970.

Sayward, Dorothy Steward, *Comfort Magazine, 1888-1942: a history and critical study*, University of Maine Studies, Second Series, No.75, Orono, Maine, 1960.

Schacht, John H., *The Journals of Opinion and Reportage*, New York, 1965.

Schackleton, Robert, *The Story of Harper's Magazine 1850-1917*, New York and London, 1916.

Schell, Ernest, Edward Bok and the Ladies' Home Journal, *American History Illustrated*, Feb. 1982, pp16-23.

Schiller, Herbert, *The Mind Managers*, Boston, 1973.

Schlereth, Wendy Clauson, *The Chap-Book. A Journal of American Intellectual Life in the 1890s*, Ann Arbor, Mi., 1982.

Schmidt, Dorey (Ed.), *The American Magazine 1890-1940*, Wilmington, Delaware, 1979.

Schmidt, Dorothy, Magazine, Technology and American Culture, *Journal of American Culture*, 3, Spring 1980, pp3-16.

Schmidt, Herman J., American and European Process Notes, *The Process Year Book*, Vol.7, London, 1901, pp65-72

Schramm, Wilbur (Ed), *Mass Communications*, Urbana, Ill., 1960.

Schreiner Jr, Samuel A., *The Condensed World of The Reader's Digest*, New York, 1977.

Schuwer, Philippe, *Histoire de la Publicité*, Geneva, 1965.

Sedgwick, Ellery, *The Happy Profession*, Boston, 1946.

Seebohm, Caroline, *The Man Who Was Vogue*, New York, 1982.

Seymour-Ure, Colin, *The Political Impact of Mass Media*, London and Beverly Hills, Calif., 1974.

Shand, James, The Significance of American Periodicals, *The Penrose Annual*, Vol.41, London, 1939, pp61-64.

Shattock, Joanne and Wolff, Michael, *The Victorian Periodical Press: Samplings and Soundings*, Leicester And Toronto, 1982.

Sherman, Sidney A., Advertising In The United States, *Publications Of The American Statistical Association*, Vol.7, December 1900.

Shorter, Alfred Henry, *Papermaking in the British Isles*, Newton Abbot, 1971.

Shorter, Clement, *C.K.S. An Autobiography*, Edited By J.M.Bulloch. London, 1927.

Simonis, H., *The Street of Ink*, London, 1917.

Sinclair, Andrew, *Corsair. The Life Of J.Pierpont Morgan*, Boston And Toronto, 1981.

Sipley, Louis Walton, *A Half Century Of Color*, New York, 1951.

Smith, Anthony, *The Newspaper: an international history*, London, 1979.

Smith, David C., *History of Papermaking in the United States (1691-1969)*, New York, 1970.

Smith, M Dwayne and Matre, Marc, Social Norms and Sex Roles in Romance and Adventure Magazines, *Journalism Quarterly*, Vol.52, Summer 1975, pp309-315.

Snedecor, George W., *Statistical Methods*, Ames, Iowa, 1950.

Snow, Ashleigh, Zinco-chromatic Methods In The U S, *The Process Year Book For 1896*, Vol.2, London.

Starch, Daniel, *Consumer Magazine Report*, New York, 1940.

Steinberg, Salme H., *Reformer in the Market Place: Edward Bok and the Ladies Home Journal*, Baton Rouge and London, 1979.

Stempel, Guido H. and Westley, Bruce H (eds.), *Research Methods in Mass Communication*, New Jersey, 1981.

Stern, Madeleine Bettina, *Publishers for Mass Entertainment in Nineteenth Century America*, Boston, 1980.

Stern, Madeleine Bettina, *Purple Passage*, Oklahoma, 1953.

Stone, Lawrence, Literacy and Education in England, 1640-1900, *Past and Present*, Vol.42, Feb.1969, pp69-139.

Stouffer, Samuel A. et al, *Measurement and Prediction*, Princeton, 1959.

Sullerot, Evelyne, *La Presse Feminine*, Paris, 1963.

Sullivan, Mark, *National Floodmarks*, New York, 1912.

Summers, M., John Dicks, *Times Literary Supplement*, London, November 7, 1942.

Sutcliffe, Frank M., 'Process' from the Photographic Point of View, *The Process Year Book for 1898*, Vol.4, London, pp22-24.

Swanberg, W. A., *Henry Luce and His Empire*, New York, 1972.

Sykes, Philip, *Albert E Reed and the Creation of a Paper Business 1860-1960*, Privately Produced, 1982.(Only known copy held by the British Library)

Symon, James David, *The Press and Its Story*, London, 1914.

Symons, Julian, *Horatio Bottomley*, London, 1955.

Tarbell, Ida M., *All in a Day's Work*, New York, 1939.

Tarible, L., *Les Industries Graphiques*, Privately Published, Paris, 1952.

Taylor, Henry Archibald, *Robert Donald*, London, 1934.

Tebbel, John, *The American Magazine*, New York, 1969.

Tebbel, John, *George Horace Lorimer and the Saturday Evening Post*, New York, 1948.

Thayer, John Adams, *Astir*, Boston, 1910.

Thayer, John Adams, *Out Of The Rut*, New York, 1912.

Thevoz, Fred, Colour Photogravure, *Penrose's Pictorial Annual*, Vol.28, London, 1926, pp81-84.

Thevoz, Fred, The Graphic Arts in France, *Penrose's Pictorial Annual*, Vol.37, London, 1935, pp147-148.

The Newspaper Press Directory and Advertisers' Guide, London, 1953 et seq.

The Art Of Radio Times, London, 1981.

Thomas, W.L., The Making of the 'Graphic', *The Universal Review*, Vol.2, No.5, September 1888, London, pp80-93.

Time Inc., *Writing for Fortune*, New York, 1980.

Tooker, L. Frank, *The Joys and Tribulations of an Editor*, New York, 1924.

Towne, Charles Hanson, *Adventures in Editing*, New York and London, 1926.

Twyman, Michael, *Printing 1770-1970*, London, 1970.

Tye, J. R., *The Periodicals of the Nineties*, Oxford, 1974.

Unger, Leonard (Ed.), *American Writers*, Vol. 2, New York, 1974.

United States Bureau Of The Census, *Historical Statistics Of The United States, Parts 1 and 2*, Washington, DC, 1975.

United States Department of Commerce, *United States Census of Manufactures*, Washington, DC, various dates.

Verfasser, Julius, *The Half-tone Process*, London, 1904.

Vidal, Leon, Applications and Progress of Photo-Mechanical Processes in France, *The Process Year Book For 1896*, Vol.2, London.

Villers, Frederic, *Pictures of Many Wars*, London, 1902.

Vincent, David, *Literacy and Popular Culture, England, 1750-1914*, Cambridge, 1989.

Vizetelly, Henry R., *Glances Back Through 70 Years*, London, 1893.

Wadsworth, Alfred Powell, Newspaper circulation 1800-1954, *Transactions of the Manchester Statistical Society*, 1954-5.

Wainwright, Loudon, *The Great American Magazine*, New York, 1986.

Wakeman, Geoffrey, *The Production of Nineteenth Century Colour Illustration*, Loughborough, 1976.

Wakeman, Geoffrey and Bridson, Gavin D. R., *A Guide to Nineteenth Century Colour Printers*, Loughborough, Leics. and London, 1975.

Walker, John Brisben, In Memoriam: Edward Dwight Walker, *The Cosmopolitan*, Vol.9, No.4, New York, August 1890.

Wallace, N. L., Life production, *The Penrose Annual*, Vol.42, London, 1940, pp108-110.

Wallis, L.W., *A Concise Chronology of Typesetting Developments 1886-1986*, London, 1988.

Waples, Douglas, Berelson, Bernard and Bradshaw, Franklin, *What Reading Does to People*, Chicago, 1940.

Wassersrom, William, *The Time of The Dial*, New York, 1964.

Waugh, Colton, *The Comics*, New York, 1947.

Weber, Wilhelm, *A History of Lithography*, London, 1966.

Weiss, Herbert L., *Rotogravure and Flexographic Printing Presses*, Milwaukee, Wi., 1985.

Weitenkampf, Frank, *American Graphic Art*, New York, 1924.

Westberg, C. A., The Claybourn Process and 'wet' colour printing, *Penrose's Pictorial Annual*, Vol.28, London, 1926, pp91-95.

Whetton, Harry, The Meisenbach Company Ltd., *The British Printer*, Vol7, No.39, May-June 1894, pp165-177.

White, Cynthia Leslie, *Women's Magazines 1693-1967*, London, 1970.

Wiborg, Frank B., *Printing Ink: a history with a treatise on modern methods of manufacture and use*, New York, 1926.

Wiener, Joel H., *The War of the Unstamped*, Ithaca and London, 1969.

Williams, Raymond, *The Long Revolution*, London, 1961.

Williamson, Jeffrey G., *Late Nineteenth-Century American Development: a general equilibrium history*, Cambridge, 1974.

Williamson, Oliver E., *Markets and Hierarchies*, New York, 1975.

Wilsher, Peter, *The Pound in your Pocket 1870-1970*, London, 1970.

Wilson, Charles, *First with the News. The History of W.H.Smith 1792-1972*, London, 1985.

Wilson, Charles, *The History of Unilever*, London, 1954.

Wilson, Harold S, *McClure's Magazine and the Muckrakers*, Princeton, 1970.

Wolseley, Roland E., *The Magazine World*, New York, 1951.

Wolseley, Roland E., *Understanding Magazines*, Iowa, 1965.

Wolseley, Roland E., *The Black Press, U S A*, Iowa, 1971.

Wood, Clement, *Bernarr Macfadden*, New York, 1929.

Wood, Franklin, A Century of Progress in the Graphic Arts, 1842-1942, *The British Printer*, Vol.55, no.329, London, March 1943.

Wood, James Playstead, *The Story of Advertising*, New York, 1958.

Wood, James Playstead, *Of Lasting Interest*, New York, 1958.

Wood, James Playstead, *Magazines in the United States*, New York, 1971.

Wood, James Playstead, *The Curtis Magazines*, New York, 1971.

Wyman, Phillips, *Magazine Circulation : an outline of methods and meanings*, New York, 1936.

Yoxall, Harold Waldo, *A Fashion of Life*, London, 1966.

Zeldin, Theodore, *France 1848-1945*, Vol.11, Intellect, Taste and Anxiety, Oxford, 1977.

Zeraffa, Michel, La Nouvelle Revue Française de 1910 à 1914, *L'Année 1913*, Paris, 1971, pp 1089-92.

Zimet, Sara Goodman, *Print And Prejudice*, London, 1976.

van Zuilen, Antoon J., *The Life Cycle of Magazines*, Uithoorn, Holland, 1977.

3^{mme} Annuaire Général et International de la Photographie, Paris, 1894.

Index